Faith in the family

A lived religious history of
English Catholicism, 1945–82

Alana Harris

Manchester University Press

Copyright © Alana Harris 2013

The right of Alana Harris to be identified as the author of this work has been asserted by her in accordance with the Copyright, Designs and Patents Act 1988.

Published by Manchester University Press
Altrincham Street, Manchester M1 7JA, UK
www.manchesteruniversitypress.co.uk

British Library Cataloguing-in-Publication Data is available

Library of Congress Cataloging-in-Publication Data is available

ISBN 978 1 7849 9365 8 *paperback*

First published by Manchester University Press in hardback 2013

This edition first published 2016

The publisher has no responsibility for the persistence or accuracy of URLs for any external or third-party internet websites referred to in this book, and does not guarantee that any content on such websites is, or will remain, accurate or appropriate.

Printed by Lightning Source

*For my grandmother and mother,
who formed me in the family of faith*

Contents

List of illustrations	*page* viii
Acknowledgements and author's note	ix
1 Introduction: A Vatican rag	1
2 English Catholicism reconsidered: Beyond 'ghettos' and 'golden ages'	32
3 Gatherings at the family table: The liturgy, the Eucharist and Christ our brother	57
4 'A model for many homesteads': Marian devotion, the Holy Family and Catholic conceptions of marriage and sexuality	130
5 'Plaster saints' or 'spiritual friends'? St Thérèse of Lisieux, St Bernadette Soubirous and the Forty Martyrs	202
6 Conclusion: Hymns ancient and modern	258
Appendix: Oral history interviews	271
Select bibliography	279
Index	300

Illustrations

3.1 Visual representation of the role of believer, priest and God in the action at the altar, from Grace Hurrell, *The Church's Play* (London: Sheed and Ward, 1945) — page 66

3.2 Cartoon entitled 'Thou Shalt not have Strange Gods Before Me', depicting the Sacred Heart triumphant over various demagogues and ideologies, from the *Catholic Times*, 23 March 1956, 7 — 71

3.3 'Make Room Luv!', from *The John Ryan Ecclesiastical Fun Book* (Great Wakering: Mayhew-McCrimmon, 1973), n.p. — 113

4.1 A Durham miner (with Father Patrick Peyton) leading his family in the rosary, from 'Crusader for Prayer', *Picture Post*, 26 July 1952, 5 — 149

4.2 St Joseph the worker and May Day comrade, from the *Catholic Times*, 6 May 1955, 9 — 153

4.3 Consternation about *Humanae Vitae*, from the *Catholic Herald*, 2 August 1968, 1 — 165

5.1 Commissioned painting of the Forty Martyrs by Daphne Pollen, from the *Universe and Catholic Times*, 10 July 1964, 1 — 238

The author has endeavoured to secure all necessary copyright permissions and disclaims any intention to infringe the copyright of any unidentified first owner. She is willing to acknowledge any such rights holder, should they make themselves known.

Acknowledgements and author's note

As this book is a sustained enquiry into the 'household of faith' surrounding and supporting English Catholics in the latter part of the twentieth century, so too has its evolution and completion been attributable to a congruent 'family of faith' who have encouraged and sustained the author throughout its production. It is a great pleasure to acknowledge the many people who have supported this research over the years, and have helped me to keep body, mind and spirit together throughout the process.

Since it began its life as an Oxford doctoral thesis, a primary debt of gratitude for this final product is owed to my former supervisor, and now mentor, friend and research collaborator, Jane Garnett. Her unfailing help and intellectual encouragement have sustained me through the various phases of the research process, and I am delighted to pass on here grateful and affectionate thanks.

Financial and institutional support to undertake the project was initially provided by a *Newman College Archbishop Mannix Travelling Scholarship* and the *University of Melbourne Rae and Edith Bennett Travelling Scholarship*. Appointments as a Sub-Dean and Senior Scholar at Wadham College, and then as the Hardie Fellow at Lincoln College, aided the completion process and the transition to a monograph. A period of sabbatical leave from my current Fellowship at Lincoln, and the collegial support of my colleagues there, including Susan Brigden and Perry Gauci, has greatly helped with the final stages of the writing process.

Appreciative thanks go to the archivists and librarians, particularly in the Upper Reading Room of the Bodleian library, who have enabled access to the source materials and archival collections utilised throughout this research. I am especially grateful to Father David Lannon for his hospitality and good cheer on my archival visits to Burnley, and for expert assistance from Meg Whittle at Liverpool and other archivist staff at Birmingham, Westminster, Farm Street and the Catholic Truth Society.

Particular thanks are owed to Father Simon Firth and (the late) Canon Joseph Carter who allowed me to undertake research within their parishes. To the men and women who spoke to me on these trips to Trafford Park and Crumpsall, I pass on my heartfelt thanks for their generosity and trust in sharing with me their life stories and their faith.

Research and writing can be a solitary exercise, made palatable by the camaraderie and conviviality of fellow travellers and surrogate family. For their intellectual companionship and congenial diversions in Oxford, many thanks go to Mark Abrahamson, Nazneen Ahmed, Anne Bush, Elin Hellum, Christian Lübbe, Marcia Dixon (up north), Frances Flanagan, Matthew Grimley, Max and Hannah Skoda and Rafal Stepien. Support from antipodean outposts came from Danielle Conroy, Andy Hamilton SJ, Katharine Massam, Tom Moloney, Josie Vains, Virginia Wise, and the Harris family. It is a source of sadness that my mother did not live to see this book come to fruition, but her influence permeates its pages, and I dedicate it to her. In recent times, the Folkards in Norfolk have provided a haven when much needed, and have wholeheartedly welcomed me into their family, for which I am so very grateful.

Finally, to my darling husband Tim, who has walked this journey with me (over difficult terrain) and proofread so valiantly. Without his faith, love and support, none of this would have been possible.

Author's note

The oral history interviews undertaken were recorded in MP3 format, fully transcribed and the minutes and seconds that elapsed within the interviews quoted are referenced. Fuller details are given in the Appendix.

Chapter 1

Introduction

A Vatican rag

First you get down on your knees
Fiddle with your rosaries ...
           (TOM LEHRER, 'VATICAN RAG')

Responding to 'another big news story of the year [namely] the ecumenical council in Rome, known as Vatican II',[1] American singer/songwriter and erstwhile distinguished mathematician Tom Lehrer produced his 'Vatican rag' in 1964–65 for the US version of the British satirical TV programme *That Was The Week That Was*. Prefaced in an introductory commentary to a 1966 performance as his own modest response to the Council's objectives to 'introduce the vernacular into portions of the mass, to replace Latin, and to widen somewhat the range of music permissible in the liturgy', he offered this as an example of re-doing 'liturgical music in popular song form' so as 'to sell the product, in this secular age'.[2] The song's notoriety in Britain was assured by Lehrer's regular slot as resident musical satirist on the irreverent weekly comedy programme *The Frost Report* (1966–67), an apt companion piece to his compositions for the episode on 'Sin' running on 17 March 1966.[3] Whether given comedic (and caustic) treatment in this forum, or more serious theological consideration in Malcolm Muggeridge's documentary *The English Cardinal: A Personal View of John Carmel Heenan*, which followed *The Frost Report* on Thursday 21 April 1966,[4] the Second Vatican Council was big news in Britain, as elsewhere, and elicited vastly different responses from those interrogating the 'dramatic changes' taking place within the Catholic Church in the 1960s.

Overtly political and intentionally provocative, Lehrer's parodic litany of all things Catholic provides an unexpected, but nevertheless pertinent, beginning to this examination of English Catholicism in the period after the Second World War and the religious changes in Britain in the decades that followed. As a starting point, in a pithy and irreverent fashion, it identifies many of the popular pieties, ritualised devotions and forms of spirituality that are examined throughout this book – the mass and the Eucharist, the rosary and associated Marian devotions, votive candles and devotions to the saints. The stimulus for the song – the intense media interest created by the gathering of the world's Catholic bishops in Rome for the Second Vatican Council (1962–65) – is the key backdrop to this study of the transformations in English Catholic spirituality, social identity and popular religion from 1945 onwards. Also implicit in Lehrer's lyrics are some of the chief preoccupations of the chapters which follow, which include the changing and vexed relationship between lay spirituality and autonomy, clerical identity and professional authority, as well as Roman centralisation and papal direction during the period. Most importantly, these issues were articulated by Lehrer in the midst of the 1960s and in a forum often associated with the 'counter-cultural' movement. This decade emerges in this study, as in many others, as a hinge-point, raising broader questions about the place of organised religion within British society, where there was an increasing scepticism and irreverence for traditional customs and beliefs, and growing affluence and consumption. Whilst Lehrer may have initially addressed his analytical jibes to an American audience, the shifts in Catholic culture that he described were international in character and not just institutional changes inaugurated by the Council, but also responses to global societal pressures. Finally, and most appropriately to one of the central themes of this exploration, Lehrer's 'Vatican rag' alludes to the astonishment, indeed near-incredulity, of many observers in confronting the 'modernisation' of an institution which had presented itself, most vociferously over the previous hundred years, as immutable and infallible.

This study considers the multiplicity of reasons for these changes to Catholicism in England in the latter half of the twentieth century, encompassing the post-war years through to the National Pastoral Congress in Liverpool in 1980. It focuses on 'English Catholicism', encompassing Catholics living in this region of Britain across different ethnic backgrounds, in contrast to the distinctive forms of Catholicism found in Scotland, Wales or, most particularly, in Ireland.[5] These transformations in the religious identities and devotional practices of English Catholics over nearly forty years, or three different generations, are situated within the broader cultural context of changes within British society during this period, and the scale and importance of these shifts, for the institutional church and the laity, are evaluated. While acknowledging that there were important changes and marked shifts in practice during these years, one of the central arguments of this book – in contrast to much of the existing historiography – is its evaluation of little-appreciated elements of continuity within English Catholic culture and popular religiosity, at a grass-roots level, throughout. It therefore views the years surrounding the Council as a distinct historical moment – a time of social transition but, more importantly, one that deliberately and self-consciously articulated and embraced notions of 'revolution', innovation and societal transformation that had a wider cultural salience. This orientation, reflected in the perspectives of the majority of the Council Fathers gathered, as well as the reformist movements mobilised within most Western European societies, allowed space for the vocalisation and tentative realisation of a variety of reforms. It is argued here that these were reorientations and reconfigurations that were in train well before the Second Vatican Council, but which were acknowledged and partially implemented in the 'opening' or 'window of change' (as Pope John XXIII designated it when calling the Council) which allowed a period of licensed social, religious and cultural ferment. As Cardinal Heenan, Archbishop of Westminster, reflected in his autobiography, these developments were 'the result not so much of the Council as of the conscious turning away from authority in the years following the Council – a phenomenon not exclusively religious'.[6]

Rather than interpreting this period as a time of caesura or rupture, especially through an over-emphasis on the social dislocation of the 1960s, this book reinterprets these movements as modulations or gradual, non-linear modifications of Catholics' understandings of their identities, beliefs and practices. The generation of English Catholics who attended Cameron Mackintosh's 1980 West End musical review of Lehrer's work *Tomfoolery*[7] may not have regularly 'fiddled with their rosaries' nor recently darkened the door of a 'small confessional'. Nevertheless, despite some unmistakable differences in the cultural accoutrements of Catholicism, and lasting reappraisals of elements of its sacramental system, this study argues that a form of distinctive Catholic identity evoked by the 'Vatican rag' continued to resonate with a post-conciliar generation of Catholics. Such churchgoers (and those who identified as 'cultural Catholics') towards the end of the twentieth century articulated markedly different understandings of the institution and its imperatives from those of their forebears. Nonetheless, they felt themselves to be part of a 'family of faith' in clear continuity with the 'Faith of Our Fathers' – to borrow the title of an older, but no less controversial, and provocative, musical jibe at the establishment from Father Faber (1849).[8] In charting these discursive and societal shifts, as well as more stable and sustained cultural and devotional sensibilities in the chapters that follow, this study focuses on the Catholic family as an interpretative metaphor and a subjective actuality. This chapter commences with a short, partial, but essential introduction to the Second Vatican Council, and then outlines the methodologies and sources to be employed throughout this study, foregrounding the lived religious experiences of Catholics before and after the Council, and situating these discussions within broader debates in the mainstream twentieth-century historiography about secularisation, the sixties, and shifting gendered identities.

*

The Second Vatican Council, the twenty-first ecumenical council of the Roman Catholic Church, was announced by Pope John XXIII on 25 January 1959 and convened, after four years of preparation, on 11 October 1962. Unlike previous Councils held to combat heresy or to hone doctrinal propositions, this gathering in Rome of about 2,500 bishops from around the world was centred around a programme which John XXIII defined as '*aggiornamento*' (translated as 'updating'). In his opening address, the Pope denounced those 'prophets of doom' continually warning that the modern world is 'full of prevarication and ruin'.[9] Instead, he insisted that at the heart of the Council's work was 'Christ … ever resplendent as the centre of history and life' and that 'by bringing herself up to date where required, and by wisely organising mutual cooperation, the Church will make individuals, families and peoples really turn their minds to heavenly things'.[10]

The Council ran over four sessions until 8 December 1965, the last three sessions under the leadership of Pope Paul VI, and ratified sixteen documents immensely affecting most areas of the Catholic Church's life. One of the foremost religious chroniclers of the Council, Giuseppe Alberigo, evaluated the Council's significance as 'the most important event in the history of the Roman Catholic Church since the

Protestant Reformation'.[11] An Anglican observer at the Council, Bishop John Moorman of Ripon, concurred and went further in asserting that 'there can be no doubt that this Second Vatican Council will, in future, be regarded as one of the turning-points in the history of the Christian Church, not only of the Church of Rome'.[12] The Council's pronouncements on biblical scholarship, the nature of the church and its authority, relations with other Christian churches, and indeed with non-Christians and the modern world, are all important components justifying such assessments. This book, however, focuses on changes in three particular areas of Catholic sacramental practice and devotional life – namely the liturgy and understandings of the Eucharist, devotion to Mary (and Joseph as the foster-father of Jesus) and the importance of the cult of the saints.

In speaking about events in Rome in 1870, known as 'Vatican I', when a gathering of the world's bishops in Rome ratified a declaration of papal infallibility, Cardinal Newman took a long historical perspective when wryly observing that 'there has seldom been a Council without great confusion after it'.[13] Such an assessment is also apt when considering this next conciliar event a century later, with such difficulties encompassing not only the intention of the decrees and their translation, but also their subsequent understanding, and varied implementation, internationally.[14] Whilst the Dogmatic and Pastoral Constitutions, Decrees and Declarations of the Second Vatican Council are easily cited, described and referenced, their interpretation has given rise to personalised polemics, polarised perspectives and ongoing interdenominational politics rendering near-impossible any neutral interpretation of the Council and its legacy. As John O'Malley SJ has observed, as a '"meeting" like no other, vast in proportions and wide-ranging in scope', it is not surprising that 'interpretations have emerged that seem almost to contradict one another and that are not always innocent of agenda'.[15] These interpretative difficulties have a particular salience in view of contemporaneous commemorative activities marking the fiftieth anniversary of the Council and its legacy at the present,[16] and are given added piquancy when viewed through the pontificates of Pope John Paul II, and particularly Benedict XVI, who have sought to craft an authoritative understanding of Vatican II and its 'spirit', stressing a 'hermeneutic of continuity'.[17] Such theological, doctrinally orientated interpretations are sometimes juxtaposed with the scrupulously detailed, socio-historic commentaries of Alberigo and other,

'Bologna-school' inspired scholars,[18] or the theologically progressive strands of North American Catholicism that draw authority and sanction for present-day activism through reference to conciliar changes.[19] This book eschews either approach through adopting a 'lived religious history' methodology, which takes seriously the immediate period of conciliar 'reception', that is from 1964 until the early 1970s, when contemporary interpreters were caught up in the whirlwind of events and, whether supportive or despairing of the changes, used a discursive register of radical discontinuity, and revolutionary change, to narrate the momentous changes under way.[20] However, through concerted attention to the embodied practices, domestic pieties, and life histories of ordinary English Catholics negotiating, interpreting or ignoring the impact of the Council on their own spiritual lives and self-identities, it also seeks to situate this event within the *longue durée* of the second half of the twentieth century. Examining longer-term trends in Catholic devotional life, and the place of Catholics within English society, broader causal explanations for change emerge, as well as considerable continuities that require recognition for a textured, grass-roots and comprehensive reappraisal of Vatican II and its effects.

On the assessment of the most internationally influential British theologian of the period, Bishop Christopher Butler, it was Vatican II's declaration on the liturgy which 'has affected ordinary churchgoing Catholics more, perhaps, than any other of the conciliar documents', because such changes were practically negotiated by the people in the pew, each week at mass.[21] The Constitution on the Sacred Liturgy, known by its opening words *Sacrosanctum Concilium*, was amongst the first of the Council's documents to be approved, on 4 December 1963 by an overwhelming majority of bishops, with the stated intention of taking 'steps towards the renewal and growth of the liturgy'.[22] Outlining this programme of adaptation, change and improvement to enable 'all believers to be led to take a full, conscious and active part in liturgical celebration',[23] the Constitution stressed on the one hand that 'the use of the Latin language is to be maintained in the Latin rites',[24] yet acknowledged that 'in the mass, the administration of the sacraments, and in other parts of the liturgy, there cannot at all infrequently exist a practice of using the local language, a practice which is really helpful among the people'.[25] The liturgical movement, following the efforts of Dom Lambert Beauduin on the continent earlier in the twentieth century,[26] had been exploring ways in which 'active participation' by the laity could be encouraged. But in a British context, liturgical experimentations were slower to develop, though clearly under way prior to the Council through gatherings such as that at Stanbrook Abbey in 1942.[27] Publicly endorsing such initiatives, *Sacrosanctum Concilium* advocated that 'it should therefore become possible for more scope to be given for such practices', and the document provided general guidance as to the parts of the mass and other sacraments in which the local language could be incorporated. It also recommended a 'revision of the way the mass is structured ... so that it becomes easier for the people to take a proper and active part'.[28] Implementation of these principles commenced with the *motu proprio*, *Sacram Liturgiam*, issued by Pope Paul VI on 25 January 1964, and further documents followed, extending the role of the vernacular in the liturgy, and introducing other changes to the liturgical setting and practice, including to church architecture, the location of the altar and liturgical music.[29] These developments culminated in the promulgation of the much-debated Apostolic Constitution *Missale Romanum* on 3 April 1969, which ushered in a new order of mass, replacing the Tridentine Rite promulgated by Pope Pius V in 1570 in response to many of the challenges of the Protestant Reformation.[30] Reflecting on these changes, the church historian Adrian Hastings acutely observed that:

> when one considered that the Latin mass had remained almost unchanged for more than five hundred years, that its revision constituted one of the most burning issues of the Reformation and one which Rome had been adamant in refusing, then the speed and decisiveness of liturgical reform in the 1960s becomes really amazing.[31]

This unfreezing of a liturgical tradition, which had seemed sacrosanct and immemorial, beyond question or change, was met with particular consternation by some English Catholics,[32] who were less liturgically adventurous than their continental counterparts and historically predisposed to the preservation of traditional practices (and Latin) as a marker of identity, continuity and distinctiveness, compared with the Church of England.[33] As the English bishops acknowledged contemporaneously, the implementation of the liturgical decree 'has launched a movement which will uproot all kinds of age-old habits, cut psychological and emotional ties [and] shake to the foundation the ways of thought of three or four million Catholics'.[34] While the liturgical changes did strike a deep chord, testified by the fact that for a time they rivalled the weather as a topic for conversation (in the estimation of a Benedictine priest), this cleric was also at pains to recount that most people were 'amazingly good tempered about it all'.[35]

These changes to old habits and emotional ties extended beyond the liturgy to include a marked shift in the theology surrounding Mary, which had previously been treated as a somewhat discrete doctrinal teaching, isolated from theological developments surrounding Christ, the Holy Spirit and the Church.[36] Deemed one of the most controversial decisions of the Council,[37] the closely contested decision of the world's bishops to incorporate their pronouncements on the Virgin Mary within the broader Dogmatic Constitution on the Church had an important impact on theological interpretations, and clerical encouragement, of Marian devotions, which are explored in chapter 4. Drawing extensively upon patristic teaching, *Lumen Gentium* (pronounced on 21 November 1964) enunciated a clear and coherent doctrine of the mother of God as 'the type of the church ... in the order of faith, charity and perfect union with Christ' and as an exploration of 'the mystery of the church, which is also rightly called mother and virgin'.[38] Mindful of the divergence of opinion amongst contemporary theologians and within the Council itself, this Dogmatic Constitution sought to redirect all discussion of 'the maternal role of Mary', and her titles of 'advocate, benefactress, helper and mediatrix', in a strong statement on the unique mediation of Christ. In its explanation of the manner in which, just as the priesthood of Christ might be 'shared in a variety of ways both by ministers and by the faithful people', it made implicit reference to Mary so that 'the one mediation of the redeemer does not rule out, but rouses up among creatures, participation and cooperation from the one unique source'.[39] This express re-coupling of Mariology to Christology, intended to keep over-zealous Marianism under control, was reinforced by a discussion of the Virgin Mary as a type of first apostle, or an exemplar to 'the whole community of the elect as the model of virtues'.[40] The Virgin Mary should therefore inspire all to work together in 'the church's apostolic mission for the regeneration of humanity', and function as a sign of 'hope and comfort for the pilgrim people of God'.[41] The restated emphasis on the Virgin Mary's maternal role continued to inform this theological reorientation, with the relationships between the faithful and the mother of the Saviour re-cast in familial and filial language, and

Introduction

consideration of 'our separated brothers and sisters'. These ecumenical sensitivities resulted in a stern warning about the bounds of orthodoxy surrounding Mary's special cult,[12] and an exhortation to 'theologians and preachers of the divine word carefully to avoid all false exaggeration and equally a too narrow mentality in considering the special dignity of the mother of God … [which] might lead our separated brothers and sisters or any other people into error concerning the true teaching of the church'.[13] The result was that most theologians, and indeed some of the faithful in the pews, avoided sustained reflection on Mary in the immediate wake of the Council. Instead, they redirected their efforts into areas of uncontroversial ecumenical development and practical Christian collaboration.

Whilst much of the impetus within the Second Vatican Council involved a reconsideration of the earthly apostolate of the laity (*Apostolicam Actuositatem*, 18 November 1965) and their mission in the world (*Gaudium et Spes*, 7 December 1965), the continuing importance of the communion of the elect in heaven was also explicitly acknowledged within *Lumen Gentium*. In a section devoted to the 'eschatological character of the pilgrim church and its union with the heavenly church', the Council considered the 'fraternal solicitude' of the apostles, martyrs and those 'whom the outstanding practice of the Christian virtues and the divine charismata recommend to the pious devotion and imitation of the faithful'.[14] Consonant with the teachings on Mary, the doctrine of the communion of saints was also included as an element within a redefined ecclesiology, with the unity between the communion of saints in 'their homeland', and their 'brothers and sisters' on earth, presented as a way of consolidating the holiness and health of the whole church, and of bringing the Christian communion of earthly pilgrims closer to Christ.[15] The saints were commended not only as exemplars, but as actors to be invoked through prayer, and approached for helpful assistance in obtaining blessings from God.[16] Through the saints' manifold examples, Christians would be:

> educated in the safest way by which, through the world's changing patterns, in accordance with the state and condition of each individual, we will be able to attain perfect union with Christ and holiness. In the lives of those who, while sharing our humanity, are nevertheless more perfectly transformed into the image of Christ (see 2 Cor. 3,18), God makes vividly manifest to humanity his presence and his face.[17]

The stress in this short but very dense teaching on eschatology and sanctity is identifiably Christological – for the union with the church in heaven 'is realized in the most noble way' in the 'sacred liturgy' and the 'Eucharistic sacrifice',[48] and any 'abuses, excesses or deficiencies that may have crept in here and there' obscuring this full praise of Christ and God, should be excised or corrected.[49] The faithful were to be taught that the 'cult of saints does not so much consist in the multiplicity of external acts, but rather in the intensity of our active love'.[50] This is a love of:

> these friends and coheirs of Jesus Christ who are also our sisters and brothers … For every authentic testimony of love that we offer to the saints, by its nature tends towards Christ and finds its goal in him who is 'the crown of the saints,' and through him to God, who is wonderful in his saints and in them is glorified.[51]

As a practical example of this regulation of 'external acts', *Sacrosanctum Concilium* cautioned against the excessive or heightened presentation of 'worshipful symbols in church', lest they 'excite sensationalism among the Christian people or pander to a devotion that is not quite right'.[52] Moreover, in a section on the liturgical year, as the feasts of the saints 'proclaim what are in fact the wonders of Christ', the celebration of such feast days should not be given more weight or obscure 'the actual mysteries of salvation'.[53] It was the practical implementation of these sorts of instructions, as part of a wider architectural reorientation of Catholic churches,[54] which led to the removal of the statues of saints within many churches, and the changed use of side chapels and shrines. Moreover, it also prompted the reorganisation of the calendar of the saints in 1970, which reduced the number of saints' feast days for the universal church, excising those with local cults or uncertain historical lineages, such as the popular but probably mythical St Christopher.

Faith in the family and lived religion: metaphors, methodologies and sources

In seeking to describe the relationship between God, the individual believer and the community of the faithful, familial analogies pervade the Jewish scriptures and the New Testament, refined and developed through centuries of Christian piety and church teaching.[55] From these scriptural underpinnings, and developments in church tradition, historians of Catholicism in North American, European and British contexts have explored the continued utilisation of, and emphasis upon, familial analogies in the popular piety, devotional practices and religious imaginations of the laity in the late nineteenth and early twentieth centuries.[56] As American historian Ann Taves has observed of American Catholics' constructions of their relationship with the divine, 'everyone takes on a familial role: God is the father, Mary the mother, and Jesus the elder brother to all the angels, saints and other Catholics, both living and dead'.[57] This metaphorical understanding is founded on an affective appreciation of the intimate and domestic interactions between the communion of the faithful and these spiritual persons, reinforced in many Catholic homes (then as now) in material and spatial terms. This creates, as American priest-sociologist Andrew Greeley puts it, a 'Catholic imaginary',[58] materialised through paintings and images of Christ, Mary and the Holy Family, statues of the saints, and a variety of devotional objects not only for church use, but displayed within the family home.[59] Far from signalling a break from this approach, the Second Vatican Council reinforced this metaphor through its decrees, speaking for example in *Lumen Gentium* about 'the family, in which are born citizens of human society who, by the grace of the holy Spirit, are raised by baptism to the status of heirs of God to carry on his people through the centuries. This is, as it were, the domestic church'.[60]

Moving from this institutional, collective and episcopal statement in 1964, the currency of this metaphor in an English Catholic context was reaffirmed over fifteen years later, at a local level, through the National Pastoral Congress (NPC) in Liverpool in 1980. At this unprecedented gathering of over 2,000 clerical and lay representatives of the Catholic Church in England and Wales, which assembled in a synod-like forum to evaluate the state of the contemporary church, and to translate the Council's theological musings into a practical, action-orientated programme, its members restated:

> The Church is a *family*. The way we work with one another in the Church should show the unity, love and acceptance of one another, which is central to family life. Also, the family is the domestic church: these loving, caring qualities, which are shown in family life, should find parallel expression at three different levels:

(a) the mutual love of God and man, or of Christ and the Church;
(b) in the family;
(c) this same love and concern should radiate out into our lives both in the Church and in the secular world.[61]

As the NPC was at pains to stress, this understanding of the family is threefold, encompassing the divine, heavenly family (the Triune God, as well as Mary and the saints), the earthly family bound by kinship, and the 'familial' relationships believed to exist between Christians, and indeed beyond. It formed part of an inclusive call to recognise the consequences of conceiving of all peoples as part of the 'human family'.

This *topos* of the 'holy family' has remained central to the aspirations, understanding and self-identification of Catholics in England in the latter half of the twentieth century and it therefore offers a fundamental metaphorical framework for this lived religious history of English Catholics, before and after the Second Vatican Council. Nevertheless, the chapters that follow also contend that such overarching continuity must be situated against the considerable diachronic changes in the meanings and constructions of familial life in Britain in the latter part of the twentieth century. The use of the metaphor of the 'household of faith' as an interpretative device for structuring each chapter and its analysis, therefore, situates questions of change and continuity in the beliefs and practices of English Catholics within a broader and evolving historiography of the family developed by historians of intellectual, social, cultural and gender history.[62] Beyond some recent and important interventions by Callum Brown,[63] Hugh McLeod[64] and Sue Morgan,[65] for reasons that will be explored more fully in chapter 2, most histories of twentieth-century Britain fail to acknowledge the continued salience of Christian (and especially Catholic) frameworks and precepts to evolving concepts of marriage, gender identities and roles, and sexuality. Given the historically mutually supportive relationship between the institutions of the family and the church across the centuries, it is indeed surprising, as one American sociologist of religion has observed, that 'even the most informed discussions on the restructuring of religion and society ... since the 1950s give amazingly little attention to family-based changes'.[66] This book foregrounds the family not only as a site for religious formation and gendered identity construction but as a lens for analysing wider socio-religious changes relating to socialisation, generational transmission, and competing religious and spiritual discourses.

As will be apparent, this interpretative lens of the 'household of faith' is a rich, multifarious and multi-layered metaphor that provides a flexible mechanism for identifying transformations, new configurations, and indeed continuities in the faith lives and social situations of English Catholics across the twentieth century. In the first instance, it is useful in foregrounding this 'domestic church', forged through blood ties or marriage, where cultural and religious affiliations are interwoven with other facets of identity formation and self-expression. Nevertheless, when extended under the rubric of the 'family of the faithful', this framework may also encompass the concentric circles of relationships surrounding and beyond the nuclear family, illuminating the role of voluntary church organisations (such as the Young Christian Workers (YCW) and other youth confraternities) and church institutions (such as the school or the parish) as supplementary, communal locations in which believers were inculcated in the faith and performed, and transmitted, collective memories of its traditions and practices.[67] In this respect, it shares the approach of many historians of Victorian religion who have looked to the networks of relationships and associational membership that sustained different forms of Catholic identity and popular religiosity following Catholic emancipation.[68]

Nevertheless, this analysis diverges sharply in other respects from the ways in which the 'family' has been conceived and analysed within much of this historiography, namely when packaged into analytical frameworks which reinforce the notion of separate domestic and public spheres,[69] or as identifiable with a form of feminised piety, closeted domesticity, and middle-class morality. Typical of this prevalent characterisation of the nineteenth-century 'angel in the house', but filtered through an (American) Catholic lens, is Jay Dolan's pejorative dismissal of devotions such as the rosary, the Sacred Heart and the cult of saints as anti-modern and 'riddled with emotionalism and sentimentalism, qualities identified as feminine'.[70] Even within those histories which eschew these maximalist assessments of the 'feminisation' of Victorian Christianity and modernisation narratives, most existing studies proceed on the presumption that nineteenth-century women had an inherent interest, and greater involvement, in religion than their menfolk and that this increasing identification of Christian spirituality with the feminine led to the further alienation of an industrialised, 'masculine' working class.[71] It is this analytical tradition, explored in detail in the next chapter, which underpins Brown's extension of a highly gendered form of nineteenth-century 'discursive Christianity' into the twentieth century, leading to his apocalyptic pronouncement of the collapse of the churches in the 1960s upon the advent of the women's liberation movement and widespread female integration into the public sphere and a previously male workplace.[72] Given the general tendency of this historiography to be predicated on an 'Evangelical Protestant norm', the exceptionalism of Catholicism in terms of gender balance has been sometimes grudgingly acknowledged in studies of religious revival,[73] Catholic working-class leisure, or labour politics.[74] However, this debate about an inherent female religiosity, and the irreligion of working-class men, interlaced as it is with the presumptions of the secularisation thesis,[75] is being increasingly subject to wholesale revision and reappraisal,[76] and chapter 2 seeks to extend this critique. The framework of the 'household of faith' utilised in this study builds upon a much broader understanding and expression of gendered religiosity, encompassing both men and women, and attentive to other identity-shaping categories such as class and ethnicity. While sensitive to the central role that is often played by women, and mothers, in the transmission of religious culture, it also examines other areas of inter-generational authority (and contestation), such as the place of priests, and fathers, church congregations and parish associations, as well as neighbourhood and ethnic communities.

In undertaking this study of the social and spiritual identities of English Catholics, this book situates itself methodologically within an innovative, emerging literature that seeks to map the contours of 'belief' as a category of analysis, and to explore the 'lived religious experiences' of the laity and their popular religious practices.[77] Adopting the concept of 'everyday religion', sociologists and anthropologists like Ammerman,[78] McGuire[79] and Giordan draw attention to the role of the domestic, the prosaic, and the material when appraising the contemporary vitality of prayer, and religious expression, outside church membership and practice.[80] Recent scholarship by Asad and Mahmood (beyond a Christian framework) has also identified the need to engage with subjective understandings of religious identity and agency distinct from institutional (and secular liberal) settings through the study of life narratives,[81] in tune with the premium on 'experience' placed by Charles Taylor in his path-breaking exploration of the complexion and contradictions surrounding religion with Western Europe's 'secular age'.[82]

My exploration of the lived religious experiences of English Catholics across the latter decades of the twentieth century employs this mixed, multi-disciplinary methodology through attention to written sources, material practices, oral histories and life narratives, which understand religious beliefs as lived, experiential and everyday. It also chimes with broader trends in cultural and intellectual history towards a study of the subjective and embodied, as well as the linguistic and the representational.[83] Drawing upon the insights of Robert Orsi, one of the foremost practitioners of this historical methodology, religion is identified as 'a form of cultural work … [encompassing] institutions *and* persons, texts *and* rituals, practice *and* theology, things *and* ideas'.[84] This is also a perspective endorsed by Sarah Williams in her influential study of religious belief and culture in late nineteenth- and early twentieth-century Southwark,[85] for 'so long as we persist in searching for the religious in social phenomena alone, belief will continue to elude' the historian, and the historiography will continue to prioritise 'social structures and institutions over and above mentalities and cultures'.[86] As Orsi has most recently argued, such a methodological approach to the study of Catholicism fundamentally critiques Weberian and Durkheimian explanations of religious change, and the constraining academic paradigms surrounding 'secularisation' and 'modernity',[87] as well as most existing histories of the impact and spiritual legacy of the Second Vatican Council. It seeks to engage with 'the God-tangles of actually lived lives',[88] through recognising that Catholic spirituality and devotional practice before (as after) the Second Vatican Council did not constitute a coherent, consistent and homogeneous entity, forged entirely by institutional direction and clerical instruction. Rather, it has always been a complex and flexible idiom, capable of adaptation and diverse application, sometimes in an internally contradictory fashion.[89] Such an approach breaks down the dichotomous, structural oppositions, often drawn in studies of 'popular religion', between high and low culture, between clerisy and laity, between the public and private.[90] It is, rather, an approach that seeks to chart, through the difficult and imprecise process of searching for new sources, and re-reading old ones with fresh eyes, the ambivalences and contradictions in the beliefs and practices of the ordinary 'person in the pew'.[91]

Groundbreaking studies employing this methodological approach to twentieth-century Catholicism have been chiefly confined to a

North American context, exemplified in the work of historians such as O'Toole,[92] Tentler,[93] Gauvreau and Christie[94] and, most pertinently for present purposes, by Timothy Kelly in his fascinating exploration of the way Catholics in Pittsburgh prepared for, and responded to, the Second Vatican Council between 1950 and 1972.[95] Kelly's interest in the changing religious, social and cultural sensibilities of the laity in this American diocese parallel many of the preoccupations of English Catholics described in this study, but his findings of a 'dramatic change' within the Catholic Church in America from 1950, and the decline of Catholic devotionalism for practices that 'resonated more with their lived experiences', diverge sharply from my analysis, which stresses gradual transformation, shifting doctrinal and devotional emphases, and a spectrum of lay responses to conciliar impulses and imperatives. Underpinning this differentiation is the recognition, to be explored more fully in a forthcoming internationally comparative volume edited by Matovina, Cummings and Orsi (to which I am a contributor),[96] that there are many 'lived religious histories' of the Second Vatican Council. Such an approach acknowledges that the conciliar moment, as a transnational event with localised consequences, was experienced differently throughout the world, and may be best explained through close-grained studies which are sensitive to the divergent social histories, and particularised expressions of Catholicism, in different national (and indeed diocesan) contexts.[97]

This study seeks to address a very noticeable gap, indeed a gaping lacuna, in twentieth-century historiography through responding to calls to redress the paucity of 'research-based evidence about English Catholicism in the second half of the twentieth century'[98] and to produce a study 'which places devotion in the solid context of Catholic community history'.[99] It builds upon Mary Heimann's foundational exploration of Catholic religious expression and social identity within nineteenth-century England,[100] and extends these narratives into the later twentieth century, thereby speaking to a wider literature on the place of Christianity in post-Second World War British society, and the underestimated importance of Catholics throughout this period as either 'Britain's largest minority'[101] or England's largest religiously observant church community.[102] It seeks to escape from existing (often nostalgic and biographically inflected) accounts that draw a sharp, reductive contrast between 'pre-conciliar' and 'post-conciliar' Catholicism, to sketch a picture of staggered change (both reactive and responsive), of devotional innovations, renovations

Introduction 17

and demolitions, and of cross-generational, gendered conflict and continuities, which echo and illuminate afresh related trends in post-war English society.

In charting the lived religious experiences of Catholics in England from the post-war period towards the start of John Paul II's pontificate, this book draws upon a vast range of written, visual and oral sources, with widely diverse authorships and audiences, origins and institutional status. The foundations of this study have included consultation of a wide range of papal encyclicals, Vatican pronouncements and pastoral directives across the twentieth century, with a particular concentration on the decrees of the Second Vatican Council (1962–65). These sources provide fundamental information about the institutional structures and sacramental systems operational in the Church, as well as the formulations of theological 'orthodoxy' articulated throughout the period. This institutional bedrock is augmented by close consideration of the national context, spanning the leadership of four different Archbishops of Westminster – Cardinal Bernard Griffin (1943–56); Cardinal William Godfrey (1956–63); Cardinal John Heenan (1963–75) and Cardinal Basil Hume (1976–99). The implementation, interpretation and interrogation of the Church's traditions, teachings and pastoral imperatives are partially accessible through the personal papers of these bishops, and for this reason a variety of diocesan archives have been consulted, including those of the Archdioceses of Westminster, Birmingham and Liverpool, but with a particular focus on the Diocese of Salford, for reasons explained below. These repositories have been supplemented by use of the archives of various religious orders, church committees and organisations, and some local parishes and shrines.

To these institutionally derived textual sources I have added the vast publication list of the Catholic Truth Society (CTS), accessible through copyright libraries, but also through the CTS index of all publications and book repository held in Vauxhall, London. Established in 1868 by the then Bishop of Salford (and later Archbishop of Westminster) Henry Vaughan, with the aim of catechesis and evangelisation, and with a mass circulation of near two million pamphlets per annum in 1951,[103] these pamphlets were designed with a view to accessibility and the instruction of 'ordinary' Catholics in the faith. While representing an idealised, and institutionally underwritten presentation of Catholic belief and practice, this body of cheap, accessible and popular advice literature provides an insight into the reading tastes of a large group of Catholics in England, and the types of understandings of Catholic doctrine and devotions which circulated in the period.

Other Catholic newspapers and magazines have also formed an important component of this study, particularly as throughout most of the twentieth century control of the weekly Catholic press remained, remarkably, in the hands of the laity. The sole exception to this rule was the *Catholic Times*, which ran from 1933 until its 1962 merger with *The Universe*.[101] Broadly speaking, these newspapers reflected distinctive constituencies within the English Catholic community, especially given the noteworthy continuities in the editorship of some of the largest circulating and most influential weeklies. The largest of these was *The Universe*, which had an enormous circulation of 300,000 in the mid-1950s.[105] This made it one of the most widely read religious newspapers in the world. Between 1963 and 1973, its distribution halved to 179,696 and its readership had shifted to encompass a much higher socio-economic bracket and a centrist-conservative perspective, with over two thirds of its readership aged over 55 years.[106] In contrast, the *Catholic Herald*, under the editorship since 1934 of Lancastrian-born and Stonyhurst-educated Count Michael de la Bédoyère,[107] straddled a working-class and middle-class audience with a peak circulation in the 1950s of around 100,000.[108] Balancing a mixture of news, often filtered through a strongly anti-communist perspective, with challenging and controversial opinion columns, the paper was anathema to many of the bishops and clergy and, at times, was banned in certain dioceses and parishes.[109] On the change of its editorship in 1962, it sought to continue this editorial policy, stating its aim to place 'world events in a Christian context' as well as to 'ventilate opinions which are, perhaps, somewhat in advance of those accepted by the general body of Catholics in this country at any given time'.[110]

Much more acceptable to the mainstream church was *The Tablet*, described by the ex-Jesuit journalist and Heythrop librarian turned church historian Michael Walsh as 'part of the furniture of Catholic middle-class households'.[111] Adopting a 'less churchy' but mostly conventional style under the editorship of Douglas Woodruff (1936–67),[112] it evolved into a forum for intelligent opinion pieces by distinguished Catholic writers. Its peak circulation of around 13,000 in the early 1960s belied the level of its influence in clerical circles (within and outside the Catholic Church), amongst students of foreign affairs, and within an active, opinion-setting

Catholic intelligentsia. Following a change in editorial direction in 1967, under the leadership of Tom Burns (who remained in office until 1982), the weekly became a forum for Catholic 'progressives', particularly agitated by the encyclical on contraception (*Humanae Vitae*, 1968) and supportive of the liturgical changes.

Editorials, opinion pieces and correspondence columns from each of these newspapers, given their importance in informing and edifying a wide cross-section of the Catholic population,[113] provide invaluable material which chimes methodologically with recent studies of the mainstream media by Adrian Bingham exploring the role of the press, from the interwar period onwards, in reshaping gender roles and notions of subjectivity and morality.[114] Particular attention in this lively, dynamic and heavy-hitting Catholic media has been given to the exchange of perspectives in letters pages, allowing some engagement with the opinions of those who were not part of an educated and articulate Catholic elite (who mostly authored leaders and opinion pieces).[115] To these widely accessible publications have been added a variety of monthly magazines, ranging from highbrow and theologically literate offerings such as *Downside Review*, or *Blackfriars*, through to the story pages of the *Catholic Fireside*, the Salford Catholic Rescue Society's devotional magazine *The Harvest* and the popular Redemptorist-run devotional magazine *Novena*, which began in 1951 as a family-orientated magazine and in 1974 had a circulation of 26,000, boasting full-colour supplements and an unabashedly 'low-brow image'.[116]

The final strand of source material utilised throughout consists of case studies, supported by a range of archival and textual materials as well as oral history narratives, centred on the Diocese of Salford under the leadership of Bishops Henry Marshall (1939–55), George Beck (1955–64) and Thomas Holland (1964–83)[117]. Within modern British historiography, Manchester has an iconic status as a quintessentially 'modern', dynamic city[118] – one of the key sites of the 'industrial revolution' and subject to unprecedented growth in the nineteenth century (with concurrent issues of inward migration and working-class poverty), as well as being at the forefront of experimentations with new intellectual and political movements, in strong part prompted by a liberal, non-conformist agenda.[119] It is therefore unsurprising that the city has considerable significance, and an emblematic status, for historians concerned with the 'traditional' working classes in Britain.[120] Given that much of this earlier historiography was filtered through a Marxist or modernist teleology, stressing the disaffection of the working classes and the fading of religious conviction, there has, however, been little sustained attempt to examine the intersections of religion, gender, class and culture in the communal life of the city.[121] This is even more pronounced in respect of the city's Catholic community, despite statistical surveys which indicate that practising Catholics comprised over 18% of the Mancunian population, as opposed to a national average of 10%, and that the North West region had the highest level of churchgoing throughout the country in 1979.[122] While Connolly,[123] Fielding[124] and now Wildman[125] address some of these shortcomings, this startling inattention to Mancunian Catholic culture is also attributable to wider historiographical propensities, considered in the chapter following, to treat Catholicism as a marginal, foreign and aberrant exception to mainstream religion, quarantined within the 'ghetto' of separate institutions, and characterised as the imported religion of an immigrant, mostly Irish, underclass. For this reason, Liverpool and Glasgow have been perceived as the 'archetypal' Catholic cities, and deemed the legitimate exemplars of Catholicism in Britain with their sectarian histories,[126] large Irish-Catholic immigrant communities[127] and distinctive working-class parishes.[128]

This book vigorously contests such a 'ghettoised' characterisation of Catholicism, seeking to bring it into the mainstream of modern British history and broadening the discussion of the denomination away from its construction as a 'religion of immigrants' within confined, and 'aberrant', urban centres. This specific focus on Mancunian Catholicism elicits a picture of a community comprised of a large number of first- and second-generation Irish Catholics, who drew upon this 'ethnicity' to different degrees, but also 'English' Catholics (who might themselves have had Irish antecedents) and smaller communities of Polish and Italian migrants fleeing post-war Europe. Unlike the sectarian strains and tribal triumphalism that has characterised histories of Merseyside and the Clyde, the Catholics of Manchester were ethnically mixed in the post-war period, enjoyed mostly harmonious relationships with their non-Catholic neighbours, and were chiefly concentrated in the manual or clerical occupational classes.[129] Nevertheless, as around one quarter of the total Catholic community in England during this period *was* concentrated in the north of the country (encompassing Liverpool, Lancashire and Salford), this snapshot of a confident and distinctive northern Catholicism nuances the broader conclusions about English Catholicism as a whole advanced throughout this book.[130]

Introduction

Nineteen life histories, employing an informal, unstructured oral history methodology,[131] and informed by theoretical perspectives relating to individual and collective memories,[132] and the collective shaping of these source-scripts by interviewer as well as interviewee,[133] have been utilised throughout this book. Short biographies for each of these interviewees, spanning family background, socio-economic situation and spiritual formation, as well as information about the two Catholic parishes from which participants were drawn, are provided in the Appendix. Given that issues of belief, cultural mores and intimate domestic practices are often only obliquely accessible through written sources,[134] much like considerations of sexuality[135] and gendered class identity,[136] this research responds to an increasing imperative to capture dimensions (across three distinct generational backgrounds) of the lived religious experiences of Catholic men and women in the years surrounding the Council.[137] As interviews conducted specifically for this study, with the informed consent of all participants, who are named (in short form) throughout, these autobiographically centred conversations have provided rich and highly textured explorations of belief, gender identity, experiences of family life and responses to Catholic institutional cultures which are only obliquely referenced, usually because they are of peripheral interest, within existing oral history repositories such as the Elizabeth Roberts archive (in the Centre for North-West Regional Studies)[138] or the Millennium Memory Bank.[139] In reading together the institutional documents, archival sources, popular pamphlets and press materials, with the oral history testimonies and performed practices of a selected group of Mancunian Catholics, the analysis that follows seeks to listen attentively to a 'popular or lived remembering [which] is inevitably shadowed by scripted memories' but which might nevertheless offer access to 'subterranean levels of the religious experience of modernity'.[140] Through examining the ways in which these various sources and voices inform and illuminate each other, this book seeks to articulate an untold history of the lived religious experiences, and popular devotional practices, of English Catholics before and after the Second Vatican Council.

Chapter 2 begins with a 'collective portrait' of the English Catholic 'family of the faithful' in the years immediately following the Second World War, surveying the existing histories of English Catholicism and their tendency to present a picture of a 'Catholic ghetto' or 'Golden Age'. It then explores the ways in which members of this community wrote contemporaneously about the Second Vatican Council, and their reactions to the 'doings in Rome' in the early 1960s. In situating this study of English Catholicism within a broader 'mainstream' historiography of the post-war period, this chapter triangulates its analysis against important debates between modern, twentieth-century historians about secularisation and religious diversity, fundamental shifts in morality, the erosion of respect for authority and tradition associated with the 1960s, and shifting leisure cultures and social mobility.

Chapter 3 then moves to a more particularised character study of the 'family of the faithful', through examining the encounter of English Catholics with Christ their brother in his different guises as Christ child, suffering Saviour and Sacred Heart. Nevertheless, the pre-eminent forms for this incarnated relationship were the mass and host and, through an exploration of the marked changes to the liturgy, this chapter illuminates associated and little-recognised shifts in Eucharistic theology. It argues that whilst these 'gatherings at the family table' articulated a transformed understanding of this encounter with Jesus, and utilised different tropes over this period, the mass and the Eucharist remained at the centre of English Catholic devotional life.

Chapter 4 offers a detailed study of Marian devotion and the reverence for St Joseph expressed in the context of the Holy Family. It explores the ways in which these heavenly personages functioned as ideals and models for rightly ordered, but societally adaptive, understandings of femininity, masculinity and the conjugal relationship. It then concentrates on an aspect of married life, sexuality, which underwent rapid transformation in the post-war period. It illuminates the shifting understandings, across the theological spectrum, of gender roles and married life from the 1950s onwards, and the way in which the sacramental model of the 'body of Christ' was mobilised as a more flexible and workable resource than the 'Holy Family' in responding to, and reconstructing, a Catholic perspective on the role of sex within married life. During a period of intense gender transition from the late 1960s onwards, Marian devotions slipped out of the institutional frame, but moving into the papacy of John Paul II they were increasingly reinterpreted and repackaged by the church and the laity in ways that might again resonate with gender roles and social expectations towards the end of the century.

Chapter 5 addresses the shifting hagiographical traditions surrounding St Thérèse of Lisieux and St Bernadette Soubirous as two prominent examples of the changing Catholic engagement with their 'sisters' in the 'communion of saints'. It argues that there was a movement from the presentation of these saints as exemplary character models of obedience and sacrifice towards accounts that placed a greater premium on each saint's historicity and personality within an explicitly psychological framework. The underpinnings of this shifting emphasis, and the outworkings of this interrogation of the role and importance of the saints within contemporary English Catholicism, are explored in the devotional cults that attached to both saints. The emphasis upon an experiential, 'this-worldly' spirituality increasingly present within biographies of St Thérèse, which ensured she was enduringly popular throughout the period, is contrasted with the cause for the canonisation of the forty English and Welsh martyrs. Through surveying the ambiguous response of some of the laity to the cause, centred on ecumenical concerns, lack of individual connection and differentiation, and tales of extraordinary (rather than everyday) heroism, it also illustrates those aspects of the cult which did attain a purchase in some areas of the English Catholic community. As such, these case studies illustrate the forms of sanctity which continued to be recognised and valued as the century progressed, and the ways in which these reconstructions could form a valuable spiritual resource for English Catholics, negotiating new demands and challenges to family life.

As each of these chapters cumulatively illustrate, this lived history of English Catholicism before and after the Council seeks to acknowledge the marked shifts and challenging transformations experienced within the English church over the three decades following the Second World War, but nevertheless eschews its characterisation as another 'English Reformation' or 'fresh stripping of the altars'. There was no master-score of yesteryear, nor was this a descent into a cacophony of diverse and dissonant melodies. Rather, the rich, textured and multifaceted picture of change and continuity which emerges from this exploration of three important dimensions of the English Catholic devotional and social landscape might itself be characterised as a 'Vatican rag' – a seemingly familiar tune rendered surprisingly new, and attracting fresh attention, through the addition of a syncopated rhythm, shifted accent, modulations in key, and an updated form of presentation.

Notes

1. T. Lehrer, *The Remains of Tom Lehrer* (Audio CD, 2000), Disc 3, Track 14 and http://www.youtube.com/watch?v=pvhYqeGp_Do.
2. *Ibid.*
3. See *Radio Times*, 3 March 1966, 43; 'Tom Lehrer', *Radio Times*, 7 April 1966, 43.
4. M. Muggeridge, 'The English Cardinal', *Radio Times*, 14 April 1966, 53.
5. M. Kenny, *Goodbye to Catholic Ireland* (Rev. ed., Dublin: New Island, 2000); L. Fuller, *Irish Catholicism Since 1950: The Undoing of a Culture* (London: Gill and Macmillan, 2004); K. Kehoe, *Creating a Scottish Church: Catholicism, Gender and Ethnicity in Nineteenth-Century Scotland* (Manchester: Manchester University Press, 2009).
6. J. C. Heenan, *Not the Whole Truth: An Autobiography* (London: Hodder and Stoughton, 1971), 59.
7. See the review article by I. Wardle, 'Tomfoolery', *The Times*, 6 June, 1980, 10.
8. F. W. Faber, *Hymns* (2nd edition, London: Burns and Oates, 1849), 56.
9. X. Rynne, *Vatican Council II* (Maryknoll: Orbis Books, 1999), 46.
10. G. Alberigo and J. Komonchak (eds), *History of Vatican II: Volume II* (Leuven: Peeters, 1997), 15.
11. G. Alberigo, J-P. Jossua and J. Komonchak (eds), *The Reception of Vatican II* (Wellwood: Burns and Oates, 1987), vii.
12. J. Moorman, *Vatican Observed: An Anglican Impression of Vatican II* (London: Darton, Longman and Todd, 1967), 182.
13. H. J. Pottmeyer, 'A New Phase in the Reception of Vatican II: Twenty Years of Interpretation of the Council' in Alberigo, *Reception*, 27.
14. As the most recent, thorough and scholarly translation of the documents of the Second Vatican Council, with parallel text, all quotations are from N. P. Tanner (ed.), *Decrees of the Ecumenical Councils: Volume Two, Trent to Vatican II* (London: Sheed and Ward, 1990).
15. J. O'Malley SJ, 'Foreword' in G. Alberigo, *A Brief History of Vatican II* (Maryknoll, NY: Orbis Books, 2006), vii.
16. E.g. K. T. Kelly, *50 Years Receiving Vatican II: A Personal Odyssey* (Dublin: Columbia Press, 2012).
17. Christmas Address to the Roman Curia, 22 December 2005 – www.vatican.va/holy_father/benedict_xvi/speeches/2005/december/documents/hf_ben_xvi_spe_20051222_roman-curia_en.html and N. Ormerod, 'Vatican II – Continuity or Discontinuity? Towards an Ontology of Meaning', *Theological Studies* 71(3) (2010), 609–36.
18. Alberigo and Komonchak (eds), *History of Vatican II: Volumes I–V*; N. P. Tanner, *The Councils of the Church: A Short History* (New York: Crossroad, 2001); C. M. Belitto, *The General Councils: A History of the Twenty-One Church Councils from Nicaea to Vatican II* (New York: Paulist Press, 2002); M. Lamberigts and L. Kenis (eds), *Vatican II and its Legacy* (Leuven: Leuven University Press, 2002).
19. J. O'Malley, J. Komonchak et al. (eds), *Vatican II: Did Anything Happen?* (London: Continuum, 2008); A. Marchetto, *The Second Vatican Ecumenical Council: A Counterpoint for the History of the Council* (Scranton, PA: University of Scranton Press, 2010).

20 E.g. E. Schillebeeckx, *Vatican II: The Real Achievement* (London: Sheed and Ward, 1967); M. Novak, *The Open Church: Vatican II, Act II* (London: Darton, Longman and Todd, 1964); M. de la Bédoyère, *The Future of Catholic Christianity* (Harmondsworth: Penguin, 1968); and H. Küng, *The Catholic Church* (London: Sheed and Ward, 1967).
21 C. Butler, *The Theology of Vatican II: Revised and Enlarged Edition* (Westminster, ML: Christian Classics, 1981), 171. More recently, M. Faggioli, *True Reform: Liturgy and Ecclesiology in* Sacrosanctum Concilium (Collegeville, MN: Liturgical Press, 2012).
22 Tanner, *Decrees*, SC section 1, 820.
23 *Ibid* s. 14, 824.
24 *Ibid* s. 36.1, 828.
25 *Ibid* s. 36.2, 828.
26 A. Nichols, *Looking at the Liturgy: A Critical View of its Contemporary Form* (San Francisco: Ignatius Press, 1996); A. Reid, *The Organic Development of the Liturgy* (Farnborough: St. Michael's Abbey Press, 2004).
27 J. D. Crichton, 'The Liturgical Movement from 1940 to Vatican II' in J. D. Crichton, H. E. Winstone and J. R. Ainslie (eds), *English Catholic Worship: Liturgical Renewal In England since 1900* (London: G. Chapman, 1979), 60–78; J. D. Crichton, *A Short History of the Mass* (London: Catholic Truth Society, 1983).
28 Tanner, *Decrees*, SC s. 50, 830–31.
29 A. Hastings (ed.), *Modern Catholicism: Vatican II and After* (London: Society for Promoting Christian Knowledge, 1991).
30 J. Cordeiro, 'The Liturgical Constitution: *Sacrosanctum Concilium*' in A. Stacpoole (ed.), *Vatican II: by Those Who Were There* (London: G. Chapman, 1986), 187.
31 A. Hastings, *A History of English Christianity 1920–2000* (4th ed., London: SCM Press, 2001), 526.
32 E. Duffy, 'Rewriting the Liturgy: The Theological Implications of Translation' in S. Caldecott (ed.), *Beyond the Prosaic: Renewing the Liturgical Movement* (Edinburgh: T&T Clark, 1998), 97.
33 M. Richards, *The Liturgy in England* (London: Chapman, 1966), 3.
34 'The English Bishops on Scheme 13', *The Tablet*, 31 October 1964, 1244–45.
35 B. Innes, 'Most People are Good-Tempered about it, but – How are YOU liking the New Liturgy?', *Universe and Catholic Times*, 20 July 1965, 6.
36 S. De Fiores, 'Mary in Postconciliar Theology' in R. Latourelle (ed.), *Vatican II: Assessment and Perspectives. Twenty-five Years After* (New York: Paulist Press, 1989), 471.
37 Alberigo, *History Vol. II*, 481; Alberigo, *Brief*, 49, 68.
38 Tanner, *Decrees*, LG s. 63, 896.
39 *Ibid* s. 60 and 62, 895–96.
40 *Ibid* s. 65, 896.
41 *Ibid* s. 68, 898.
42 *Ibid* s. 66, 897.
43 *Ibid* s. 67, 897–98.
44 *Ibid* s. 50, 889.
45 *Ibid* s. 49, 889.
46 *Ibid* s. 50.2, 890.

47 *Ibid.*
48 *Ibid* s. 50.3, 890.
49 *Ibid* s. 51, 891.
50 *Ibid.*
51 *Ibid* s. 50.2, 890.
52 *Ibid* s. 125, 842.
53 *Ibid* s. 111, 839.
54 E. Harwood, 'Liturgy and Architecture: The Development of the Centralised Eucharistic Space', *Twentieth-Century Architecture* 3 (1998), 51–74; R. Proctor, 'Churches for a Changing Liturgy: Gillespie, Kidd and Coia and the Second Vatican Council', *Architectural History*, 48 (2005), 291–322.
55 A. Koschorke, *The Holy Family and Its Legacy: Religious Imagination from the Gospels to 'Star Wars'* (New York: Columbia University Press, 2000); C. Walker Bynum, *Jesus as Mother: Studies in the Spirituality of the High Middle Ages* (Berkeley: University of California Press, 1982).
56 N. Christie (ed.), *Households of Faith: Family, Gender and Community in Canada, 1760–1969* (Montreal: McGill-Queens University Press, 2002); P. Pasture and T. Van Osselaer (eds), *Households of Faith: Religion and Domesticity in Twentieth-Century Europe* (Leuven: University of Leuven Press, 2013); K. Massam, *Sacred Threads: Catholic Spirituality in Australia 1922–1962* (Sydney: University of New South Wales Press, 1996). For a discussion of this Christian propensity beyond Catholic circles, see L. Davidoff et al., *The Family Story: Blood, Contract and Intimacy* (London: Longman, 1999), 84 and M. Knight and E. Mason, *Nineteenth-Century Religion and Literature: An Introduction* (Oxford: Oxford University Press, 2001).
57 A. Taves, *The Household of Faith: Roman Catholic Devotions in Mid-Nineteenth Century America* (Notre Dame: University of Notre Dame Press, 1987), 48.
58 A. M. Greeley, *The Catholic Imagination* (Berkeley: University of California Press, 2000).
59 C. McDannell, *Material Christianity: Religion and Popular Culture in America* (New Haven: Yale University Press, 1995), 167–74; M. A. Vasquez, *More than Belief: A Materialist Theory of Religion* (Oxford: Oxford University Press, 2011).
60 Tanner, *Decrees*, LG s. 11, 858.
61 I. and O. Pratt, *Becoming the Easter People: Discussion Outlines* (London: Catholic Truth Society, 1981), 9.
62 E.g. M. Peplar, *Family Matters: A History of Ideas about Family since 1945* (London: Longman, 2002); L. Delap, *Knowing their Place: Domestic Service in Twentieth-Century Britain* (Oxford: Oxford University Press, 2011).
63 C. Brown, *The Death of Christian Britain: Understanding Secularisation 1800–2000* (2nd ed., London: Routledge, 2009).
64 H. McLeod, *The Religious Crisis of the 1960s* (Oxford: Oxford University Press, 2007), 161–87.
65 S. Morgan, '"The Word Made Flesh": Women, Religion and Sexual Cultures' in S. Morgan and J. de Vries (eds), *Women, Gender and Religious Cultures in Britain, 1800–1940* (London: Routledge, 2010), 159–87.
66 W. C. Roof, *The Spiritual Marketplace: Baby Boomers and the Remaking of American Religion* (Princeton: Princeton University Press, 1999), 217–19.

67 D. Hervieu-Léger, 'Religion, Memory and Catholic Identity: Young People in France and the New Evangelisation of Europe' in J. Fulton and P. Gee (eds), *Religion in Contemporary Europe* (Lampeter: Mellen, 1994), 125–38 and G. Davie, *Religion in Modern Europe: A Memory Mutates* (Oxford: Oxford University Press, 2000), 30, 59.

68 H. McLeod, 'Building the "Catholic Ghetto": Catholic Organisations 1870–1914' in W. J. Sheils and D. Wood (eds), *Voluntary Religion, Studies in Church History vol. 23* (Oxford: Basil Blackwell, 1986), 411–44; S. Gilley, 'Vulgar Piety and the Brompton Oratory, 1850–60' in R. Swift and S. Gilley (eds), *The Irish in the Victorian City* (London: Croom Helm, 1985), 255–66; E. Norman, *The English Catholic Church in the Nineteenth Century* (Oxford: Clarendon Press, 1984).

69 L. Davidoff and C. Hall, *Family Fortunes: Men and Women of the English Middle Class 1780–1850* (London: Hutchinson, 1987); cf. L. Delap, B. Griffin and A. Wills (eds), *The Politics of Domestic Authority since 1800* (Basingstoke: Palgrave Macmillan, 2009).

70 J. P. Dolan, *The American Catholic Experience: A History from Colonial Times to the Present* (New York: Doubleday, 1985), 231.

71 H. McLeod, *Religion and Society in England, 1850–1914* (Basingstoke: Macmillan, 1996), 65–70; 156–68; F. Knight, *The Nineteenth-Century Church and English Society* (Cambridge: Cambridge University Press, 1995), 205–06.

72 Brown, *Death*, 9–10, 220–28 and most recently – published as this book went to press and hence not incorporated into the analysis – C. Brown, *Religion and the Demographic Revolution: Women and Secularisation in Canada, Ireland, UK and USA since the 1960s* (London: Boydell and Brewer, 2012).

73 G. Parsons, 'Emotion and Piety: Revivalism and Ritualism in Victorian Christianity' in G. Parsons (ed.) *Religion in Victorian Britain: Traditions* (Manchester: Manchester University Press, 1988), 213–34.

74 S. Fielding, 'The Catholic Whit-Walk in Manchester and Salford, 1890–1939' *Manchester Region History Review* 1(1) (1987), 3–10; S. Fielding, *Class and Ethnicity: Irish Catholics in England 1880–1939* (Buckingham: Open University Press, 1993).

75 L. Woodhead, 'Gendering Secularization Theory', *Social Compass* 55(2) (2008), 187–93; M. E. Ruff 'The Postmodern Challenge to the Secularization Thesis', *Schweizerische Zeitschrift für Religion und Kulterheschichte*, 99 (2005), 385–401.

76 P. Pasture, J. Art and T. Buerman (eds), *Gender and Christianity in Modern Europe: Beyond the Feminization Thesis* (Leuven: Leuven University Press, 2012); T. Van Osselaer and T. Buerman, 'Feminization Thesis: A Survey of International Historiography and a Probing of the Belgian Grounds', *Revue d'Histoire Ecclésiastique* 103(2) (2008), 1–31.

77 T. Kselman (ed.), *Belief in History: Innovative Approaches to European and American Religion* (Notre Dame: University of Notre Dame Press, 1991); D. D. Hall (ed.), *Lived Religion in America: Towards a History of Practice* (Princeton: Princeton University Press, 1997); T. Jenkins, *Religion in English Everyday Life: An Ethnographic Approach* (Oxford: Berghahn, 1999).

78 N. T. Ammerman (ed.), *Everyday Religion: Observing Modern Religious Lives* (Oxford: Oxford University Press, 2006).

79 M. McGuire, *Lived Religion: Faith and Practice in Everyday Life* (Oxford: Oxford University Press, 2008).

80 G. Giordan, 'Toward a Sociology of Prayer' in W. H. Swatos and G. Giordan (eds), *Religion, Spirituality and Everyday Practice* (New York: Springer, 2011), 33–44; S. Schielke and L. Debevec, *Ordinary Lives and Grand Schemes: An Anthropology of Everyday Religion* (Oxford: Berghahn, 2012).

81 T. Asad, *Formations of the Secular: Christianity, Islam, Modernity* (Stanford: Stanford University Press, 2003); S. Mahmood (2005) *Politics of Piety: The Islamic Revival and the Feminist Subject* (2nd edition, Princeton: Princeton University Press, 2012).

82 C. Taylor, *A Secular Age* (Cambridge, Mass.; Harvard University Press, 2007), 4–14, 30–9.

83 P. Mandler, 'The Problem with Cultural History', *Cultural and Social History* 1(1) (2004): 94–117; M. Roper, 'Slipping out of View: Subjectivity and Emotion in Gender History', *History Workshop Journal* 59 (2005), 57–72.

84 R. A. Orsi, *The Madonna of 115th Street: Faith and Community in Italian Harlem 1880–1950* (Rev. ed., New Haven: Yale University Press, 2002), xix; R. A. Orsi, 'Everyday Miracles: the Study of Lived Religion' in Hall, *Lived Religion*, 3–21.

85 S. C. Williams, *Religious Belief and Popular Culture in Southwark c.1880–1939* (Oxford: Oxford University Press, 1999).

86 S. C. Williams, 'Victorian Religion: A Matter of Class or Culture?', *19th Century Studies* 17 (2003), 15.

87 R. A. Orsi, 'Everyday Religion and the Contemporary World: The Un-Modern, or What was Supposed to Have Disappeared but Did Not' in Schielke, *Ordinary*, 145–61.

88 T. J. Ferraro, 'Not-just-cultural Catholics' in T. J. Ferraro (ed.), *Catholic Lives, Contemporary America* (Durham, NC: Duke University Press, 1997), 14.

89 R. A. Orsi, *Between Heaven and Earth: The Religious Worlds People Make and the Scholars who Study Them* (Princeton: Princeton University Press, 2005), 45.

90 K. Thomas, *Religion and the Decline of Magic: Studies in Popular Beliefs in Sixteenth and Seventeenth Century England* (London: Weidenfeld and Nicolson, 1971); C. McDannell and B. Lang, *Heaven: A History* (2nd ed., New Haven: Yale Nota Bene, 2001); J. Garnett and G. Rosser, *Spectacular Miracles: Transforming Images in Italy, 1500–2010* (London: Reaktion Books, 2013).

91 Hall, *Lived*, pp. ix–xii.

92 J. M. O'Toole (ed.), *Habits of Devotion: Catholic Religious Practice in Twentieth-century America* (Ithaca: Cornell University Press, 2004).

93 L. W. Tentler (ed.), *The Church Confronts Modernity: Catholicism since 1950 in the United States, Ireland and Quebec* (Washington: Catholic University of America Press, 2007).

94 N. Christie, M. Gauvreau and S. Heathorn (eds), *The Sixties and Beyond: Dechristianization as History in North America and Western Europe, 1945–2000* (Toronto: University of Toronto Press, 2013).

95 T. Kelly, *The Transformation of American Catholicism: The Pittsburgh Laity and the Second Vatican Council, 1950–1972* (Notre Dame: University of Notre Dame Press, 2009) and 'Suburbanization and the Decline of Catholic Ritual in Pittsburgh', *Journal of Social History* 28(2) (1994), 311–30.

96 See http://cushwa.nd.edu/about/lived-history-of-vatican-ii-project/ and K. Cummings, T. Matovina and R. A. Orsi (eds), *A Lived History of the Second Vatican Council* (forthcoming, 2015).

97 E.g. M. E. Ruff, *The Wayward Flock: Catholic Youth in Postwar Germany, 1945–1965* (Chapel Hill: University of North Carolina Press, 2005).
98 M. P. Hornsby-Smith (ed.), *Catholics in England 1950–2000: Historical and Sociological Perspectives* (London: Cassell, 1999), xvi.
99 S. Gilley, 'A Tradition and Culture Lost, To be Regained?' in Hornsby-Smith (ed.), *Catholics in England*, 29–45.
100 M. Heimann, *Catholic Devotion in Victorian England* (Oxford: Oxford University Press, 1995) and 'Devotional Stereotypes in English Catholicism, 1850–1914' in F. Tallett and N. Atkin (eds), *Catholicism in Britain and France since 1789* (London: Hambledon Press, 1996), 13–25.
101 D. Sewell, *Catholics: Britain's Largest Minority* (London: Viking, 2001).
102 See P. Brierley, *Pulling Out of the Nosedive: A Contemporary Picture of Churchgoing: What the 2005 English Church Census Reveals* (Eltham: Christian Research, 2006).
103 'The Catholic Truth Society', *The Tablet*, 3 May 1952, 363. See also C. Collingwood, *The Catholic Truth Society* (London: Catholic Truth Society, 1955), 19, 21.
104 Crichton, *English*, 32.
105 P. Stanford, *Cardinal Hume and the Changing Face of English Catholicism* (London: G. Chapman, 1993), 11.
106 M. Walsh, *The Tablet 1840–1990: A Commemorative History* (London: The Tablet, 1990), 63.
107 See A. Boyle, 'Bedoyere, Michael Anthony Maurice Huchet de la' –www.oxforddnb.com/view/articleHL/31023?docPos=1&anchor=match.
108 Stanford, *Cardinal*, 11.
109 Crichton, *English*, 32.
110 'Building on the Past', *Catholic Herald*, 9 March 1962, 4.
111 Walsh, *Tablet*, 50, 57.
112 See A. Waugh, '(John) Douglas Woodruff', – http://www.oxforddnb.com/view/article/31856.
113 J. J. Dwyer, 'The Catholic Press, 1850–1950' in G. A. Beck (ed.), *The English Catholics 1850–1950: Essays to Commemorate the Centenary of the Restoration of the Hierarchy of England and Wales* (London: Burns and Oates, 1950), 506.
114 A. Bingham, *Family Newspapers? Sex, Private Life, and the British Popular Press 1918–1978* (Oxford: Oxford University Press, 2009).
115 P. Coman, *Catholics and the Welfare State* (London: Longman, 1977), viii. Elite counter-culture and left-wing newspapers such as *Slant* have not been included in this examination – see P. G. McCaffrey, 'Catholic Radicalism and Counter-Radicalism: A Comparative Study of England and the Netherlands' (Unpublished DPhil thesis, Oxford, 1979).
116 For a survey of Catholic press circulation see: 'A Witness to the Truth', *Catholic Herald*, 24 May 1974, 4.
117 117 T. Holland, *For Better and For Worse: Memoirs of Thomas Holland* (Salford: Salford Diocesan Catholic Children's Rescue Society, 1989).
118 As Brown puts it 'secularisation theory removes any need to ask *why* religion is declining now … because it all started so long ago in the milltowns of industrial Lancashire and Lanarkshire', Brown, *Death*, 30.

119 A. Kidd, *Manchester* (Edinburgh: Edinburgh University Press, 2002), 1; C. Makepeace, *A Century of Manchester* (Stroud: Sutton Publishing, 1999); P. Shapley, D. Tanner and A. Walling, 'Civic Culture and Housing Policy in Manchester, 1945–79', *Twentieth Century British History* 15(4) (2004), 410–34.

120 E.g. A. Davies, *Leisure, Gender and Poverty: Working-Class Culture in Salford and Manchester, 1900–1939* (Buckingham: Open University Press, 1992) and 'Saturday Night Markets in Manchester and Salford 1840–1939', *Manchester Region History Review* 1(2) (1987), 3–12.

121 E.g. A. J. Dobbs, *Like a Mighty Tortoise: A History of the Diocese of Manchester* (Littleborough: Upjohn and Bottomley, 1978); J. Jackson, *Under the Smoke: Salford Memories 1922–41* (Manchester, 1990), 5, 17; D. Lannon (ed.), *Memories of Catholic Manchester* (Wigan: North West Catholic History Society, 1997).

122 P. W. Brierley, *Prospects for the Nineties: Trends and Tables from the 1989 English Church Census* (London: MARC Europe, 1991), 20, 130, 136, 152.

123 G. Connolly, 'Catholicism in Manchester and Salford 1770–1850: The Quest for "Le Chrétien Quelconque"' (Unpublished PhD thesis, University of Manchester, 1980) and 'The Transubstantiation of Myth: Towards a New Popular History of Nineteenth-century Catholicism in England', *Journal of Ecclesiastical History* 35(1) (1984), 78–104.

124 Fielding, *Class*.

125 C. Wildman, 'The "Spectacle" of Interwar Manchester and Liverpool: Urban Fantasies, Consumer Cultures and Gendered Identities' (Unpublished PhD thesis, University of Manchester, 2007); 'Religious Selfhoods and the City in Interwar Manchester', *Urban History* 38(1) (2011), 103–23.

126 T. Gallagher, 'A Tale of Two Cities: Communal Strife in Glasgow and Liverpool before 1914' in Swift, *Irish*, 106–29; P. Waller, *Democracy and Sectarianism: A Political and Social History of Liverpool 1868–1939* (Liverpool: Liverpool University Press, 1981); J. Davies, '"Faith of Our Fathers", "Dare to be Daniel": Catholic Processions and Protestant Parades, Liverpool, 1909', *North West Catholic History* 31 (2004), 98–120 and J. Davies, 'Catholic-Anglican Relations: Archbishop Downey, Bishop David and the Decree of *Ne Temere*, 1930–1931', *Recusant History* 29(1) (2008), 101–23.

127 E.g. R. Samuel, 'The Roman Catholic Church & the Irish Poor' in Swift, *Irish*, 301–08.

128 T. Koopmanschap, 'Transformations in Contemporary Roman Catholicism: A Case Study' (Unpublished PhD thesis, Department of Sociology, University of Liverpool, 1978); F. Boyce, 'Catholicism in Liverpool's Docklands: 1950s–1990s' in Hornsby-Smith (ed.), *Catholics*, 46–66; P. Doyle, *Mitres and Missions in Lancashire: the Roman Catholic Diocese of Liverpool, 1850–2000* (Liverpool: Blue Coat Press, 2005); P. McGrail, *First Communion: Ritual, Church and Popular Religious Identity* (Aldershot: Ashgate, 2007).

129 J. Keating, 'Faith and Community Threatened? Roman Catholic Responses to the Welfare State, Materialism and Social Mobility, 1945–62', *Twentieth Century British History* 9(1) (1998), 86–108.

130 J. A. Hilton, *Catholic Lancashire: From Reformation to Renewal 1559–1991* (Chichester: Philimore, 1994); M. Morris and L. Gooch, *Down Your Aisles: The Diocese of Hexham and Newcastle 1850–2000* (Hartlepool: Northern Cross, 2000).

131 Ethics clearance received through the University of Oxford Central University Research Ethics Committee (CUREC 1/07-079).
132 E.g. L. Passerini, 'A Passion for Memory', *History Workshop Journal* 72(1) (2011), 241–50.
133 K. Anderson and D. Jack, 'Learning to Listen: Interview Techniques and Analyses' in R. Perks and A. Thomson (eds), *The Oral History Reader* (2nd edition, London: Routledge, 2006), 118; S. Chandler, 'Oral History across Generations: Age, Generational Identity and Oral Testimony', *Oral History* 33(2) (2005), 48–56.
134 S. C. Williams, 'The Language of Belief: An Alternative Agenda for the Study of Victorian Working-Class Religion', *Journal of Victorian Culture*, 1(2) (1996), 303–17.
135 K. Fisher, *Birth Control, Sex and Marriage in Britain 1918–1960* (Oxford: Oxford University Press, 2006).
136 A. Gallwey, 'Lone Motherhood in England, 1945–90: Economy, Agency and Identity' (Unpublished PhD thesis, University of Warwick, 2011).
137 J. Davies, 'Oral History: History from Below: A Review', *North West Catholic History*, 19 (1992), 54–56; P. van Rooden, 'Oral History and the Strange Demise of Dutch Christianity', *Bijdragen en Mededelingen betreffende de Geschiedenis der Nederlanden* 119 (2004), 524–51.
138 Elizabeth Roberts archive – www.lancs.ac.uk/depts/cnwrs/archives.html.
139 See http://sounds.bl.uk/Accents-and-dialects/Millenium-memory-bank.
140 R. A. Orsi, '"The Infant of Prague's Nightie": The Devotional Origins of Contemporary Catholic Memory', *U.S. Catholic Historian* 21(1) (2003), 15, 18.

Chapter 2
English Catholicism reconsidered
Beyond 'ghettos' and 'golden ages'

Fiddle with your rosaries
Bow your head with great respect
And genuflect, genuflect, genuflect

On 31 October 1949, *The Times* ran an article entitled 'Catholicism To-Day' which purported to offer a 'tentative review of the present position and immediate prospects of the largest and most influential of the Christian communions'[1] comprised of 3.5 million Catholics in the United Kingdom, and 15.5 million more throughout the British Commonwealth.[2] In a lively and often heated correspondence between Catholic and Anglican clergy and laypersons in the weeks that followed, the central preoccupations which emerged (as the Dean of Chichester pithily summarised them) centred around 'a more widespread desire for Christian co-operation on the part of Roman Catholics than some would have suspected [and] ... the principle obstacles to [such] progress'.[3] The letters explored assertions of papal authority (and the interpretation of such strictures by Catholic clergy and laity), the prospects for common prayer given the close co-operation, and shared Christian agenda, developed by the Archbishops of Westminster and Canterbury during the Second World War,[4] and the role of the Catholic Church as a bulwark against materialism and pagan communism. These discussions, on the eve of the centennial celebrations of the restoration of the Catholic Hierarchy of England and Wales in 1950, cast light on some of the immediate post-war preoccupations of this confident and rapidly growing Christian denomination, but more detail and texture is required for a 'character portrait' of this community. What were the demographics, class affiliations, ethnic backgrounds, and educational experiences of the far from homogeneous community classed as 'English Catholic' throughout this book? What were its key religious, social and political organisations, and what importance and influence did they have within, and beyond, Catholicism? Who were its leading episcopal and intellectual figures? Following on from a historiographical survey of the nature of the English Catholic community in the middle of the twentieth century, this chapter analyses existing accounts surrounding the 'reception' of the Second Vatican Council by these English Catholics, and explores the ways in which these histories diverge from the analysis adopted within this book. The final section contextualises English Catholicism within a broader 'mainstream' historiography of the post-war period, encompassing concerns about secularisation and religious diversity, and the fundamental shifts in morality and respect for authority and tradition associated with the 1960s, as well as shifting leisure cultures and social mobility.

In 1936, David Mathew penned his magisterial survey of English Catholicism from the Reformation until after the Great War under the subtitle 'Portrait of a Minority: its Culture and Tradition'. Using broad brush strokes and a necessarily impressionist, sometimes chiaroscuro, technique this chapter offers a collective 'family portrait' of English Catholics from the time of the Second World War and Beveridge Report – which transformed so many aspects of British society[5] and 'reflected and created a new climate for Catholics, no less than for other groups'[6] – until the beginning of the 1980s, under the pontificate of John Paul II. This emic bookend, for reasons that will emerge, most certainly marked a new phase in conciliar reception, and the interpretation of Vatican II, throughout the Catholic world. For English Catholics negotiating a changing Britain under Margaret Thatcher's premiership,[7] this also felt like a distinctly new era in which the Falklands war (and an earlier assassination attempt on his life) could jeopardise but ultimately not derail John Paul II's historic tour of the British Isles in 1982, the first by a pope since the Reformation.

*

Responding to the aforementioned correspondence in *The Times*, an editorial entitled 'The Church and the English' in *The Tablet* summarised the debates and drew the following conclusions:

> There was present among the Catholic contributors a feeling, not without its justification, that the Church, in its general style and methods, is still too much

the post-Tridentine Church, on the defensive, and that, particularly in this country, we are now a sufficiently large and mature body to have left behind the ghetto complexes of a poor and largely immigrant community.[8]

Calling for a reappraisal of its place in a Britain where 'people ... have to see themselves and think of themselves increasingly as European', the leader adjudged:

> It must be said that each of the three great streams which have made the English Catholic river of today has had its special inhibitions; the old Catholics had learnt a tradition of reticence, the Irish Catholics a tradition of belligerence, and the converts a tradition of avowed and sharp controversy: and the approach called for today is none of these.[9]

These reflective, but caricatured, musings on the nature of English Catholicism were timely, and no doubt in part prompted by immediate preparations for the celebration in October 1950 of one hundred years of (re-established) episcopal leadership in England and Wales. The 'Restoration of the Catholic Hierarchy' centenary events included a week of erudite lectures by prominent laymen such as Christopher Hollis MP (on politics) and J. J. Dwyer (speaking on the Catholic literary revival),[10] which supplemented the commemorative essays contemporaneously published on church institutions, diocesan development and parochial growth, under the editorship of the Bishop of Brentwood (and later of Salford and Liverpool), George Beck.[11] However the popular celebrations of this milestone, and the high-profile 'public' framing of the English Catholic community to a curious British public, was through the 'Catholic Exhibition' at Chenil Gardens in Chelsea, London, with its depiction of a potted Catholic history and a displayed replica of the Tyburn gallows and relics.[12] The other prominent event later that month was the 'Catholic Rally' at Wembley Stadium, attended by 85,000 people who watched 'lively, colourful tableaux' of 'eighteen hundred years of the Catholic history of England and Wales',[13] presented as a whiggish, triumphalist (and unbroken) narrative from the Anglo-Saxon church of Augustine and Becket, through to the English martyrs, Bishop Challoner and Daniel O'Connell. All this was centred around the parade of a papier-mâché replica of an 'Our Lady of Willesden' statue, as the original was burnt during the Reformation,[14] and readings from Cardinal Wiseman's 1850 pastoral 'From out of the Flaminian Gate' and Newman's 'Second

Spring' sermon. Involving hundreds of children's organisations (including the Children of Mary and Scouts and Guides), and flanked by legions of richly robed episcopacy and clergy, the celebrations concluded with rousing renditions of 'Faith of Our Fathers' and 'God Bless Our Pope'.

Encapsulated in both of these highly self-conscious constructions of the Catholic community are many of the contradictions inherent in providing a 'family portrait' in this period – the contrasts between its various (yet far from discrete) recusant, Irish-derived and convert strands; the relationship between the church Hierarchy and lay intellectuals; and the distinctions between institutional positions and rhetorical stances, compared with the lived realities, in Catholic homes, working-class and middle-class neighbourhoods, parochial churches, schools and confraternities. In demographic terms, there were 2,754,249 Catholics in England itself in 1950, and mass attendance was over 70%, with nearly half of this constituency concentrated in the urban, industrial centres of the north.[15] These vibrant inner city parishes built upon the historic, 'recusant' heartland of Catholicism in Lancashire commemorated by historians like J. A. Hilton,[16] Steven Fielding[17] and Peter Doyle.[18] But there was also a large, and as yet little acknowledged, concentration of Catholics – perhaps as large as 50%, and increasingly middle class and suburban – living in the south around London.[19] This was a rapidly growing community in the 1950s, buoyed by the baby boom and the post-war migration of at least 300,000 Irish jobseekers,[20] Polish refugees, and European Voluntary Workers.[21] While it is true that well into the 1950s English Catholics were still disproportionately represented in occupational class C,[22] this was also in a context in which at least 70% of the entire British population was classified as 'working class'.[23] Moreover, local Catholic communities were undoubtedly becoming more heterogeneous as a result of new opportunities after the war,[24] with social mobility enhanced by the welfare state, and the movement of a younger generation into the professions, and increasingly into the universities.[25] This trend can be traced, however, to the turn of the twentieth century, when an embryonic but expanding and highly influential Catholic middle class comprised of industrialists, trade-based entrepreneurs and professionals set up sodalities and friendly societies, agitated for (and funded) Catholic secondary schools for their children, moved into local (and sometimes national) politics, and began to manifest an increasing self-confidence in public life.[26] The image within much of the literature of an alienated Catholic working class, rendered marginal (or apathetic) in political terms and only 'de-ghettoising' with the rise of prominent individuals like William Rees-Mogg (editor of *The Times* from 1967),[27] or Norman St John-Stevas (Conservative MP for Chelmsford from 1964),[28] should be recognised as a highly reductive representation, conjured with implicit contrast to a perceived political Catholicism (both radical and conservative) on the continent.

Stemming from the greater preponderance of histories of nineteenth-century Catholicism which overwhelmingly focus on the struggle to establish and sustain state-supported Catholic education from 1870 onwards,[29] or the religiously reinforced Home Rule controversies across the century,[30] English Catholicism has tended to be caricatured as unwaveringly Ultramontane,[31] excessively sectarian[32] and riven by conflict between a working-class Irish laity and an educated middle-class, English-born Hierarchy.[33] These broad outlines tend to be extrapolated upon, and extended into, later twentieth-century descriptions of the Catholic 'ghetto', in which a costly but unequivocal commitment to Catholic schools, and a vast array of extra-parochial organisations, reinforced the distinctive religious and cultural practices of an endogamous tribe until the 'rupture' of the Second Vatican Council.[34] There is ample subject matter for such a 'fortress church' *mise en scène*, for in 1944 Roman Catholic schools were the largest providers in the voluntary sector, boasting over 1,300 institutions and serving over 300,000 pupils, with every sign of further growth and expansion.[35] As Brothers and Hickman have variously described, this system of religious education was valorised (but also evolving) as a prime site for appropriate religious socialisation, sustained by the Catholic community at considerable personal sacrifice.[36] The opposition to, and compromises extracted from, Rab Butler by the English Hierarchy (with the support of influential laymen like C. H. Sheill of the Catholic Parents and Teachers Association), in exchange for Catholic support for the passage of the 1944 Education Act, are seen as an extension of this intransigence,[37] in line with wider Catholic commitments to subsidiarity and suspicion of the welfare state.[38] The activities of a number of highly distinctive Catholic social organisations – seen to be a tentative flowering of 'Catholic Action' in an English context – reinforce this picture of a self-contained, distinctive Catholic milieu.[39] Micro-histories of the Catholic Federation,[40] Catholic Social Guild,[41] Catholic Evidence Guild,[42] Catholic Women's League[43] and the Young Christian Workers,[44] are written through an often celebratory, and implicitly comparative, lens. Such confessionally distinct activity is contrasted with the scale and vigour of twentieth-century *European* Catholicism, and its self-confident political manifestations or 'pillarisation',[15] followed by the dismantling of these separate organisational structures through the 1960s.[16] Institutional and statistical measures of strength and vibrancy are adduced to sustain this picture of a homogeneous, insular and cohesive community on the eve of the Council, with the English Catholic population growing to approach the four million mark, baptisms and marriages remaining buoyant, and conversions peaking at well over 12,000 adults per annum, continuing a rising trend from the post-war period.[17]

While sometimes presented by historians and novelists as sectarian and suffocating, this conjured Catholic 'ghetto' has also been described in some histories as vivifying, protective and insulating – a necessary condition for a unified and conformant Catholicism which had its 'golden age' with the intellectual and cultural dominance of Hilaire Belloc, G. K. Chesterton and their successors in novelists like Evelyn Waugh and Graham Greene.[18] As James Lothian has explored in his assured and insightful collective biography of '*the* English Catholic Intellectual Community'[19] – which examined the intellectual formation, and philosophical orientations, of artists like David Jones and Eric Gill, the historian Christopher Dawson, and the publishers Frank Sheed and Maisie Ward – the period surrounding the Second World War emerges as a period of political rapprochement between Catholics and other English Christians, following political conservatism and an isolationist stance during the Spanish Civil War,[50] through to the Sword of the Spirit movement[51] and post-war re-Christianisation plans.[52] In Lothian's estimation, it is this movement to interdenominational co-operation and the associated fragmentation of a 'distinctive' Catholic stance which led to the diminution of a vibrant, assured and intensely networked intellectual community. Such ambivalent, often nostalgic, reconstructions of a 'golden age', of a confident, internally consistent and unequivocally authoritarian Catholicism, are also echoed within a distinct genre of Catholic memoirs, usually centred around the transition from an infantilised childhood faith. From a long list, one could cite Monica Baldwin's *I Leap over the Wall* (1949), Karen Armstrong's *Through the Narrow Gate* (1981, revised in 1995), Anthony Kenny's *A Path from Rome* (1986) and, in its most recent iteration, Michael Hornsby-Smith's *Reflections on a Catholic Life* (2010). From such a 'portrait of a minority', rendered in terms reminiscent of a modernist lino-cut, the transition to the world of New Wave social realism in the 1960s appeared, and for some was indeed experienced, in quite stark terms. Nevertheless as McClelland and Hodgetts have shown in their authoritative collection of essays for the 150th anniversary of the Restoration of the Hierarchy in 2000, echoing but expanding upon Bishop Beck's earlier offering, a view of Catholic life across a number of different facets rather suggests the evolution of this community well before the 1960s, with pockets of resistance to change, and a cleaving to the insulating comfort of the 'ghetto' well afterwards.[53]

In the immediate period of conciliar 'reception', that is from 1964 through to the early 1970s, contemporary commentators on the Second Vatican Council wrote in the context of the exhilaration and disorientation caused by the whirlwind of events and activity in Rome and throughout the world. Whether supportive or dismayed by the changes, and expert opinion was usually thus polarised, radical discontinuity and revolutionary change were the register in which events were narrated.[54] In typically accessible and topical terms, prominent layman and prolific writer and publisher Frank Sheed[55] summarised the feelings of many English Catholics in his best-selling pamphlet *Is it the Same Church?* (1968), which opened with the observation that:

> Pope John opened the window to let in fresh air. He let in a hurricane. The interested Catholic finds himself at times not only hanging on to his hat, but hanging onto his head.[56]

As a former Jesuit, then lecturer in French at Wadham College, Oxford and later professional Vatican commentator would also observe, 'pre-conciliar' and 'post-conciliar' evolved into terms that did not simply function chronologically but were conflated with 'a difference of attitude, outlook and basic conviction so deep that it seemed the two could never be reconciled'.[57] Within this taxonomy, the period before the Council was characterised by progressives as pre-rationalist, unduly clerical and politically conservative, with the post-conciliar church being commended as more open to the world and existentialist, communal and ecumenical, scripturally sophisticated and liturgically purified. By contrast, those disturbed by the Council, and temperamentally opposed to the social and political climate of the 1960s, focused particularly on the liturgical changes as the root cause for the demise of certain Catholic ways of life, a loss of the 'numinous', the erosion of denominational distinctiveness[58] and, ultimately, the demise of the sacred.[59] Within an English Catholic context, as explored more contextually in chapter 5, the changes inaugurated by the Council were often commended or critiqued by using what I have termed a 'rhetoric of the Reformation'.[60] This was an appeal to events, personages and forms of language that actively marshalled and mobilised religious history, Catholic traditions and constructions of 'Englishness' either to interrogate or integrate the changes.

Notions of 'modernity' also provided the rhetorical meta-narrative for most existing English Catholic analysis of the Council, with an evocation of a 'sacred' past of bells, smells and fish on Fridays rendering Catholics unlike 'everyone else' (to paraphrase the English Catholic anthropologist Mary Douglas).[61] Exemplified in various guises, through the polemical railings of Alice Thomas Ellis,[62] the memoirs of the Cardinal Heenan battling the winds of change,[63] the cross-century historical parallels and childhood reminiscences of Eamon Duffy,[64] or the propensity of Catholic journalists like Edward Stourton and Peter Stanford to highlight change within an overarching master narrative,[65] the facts of decline, and the disappearance of essential features of Catholicism, have often been presented as uncontested. Adherence to this descriptive, modernist paradigm also crossed the theological, political and class spectrum, with authors like David Lodge viewing the decline of pre-conciliar rigidities as 'progress', albeit combined with a Proustian rootedness in times past.[66] Similarly, Anthony Archer, in his analysis of working-class Catholicism in Newcastle, described the liturgical changes of the Council as the imposition of a new form of middle-class elitism, and attributed decline in mass attendance from the late 1960s to working-class disaffection:

> Disconcerted Catholics might have let the rosary beads slip from their fingers but they did not take up reciting the psalms ... Before the very eyes of Catholics, enchanted, indignant or indifferent, the former things of Catholicism simply passed away. The whole glittering army of Catholic symbolism had left the field. The saints had apparently laid down their powers, whether of finding things, curing sore throats or intervening in hopeless cases ... the powerful novenas and devotions disappeared, ... to light [a candle] privately in front of a statue was no longer recommended as a sensible and natural thing to do.[67]

Whilst the narrator of *How Far Can you Go?* postulated the 'loss of the fear of hell', and the disbanding of the 'snakes and ladders of sin and atonement' in 1963,[68] Archer added to this the retreat of 'heaven' and the resulting exodus of working-class men and women from the pews.

With the emergence of a distinct school of British sociology across the course of the twentieth century, and the dominance of a social scientific, positivist perspective within the British academy from the 1960s onwards,[69] the English Catholic community, and its identity as a 'subculture', increasingly became the focus of structuralist enquiries and parish studies alike. Conor Ward, attempting to acquire an 'intimate, habitual, intuitive familiarity' with parochial life in Liverpool in 1961, surveyed the role of schools, societies and clerical leadership and undertook a qualitative statistical analysis of parishioner opinion, to build a picture of a cohesive parish community.[70] A few years later, John Hickey's *Urban Catholicism* (1967) studied the 'separate' character of the Catholic community in Cardiff, and charted the religious, national and social forces, and particularly the parish structures, which militated against involvement in the social and political life of the 'host' community. The stress on parish structures, and notions of a 'tribal identity', continued to inform Ryan's 1996 study of churches in Birmingham, and remains a salient concept in Turnham's recent exploration of lay understandings of the Second Vatican Council in the Diocese of Middlesbrough.[71]

However the leading authority in this field continues to be Michael Hornsby-Smith who, through a vast number of studies of Catholic belief, practices and parish life from the late 1980s onwards, provided a detailed picture of the changing nature of Catholic identity in the post-war period and its continued salience.[72] Utilising the tools of social science (surveys, large-sample interviews and opinion polls) to explore questions of religious meaning, belonging and commitment in the post-conciliar period, Hornsby-Smith coined the term 'customary Catholicism'[73] to encompass Catholicism 'derived from official religion without being under its control and subject to processes of trivialisation, conventionality, apathy, convenience and self-interest'.[74] Given the considerable breadth of his enquiries, Hornsby-Smith differentiated between 'core' Catholics (for example those theologically engaged elites participating in church meetings and congresses) and less engaged, practising or 'dormant' Catholics, whom he described as 'ordinary Catholics'.[75] Against empirical definitions relating to belief in God, quantification of the use of forms of prayer, and the testing of morality, sexuality and acceptance of Roman authority against orthodox doctrine and teaching, Hornsby-Smith concluded from his data that 'far from simply passively receiving an official spirituality, lay people were in the process of actively *creating* their own lay spirituality appropriate for the 1980s and 1990s'.[76] Despite the collation of a vast and impressive collection of first-person interviews and personal testimonies through his fascinating and wide-ranging studies, much of this material was used in a classificatory, issues-based, fashion, emphasising individualisation and fragmentation, without plumbing the potential depths and complexities of the 'lived experiences' of his large sample of English Catholics. Moreover, in characterising the movement from 'collective-expressive' to 'individual-expressive' religiosity or, as described in more recent work, from 'religio-ethnic identity to one of voluntary religious commitment',[77] Hornsby-Smith was dealing with 'ideal types' and dichotomous distinctions, rather than the more fluid, gradual, and sometimes contradictory transformations and modulations of identity described in the chapters that follow.

While agreeing with much of Hornsby-Smith's analysis of the changes in English Catholicism during the second half of the twentieth century, this study takes a historical rather than social scientific approach in seeking to move away from binary taxonomies surrounding the individual and communal, or sharp distinctions between the chosen and habitual devotion, instrumental and spiritual. What has emerged very strongly from Hornsby-Smith's corpus of surveys and statistical collations is a clear conclusion, consonant in fact with the overarching argument of this book, that the religious beliefs of 'ordinary' English Catholics 'do not comprise a neat, coherent and consistent system subject only to occasional instances of deviation from the official orthodoxy'.[78] However, his description of the change to a 'more pluralistic set of beliefs in the [more] voluntaristic, post-Vatican Church' is predicated on a characterisation of the period preceding the 1960s as evincing 'a relative uniformity of beliefs in a fortress Church'[79] and the moving of Catholics through social mobility and education out of the ghetto into the mainstream of British society.[80] Despite some clearly expressed reservations about the invocation of a 'golden past' of doctrinal adherence and devotional fervour, and the designation of Britain as 'secularised' without attention to signs of growth and emergent forms of spirituality,[81] the systematising descriptions and rhetorical drive of Hornsby-Smith's narrative tend towards conclusions based on the dissolution of an English Catholic subculture,[82] the loss of its distinctiveness,[83] and the observations that 'religion [now] has no significant place in the lives of most Catholics'.[84] The undeniable rapidity of decline in mass attendance from the late 1960s,[85] and the shrinking use of rites of passage such as baptism and marriage in recent decades,[86] are cited as evidence that 'secularisation gets to all religions eventually'.[87] For this reason, the work of Hornsby-Smith has been used by sociologists of religion such as Steve Bruce to assert that Christianity in Britain, in all of its manifestations including a seemingly resilient post-war Catholicism, no longer retained its importance, vitality or salience as the twentieth century progressed.[88]

Heralded by titles such as *The Making of Post-Christian Britain*[89] and more recently *God is Dead*[90] and *The Passing of Protestant Britain*,[91] many authors writing on religion in post-war England have unequivocally endorsed the classic secularisation thesis which pronounces the terminal decline of mainstream Christianity. The sharp drop in church attendance, the erosion of moral certainty and the gap between church doctrine and congregational practice are viewed by the theory's adherents as indicative of the churches' diminished power to shape popular thinking.[92] As Green has caustically argued in his most recent treatment, 'Britain had ceased to be a Christian country by 1960' and 'the passing of this Christian, Protestant identity ... amounted to the onset of secularisation: that is, to the gradual but irreversible diminution in the social significance of religion'.[93] Within his and other historians' accounts, secularisation is a *descriptive* term encompassing changes such as the demise of notions of Victorian 'puritanism',[94] and the shrinkage of voluntarism, and associational cultures,[95] across the course of the twentieth century. On the other hand for Bruce, in his most trenchant re-statement of 'an unfashionable theory', secularisation is an *explanatory* paradigm, marshalled with reference to the now-familiar statistics of 'irreversible institutional' withering, unshaken by 'residual popular religion'[96] or 'fuzzy fidelity' (to use Voas' terminology),[97] and causatively linked to the constituent features of 'modernity', namely socialisation, rationalisation, urbanisation and individualisation. In either instance, this seemingly 'commonsensical', dogmatic rendering of the modern era accounts for the absence of a religiously attuned sensibility in much twentieth-century British historiography, which has focused on the more potent themes of world wars, the welfare state, imperial decline and participatory democracy. Within much of this literature, Christianity is relegated to a footnote,[98] or treated as synonymous with the Established Church and its ecclesiastical fortunes.[99]

A reversal of this trend has been observable since the beginning of the twenty-first century with a number of publications fundamentally challenging the secularisation thesis and its circular, self-reinforcing link between 'modernisation' and religious decline. Callum Brown's immensely influential but enduringly controversial *The Death of Christian Britain* (2001, second edition 2009), forcefully contested the inevitability and chronology of the classic pattern of secularisation, and asserted that Christianity remained a resilient resource for constructing personal identity which 'mattered deeply in British society as a whole in the 1950s'.[100] Here he challenged a statistically and institutionally focused approach and instead used insights gleaned liberally from modern cultural theory to establish his overarching category of 'discursive Christianity', defined as self-subscription to protocols of personal identity deriving from Christian expectations or 'discourses'.[101] Analysing rituals, dress, popular fiction, newspapers and film, Brown convincingly demonstrated the persistence of a Christian cultural framework or 'salvation economy' well into the late 1950s, taking account of the spike in church attendance statistics in all denominations after both world wars, and paying close attention to the overwhelmingly Christian-orientated social structures and cultural mores still discernible in the middle of the twentieth century. Along with other revisionist historians such as Sarah Williams[102] and Hugh McLeod,[103] it could be argued that Brown has convincingly buried the notion that urbanisation and working-class disaffection were responsible for the onset of religious decline in the nineteenth century.[104] Moreover, Brown's account does much to move the debate beyond the 'reductionist bipolarities' of churchgoers and non-churchgoers, believers and unbelievers, which has ignored, in his words, 'whole realms of religiosity which cannot be counted'.[105] His work is therefore to be welcomed for the attention it pays to the language of those engaged in religious activities, and to the different registers in which belief may be articulated. Nevertheless, a central part of the argument of *The Death of Christian Britain*, with its focus on 'discursive Christianity', is the author's equally strong conviction of discursive failure, dated precisely to 1963, when:

> really quite suddenly ... something very profound ruptured the character of the nation and its people, sending organised Christianity on a downward spiral to the margins of social significance.[106]

He identifies this 'something' as women's disaffection with religion, induced by second-wave feminism, and the wider societal changes of the 'swinging sixties'. Brown has argued that the defection of those who once were the bulwark of popular support for organised Christianity, particularly with reference to a mostly Protestant, evangelical conversion narrative, and socially conservative ethos, plunged 'a formerly religious people … into a truly secular condition'.[107] Having apparently been written out of Brown's script, secularisation makes a sudden *deus ex machina* appearance at the eleventh hour, and the timing and gradient of secularisation are merely rescheduled.[108]

Brown's account of the effect of the 1960s on British Christianity has most recently been challenged by Hugh McLeod's masterful contextualisation of the undoubted religious changes of the period within a European and American framework, and against the backdrop of the Second Vatican Council and the Church of England's embrace of the so-called 'new morality'. Entitled *The Religious Crisis of the 1960s*, McLeod's highly significant account tackled Brown's descriptions of 'a blissful dawn' for women in the 1960s, who 'reject [wholesale] the definitions of femininity, the moral rules and the career options prescribed by the churches, and abandoned the task of passing on religious beliefs and customs to the younger generation'.[109] While acknowledging that Brown has identified a crucial dimension of religious change in this period, McLeod rejected the search for a 'master narrative' and identified a panoply of factors behind the 'revolutionary' changes of the period, ranging from theological and political radicalisation, the decline of ideologically based sub-cultures, the emergence of a distinct category of 'youth', and the rise of affluence and the burgeoning of consumption.[110] What emerged from his discussion is an account in which Christianity lost its privileged position as a '"common language", which was to some degree shared by all but the most convinced and committed unbelievers'.[111] This is an extension of his earlier work on the 'decline of Christendom',[112] which mirrored Brown's category of 'discursive Christianity' in arguing that regardless of individual beliefs, Christian language, rites, moral teachings and personnel were part of a taken-for-granted environment.[113] The pivotal period in this movement from 'Christian county to civilized country' as McLeod terms it (echoing Labour MP Roy Jenkins), was the raft of legislative changes throughout the 1960s. These piecemeal and patchy legislative reforms gradually redefined the relationship between morality and legality by prioritising individual human rights, reshaping the 'private sphere', and acknowledging religious and moral pluralism.[114] In keeping with his definition of the 'long sixties', and the work of political historians such as Mark Jarvis,[115] McLeod charted the beginning of these changes under Harold Macmillan

(1957–63). They continued with considerable speed under Harold Wilson (1964–70) with the decriminalisation of homosexuality, the availability of contraceptives for unmarried women under the NHS, and reform of the laws surrounding divorce and abortion.[116] McLeod's account has varied from many of the standard accounts of the political culture and legislative reforms of the 1960s[117] by introducing much-needed balance into the discussion of these sweeping and important changes. He considered the spectrum of Christian opinion and reaction to the reforming impulses of the period, illustrating the perspectives of liberals, conservatives and those who operated with greater regard to pragmatism than the intricacies of political theory or contemporary theology. Moreover, McLeod made an important and little-recognised argument about the role of the churches themselves, particularly the Anglican Establishment, in facilitating these legislative changes, thereby illustrating that they were piecemeal and debated, rather than part of a homogeneous 'liberalising' package.[118] His conclusion is that 'in none of these cases is there much validity in the view which sees religion and the churches as passive victims of overpowering secularizing forces'.[119] Nevertheless, what has changed, he contended, is the movement away from one set of moral principles as normative towards a more pluralistic, individualistic and consumerist society.

There is much to commend in McLeod's lively and broad-ranging account of this tumultuous period, particularly its recognition of the need to nuance the story of the 1960s through its 'discursive' constructions (as Brown would have it), or the 'lived experiences' of ordinary people from a variety of backgrounds and religious affiliations. Despite the methodological challenges arising from the use of existing, archived oral history testimonies conducted by others at differing times and for diverse purposes, McLeod's use of this material to engage with the ways in which people experienced the 1960s, and narrated their self-identities and faith perspectives, is a welcome movement away from the prevalent mythologised or institutionally derived histories of the period. Moreover, McLeod's contextualisation of these social and cultural movements on a broader, international, canvas and his sophisticated analysis of the causes of the very important religious changes that undoubtedly did take place, are a welcome addition to a developing historiography.[120] Nevertheless, there remains a tension in McLeod's continued utilisation of the metaphor of 'decline' and the language of 'crisis'. This seems to run counter to his descriptive emphases and narrative structures, which describe what might be better conceptualised as religious transformation, institutional innovation and adaptation (as well as lethargy) *and* the resilience of some aspects of religious life in the face of a number of social and cultural factors which profoundly altered the landscape of late twentieth-century Britain. While McLeod rightly highlighted an intense renegotiation of the relationship between church and state in this period, by returning in his concluding assessments to a picture of the sixties as ushering in the 'dechristianisation of Britain', he reverts to a purely institutional perspective, with a particular emphasis on the Established Church. His account therefore does not specifically tackle the ways in which forms of Christian language continued to circulate within and animate British society. As the chapters that follow contend, Christian discourses and in particular an English Catholic 'dialect' continued to be used by individuals and communities to shape and articulate a form of cultural identity within the changed context of an ethnically, morally and religiously plural Britain. For some, their vocabulary had not changed greatly from that learnt in their childhood earlier in the century, whereas others modulated their language through contemporary ecumenical, experiential and psychological terms. Yet others adopted a reconstructed Catholic identity as a form of radical, counter-cultural identification or a defensive, oppositional identity. As Brown himself has argued elsewhere in a detailed exposition of McLeod's study and his own (varying) account of 'the religious crisis of the 1960s', a more textured religious history requires consideration of religious conservatives (as well as liberals), tailored oral histories, and a close discursive analysis of the engagement of youth cultures in the 60s and 70s with religion'.[121]

In a recent study of the 'genealogy of arguments about secularization' which both located the emergence of secularisation theory within the modernist sociological projects of the 1960s and perceptively excavated Christianity's own complicity in generating narratives of secularisation, through assumptions about religious decline and renewal central to Christian soteriology, Jeremy Morris concluded that '"secularization" is a broken concept'. He argued that it is 'inapplicable to the British experience in the eighteenth, nineteenth, and early twentieth centuries, and unhelpful even in attending to the contraction of mainstream Christianity in the last half-century'.[122] He advocated the critique of monolithic notions of 'religion' itself, and urged closer attention to religious experience in its various forms, to yield an account more attuned to the contours of social change in modern Britain.[123] Jeffrey Cox, three decades on from his own pioneering account which questioned the adequacy of statistics and secularisation-based explanations for religious change,[124] has also proffered a recent assessment (in a festschrift for Hugh McLeod) on the need to 'eliminate' the 'hidden and invocatory master narrative of secularisation'.[125] This book firmly takes up this agenda, adopting 'lived religious experience' as an interpretative lens and concrete actuality in describing the complexities of beliefs and practices of Catholics in the decades following the Second World War. It co-opts an emerging strand within the sociology of religion and spirituality prioritising 'experience',[126] and the shifting of religious authority in identity formation, and decision making, from external sources to 'the self'.[127] This literature places a premium on embodiment,[128] expressive new age practices[129] and a 'questing' or 'seeking' spirituality that is self-authenticating and self-directed (within, as well as outside, institutional settings).[130] In this vein Charles Taylor, in his monumental survey of five centuries of interaction between 'secularity and belief', has designated the latter part of the twentieth century as 'The Age of Authenticity'[131] which prioritises an 'immanent frame', or 'this-worldly' order, but 'of itself leaves the issue open whether, for purposes of ultimate explanation, or spiritual transformation, or final sense-making, we might have to invoke something transcendent.'[132]

These explanatory categories from the study of contemporary spirituality have salience here because they also resonate with theological currents in the Catholic Church in the latter part of the twentieth century, perhaps best described as a shift in emphasis or accent from a soteriological framework to an eschatological framework. These theological tendencies reached their full expression in the Second Vatican Council and the work of continental theologians like Yves Congar, Marie-Dominque Chenu, Karl Rahner, Henri de Lubac, Edward Schillebeeckx and Pierre Teilhard de Chardin. As Bill McSweeny contemporaneously summarised – giving concrete examples of this movement from the soteriological to the eschatological – for English Catholics in 1980 this re-orientated perspective meant:

> a shift in emphasis from Christ's divinity to his humanity; from the Church as an institution of salvation to the Church as community; from the objective to the subjective aspects of liturgy; from God's transcendence and otherness to his presence among men and in all creation; from the resurrection as a discrete event in the past and in the future to the kingdom already present

in the world and in the process of fulfilment; from a moral theology of sin to a moral theology of human development and interpersonal relationships.[133]

The chapters that follow, examining changes in Catholic liturgical and extra-liturgical Christological practices, Marian devotions and the rosary, and the cult of the saints, explore more fully this accentuation of authenticity, self-expressiveness and a 'this-worldly' theology in the evolution, adaptation or abandonment of traditional forms of English Catholic devotional culture.

Taking a lead from Brown in the conjoining of Christian discourses to analysis of gender relations, but more influenced by the theoretical interventions of Jacqueline de Vries discussing Christianity's contribution to feminism[134] than Brown's continuing emphasis on the centrality of feminism to the 'religious crisis',[135] this book addresses Joy Dixon's invitation to 'find ways to write the history of religion and gender without allowing our analyses to collapse back into the Victorian binary of the 'secular man' and the 'spiritual woman'.[136] Inspiration for this enterprise has been taken from recent developments in gender history,[137] urban studies and explorations of immigration and religious pluralism in Britain,[138] as well as detailed social histories of the 1950s and 1960s.[139] From Claire Langhamer's *The English in Love*, which explores the evolution of marriage from a religiously sanctioned institution to a relationship based on love, sex and self-actualisation,[140] through to Clive Field's re-examination of post-war 'faith in the metropolis'[141] and Mark Donnelly's forthright reappraisal of the 1960s as neither golden age nor catastrophe, emerging histories increasingly assert that change in twentieth-century Britain should be situated as part of a longer-term continuum (even reaching back into the inter-war period).[142] Rather than engaging in what Donnelly has described as 'sterile debates about the "myth" or "reality" of the period, and contending readings of "what it was really like" back then', I too view it as more productive to look at 'a series of overlapping contexts' and the 'mobilisation and reworking' of narratives about these decades at various times and for divergent purposes.[143]

This book then, in challenging the marginalisation of English Catholicism within ecclesiastically derived narratives of 'ghettos' and 'golden ages', and moving beyond internecine struggles for ownership of the Second Vatican Council, contributes to a broader historiography re-examining change (and continuity) in the 1950s and 1960s across a longer trajectory. In doing so, it is also taking up the challenge set by Becky Conekin, Frank Mort and Chris Waters to transcend 'highly compartmentalised', disciplinary-discrete and narrowly focused histories of the years after 1945.[111] From the collective portrait of English Catholicism that this chapter has offered (and the intellectual debates and backdrops against which these constructions are projected), the following chapters offer more individualised character studies of Christ, Mary (and Joseph), and a number of saints. These further 'family' portraits are also framed by debates about class relations and internationalism, marriage (and sex), psychological knowledge and ecumenism. They are freighted by presentation through an idealised, prescriptive literature, yet also personalised, and particularised, through the interwoven and contrasting life narratives. 'Faith in the family' throughout this period is shown to be highly diverse, undergoing internal re-orientation as well as externally driven adaptation, and capable of modulation through personal, communal and civic manifestations.

Notes

1 *The Times*, 31 October 1949, 5.
2 Ibid. All correspondence reprinted in *Catholicism To-Day: Letters to the Editor* (London: Times, 1949).
3 A. S. Duncan-Jones, *The Times*, 28 November 1949, 5.
4 J. Hagerty, *Cardinal Hinsley: Priest and Patriot* (Oxford: Family Press, 2008), 303–35; T. Moloney, *Westminster, Whitehall and the Vatican: the Role of Cardinal Hinsley 1935–43* (Tunbridge Wells: Burns and Oates, 1985).
5 S. Parker, *Faith on the Home Front: Aspects of Church Life and Popular Religion in Birmingham, 1939–1945* (Oxford: Peter Lang, 2005).
6 Keating, 'Faith', 86.
7 M. Grimley, 'Thatcherism, Morality and Religion' in B. Jackson and R. Saunders (eds), *Making Thatcher's Britain* (Cambridge: Cambridge University Press, 2012), 78–94; L. Filby, 'God and Mrs Thatcher: Religion and Politics in 1980s Britain' (Unpublished PhD thesis, University of Warwick, 2010).
8 *The Tablet*, 3 December 1949, 368.
9 Ibid.
10 *Catholic Herald*, 29 September 1950, 9.
11 Beck (ed.), *The English Catholics*.
12 *The Tablet*, 20 May 1950, 408.
13 '"Papal" Pageant in Wembley Sun', *Catholic Herald*, 6 October 1950, 1.
14 N. Schofield, *Our Lady of Willesden: A Brief History of the Shrine and Parish* (London, 2002).

15 *Catholic Directory 1950* (London: Burns and Oates, 1950), 571.
16 Hilton, *Catholic Lancashire*.
17 Fielding, *Class*.
18 Doyle, *Mitres*.
19 J. Hagerty, *The Catenian Association: A Centenary History* (Coventry: Catenian Association, 2008), 123.
20 K. Ziesler, 'The Irish in Birmingham 1830–1970' (Unpublished PhD thesis, University of Birmingham, 1989) who suggests at least 90–100,000 came between 1941 and 1945 – see Keating, 'Faith', 105, fn 155.
21 A. Rea, *Manchester's Little Italy: Memories of the Italian Colony of Ancoats* (Manchester: Neil Richardson, 1988); L. Ryan, 'Family Matters: (E)migration, Familial networks and Irish women in Britain', *Sociological Review* 52(3) (2004), 351–70; K. Sword, J. Ciechanowski and N. Davies, *The Formation of the Polish Community in Great Britain 1939–50* (London: University of London, 1989).
22 Keating, 'Faith', 101.
23 On the difficulties of defining 'class', but a discussion of various indices which tend towards the view that the working class were around three quarters of the population until the latter half of the twentieth century, see J. Bourke, *Working Class Cultures in Britain 1890–1960: Gender, Class and Ethnicity* (London: Routledge, 1994), 2–22.
24 Coman, *Welfare*.
25 Newman Demographic Survey, *Catholics in the Universities: the Next Decade* (London: Newman Demographic Survey, 1960).
26 P. Lane, *The Catenian Association, 1908–1983: A Microcosm of the Development of the Catholic Middle Class* (London: Catenian Association, 1982); A. Harris, '"The People of God dressed for dinner and dancing"? English Catholic Masculinity, Religious Sociability and the Catenian Association' in S. Morgan and L. Delap (eds), *Men, Masculinity and Religious Change in Britain Since 1900* (London: Palgrave, 2013), chapter 2.
27 W. Rees-Mogg, *A Humbler Heaven: The Beginnings of Hope* (London: Hamish Hamilton, 1977) and *Memoirs* (London: HarperPress, 2011).
28 N. St John-Stevas, *Before the Sunset Fades: An Autobiography* (London: Harper Collins, 2009).
29 D. Lannon, 'Financing Catholic Schools: Two Aspects of the Situation in 1900' in J. A. Hilton (ed.), *Turning the Last Century: Essays on English Catholicism c.1900* (Wigan: North West Catholic History Society, 2003), 27–46; E. G. Tenbus, *English Catholics and the Education of the Poor, 1847–1902* (London: Pickering Chatto, 2010).
30 E. Larkin, *The Roman Catholic Church and the Home Rule Movement in Ireland* (Dublin: Gill and Macmillan, 1990).
31 Parsons, 'Emotion'; Gilley, 'Vulgar'; cf. Heimann, *Catholic*.
32 Davies, 'Faith of Our Fathers'; F. Neal, *Sectarian Violence: The Liverpool Experience 1819–1914* (Manchester: Manchester University Press, 1988).
33 E.g. M. Hickman, 'The Religio-Ethnic Identities of Teenagers of Irish Descent' in Hornsby-Smith (ed.), *Catholics*, 182–97. cf. D. Jodock (ed.), *Catholicism Contending with Modernity: Roman Catholic Modernism and Anti-Modernism in Historical Context* (Cambridge: Cambridge University Press, 2000).

34 E.g. G. Scott, *The R.C.s: A Report on Roman Catholics in Britain Today* (London: Hutchinson, 1967); K. Aspden, *Fortress Church: The English Roman Catholic Bishops and Politics, 1903–1963* (Leominster: Gracewing, 2002).
35 S. Green, *The Passing of Protestant Britain: Secularisation and Social Change c. 1920–1960* (Cambridge: Cambridge University Press, 2011), 232.
36 J. Brothers, *Church and School. A Study of the Image of Education on Religion* (Liverpool: Liverpool University Press, 1964); M. Hickman, *Religion, Class and Identity: The State, the Church and the Education of the Irish in Britain* (Aldershot: Avebury, 1995).
37 J. Davies, 'L'Art du Possible: The Board of Education, the Catholic Church and Negotiations over the White Paper and the Education Bill 1943–44', *Recusant History* 22(2) (1994), 231–50; K. Elliott, 'A Very Pushy Kind of Folk: Educational Reform 1944 and the Catholic Laity of England and Wales', *History of Education* 25 (2006), 91–119.
38 Coman, *Welfare*.
39 J. Pereiro, 'Who are the Laity?' in V. A. McClelland and M. Hodgetts (eds), *From without the Flaminian Gate: 150 Years of Roman Catholicism in England and Wales 1850–2000* (London: Darton, Longman and Todd, 1999), 167–91.
40 P. Doyle, 'The Catholic Federation 1906–29' in Sheils, *Voluntary*, 461–76.
41 J. M. Cleary, *Catholic Social Action in Britain 1909–1959: A History of the Catholic Social Guild* (Oxford: Catholic Social Guild, 1961); P. Doyle, 'Charles Plater SJ and the Origins of the Catholic Social Guild', *Recusant History* 21 (1993), 401–17; J. Keating, 'Making a Catholic Labour Activist: The Catholic Social Guild and the Catholic Workers' College 1909–39', *Labour History Review* 59(3) (1994), 44–56.
42 D. Campbell, 'The Catholic Evidence Guild: Towards a History of the Laity', *Heythrop Journal* 30(3) (1989), 306–24.
43 P. Kane, '"The Willing Captive of Home?": The English Catholic Women's League, 1906–1920', *Church History* 60(3) (1991), 331–55. See also F. Mason, '"The Newer Eve": The Catholic Women's Suffrage Society in England 1916–23', *Catholic Historical Review* 72 (1986), 620–38.
44 S. Collins and M. P. Hornsby-Smith, 'The Rise and Fall of the YCW in England', *Journal of Contemporary Religion* 71(1) (2002), 87–100; C. Walker, *Worker Apostles: The YCW Movement in Britain* (London: Catholic Truth Society, 1994).
45 J. Keating, 'The British Experience: Christian Democracy without a Party 1910–60' in D. Hanley (ed.), *Christian Democracy in Europe: A Comparative Perspective* (London: Pinter, 1994), 168–81.
46 S. Hellemans and J. Wissink (eds), *Towards a New Catholic Church in Advanced Modernity: Transformations, Visions, Tensions* (Münster: LIT Verlag, 2012).
47 *Catholic Directory 1964* (London: Burns and Oates, 1964), 769.
48 For a highly readable 'who's who' of late twentieth-century prominent English Catholics, see Sewell, *Catholics*.
49 J. Lothian, *The Making and Unmaking of the English Catholic Intellectual Community, 1910–1950* (Notre Dame: University of Notre Dame Press, 2009); A. Hastings (ed.), *Bishops and Writers: Aspects of the Evolution of Modern English Catholicism* (Wheathamstead: Anthony Clarke Books, 1977); J. Pearce, *Literary Converts: Spiritual Inspiration in an Age of Unbelief* (London: HarperCollins, 1999).

50 M. Conway and T. Buchanan, *Political Catholicism in Europe, 1918–65* (Oxford: Oxford University Press, 1996), chapter 8.
51 M. Walsh, *From Sword to Ploughshare: Sword of the Spirit to Catholic Institute for International Relations 1940–80* (London: Catholic Institute for International Relations, 1980); S. Mews, 'The Sword of the Spirit: A Catholic Cultural Crusade of 1940', *Studies in Church History* 20 (1983), 409–30.
52 M. Walsh, 'Ecumenism in War Time: The "Sword of the Spirit" and "Religion and Life" 1940–45', *Heythrop Journal* 23 (1982), 243–58; M. Grimley, 'The Religion of Englishness: Puritanism, Providentialism and "National Character", 1918–45', *Journal of British Studies* 46 (2007), 884–906.
53 M. Walsh, 'Catholics, Society and Popular Culture' in McClelland and Hodgetts, *Flaminian Gate*, 346–70.
54 E.g. E. Schillebeeckx, *Vatican II – A Struggle of Minds and Other Essays* (Dublin: Gill, 1963); Novak, *Open*; Bédoyère, *Future*.
55 M. J. Weaver, 'Sheed and Ward', *U. S. Catholic Historian* 21(3) (2003), 1–18.
56 F. Sheed, *Is it the Same Church?* (London: Sheed and Ward, 1968), xvi.
57 P. Hebblethwaite, *The Runaway Church* (London: Collins, 1975), 9.
58 H. R. Williamson, *The Modern Mass: A Reversion to the Reforms of Cranmer* (Chumleigh: Britons, 1969) and *The Great Betrayal: Some Thoughts on the Invalidity of the New Mass* (Chumleigh: Britons, 1970).
59 L. Boyer, *The Decomposition of Catholicism* (London: Sands, 1970).
60 A. Harris, 'A Fresh Stripping of the Altars? The Reactions of English Catholics to the Second Vatican Council and Liturgical Change' (Unpublished MSt dissertation, University of Oxford, 2004).
61 M. Douglas, *Natural Symbols: Explorations in Cosmology* (London: Harmond, 1973), 67.
62 A. T. Ellis, *Serpent on the Rock* (London: Hodder and Stoughton, 1994) and *God has Not Changed* (London: Burns and Oates, 2004).
63 Heenan, *Not the Whole Truth*; J. Hagerty, *Cardinal John Carmel Heenan* (Leominster: Gracewing, 2013).
64 E. Duffy, *Faith of Our Fathers: Reflections on Catholic Tradition* (London: Continuum, 2004).
65 Stanford, *Hume*; E. Stourton, *Absolute Truth: The Catholic Church in the World Today* (London: Viking, 1998).
66 D. Lodge, *Paradise News: A Novel* (Secker & Warburg, 1991), 56–59, 189–92, 257, 354–56 and *Therapy: A Novel* (London: Secker & Warburg, 1995), 232–54, 267, 290–91. See also D. Spencer, 'The Second Vatican Council and the English Catholic Novel' (Unpublished PhD thesis, University of Liverpool, 1996).
67 A. Archer, *The Two Catholic Churches: A Study in Oppression* (London: SCM Press, 1986), 132.
68 D. Lodge, *How Far Can you Go?* (London: Secker & Warburg, 1980), 79.
69 M. Savage, *Identities and Social Change in Britain since 1940: The Politics of Method* (Oxford: Oxford University Press, 2010).
70 C. K. Ward, *Priests and People: A Study in the Sociology of Religion* (Liverpool: Liverpool University Press, 1961), 130.
71 Margaret Turnham, 'Roman Catholic Revivalism: A Study of the Diocese of Middlesbrough, 1779–1992' (PhD thesis, University of Nottingham, 2012).

72 See M. P. Hornsby-Smith, *Roman Catholics in England: Studies in Social Structure since the Second World War* (Cambridge: Cambridge University Press, 1987); *The Changing Parish: A Study of Parishes, Priests and Parishioners after Vatican II* (London: Routledge, 1989); *Roman Catholic Beliefs in England: Customary Catholicism and Transformations of Religious Authority* (Cambridge: Cambridge University Press, 1991).
73 Hornsby-Smith, *Roman Catholic Beliefs*, 3.
74 *Ibid*, 21.
75 *Ibid*, 29.
76 *Ibid*, 60. See also B. McSweeney, *Roman Catholicism: The Search for Relevance* (Oxford: Basil Blackwell, 1980).
77 M. P. Hornsby-Smith, 'The Changing Identity of Catholics in England' in S. Coleman and P. Collins (eds), *Religion, Identity and Change: Perspectives of Global Transformations* (Aldershot: Ashgate, 2004), 47 and Hornsby-Smith, *Roman Catholic Beliefs*, 9.
78 Hornsby-Smith, *Roman Catholic Beliefs*, 215.
79 *Ibid*. See also Aspden, *Fortress*.
80 M. P. Hornsby-Smith, 'Into the Mainstream: Recent Transformations in British Catholicism' in T. M. Gannon (ed.), *World Catholicism in Transition* (New York: Macmillan, 1988), 228.
81 M. P. Hornsby-Smith, 'Recent Transformations in English Catholicism: Evidence of Secularization?' in S. Bruce (ed.), *Religion and Modernization: Sociologists and Historians Debate the Secularization Thesis* (Oxford: Clarendon Press, 1992), 122.
82 Hornsby-Smith, *Roman Catholics in England*, 208–14.
83 Hornsby-Smith, *Roman Catholic Beliefs*, 8.
84 *Ibid*, 221. See also his critique of Grace Davie in 'Believing without Belonging? The Case of Roman Catholics in England' in B. R. Wilson (ed.), *Religion: Contemporary Issues. The All Souls Seminars in the Sociology of Religion* (London: Bellew Publishing, 1992), 134.
85 Catholic Sunday mass attendance has dropped by 30% since 1961 to 995,000 people in 2001 – see T. Horwood, *The Future of the Catholic Church in England* (London: Laicos Press, 2006), 13, and McLeod, *Religious Crisis*, 65.
86 Infant baptisms have fallen by 61% and marriages within the church by 78% since 1958 – see A. E. C. W. Spencer (ed.), *Pastoral and Population Statistics of the Catholic Community in England and Wales, 1958–2002* (Taunton: Pastoral Research Centre, 2004), 1.
87 Bruce, *Religion and Modernization*, 4.
88 S. Bruce, *Religion in the Modern World: From Cathedrals to Cults* (Oxford: Oxford University Press, 1996), 123–24 and *Secularization: In Defence of an Unfashionable Theory* (Oxford: Oxford University Press, 2011), 70, 74.
89 A. Gilbert, *The Making of Post-Christian Britain: A History of the Secularization of Modern Society* (London: Longman, 1980).
90 S. Bruce, *God is Dead: Secularization in the West* (Oxford: Blackwell, 2002).
91 Green, *Passing*.
92 S. Bruce, *Religion in Modern Britain* (Oxford: Oxford University Press, 1995), 234.
93 Green, *Passing*, 32.
94 *Ibid*, 135–79.

95 F. Prochaska, *Christianity and Social Service in Modern Britain: The Disinherited Spirit* (Oxford: Oxford University Press, 2006).
96 S. Bruce, 'Secularisation, Church and Popular Religion', *Journal of Ecclesiastical History* 62(3) (2011), 543–61.
97 D. Voas, 'The Rise and Fall of Fuzzy Fidelity in Europe', *European Sociological Review* 25(2) (2009), 155–68; D. Voas and A. Crockett, 'Religion in Britain: Neither Believing nor Belonging', *Sociology* 39(1) (2005), 11–28.
98 E.g. P. Clarke, *Hope and Glory: Britain 1900–1990* (London: Allen Lane, 1996), 161–6; A. Marr, *The Making of Modern Britain: From Queen Victoria to VE Day* (London: Pan Books, 2009), 404; D. Kynaston, *Family Britain: 1951–7* (London: Bloomsbury, 2009), 531–8.
99 E.g. J. Obelkevich, 'Religion' in F. M. L. Thompson (ed.), *The Cambridge Social History of Britain 1750–1950: Volume 3, Social Agencies and Institutions* (Cambridge: Cambridge University Press, 1990), 311–56; J. Maiden, *National Religion and the Prayer Book Controversy, 1927–8* (Woodbridge: Boydell Press, 2009); J. Wolffe (ed.), *Religion in History: Conflict, Conversion and Co-existence* (Manchester: Manchester University Press, 2004); M. F. Snape, *God and the British Soldier: Religion and the British Army in the First and Second World Wars* (London: Routledge, 2005).
100 Brown, *Death*, 7, 9. See also C. Brown, *Religion and Society in Twentieth-Century Britain* (Harlow: Longman, 2006).
101 Brown, *Death*, 12.
102 Williams, *Religious Belief*.
103 H. McLeod, *Religion and the People of Western Europe 1789–1989* (Oxford: Oxford University Press, 1997).
104 Brown, *Death*, 8–9.
105 *Ibid*, 12.
106 *Ibid*, 1.
107 *Ibid*.
108 Brown had previously identified decline from 1914; see C. Brown, 'A Revisionist Approach to Religious Change' in Bruce, *Religion and Modernization*, 53.
109 McLeod, *Religious Crisis*, 13.
110 *Ibid*, 15.
111 *Ibid*, 264.
112 H. McLeod and W. Ustorf (eds), *The Decline of Christendom in Western Europe, 1750–2000* (Cambridge: Cambridge University Press, 2003).
113 McLeod, *Religious Crisis*, 265.
114 *Ibid*, 215.
115 M. Jarvis, *Conservative Governments, Morality and Social Change in Affluent Britain, 1957–1964* (Manchester: Manchester University Press, 1995).
116 McLeod, *Religious Crisis*, 217–26.
117 E.g. A. Marwick, *The Sixties: Cultural Revolution in Britain, France, Italy and the United States, c.1958–c.1974* (Oxford: Oxford University Press, 1998), 247–87, 679–724 (and the limited discussion of religion, 33–5, 501); C. Davies, *The Strange Death of Moral Britain* (London: Transaction Publishers, 2004) and H. Cook, *The Long Sexual Revolution: English Women, Sex and Contraception, 1800–1975* (Oxford: Oxford University Press, 2004).

118 McLeod, *Religious Crisis*, 220-21. Also G. Parsons, 'How the times they were a-changing: exploring the context of religious transformation in Britain in the 1960s' in Wolffe (ed.), *Religion in History*, 161-89 and G. Parsons (ed.), *The Growth of Religious Diversity: Britain from 1945, Volume III* (1994), 125-263.
119 McLeod, *Religious Crisis*, 233.
120 E.g. M. Grimley, 'Law, Morality and Secularisation: The Church of England and the Wolfenden Report, 1954-1967', *Journal of Ecclesiastical History* 60(4) (2009), 725-41; L. Woodhead and R. Catto (eds), *Religion and Change in Modern Britain* (London: Routledge, 2012).
121 C. Brown, 'What was the Religious Crisis of the 1960s?', *Journal of Religious History* 34(4) (2010), 479.
122 J. Morris, 'Secularization and Religious Experience: Arguments in the Historiography of Modern British Religion', *Historical Journal* 55(1) (2012), 195-219.
123 Ibid, 212-15.
124 J. Cox, *The English Churches in a Secular Society: Lambeth 1870–1930* (Oxford: Oxford University Press, 1982).
125 J. Cox, 'Towards Eliminating the Concept of Secularisation: A Progress Report' in C. Brown and M. Snape (eds), *Secularisation in the Christian World: Essays in Honour of Hugh McLeod* (Farnham: Ashgate, 2010), 19. See also D. Endozoin, '"The Cause is not Quite what it Used to Be": The Return of Secularisation', *English Historical Review* CXXVII (525) (2012), 377-400.
126 G. Lynch, *After Religion: 'Generation X' and the Search for Meaning* (London: Darton Longman and Todd, 2002); G. Lynch, *The New Spirituality: An Introduction to Progressive Belief in the Twenty-First Century* (London: I. B. Tauris, 2007). G. Davie, P. Heelas and L. Woodhead, *Predicting Religion: Christian, Secular and Alternative Futures* (Aldershot: Ashgate, 2003).
127 P. Heelas, S. Lash and P. Morris (eds), *Detraditionalization. Critical Reflections on Authority and Identity* (Oxford: Blackwell, 1996).
128 E. Sointu and L. Woodhead, 'Spirituality, Gender, and Expressive Selfhood', *Journal for the Scientific Study of Religion* 47(2) (2008), 259-76.
129 P. Heelas and L. Woodhead, *The Spiritual Revolution: Why Religion is Giving Way to Spirituality* (Oxford: Blackwell, 2005).
130 Roof, *Spiritual*, 75. See also R. Bellah, *Habits of the Heart: Individualism and Commitment in American Life* (Updated ed., Berkeley: University of California Press, 1996), 221, 235; R. Wuthnow, *After the Baby Boomers: How Twenty- and Thirty-Somethings are Shaping the Future of American Religion* (Princeton: Princeton University Press, 2007), 13-16; R. Flory and D. E. Miller, *Finding Faith: The Spiritual Question of the Post-Boomer Generation* (New Brunswick: Rutgers University Press, 2008).
131 Taylor, *Secular*, 473-504.
132 Ibid, 594.
133 McSweeney, *Roman*, 112.
134 J. de Vries, 'More than Paradoxes to Offer: Feminism, History and Religious Cultures' in Morgan and de Vries, *Women*, 188-210.
135 Brown, 'Religious Crisis', 477; 'Women and Religion in Britain: An Autobiographical View of the Fifties and Sixties' in Brown and Snape, *Secularisation*, 159-74 and

'Gendering Secularisation: Locating Women in the Transformation of British Christianity in the 1960s' in I. Katznelson and G. Stedman Jones (eds), *Religion and the Political Imagination* (Cambridge: Cambridge University Press, 2010), 275–94.

136 J. Dixon, 'Modernity, Heterodoxy and the Transformation of Religious Cultures' in Morgan and de Vries, *Women*, 212.

137 'Gender and Religion Special Issue', *Gender and History* 25(3) (2013) (edited by J. DeGroot and S. Morgan); A. Wills, 'Delinquency, Masculinity and Citizenship in England, 1950–70', *Past and Present* 187(1) (2005), 157–85; C. Langhamer, 'Sexual Politics in Mid Twentieth-Century Britain: Adultery in Post-war England', *History Workshop Journal* 62(1) (2006), 86–115; S. Brooke, 'Gender and Working Class Identity in Britain during the 1950s', *Journal of Social History* 34(4) (2001), 773–95.

138 M. Grimley, 'The Church of England, Race and Multiculturalism, 1962–2012' in J. Garnett and A. Harris (eds), *Rescripting Religion in the City: Migration and Religious Identity in the Modern Metropolis* (Farnham: Ashgate, 2013), chapter 12; Panikos Panayi, *An Immigration History of Britain: Multicultural Racism since 1800* (Harlow: Pearson Longman, 2010); D. Goodhew (ed.), *Church Growth in Britain: 1980 to the Present* (Farnham: Ashgate, 2012).

139 D. Sandbrook, *Never Had it So Good: A History of Britain from Suez to the Beatles* (London: Little, Brown, 2005); *White Heat: A History of Britain in the Swinging Sixties* (London: Little, Brown, 2006); P. Hennessy, *Having it So Good: Britain in the Fifties* (London: Allen Lane, 2006); D. Kynaston, *Austerity Britain, 1945–1951* (London: Bloomsbury, 2007).

140 C. Langhamer, *The English in Love: The Intimate Story of an Emotional Revolution* (Oxford: Oxford University Press, 2013).

141 C. D. Field, 'Faith in the Metropolis: Opinion Polls and Christianity in Post-war London', *London Journal* 24(1) (1999), 68–84 and '*Puzzled People* Revisited: Religious Believing and Belonging in Wartime Britain 1939–45', *Twentieth Century British History* 19(4) (2008), 446–79.

142 See N. Thomas, 'Will the Real 1950s Please Stand Up? Views of a Contradictory Decade', *Cultural and Social History* 5(2) (2008), 227–36.

143 M. Donnelly, *Sixties Britain: Culture, Society, Politics* (Harlow: Pearson Longman, 2005), 196–7.

144 B. Conekin, F. Mort and C. Waters (eds), *Moments of Modernity: Reconstructing Britain 1954–1964* (London: Rivers Oram, 1999), 20.

Chapter 3

Gatherings at the family table

The liturgy, the Eucharist and Christ our brother

Drink the wine and chew the wafer
Two, four, six, eight
Time to transubstantiate

In his popular pamphlet examining the ways in which 'the Catholic world [we] knew seems to have been turned upside down – and so quickly', Frank Sheed presciently recognised that, of all the changes instituted around the time of the Council:

> for the man-in-the-pew the question 'Is it the same Church?' often enough boils down to the question 'Is it the same Mass?'[1]

Writing two decades later in 1986, Cardinal Joseph Cordeiro would concur, suggesting that the average '1960s Catholic' transported into the present would be 'startled out of his wits', for in the ways in which 'he prayed and sang and bowed his head in the house of God', he would detect a 'revolution in his mode of worship'.[2] These representations of the radical liturgical transformations wrought by the Council – one by an opinion-setting layman and the other by a high-ranking cleric involved in the conciliar reforms – share a common recognition that 'it is the mass that matters'.[3] In their assessment, echoed by many other commentators, the movement from Latin to English, the changed responses and postures during the service and the introduction of communion in both kinds ('drink the wine and chew the wafer'), represented a radical transformation in English Catholics' spiritual and devotional life. And so it did, on one reading. The Mancunian Catholic attending, perhaps sporadically, her parish church in 1980 would encounter a new rite, celebrated in her own language and conducted by a priest facing the congregation from an altar in the centre of the church. Whereas she may have previously recited her rosary during mass, or followed the priest's words and gestures with a missal, now she was expected to respond, and might be called upon to read a passage from the Old Testament or Epistles, or to minister communion to her co-worshippers.

Important as it is to note the scale and magnitude of these widespread transformations in liturgical rote and rite, this chapter moves beyond a meticulous recitation of the intricacies and minutiae of these rubrical adaptations. While registering the impact of these changed habitual practices on ordinary English Catholics, it contends that this preoccupation with the external aspects of these reforms has distracted attention from a more interesting transformation in the conceptualisation of the mass, and one, moreover, which predated the liturgical edicts of the 1960s. The nature and dimensions of this re-orientation may be appreciated by using as an exemplar a widely distributed tract by one of Britain's best-known catechists and social commentators,[4] Canon F. H. Drinkwater. Seeking to encourage a wide Catholic audience in 1957 to re-examine the mass and re-conceptualise it as a 'drama of redemption in five acts',[5] the Birmingham priest drew particular attention to the concluding 'communion' scene, when:

> The Sacrifice-prayer is ended ... the altar becomes the Family Table of God; and we are gathered round it, daring to address Him together as 'Our Father, who art in heaven ...'[6]

This popular publication was symptomatic of a burgeoning number of prescriptive pamphlets in the post-war period that translated the insights of the liturgical movement to a wider English Catholic audience. Within this tract, Canon Drinkwater concluded:

> We are all family here – brothers and sisters. No rich or poor, no black or white or yellow ... Just God's children asking Him for our daily bread, sharing it on equal terms. ... At the Consecration, the moment of Sacrifice, we were concerned primarily with our relationship to God – creaturehood. Communion settles our relation towards one another – brotherhood with Christ our Brother as the vital centre.[7]

While written to educate his audience about the elaborate rubrics and rhetorical flourishes of the Latin Tridentine mass, this form of catechetical exposition was representative of an increasing emphasis, made palpable after the Council, upon the laity's active participation in the mass and an appreciation of the social and communal consequences of the Eucharist. Underpinning this shift in 'theological accent' from a salvation-focused, sacrificial interpretation towards a more eschatological, 'this-worldly' and redemptory understanding of the Eucharist is an enduring emphasis upon the liturgy as the site for a renewal of a personal relationship with Christ. This continued to be expressed through a fraternal metaphor but was increasingly articulated, as the century progressed, in an understanding of the Eucharist as an encounter with Jesus at a sacred *banquet* or *meal*. Whilst the Eucharistic rhetoric of the earlier part of the century encouraged Catholics to envisage themselves as witnesses to the passion at the foot of the cross, as the century progressed this enduring centre and purpose of the mass was re-visioned as a gathering of brothers and sisters, with Jesus, at the family table.

This chapter begins with an examination of the ways in which English Catholics in the mid-twentieth century conceptualised their relationship with Christ as brother through a variety of guises: the Christ-child, the suffering Saviour and the 'Sacred Heart'. Supplementary to these personalised manifestations, made accessible to the laity when embodied in 'statues' and 'stations' at home or in church, the host remained the most potent visual mode for imagining and embodying an encounter with Christ. In this respect, the mass, and related extra-liturgical devotions such as benediction, were recognised as at the heart of an incarnate Catholic lived religiosity and popular spirituality. It is here that a more marked, and little appreciated, transformation was indeed taking place throughout the 1940s and 1950s, manifested through the discernible shifts in Eucharistic theology initiated by the liturgical movement, gradually disseminated throughout academic circles and embodied within some influential papal encyclicals by the middle of the century. In this changing emphasis, identifiable within the prescriptive literature and increasingly within lay perceptions of the mass as a sacred meal rather than sacrifice, it is also possible to see a context for changed understandings of the place of Catholicism within English society and the cultural preoccupations of the post-1960s generations.

Working from the premise that there is an inescapable link between the form of prayer and the shape of belief, this chapter focuses upon the transformed understandings of the actions centred upon the liturgical table through the second half of the twentieth century. In seeking to facilitate an authentic, personalised and experiential encounter with

God, many English Catholics increasingly drew upon the gospel image of Holy Thursday rather than Good Friday; a redeeming Christ of the Last Supper, rather than the Saviour crucified at Calvary, was embraced as a more accessible and workable trope for realising their relationship with God and their responsibilities in the world. As this chapter charts, in their gatherings around the altar and the ways in which this fraternity was articulated outside the mass, English Catholics across the century continued to prioritise an intensely incarnational and relational understanding of their faith, articulated through re-conceptualised familial metaphors and expressed through embodied ritual practices. The movement from Christ as child, suffering Saviour and Sacred Heart to 'fully human' person, bridegroom and comrade was both reactive to and reflective of the changed social context of Catholics in England as the century progressed.

Brother Jesus and His siblings: Christ as child, suffering Saviour and the Sacred Heart

In a series of sermons written during the last days of the war for evacuated schoolgirls sheltering at the Exton Rutland Assumption Convent, Monsignor Ronald Knox[8] sought to instruct his temporary charges by exhorting them to recognise:

> You, as a Christian, are the sister of Jesus Christ, and therefore our Lady is your Mother. I suppose it was because he wanted us to see that that our Lord gave her to St. John from the Cross.[9]

Writing in a similar vein but for a larger audience in a liturgical publication serialised in *The Tablet* in 1947, Knox – then Catholic Chaplain to the University of Oxford – developed the concept of the 'household of faith' urging English Catholics to understand that 'from the offertory onward the Mass was to be entirely a family affair'.[10] The ways in which this 'familial' encounter was to be understood and experienced were elaborated, around the same time, by his influential colleague the Apostolic Delegate to Great Britain (and later Archbishop of Westminster), William Godfrey. In a tract that urged the faithful as children of God and brothers of Jesus, to imitate 'as far as we are able [the] union of the heart of Mary with her Maker',[11] the means for this indwelling with Christ and incorporation into a relationship with the Holy Family was identified as:

> [t]he physical union … made possible for us each morning when after Holy Communion the Incarnate Word deigns to abide close to our own heart … the privilege which Our Lady enjoyed for nine months is mirrored by the ineffable union of Jesus with us when He comes to us in the Blessed Sacrament.[12]

As these three contemporaneous extracts encapsulate, mid-century Catholicism employed a number of dense yet flexible theological concepts, centred upon the incarnation and articulated through concepts of embodiment and transubstantiation, through which English Catholics were encouraged to experience their relationship with their brother Jesus. In describing and analysing this spiritual landscape, this section explores the various strands of this immanent Christology and fleshes out three prominent models or manifestations of the incarnate Christ that the laity deployed to articulate an affective relationship with their Saviour. These Christological modes were customised and mobilised, by both clergy and laity, in response to personal temperament, generational needs, and wider societal preoccupations.

Drawing upon a longstanding tradition of veneration of the infant Christ and apocryphal stories of his childhood which attained a particular popularity in the nineteenth century, devotional writings and instructional pamphlets in the twentieth century continued to emphasise this 'holy childhood' as an appropriate model for all Catholics, but particularly for the socialisation of boys and girls. In a 'meditation' intended for, though perhaps not readily comprehensible by, a young audience, Mary Tindall ventriloquised the Catholic child using first person language:

> If I look very hard at the Tabernacle on the Altar and take no notice of anyone in the Church, I shall be able to remember that Jesus has promised to be waiting there especially to talk to me and to listen to me … [and] I will think about His Childhood and try to be like Him.[13]

A more effective catechetical strategy was adopted by the prolific Canon Drinkwater who moved on to liturgical writings from his perennially popular *Catechism Stories* (1948). In a tale constructed for teachers of religion seeking to expand upon rote learning of the *Penny Catechism*, when explaining the meaning of proposition 38,[14] he offered a contemporary parable perhaps with the recent images of wartime civilian displacement in mind:

> *Christ is our Elder Brother*
> A lady met a little boy of seven carrying a heavy baby in his arms. He looked tired and his thin arms did not look strong enough to bear the weight of the younger child.
> 'Isn't he too heavy for you?' the lady asked him kindly.
> 'Oh no, he's my *brother*,' the little boy replied. He seemed surprised at the idea that the little brother whom he loved could be a burden.
> And that is the way Our Lord feels about us.[15]

Other catechists seemed to show an awareness of the mid-century advances in child pedagogy and psychology when advocating an experiential, tactile approach to learning. For example another clerical teacher, Father Greenstock, recognised that 'the child finds it much easier to assimilate things through the senses of sight and touch at first',[16] and therefore advocated a creative and tangible approach such as a 'religious scrap-book' with scenes from the nativity, the Holy Family and Christ's boyhood, illustrating that 'like your own child, Christ was once a baby'[17] and part of a wider, cross-generational family. Numerous publications supplied parents with 'Prayers to the Infant Jesus' to be taught to their children. Young boys and girls were to be assured of the constant presence of their 'sweet brother' and in first person language should articulate their aspiration to exemplary conduct so that they might 'never … make Thy dear Heart sore'.[18] But recognising that formulaic prayer might be off-putting for children, for whom 'the rosary is often meaningless', the Prior of Blackfriars in Oxford and formidable preacher Bede Jarrett counselled a story-driven approach. He urged a focus on 'the character of Christ' which 'can be of interest as well as help to a child', through:

> the stories of the Gospel, the scenes, the parables, His patience, courage, endurance, fortitude, truthfulness, fearlessness, His love of birds and the harvest, His choice of carpentering, His love of the sea and the hills and the gardens at night for praying in, His forgiveness … teach him to pray by showing him how to form his own prayers, how to ask and thank and praise, how to be silent and listen, how to gaze at Christ.[19]

Adopting an early form of the later mainstreamed 'narrative theology' methodology popularised by theologians such as the French Jesuit Henri de Lubac, Jarrett offered to his readers a character profile of the

Gatherings at the family table

good Christian as an *alter Christus*, formed in the likeness of the child of Nazareth. For, as the regular 'home section' advice columnist 'Marguerite' wrote in 1952 in her column aimed at children and mothers in the mass-circulated, affordable family journal, *Catholic Fireside*:

> To imitate Christ should be the goal of every Christian. To think like Him, act like Him, speak like Him. To look upon the world with His eyes, to see humanity from His viewpoint, to desire it and, above all, to desire and obey, like Christ, His Father's Word.[20]

This emphasis on Christ's personal biography, stressing 'the Jesus of history' and his complete humanity (but virtuous boyhood), was a Christological imperative found in various manifestations across the theological spectrum of Catholic thought and communicated to English Catholics of all classes through a variety of media. Therefore, despite marked differences in rhetorical style, and audience, Father S. B. James' reflections on the Feast of the Holy Family in 1945 for the liberal-minded and educated middle-class readership of the *Catholic Herald* could be likened to those of 'Marguerite' in stressing Christ's relationship to God the Father, his emotional and moral life, and his role as an exemplar for men, women and Catholic youth:

> Jesus, we may assume, was like other Jewish boys of his age, but doing ordinary things in an extraordinary way … [illustrating] the perfection of a life lived strictly within the narrow limits of a Jewish craftsman's home in a small provincial town. We are thus encouraged to ponder the possibilities as regards sanctity of even the humblest domestic circle.[21]

For English Catholics, like their compatriots, six years of war and continuing economic austerity and food rationing well into the 1950s had narrowed many people's concerns to a focus on the preservation of a humble domestic circle. These messages about the holiness of simplicity and an everyday sanctity chimed well with the national sentiment.

Central to this conception of Jesus as 'child' within the religious literature, theological commentaries and devotional aids was a near-equal emphasis on the role of the Virgin Mary. Instructional holy cards exhorted the young Catholic to imagine him/herself, like Jesus, at Mary's knee. Another dimension of this conjoining of Mariology with an incarnational Christology was a likening of the indwelling of Christ in the believer (through reception of the Blessed Sacrament) to the indwelling of Christ within the pregnant Miriam of Nazareth. The implications of these metaphorical analogies were perhaps most clearly expressed and evocatively elucidated by one of the best-selling religious authors of the 1940s, Caryll Houselander.[22] Widely known and revered by the English Catholic community as a theologically astute laywoman, sculptor and mystic, Houselander mused:

> He was dumb, her voice was His voice. He was still, her footsteps were His journeys. He was blind, her eyes were His seeing. His hands were folded, her hands did the work of His hands ... This was a foreshadowing of what the Incarnation would mean for us; for in us, too, Christ rests as He rested in Mary.[23]

For English men and women, bound as siblings of Christ through the common motherhood of Mary as an archetypal encounter between the faithful and God, there was the promise of new creation, personal transformation and society's redemption when:

> mankind
> born again
> was laid in her arms,
> in the body of her dead child.[24]

Whilst the dimensions of this form of Mariology within the context of post-war society and its implications for English Catholics' understandings of femininity and maternity are explored in greater detail in the next chapter, it is important to note this nexus within the Catholic religious landscape so as to avoid drawing an artificial distinction between Mariology and Christology. This popular form of devotional writing which inserted the devout believer into the stories of the annunciation, the familial sojourn in Nazareth and the passion narratives illustrated a distinctively Catholic conception of the sibling relationship between the Christian and his or her Saviour, sometimes refracted through Mary (and the other saints) who functioned both as facilitators and exemplars of this relationship.

Understandings of Christ as child were supplemented by the teachings, primarily for children preparing for first communion, about Christ as child-like and vulnerable when 'really present' in the host. This conceptualisation was most dramatically depicted in the visceral and maternal imagery employed by the eminent theologian Canon Eugene Masure, writing for a theologically informed and sophisticated audience, when likening the effect of the consecration to:

> a mould break[ing] when the statue which it outlined is disengaged from it, or rather (Christ, who spoke in such respectful terms of the pains of childbirth, pardon us this comparison) like a mother who dies in bringing her child into the world. Thus the sign changes its content and value at the moment when it reached the end of its ritual course.[25]

A similar understanding, yet one packaged for a youthful audience with a less analogical theology, was communicated to English Catholics in laywoman Grace Hurrell's talks for first communicants. Assuming the voice of 'Father Smith', perhaps for purposes of authority when passing on instructions about the etiquette for reception of the host ('do not swallow immediately and do not use one's teeth to chew as with ordinary food'), Hurrell likened the new communicant, 'John', to 'the Tabernacle where Our Lord was'.[26] This encounter with Christ, mediated through the Eucharist, was also evocatively depicted in an illustration accompanying another of her pamphlets on the liturgy, in which a young boy wearing shorts mirrored the posture of Christ crucified in an embrace of the host (Figure 3.1).

These teachings on the tangibility of the real presence persisted in catechetical practice in Lancashire well into the 1970s, illustrated by Bernie's reflections on his preparations for his first communion:

> BB: I was always taught never to chew – 'it's biting Our Lord' (laughs). That's what I was told, 'It's like biting Our Lord'.[27]

Clergy also penned instructional tracts for parents (usually expressly contemplated as mothers) seeking to impart the 'reality of his Presence by your example', through teaching their children:

> Jesus is in the tabernacle just as truly as He was in the stable, with His Mother and St Joseph. That He is just as present to the child during one of those little visits to the church as you are when you have him on your knee: that the church is Jesus' home, where He lives and where He loves to see and talk to His friends, and so on.[28]

This explicit recognition of the 'real presence', manifested through the popular Catholic devotionals of adoration and benediction of the Blessed Sacrament discussed later in this chapter, was nevertheless pre-eminently

3.1 Visual representation of the role of believer, priest and God in the action at the altar, from Grace Hurrell, *The Church's Play* (London: Sheed and Ward, 1945), n.p. [Reproduced with permission from Continuum, London and The Bodleian Libraries, The University of Oxford, shelf number 13215 e.465]

available through the mass. In a poem written in 1950 for the Feast of Corpus Christi, the layman Gavin Dyer echoed Canon Masure in his description of the act of creation within the rite of consecration:

> A priest whispers over a wafer: God waits without
> creation's court till His creatures call Him to enter,
> wholly humbling Himself to heavy human hands.
>
> ...
>
> O Child of the Tabernacle, King and climax of creation,
> Suffer us exiles to share in the seraph's rapture, and raise
> up, up, with the paeans of paradise this pauper's penny of praise.[29]

This reflection on the mysterious transformation of wafer to flesh, the translocation of heaven and earth, and the unresolved juxtaposition between creature and seraph, child and king, encapsulated the spectrum of experiential encounters with 'brother Christ' made available to the pre-conciliar Catholic in the mass and through the host.

As a Christological image well adapted to present-day needs shaped by a war fought on the domestic as well as international fronts, English Catholics also had recourse to another longstanding but potent representation of Christ as the crucified Saviour.[30] The wide societal resonance of a frail, suffering yet compassionate God-man who provided inspiration through courageously enduring unfair trials, excruciating pain and a bloody death was intuitively recognised by Caryll Houselander, who in 1943 wrote *This War is the Passion*. In a series of spiritual reflections, written under lamp-light security, she offered an alternative, eschatological reading of the 'bitterness, hatred and ruin' of the world around[31] and an interpretation of the Stations of the Cross expressly set in the Britain of the Blitz, so that English Catholics could learn the passion of Christ through the adventures of their own hearts.[32] Poets also drew upon the passion, and its recapitulation in the sacrifice of the mass, to interrogate and integrate the psychological suffering and physiological wounds inflicted by war, such as John Murphy's 1949 reflection for Armistice Sunday:

> Blitz has a sullen sort of end, like curs
>   That bark a bit when barking themes are done ...
> When the All-clear
>   Finds us alive – a cosy privilege.

> And soon, tranquil at Mass, one understands
>   The night: our sore extremities were but
> His body, mystical, with aching hands
>   And feet, our cause His side …
> Whose heart is where the altar candles glint,
>   Like trinkets on the wrists of Liturgy.[33]

A decade after the conflict, when Britain was on the road to reconstruction, the Bishop of Salford urged parents to set the Stations of the Cross (a devotional practice of fourteen 'stations', usually depicted on plaques, representing events that occurred before the crucifixion) in a domestic setting, speaking to their children about the sufferings of the Lord so that they might 'deny themselves in little things so as to follow gradually in His footsteps'.[34] Refuting the need for elaborate instructions, Bishop Holland extolled the 'simply homely words of a good father and mother', and their example in standing before each Station of the Cross, speaking of the passion narrative, and giving to their child 'the example of the self denial which Our Lord has given to all of us in His life'.[35] The central element in the prayers of the Stations of the Cross was the encouragement of a spiritual and bodily emulation of Christ and the internalisation of the gospel narratives. As Houselander reflected, the fact that the gospel reading on the day the war broke out was the Sermon on the Mount led her to conclude:

> On the day war is declared, knowing all the difficulties in our way, Christ repeats the gentlest of His words, which are also the most uncompromising, which have been the most consistently avoided ever since He uttered them, by all but the saints.[36]

This emphasis on self-abnegation and sacrifice, endurance and emulation was made even more explicit and palpable in Peter Winckworth's 'Meditation on the Stations of the Cross in time of war'. In his reflection on the eighth station (The women of Jerusalem mourn for Jesus), he wrote, in the light of the resurrection:

> What is lost, dear mother, if your son
> Has died, but in death found life;
> Weep not.
> What is lost, dear friends,

If our homes are bombed,
Our children gassed,
Our favourite things destroyed,
If our souls remain in God's keeping,
And the faithful departed find peace,
Weep not.
Weep only that we have not trusted,
Weep only that we have not prayed.[37]

Stressing the sanctified example they followed, and the glorious promise made available through the martyr's sacrifice, he justified his uncompromising message with the conclusion:

They have trod the way,
Through the cannon to His Justice,
Through the air raid to His Heaven
Through the mud of war to His white Tomb.[38]

In situating the present sufferings of the world explicitly within the gospel narrative and devotional practices focused on the passion, Catholics were offered a long-established framework and rich repository to draw upon in times of hardship, suffering and loss. For as Houselander surmised:

If a human creature grows to his full stature of Christhood, then he will most inevitably experience those things which Christ did, in His earthly life … temptation, poverty, homeless and destitute, without recognition … forsaken.[39]

Through this suffering and apparent failure, Houselander reminded her readers that they 'will be linked with Christ's suffering and His power of redeeming', from 'a child's first fall on the gravel-path or his first homesickness at school, to the soldier's death on the battlefield, should that be asked'.[40] These immediate, accessible and intensely mystical writings by Sheed and Ward's best-selling author, which evoked a compassionate and suffering Christ within an ordinary and recognisably contemporary context, clearly appealed to a wide Catholic reading public yearning for spiritual succour and personal reassurance.

Blessed assurance was also offered to Catholics through another Christological model available for emulation and reliance – devotion to the Sacred Heart of Jesus. While founded within an ongoing historical tradition that stressed Christ's love and compassion, this devotional form obtained widespread popularity in the seventeenth century following a series of apparitions to the French nun Margaret Mary Alacoque, who was canonised in 1920.[41] The widespread popularity of the devotion she inaugurated continued in Britain well into the second half of the twentieth century,[42] and centred around a re-appreciation of the enduring love of the resurrected Christ and the wounds caused to Him by humanity's unrequited affections and their unceasing wrongdoing. Practice of the devotion therefore focused on the union of the believer with Christ in love (through frequent reception of Holy Communion: principally nine times on the 'first Fridays' of consecutive months) and through reparation for sin (through prayer and penance). Commemorating the centenary of the establishment of the official feast day by his predecessor, Pope Pius XII surveyed the history of the devotion in 1956 in his encyclical *Haurietis Aquas* and urged a 'more vigorous zeal in promoting this most attractive form of piety' as a means 'towards the attaining of Christian perfection'.[43] Making reference to the 'present-day needs of the Church and the human race [when] so many evils meet our gaze – such as cause sharp conflict among individuals, families, nations and the whole world', the chief evils subject to the pontiff's scrutiny were communism and other forms of secular materialism. Such targets were addressed through instructional pamphlets[44] and cartoons, like the one reproduced in the *Catholic Times* on 23 March 1956, which graphically depicted a triumphant but grieved Christ towering over the broken idols and the flawed, rival utopian ideals of enlightenment thinkers, revolutionaries and Marxist leaders (Figure 3.2).

Cold War insecurities were not, however, the only papal preoccupations mirrored in the document, as the encyclical manifested an express concern to demonstrate the relevance, rationality and historical (as well as biblical) authenticity of prayers to the Sacred Heart against the charges of 'sentimentalism' levelled by those who:

> See it rather as a type of piety nourished not by the soul and mind but by the senses and consequently more suited to the use of women, since it seems to them something not quite suitable for educated men.[45]

Stressing that devotion to the Sacred Heart is 'worship of the love with which God, through Jesus, loved us, and at the same time, an exercise of our own love by which we are related to God and to other men', Pius XII sought to fasten this devotion securely to the incarnation as a practical,

Gatherings at the family table 71

3.2 Cartoon entitled 'Thou Shalt not have Strange Gods Before Me', depicting the Sacred Heart triumphant over various demagogues and ideologies, from the *Catholic Times*, 23 March 1956, 7. [Reproduced with permission from the *Universe and Catholic Times*, Manchester and The Bodleian Libraries, The University of Oxford, shelf mark N.11132 b.3]

'masculine' means for the sanctification of the modern world. As such, his pronouncement echoed the perceived discomfort with the designation of other, Marian, devotions as affective and therefore 'feminine'. There were also simultaneous attempts to reconfigure a Marian 'masculinity' and St Joseph as a model male worker and potent counterfoil to class conflict and social grievance, as the next chapter explores.[46]

Despite these institutional efforts to craft a particular interpretation and utilisation of the devotion to the Sacred Heart – which arguably was the cause of its partial fall from favour when Cold War insecurities subsided – this form of devotion prioritised a personal relationship with Christ and one therefore explicitly available for a domestic piety beyond the control of the clergy. As Peter Gay has observed in his extensive study of Christological trends in the later nineteenth century, an intensely incarnational religiosity with its focus on the 'manliness' of Christ also had the capacity to prioritise the 'feminine' through reference to characteristics such as tenderness, thoughtfulness and compassion.[47] Within certain devotional writing (and images) during the early twentieth century, it is possible to see the further extension of such trends through Jesus' portrayal as a friend and lover.[48] For example, in addressing an educational pamphlet to an audience of Catholic schoolgirls in 1930, its three lay female authors urged them to think beyond their girlish fantasies and eventual 'lawful human loves' to 'the Love of Christ our Lord', for:

> Only God is always just right. Friendship with him is a wonderful thing, for he is as tender as a woman and as comradely as a man. He, the Maker of all loves and friendships, is the only completely satisfying Being.[49]

This implicit link between 'lawful human loves' and the love of Christ was also tacitly drawn by Ancoats-born John, who worked throughout his adult life as an electrician and married in 1955. When asked about the popularity of devotion to the Sacred Heart, he began to recite a rote prayer associated with the 'Enthronement of the Sacred Heart in the Home'.[50] This was an extra-liturgical ritual, which consisted of a blessing by the priest of the devotional picture and its installation in a position of honour by the designated 'head of the house'.[51] As such, it was a form of domestic piety repeatedly urged upon Mancunian Catholics by Bishop Marshall of Salford[52] and later linked to the Crusade for Family Prayer.[53]

In his oral reflections, John then spoke about the location of this picture of the 'Sacred Heart' in 'the bedroom. Over our, over my wife's dressing table'.[51] The 'blessings on the house' that he attributed to this devotional image reached right to the heart of his home – the bedroom he shared with his wife – and through this pictorial representation, Christ was adjacent to and overlooking the matrimonial bed. For other lay Catholics, this form of devotion might also offer a personalised encounter with Christ outside the mass. Such was the case for Caryll Houselander who wrote in her autobiography about her domestic piety:

> God, whom I did know to be everywhere, was also localized on my altar, a feeling no doubt produced by the huge shadow of the Sacred Heart [statue] thrown on the wall by the crimson lamp burning in the darkness.[55]

These sentiments were echoed by Mitzi, born of post-war Irish immigrant parents and growing up in Manchester and Sale in the late 1950s and early 1960s. She too recalled:

> MS: (The Sacred Heart), Oh, we used to have that on the wall. With a little fire, with a little candle burning in front, with the little red heart. That used to be on the wall in every Catholic house, didn't it?[56]

Further extending upon these themes of the spiritual (and embodied) union between the believer and God in the Sacred Heart, in ways which anticipated the later insights of feminist theologians in the 1970s, Houselander wrote elsewhere about a Saviour who transcended gender and offered a solution to the widespread desire for security:

> Our rest in a world that is full of unrest is Christ's trust in His Father, our peace in a world without peace is our surrender, complete as the surrender of the sleeping child to its mother, of the Christ in us to God who is both Father and Mother.[57]

Themes of peace and prosperity also characterised the 1948 Joint Pastoral Letter on the Sacred Heart by the English and Welsh Bishops, who stressed this devotion as a palliative to 'the world's miseries … discontent and disorder' and as the means to 'restore true peace to the world'.[58] Urging a recognition of Christ in our neighbours, the bishops linked the feast of the Sacred Heart to 'those who are suffering hunger and misery; and for the millions who are oppressed with anxiety and fear of the future', advocating Christ's 'reign in every family and in every home' and his rule in 'national life and international affairs'.[59] This explicit link between the 'private' and 'public' spheres, sanctifying the domestic realm and the relationships within it, allowed Catholics to recognise Christ under their roof, sharing their firesides, and from there to build up the Kingdom of Heaven on earth.[60]

Nevertheless, as the century progressed, even the clergy most associated with the promotion of the devotion were beginning to ask questions about it and its representation by 'the blue-and-red statue that may not attract or the picture that may repel'.[61] Instead, a Jesuit commentator sought to redefine the Sacred Heart as a symbol which:

> enshrines the love of the most devoted friend and the most affectionate brother, of the true lover for his life-long beloved, of a mother for a dear son. And His love covers the world in its unifying embrace: the outcast and the abandoned, rich and poor, the unwanted and the unlikable, those whose colour and code and culture are not our own.[62]

This was a movement towards a re-presentation of this devotion in terms which addressed the suffering and injustices recently highlighted by a war that had exposed, tragically and brutally, the consequences of distinctions based on race and religion.[63] Similar movements to reframe Christology with an expressly experiential, worldly and eschatological cast were also taking place within liturgical circles and in explicit reflection upon Eucharistic theology.[64] Canon Drinkwater, in yet another commentary on the liturgy in 1948, emphasised the mass and communion as the chief means through which Catholics should 'let [God's] Mind be in all your thoughts and your hearts be always in His Sacred Heart'.[65] Those directly concerned with catechesis and conversion, such as the former head of the Catholic Missionary Society and now Archbishop of Liverpool John Heenan, were also seeking to absorb the Sacred Heart devotions within a wider understanding of the Eucharist:

> Reduced to practical terms devotion to the Sacred Heart means devotion to the Blessed Sacrament on the Altar. ... [because] for members of the household of Faith every other union besides Holy Communion is a second best.[66]

Therefore alongside papal attempts to reconfigure the devotion for a postwar society in an ideologically combative guise, there were others within the Hierarchy who thought it better to concentrate their efforts on reframing the liturgy and Eucharistic theology. Some historians have argued,

Gatherings at the family table 75

through an American Catholic lens, that this represented an attempt to bolster 'a gendered distinction between the private and the public realm … proclaiming the ascendancy of the male over the female [and] the priesty over the lay'.[67] Yet as this discussion has illustrated, alongside other studies of the Sacred Heart within European Catholicism,[68] there was a complex interplay between the different clerical injunctions and lay applications surrounding this cult, and the blurred categories of masculinity and femininity, private and public, that were invoked through this devotional practice. Whilst certain Christological tropes, such as the Christ-child, the suffering Saviour and the Sacred Heart, had started to recede from the devotional scene as the century progressed, other Christocentric understandings, primarily centred on the Eucharist, emerged as spiritual analogies which resonated with and reassured English Catholics. This incremental and gradual transformation, manifest through practical arguments about the form and function of the mass (including the use of missals, dialogue masses and frequent communion), was primarily focused on the believer's relationship to Christ and the gathered congregation through reverence for and reception of the host.

The Mass and the Eucharist: sacrifice or sacrament, immolation or meal?

In his widely read pamphlet entitled *What is he doing at the Altar?* the well-known Jesuit Father C. C. Martindale[69] addressed in direct and accessible language the perceived consternation of the layperson – Catholic as well as non-Catholic – when seeking to understand the Latin Tridentine mass. As one of the first commentators attempting to communicate the theological insights of the liturgical movement to an English Catholic audience, Martindale's 1931 commentary centred on the Eucharistic consecration and an understanding of the mass as a 'sacrifice':

> [I]f we join our hearts and minds and wills to His, we become so closely united with Him as to be closer even than brothers; we become, as it were, one person with Him: in looking upon Him, God sees us: in looking upon us, He sees His own Son, Jesus Christ.[70]

In this understanding of 'sacrifice', expounded in a publication two years earlier, he contended that the commonly circulating understanding of sacrifice was inverted within the mass – rather than a 'doing without', this sacrifice enriches us, as it is an acquiring of Christ that rids us of the effects of our sins.[71]

A generation later, another Jesuit (headmaster at Stonyhurst, then Superior at Farm Street from 1950) continued this educative trend in a series of pamphlets explaining the various phases of the mass and offering the layperson a first step 'to intelligent and profitable sharing in the Mass'.[72] Father McEvoy's *New and Easy Way at Mass* reflected a modern preoccupation with efficiency, time management and functionality, breaking the mass into segments and highlighting in particular the 'eighteen minutes you are mostly concerned with the Chalice and the Host with which three things apposite must be done', namely the sacrificial preparation, the sacrificial action and the sacrificial banquet.[73] Reinforcing these theological insights, but using metaphorical language far more likely to resonate with an audience of ordinary Catholics, laywoman Caryll Houselander offered her own description of the mass:

> He is lifted up in the priest's hands, sacrificed. God accepts the sacrifice and gives Christ back to us, He is lowered in the altar; He who was taken down from the Cross is given to us in Communion; buried, laid to rest in our hearts.[74]

Within these various accounts, representative of much of the liturgical commentary and instructional literature of mid-century, the institution of sacrifice remains one of the dominant features of Catholic theology and practice.[75] Moreover, in the popular understanding, as well as the earliest theological writings stressing greater liturgical participation, the sacrament of the Eucharist remained ritually distinct from the liturgical action of the 'sacrifice',[76] reinforcing the distinction between mass and Holy Communion, and reflected in the widely understood conception of a 'spiritual communion' (namely, participation in the mass, even if unable or unwilling to receive the host). Within these categories, the mass was something performed by the priest on behalf of the laity, and for the person in the pew it was a temporal as well as physical site for their own personal devotions, such as 'telling the rosary', recitation of set prayers or the reading of the missal. These devotions, and the reception of communion within the liturgy (or on other occasions) were the primary means for maintaining the believers' relationship to God.

These prevalent distinctions were increasingly being critiqued and challenged by the middle of the twentieth century not only by those most intimately involved in liturgical study and development,[77] but also within accessible instructional material – illustrated, for example, in Grace Hurrell's addresses to communicant-in-training 'John' (assuming the voice of his 'mother'):

> Now here is something for you to learn. The name of the Sacrament that we called the **Blessed** Sacrament, because it is Our Lord Himself, is the **Sacrament of the Holy Eucharist**. The word Eucharist means thanksgiving, and I want you to remember that the Holy Eucharist is a **Sacrifice** as well as a **Sacrament**. It is what **we** offer to God, in Sacrifice, and what God gives to **us**, as a Sacrament, to be Food for our souls (original emphasis).[78]

As 'John' was didactically lectured about the corporate nature of this 'food for our souls', one of the foremost English theologians (and editor of *The Downside Review*), Dom Illtyd Trethowan, also sought to expound this emphasis to the magazine's circulation of clergy, theologians and educated middle-class laity:

> Holy Communion is not a private devotion. … Holy Communion joins us together, if we will only make *use* of it, into the only indissoluble union, the bond of Christ. This is the only solution to human conflicts which strike down to the root of things.[79]

In his emphasis on the intensely communal nature of 'the Communion of Christian *Sacrifice*' and its implications for humankind outside a church context, Dom Illtyd would anticipate many later developments in Eucharistic theology. Moreover, in the context of increasing theological and liturgical reflection on the 'use' of the liturgy as the century progressed, the debates in the Catholic press and instructional literature would turn on how this 'bond of union' was forged and the role of a more engaged and active congregation in its creation.

Advocated by liturgists from the 1920s and increasingly adopted by an educated laity, the use of a missal was one of the earliest means advocated to encourage greater corporate engagement in the mass and to ensure the laity's comprehension and attention during worship. Adrian Fortescue's *Roman Missal* (1915) became the standard text for 'following the mass', but multiple versions followed complete with illustrations, explanations, scripture readings and parallel translations.[80] Such tools for understanding the Latin scripture readings, as well as the historical evolution and complex rubrics within the liturgy, became commonplace within parish churches in the post-war period, particularly amongst a younger generation of Catholics and extending beyond their initial adoption by an educated middle class.[81] Eighty-five-year-old Kathleen still retains a treasured and inscribed *My Small Missal* which was a parting gift conveyed 'with all good wishes for her future welfare' from her old head teacher when she left St Antony's School, Trafford Park in 1937 for the world of factory work.[82] Nevertheless, considerable scepticism about the necessity and accessibility of this innovation remained, illustrated in an address by the Bishop of Salford to a Clergy Deanery Conference in 1944:

> [T]he use of the Missal is an excellent practice, for those who can follow and understand it (even in the vernacular); but a great variety of practice may be allowed and even encouraged, so long as the main purpose is achieved (e.g. the Rosary may help the faithful to assist at Mass in the spirit of Mary at the foot of the Cross, for which no disposition could be better).[83]

Some liturgists also objected to the increasing insistence in many quarters that 'one *must* follow all of the prayers in the Missal', for 'not only the ordinary simple-minded Catholic, but many of the most spiritually minded people, who are far advanced in the ways of prayer, would find the Missal more of a hindrance than a help'.[84] Despite these hesitations, and clear differences of opinion about what 'active participation' in the mass required, Bishop Marshall's Clergy Deanery address in 1944 went on to discuss the ways in which the 'priesthood of the laity' and their 'offering of the mass' should be correctly understood. As such, it illustrates the inroads made by the European liturgical movement throughout the country even at this lower-level gathering for Mancunian priests.

Similar debates about participation in the mass also centred on the increasing liturgical experimentation with the 'dialogue mass', in which the whole congregation, not just the altar server, answered the priest in those parts of the mass calling for a sung or spoken response. Following on from its first explicit approval at Malines in 1922, the Sacred Congregation of Rites explicitly approved the practice on 30 November 1935, subject to the approval of local hierarchies. Whether the implementation of the Latin dialogue mass really made much difference to the laity's involvement in, and comprehension of, the priestly act of consecration is, however, thrown into question by the recollections of retired university academic Richard (born in 1947):

RD: Yeah. I mean they knew the rote. I mean, I'll tell you a lovely story. My uncle Leo used to serve mass right, and he served with a German priest in Eccles. And Leo said he used to have chickens in the backyard, right? So do you know the Latin mass? [AH: mm] *'Et cum spiritu tuo'*. Right, so he used to do, can't remember (pause): *'Dominus vobiscum. Et cum ...'*. So he used to turn around (and say) *'Dominus vobiscum. Et cum spiritu tuo'*. And he used to – Leo said he used to turn around at a set time in the mass and he used to say 'Go and feed the chickens Leo'. And everyone used to reply: *'Et cum spiritu tuo'*. And Leo used to go out and feed the chickens and come back. 'Cause nobody knew, 'cause he said it in a German accent, 'Go and feed the chickens'. They just thought he was saying *'Dominus vobiscum'*. So that to me typifies what the Latin mass was about (both laugh). It is, isn't it? It's perfect.

AH: And a missal just didn't help with any of that?

RD: No! Rubbish! Nobody ... hah. The goody two-shoes read the missal. Nobody read the missal. Come on![85]

Whether responses in the vernacular would have challenged this clerical flexibility and the associated congregational incomprehension of a 'thick German accent' is another matter, but by the middle of the century many English Catholics were fiercely debating the advantages and limitations of dialogue mass in English. Alongside news of air-raids on cathedral cities and U-boat sea battles, the correspondence columns of the *Catholic Herald* witnessed great excitement and agitated opinion when Father Martindale floated the idea of the use of English responses in the mass.[86] These debates gathered momentum in the post-war period, generating a prominent symposium and proceedings on English in the liturgy,[87] a vast correspondence in *The Tablet*[88] and the increasing circulation of literature on the liturgy, such as *The Work of Our Redemption* (1953) by the English Jesuit Clifford Howell, which made the best-seller lists in Britain and the United States. In a letter to *The Tablet* in 1953 responding to the impact of this book on his understanding of the liturgy, the Isle of Wight resident W. E. W. Crealock recanted from his earlier, published objections to the dialogue mass:

> True, my prejudices are unchanged. I like to listen to 'A sacred glee-club performing to an audience of deaf mutes'. I distrust my own voice and dislike my neighbour's if untrained, and I cherish the familiar in a world of change. But, if changes in the liturgy mean a more perfect worship by the Mystical

Body, and the rousing of the apathy of backbenchers like myself, then let us have changes. ... Anyhow, if I am told to sing, my neighbours will be provided with a splendid opportunity of acquiring merit.[89]

While he would have agreed with this layman on the diversity of ways to acquire merit – including holy patience with out-of-tune singing – Father Thomas Holland (as he then was) perhaps had his future Diocese of Salford in mind when he urged liturgists to take account of 'differences in intelligence, culture and legitimate custom'. When writing a scathing review of *The Work of Our Redemption* for *The Catholic Gazette* in 1954, Holland stressed that:

> one advantage of the present Mass-liturgy is that all *can* be present at the Holy Sacrifice at their own understanding and level of devotion ... If no more awareness is present in the faithful than that they are ... offering themselves with Christ as His members, there is a true participation in the Sacred Mysteries.[90]

Reminiscent of the approach of the preceding Bishop of Salford, with an eye to the more simple-minded faithful of Manchester, Holland, like Marshall, illustrated a conservatism common to many in the English Hierarchy when confronting liturgical innovation and participatory experimentation in their dioceses.

While Thomas Holland identified 'true participation' through the laity's appreciation of the Holy Sacrifice at which they were present, much liturgical thinking also stressed frequent communion as another guarantee of participation. Indeed, as his far from radical predecessor in the See of Salford observed, 'the fact the faithful have the right to receive Holy Communion is in itself a proof that they offer the sacrifice'.[91] Following on from Pope Pius X's encouragement of frequent reception at the beginning of the twentieth century,[92] and with the adjustments of the Eucharistic fasting provisions in 1953 and 1957, some of the restrictive bodily and spiritual regimes surrounding the Eucharist were beginning to be relaxed after the Second World War. Yet the laity's participation through reception of the host still remained universally low: as Peter (born in 1944) reflected, implicitly contrasting the Eucharistic reception practices of his childhood with those of the children he taught as a deputy head teacher:

> PK: You weren't encouraged to go as often. I mean, that was ... the view was that if you went to mass every week, but if you went to Holy Communion once a month, you're all right.

Gatherings at the family table

AH: And if you went more than once a month?

PK: Well, 'Holy Jo', or saint or … And it's only because… The altar servers, we went weekly. If you served you went to Holy Communion. But you weren't necessarily on the same mass either, and you weren't necessarily on every week.[93]

Despite this improvement in the frequency of communion from earlier in the century, weekly communicants remained rare, and spiritual scruples led many to receive pre-consecrated hosts outside the context of mass, usually immediately after confession.[94] A similar practice seems to have applied in America[95] and Australia[96] and was perhaps well summed up by the Dominican author and preacher Edwin Essex, who observed of the current English practice, in correspondence to *The Tablet* in 1953, that:

> it may be true that some communicants never associate their personal reception of the sacrament with the sacrificial action of the Mass, and rarely advert to the fact of the mystical union of Christ and the Church.[97]

As the twentieth century progressed, the institutional church's expressed understandings, as well as the experiences of a cross-section of the laity, were undergoing considerable transformation and re-articulation. This increasing disjunction between the mass conceptualised as a 'sacrifice' (a witnessed immolation) compared with a 'sacrament of communion' (such as a communal, participatory meal) was most manifest in devotions centred on reverence for the host, including the extra-liturgical devotions of adoration and benediction.

There is no better example of the tensions, cross currents and countervailing trends in liturgical practice and Eucharistic emphasis in the mid-twentieth century than a comparison of two of Pope Pius XII's most important encyclicals, *Mystici Corporis Christi* (1943) and *Mediator Dei* (1947). Written within five years of each other and in sight of the searing images of 'cities, towns and fertile fields … strewn with massive ruins and defiled with the blood of brothers',[98] the later encyclical was characterised by strongly 'sacrificial' language and emphatically reinforced the Council of Trent's pronouncement that the God-man is 'truly, really, and substantially' present under the appearance of bread and wine.[99] This insistence on a hieratic (yet witnessed) act gave rise to certain understandings about the sacred 'otherness' of the host and its visual adoration. In contrast, the Pope's earlier pronouncements in *Mystici Corporis Christi* utilised the metaphor of a sacramental meal and a this-worldly, redemptive frame when exploring the believer's redemption in Christ. It was these latter emphases that were to be developed as the century progressed and which led to a greater stress on participation and understanding of the sacramental. Despite their marked differences, both of Pius XII's encyclicals were important precursors to the formulation of *Sacrosanctum Concilium* (1963) at the Second Vatican Council, in their refinement of the incarnational theology of the 'Body of Christ', in both Eucharistic and ecclesiological terms.

Insisting that the mass was 'no mere empty commemoration of the passion and death of Jesus Christ, but a true and proper act of sacrifice', *Mediator Dei* stressed the 'august sacrifice of the altar ... whereby the High Priest by an unbloody act of immolation offers Himself a most acceptable victim'[100] and that through 'the "transubstantiation" of bread into the body of Christ and of wine into His blood, His body and blood are both really present'.[101] This emphasis on the 'real presence' within the encyclical was, of course, a restatement of early modern Catholic orthodoxy in all its theological complexity, and was communicated to the faithful as a personalised, physical encounter with Christ to which the appropriate response, modelled by 'Our Lady at the foot of the cross', is 'awe and admiration, thanksgiving and penance'.[102] The responses of an older generation of the Mancunian laity illustrate this mixture of 'awe and admiration', 'thanksgiving and penitence' as well as an inchoate understanding of the full implications of transubstantiation. Kathleen, for example, recollects the commission of a terrible 'sin' when accidentally wearing a special pair of gloves received as a Christmas present to the altar rail.[103] In a similar vein, she then spoke of the practice of a friend's mother in Trafford Park who would:

> KF: make you have a drink of water, you know, to wash your mouth out after you'd had the communion.
> AH: Why was that?
> KF: I don't know. To clear your mouth, I don't know. We wouldn't go on top of the – ... yeah ... sometimes I do it myself now. When I go home I'll have a drink of water.[104]

This reverence for the received host, for example by not putting ordinary food 'on top', was heightened for altar boys in their immediate proximity to the consecrated 'body of Christ'. Given that such access to the altar was forbidden to all other members of the laity, the nearness of the host brought familiarity but also an investment in preserving its sacral 'otherness'. This relationship of visual presence, but physical distance, was expressed in a number of strictly internalised prohibitions against physical contact with the host, the chalice and various sacred objects and vestments. Tony (born in 1943) who served on the altar in an Irlam parish well into his twenties was typical in voicing such understandings:

> TC: But when we were altar boys, to touch the chalice – you weren't allowed to touch the chalice, er, you know, anything like that. And if you touched the host, you know, it was sacrosanct that – you know, you don't touch.[105]

The consequences of 'touching' upon those who grew up with this demarcation of the sacred and the embedded understandings of the relationship of the laity to the mass and the Eucharist can be seen in the oral testimony of Francis, who was born in 1928 and served on the altar at a church in Lower Broughton with his brother, who later went on to the priesthood. Reflecting on this altar service, which ceased upon his own marriage aged twenty-six, Francis emotionally recalled:

> FL: As a lay person I did everything that it was possible for a lay person to do … I mean in them days you weren't technically allowed to touch anything. … (but on one occasion) this strange priest was saying mass and I was serving mass. And when he came to open the Tabernacle – it had a little knack – if you turned the handle first and put the key in it wouldn't turn, and he was there for about two minutes. And I didn't know what to do – I was sort of spellbound. I thought 'He wants to give communion out and he can't get it out. I know what's happened'. So of course I plucked up courage, went up, turned the handle back, turned the key, turned the handle and I actually opened the Tabernacle (sobs).[106]

Whilst Francis presents this 'touching' as expedient and exceptional, particularly given the public nature of the mass, earlier in his interview Francis recounted fetching the chalice and monstrance for his usual (but often forgetful) priest,[107] and presumably had some personal experience of the 'knack' of opening the tabernacle door. As a foil to traditional historical accounts of pre-conciliar devotional life which have stressed the passivity of the laity, the hieratic nature of the mass and the strict policing of the boundaries of the 'sacred' and 'secular', Francis' recollections suggest a greater degree of (male) lay involvement than is often recognised and the negotiated permeability of these boundaries.

Reverence for the visual holiness of the host was also, of course, reinforced by the common practice of benediction. Established as a popular devotional in the nineteenth century (though with a longer history related to Corpus Christi)[108] and recommended by Pope Pius XII in *Mediator Dei* as a 'praiseworthy and indispensable' personal piety, which 'spring[s] from the inspiration of the liturgy', it allowed the believer to 'enjoy the intimacy of His [Christ's] friendship'.[109] As a form of lay religiosity that was sensory, communal and intensely ceremonial, benediction continued to be an intrinsic part of Catholic devotional life well into the mid-twentieth century.[110] An appreciation of the numinous and extra-ordinary was reinforced by this immensely popular extra-liturgical practice, which consisted of much loved litanies and hymns (such as *Tantum Ergo* and *O Salutaris Hostia*) before the Blessed Sacrament exposed on the altar in a monstrance surrounded by candles.[111] At the end of this brief ceremony, usually celebrated on a Sunday afternoon or early evening, the priest, garbed in a 'humeral veil', took the monstrance and made the sign of the cross in silence over the kneeling congregation.

Reminiscences of childhood Catholicism from earlier in the twentieth century often make reference to this very tangible, corporeal and incarnational form of devotion to Christ, which evoked:

> a memory of … the host, larger than the ones you received, white, crisp, the Body of Christ. Round like the moon, rising above the congregation, 'exposed' for all to gaze upon in absolute reverence. The Body of Christ 'exposed' in benediction, a vaguely, deeply sensual act.[112]

Tom, born in 1946 in Trafford Park where he still worships today, spoke in committed but less poetic terms of his memories of the quiet reflective time provided during benediction, and also drew an interesting, non-Eucharistic contemporary parallel:

> TF: Benediction was something special. It was a different, different mass. A different thought process. (Pause) Everything what went (sic) with it. Like, you know, the incense and all that kind of thing what went on. It was something different I suppose. But you was brought up to actually, you know, you *must* go to mass. Where now you go because you choose to go. But like if you compare sort of benediction say with … probably I

would liken it now maybe to a Taizé service, which I think is something special again.[113]

For Tom, benediction (like Taizé services now)[114] functioned as a form of experiential spirituality that was chosen and meditative and roused the emotions through music and incense. Long-serving altar boy Tony, whilst confessing a common tussle on Sunday afternoons between duty and pleasure, benediction and his (unsatisfied) boyish preference for football, reflected:

> TC: [Y]ou looked at it, venerating Him in the monstrance and things like that. And, of course, it's your Catholic belief, isn't it, that 'There's Christ, and he's giving me a blessing' ... You came out of benediction feeling a lot better than you went in.[115]

However, for some Catholics of this same generation, such as Richard, whose mother was a convert to Catholicism and who revels in a more rationalistic temperament, benediction was incomprehensible:

> RD: I don't know. I wouldn't know. No idea. No idea what the premise of benediction was. Benediction was just something that occurred and there was lots of incense and that's it. That's all benediction meant to me. Wasn't very deep.[116]

A generation on, Mary (born in 1967), has developed her understanding and appreciation for benediction only very recently, and her reflections on her childhood echoed Richard's confusion about the function of this devotional:

> MH: Well, I remember being a child and not having a clue what was going on. All I used to know was that we used to have all this smoke (laughs) and the priest used to be there with and then he used to go out. I don't think I even knew at the time he was taking the Blessed Sacrament out of the Tabernacle. It was one of those things that you had to go to.[117]

As these reflections from Catholics across a generational and spiritual spectrum illustrate, this was a form of 'religious exercise' which appealed to particular tastes and temperaments and was not always, despite Pius XII's exhortations, recognised as a practice which 'spring[s] from the inspiration of the liturgy' and which enabled Catholics to 'live the life of the liturgy'.[118] Nevertheless, as a voluntary devotion that remains part of the repertoire of Catholic devotional life, this was an extra-liturgical activity available to nourish the spiritual life of some Catholics, even if re-assessed after some years of non-practice by younger Catholics like Mary (perhaps through the clerical re-emphasis stemming from the 1990s).

Contemporaneous with this prominence given to the 'body of Christ' as subsisting in the observed and revered host, theological reflections were also beginning to evince an emphasis upon the Church *itself* as the 'body of Christ'. Deriving from a re-appreciation of the gospel witness and Pauline letters, within this notion the 'body' was comprised of the worshipping faithful with Christ, ever incarnate and active, as its Head. Such a shift was most prominently identifiable within the encyclical *Mystici Corporis Christi* (1943), published before *Mediator Dei* and reflective of this gradually evolving ecclesiology. Written in the year when the war in Europe reached a decisive turning point, atonement and sacrificial language were sensitively muted, and the Eucharist was described as an occasion through which 'the faithful are nourished and strengthened at the same banquet and by a divine, ineffable bond are united with each other and with the Divine Head of the whole Body'.[119] Within this encyclical the accent was upon the corporeal, the communal and an interiorised, consuming relationship with Christ, who:

> permeates His whole Body and nourishes and sustains each of the members according to the place they occupy through the body, in the same way as the vine nourishes and makes fruitful the branches which are joined to it.[120]

The encyclical highlighted the Eucharist as the supreme instance of intimate union between the 'mystical Body with its Head' and the occasion at which 'this union during this mortal life reaches, as it were, a culmination'.[121] In this sensual, organic analogy, likening the link between Christ and the Church to that between the head and its members, or a 'bride and bridegroom', there was a newer emphasis on Holy Communion as a unifying meal – symbolic of the 'unity of the church' as bread is comprised of many grains.[122] A decade later in *Christus Dominus* (1953) and *Sacram Communionem* (1957), which relaxed the periods of fasting before reception, this re-emphasis upon the Eucharist as nourishment and food was extended in speaking of frequent visits to the 'sacred Table' for those that 'hunger for the heavenly Bread and ... thirst for the Sacred Blood'.[123] Whilst throughout the 1950s the rhetoric of witnessed 'sacrifice' remained present within strains of institutional teaching on the mass and the Eucharist (such as *Mediator Dei*), there was an inexorable interpretive shift, as demonstrated in *Mystici Corporis Christi*, towards a theology of the sacred meal at which people participated and ate.

In translating these trends in somewhat rarified ecclesiastical and Eucharistic theology to a lay and youthful audience, the then head of the Catholic Missionary Society Father John Heenan drew upon the language of *both* Calvary and the Cenacle (the upper room), sacrifice and supper, to communicate his conviction that '[t]he Mass is not something we look at; it is something we do'.[124] A more emphatic position was discernible, however, in the trenchant observations of the liturgist Clifford Howell SJ that the previous piety, stemming from the medieval period, was centred 'on "seeing the Host"' and was fundamentally misconceived, for:

> Instead of the Mass being an approach by man through Christ to God, it became ... an approach by God to man, an 'epiphany', the irruption of God into this world, the coming of God to man in the Sacred Host.[125]

What was required, he insisted, was the recognition of the 'real nature of the liturgy as communal prayer, communal instruction, communal offering and communal meal'.[126] Another strong advocate of liturgical reform, Michael de la Bédoyère, drew upon the liturgical practice in France where mass was celebrated facing the people to reduce 'the centuries between ourselves and the Last Supper' and to reinforce 'the community of all the faithful with the priest round the altar of solemn sacrifice'.[127] Whilst debates raged within the erudite pages of the Benedictine *Downside Review* about transubstantiation, immolation and the nature of the Eucharist as our gift to God,[128] these insights were also percolating through popular literature. In slightly patronising tones, Grace Hurrell told her youthful audience that:

> When we want several people to meet and become friends, we often give a party and invite them all to meet at a meal ...
>
> That is why our Lord invented the spiritual banquet we call the Holy Eucharist, and it is at this festive meal that we are meant to increase our love for the other members of our Lord's Body, the Church. For at the Holy Sacrifice, especially when we receive Holy Communion, we feast together with the saints, as well as with our Lord.[129]

Reflecting similar concerns, but also reifying contemporaneous (and perhaps middle-class) concerns about the changes in post-war society and family life, Monsignor Knox was more expansive in drawing upon the metaphor of a meal to elucidate the function of the Eucharist:

> [T]he old kind of family meal did bring with it the sense of a family reunion. Papa was carving and Mamma got half the breast ... Day after day you share the same food, and it drove home to you the fact that you were a single family. Nowadays, when you go into a snack bar and scoop up a bit of spam and a couple of parsnips for yourself, I dare say it's different ... [But] Our Lord said 'My friends shall have a feast of home reunion like that. ... *All* my friends shall be one family, and have one common meal, going on *all* over the world, going on *all* the year round.' So he instituted the Holy Eucharist.[130]

Whilst giving priority in order and substance to this explanation of the mass in his narrative, four pages later Knox nevertheless drew upon the cross and Calvary to explicate the nature of the sacrifice of the mass. The co-existence, and indeed compatibility, of these very different ideas of the mass was recognised by other systematic theologians and reformist liturgists working at the time, such as the Jesuit John Coventry who insightfully observed:

> [N]o age can grasp the *whole* of the Gift – Real Presence, Sacrifice and Sacrament ... He has placed the emphasis on the aspect of it which appeals most to His needs or insight. Now it may be the meal of unity in Christ; now the life-giving Flesh and Blood ... The thought of the Person present may dominate, or His original action where He is here re-presented. Now awe dominates, now homeliness. What matter? The *thing done*, the *Gift itself*, remains unchanged and contains all this and more. Hence we can neither look forward nor backward for the complete and perfect ritual for Mass.[131]

As a theological reflection this remains a satisfactory explanation for the differing figurative metaphors used within Catholic commentary and religious practice in the mid-twentieth century. Nevertheless, a historical account must move beyond these models to understand why certain understandings of the central action of the mass 'now dominate' and came to appeal more to the 'needs or insights' of the faithful. It is to this task – the predominant emphasis on the Eucharist as an eschatological banquet or sacred (family) meal identifiable from the 1950s and overwhelmingly prominent in the post-conciliar theology – that this discussion now turns. It will consider the gradual but ultimate dominance of this understanding of the Eucharist, its reinforcement through Pope Paul VI's new liturgical rite, and the reasons (including the ecumenical context) for a de-emphasised sacrificial understanding.

Writing in 1958 for the missiologically focused *Catholic Gazette*, one of England's best-known theologians and editor of a provocative intellectual monthly, *The Clergy Review*, wrote of the Eucharist's dual and dynamic purpose: 'to bring Christ to us in the act of sacrifice and to give Him to us as the food of our Christian life'.[132] In an earlier companion article, Father Charles Davis explained that Christ 'chose for His sacraments certain basic human actions', converting the common action of bathing into the sacrament of baptism, and encouraged the discernment, beyond the priestly elements, of 'the basic shape of this sacrament [as] ... a meal' and 'the natural means of expressing and strengthening other social relationships'.[133] As a *peritus* (theological expert) at the Second Vatican Council some six years later, before his dramatic defection from the Catholic Church outlined in *A Question of Conscience* (1967),[134] Davis played a part in the restatement of the 'holy mystery' in *Sacrosanctum Concilium* (1963):

> Our saviour inaugurated the eucharistic sacrifice of his body and blood at the last supper on the night he was betrayed, in order to make his sacrifice of the cross last throughout time until he should return; and indeed to entrust a token to the church, his beloved wife, by which to remember his death and resurrection. It is a sacrament of faithful relationships, a sign of unity, a bond of divine love, a special easter meal.[135]

Drawing upon the implicit legacy of *Mediator Dei*, the Eucharist was nevertheless re-conceived in dynamic, interpersonal and this-worldly terms, with a marked emphasis on the formation of Christian community and the celebration of a sacramental meal, as well as the effecting of an atoning sacrifice. Codifying these developments, the Sacred Congregation of Rites issued an *Instruction on Eucharistic Worship* in May 1967, which definitively stated that 'the Mass, the Lord's Supper, is at the same time and inseparably':

- A sacrifice ...;
- A memorial of the death and resurrection of the Lord, ...
- A sacred banquet in which, through the communion of the Body and Blood of the Lord, the People of God share the benefits of the Paschal Sacrifice, renew the New Covenant ... and anticipate the eschatological

banquet in the kingdom of the Father, proclaiming the Lord's death 'till His coming'.[136]

It is telling that while it retained the terminology of Calvary and sacrifice, and asserted that 'the sacrifice and sacred meal belong to the same mystery', the predominant emphasis of the *Instruction* is on the 'Lord's supper' and the 'celebration of the memorial' in which 'the Church is nourished by the bread of life which she finds at the table both of the Word of God and of the Body of Christ'.[137] In the implementation of the extensive liturgical reforms and ritual changes following the Council, the main characteristics of the renewed rite were seen to lie in its conception as a sacred meal, or more precisely, 'a ritual meal of a sacrificial nature'.[138]

This transition in Eucharistic theology is most clearly appreciated in many of the catechetical programmes for schools and educational commentaries published which sought to inculcate an updated, active and corporate liturgical enthusiasm to the laity. For example, in his chatty 1964 commentary, Canon Drinkwater emphatically stated:

> The Mass, from the *Pater Noster* onwards, is just a Family Meal, at God the Father's Table. ... People may go to the same cinema for years and never get to know each other ... But the Mass is not something we go to watch or listen to. It is something we are doing ourselves or should be. Even a third-rate sort of Catholic does not sit through Mass like a film-show: he stands up at the gospel, signs himself with crosses, kneels at the Consecration, perhaps even breathes a prayer or two. ... The very fact of being at Mass together, all friends of Jesus Christ, ought to make us ready to be friends together after Mass, to speak to each other, to be ready to work and play together.[139]

The impact of the liturgical renewal was also palpably apparent in publications like *The Harvest*, an organ of the Salford Diocesan Rescue Society, which underwent a metamorphosis from a pious monthly devotional magazine to an illustrated quarterly which, upon its re-launch, ran a three-part series by Father Michael Child on 'The People's Mass'. Breaking down the Tridentine mass (which was increasingly being celebrated in English) into its constituent parts, Father Child's third article offered an illustrated explanation of the 'Offertory, Eucharist, Communion & Mission' and the role of the laity within a liturgical action that permeated everyday life.[140] In an illustration accompanying the article, the Eucharist is represented by showing Christ from the cross overlooking a modern-day cityscape, and the 'mission' of the Church embodied in a nuclear family, leaving an architecturally experimental church building (evocative of Liverpool Cathedral, which opened in the same year), to take the familial message into the world.[111] Fifteen years later, within a 'First Communion workbook' published for school children by the Catholic Truth Society, this doctrinal and iconographic presentation of Holy Communion as a family meal had fully converged, with illustrations of the family at dinner directly echoing the 'universal family of God coming together to the table of God'.[112]

Such a discernible shift in emphasis was also present in the Eucharistic theology of a post-1960s generation of Mancunian laity such as Mary, who explained her understanding of the Eucharist as creating an existential, experiential link between the believer and Jesus:

> MH: [B]asically like having the communion – we have to have bread and water to live. We need Jesus as well, for our spiritual wellbeing. So I suppose in that way, that's the way I look at it now.[113]

Expanding upon her understandings and the way she communicates these within the sacramental programme she leads in a local Catholic school, Mary used concepts reminiscent of Grace Hurrell's, but updated for a contemporary, northern context:

> MH: I mean the children are only seven and eight so the simplest way you can explain it to them is 'You've got to eat, like, your fish and chips, haven't you? You've got to have your glass of coke or whatever to live. You've got to eat.' And just as you've got to eat – you need to (feed) your soul. ... It's like going to a party and then not going to enjoy the food and having a celebration if you don't go and have communion.[114]

Nevertheless the concept of 'transubstantiation' had not totally disappeared from this reframing of the Eucharist as a meal. Peter, born in 1944, recounted the discussions in a lay group in the early 1970s ('the Patricians', of which he is still a member) which explored the differences between the Catholic 're-enactment' of the Last Supper, giving rise to the 'real presence', and an Anglican 'commemoration'.[115] For the theologically alert eighteen-year-old Patrick (who is Mitzi's son) there is a struggle, but also a faith-based obedience, in his wrestling with 'watching the priest *make* the bread and wine into the Body and Blood'[116] and asking '"Do I actually believe that I'm ingesting part of the Son of God during Communion?"'[117]

The questions, difficulties, conundrums and faith-based affirmations of Catholics when confronted with the doctrine of transubstantiation have not disappeared, but are now framed more by the analogy of a redeeming meal than a salvific recapitulation of the passion.

There were a number of factors underpinning this shift in Eucharistic metaphor, not least of which was the movement away from a narrowly Christological and soteriological focus towards viewing the Eucharist as both the recapitulation of the Last Supper and celebration within the context of the entire liturgy by the worshipping church community. As Robert Daly, writing on post-Tridentine Eucharistic theology expressed it, '*in persona Christi*' was increasingly interpreted as '*in persona Christi capitis ecclesiae*' and '*in persona ecclesiae*'.[148] This trend was reinforced by the implementation of the new liturgical rite, Pope Paul VI's *Missa Normativa* (1969), which is chiefly known for its enshrinement of the vernacular but which also introduced new versions of the Canon that were spoken aloud and were addressed, with places for response, to the congregation by a priest facing the people. Liturgists supportive of this new ritual suggested that while the notion of sacrifice had been retained, the central themes of the new Eucharistic prayers were the memorial, thanksgiving and a new creation.[149] However, not all the laity were initially impressed with the changes, with Francis' wife Kathleen recalling:

> KL: Oh yes, I didn't like the English mass at first. It took me a long, long time. I didn't understand the Latin, but I knew by heart some of the prayers that were said. I couldn't translate them for toffee. It's only in recent times that I've thought: 'What if they said they'll change it back?' I don't think I'd like to go back now.[150]

The basis for Kathleen's objection, common to many ordinary English Catholic laity, was chiefly the disruption of habitual, ritualistic (and linguistic) forms and the common (but confused) conflation of the movement to the vernacular with the implementation of the new Roman liturgy.[151]

Sometimes a well-informed and theologically articulate laity did not like the new mass either, discerning within it a substantial change in liturgical theology. Representative of those writing to their pastors to express their misgivings about the new Eucharistic rites was 'Denis Sheridan Esq', who in 1969 wrote to Cardinal Heenan about the translation of '*in meum memoriam facietis*' (whilst citing Livy) and objected to 'having so much emphasis placed on the Mass as being a memorial'.[152] Stressing that the Eucharist is 'truly the living God', not merely symbolic as a 'dead monument, or a keepsake or mere trinket', he continued:

> The act of consecration at the Last Supper was no mere gesture or pious custom like a toast drunk 'To the prior and immortal memory of Good Queen Bess' but something much, much more significant.[153]

Another correspondent, also drawing upon recusant concerns, linked her opposition to the new mass specifically to Canon II, which 'omits the sacrificial aspect as the Mass … [for which] our blessed English Martyrs died … [and] which the Reformers denied so vehemently'.[154] Mrs Krynski went on to assert that this new form of Eucharistic rite was 'practically synonymous with the Anglican service [and] could be said in good conscience by one who did not believe in transubstantiation'.[155] This invocation of the English Reformation, and the accusation of undue capitulation to a Protestant understanding of the liturgy, was a frequent lament in the reactions of some lay English Catholics to the liturgical reforms,[156] and those commentators opposed to the changes often attributed the fervour for reform to a false conception of ecumenism.[157]

While it is clear that these shifts in liturgical practice and Eucharistic theology were not merely driven by ecumenical capitulation, the changed ecumenical sensibilities following Vatican II's *Unitatis Redintegratio* (1964) did allow for greater cross-denominational collaboration and the formulation of some common strategies between the Church of England and the Catholic Hierarchy. This required a focus on theological language held in common, exemplified by a shared Eucharistic theology of the 'sacramental meal', but also pursued in areas of common concern such as church attendance, the accessibility of liturgical language and the need for greater congregational participation. Whilst there was a vociferous section of the laity who objected to these changes and efforts at ecumenical convergence, the vast majority (quietly) accepted the reforms and some were equally loquacious in their zeal for liturgical renewal. One example was Mrs M. L. Bamford, who wrote a letter in 1965 forwarded to Archbishop Dwyer of Birmingham as head of the English Liturgical Commission. Prefacing her suggestions as 'very humble comments from an ignorant person', she insisted that 'all parts spoken by the people should be memorable, have a poetic quality and wherever possible should be the same as the Anglican version', with any 'fresh translation made … [in] consultation with the Anglican liturgists'.[158]

Just such a spirit of collaboration and co-operation, drawing upon a common patristic heritage and the history of liturgical development, underpinned the ecumenical activities of the Anglican-Roman Catholic International Commission (ARCIC) established by Pope Paul VI and the Archbishop of Canterbury, Dr Michael Ramsey, in 1970. One of the first documents to be produced by the commission was an agreed statement on *Eucharistic Doctrine* (1972), which proclaimed the attainment of 'substantial agreement' despite differences in traditional expression and practice of Eucharistic faith.[159] Acknowledging that 'communion with Christ in the eucharist presupposes his true presence', the document stressed this 'signification' by the bread and wine and employed the metaphors of the 'table' and the 'eschatological banquet' – consigning transubstantiation to a footnote where it was described as a doctrine affirming Christ's presence and the changed nature of the elements, but not, in 'contemporary Catholic theology ... explaining how the change takes place'.[160] Subsequent Anglican commentary on the ARCIC document stressed the agreement between Anglicans and Catholics that the Eucharist is 'the central action at the heart of the Church's life' and a 'common meal' of commitment to God, each other and the world.[161] Liberal Catholic opinion was mostly in agreement, perhaps epitomised by Bishop Christopher Butler, a prominent *peritus* to the Second Vatican Council, Chair of the English ecumenical body (English ARC), and a public personality through regular participation in Radio 4's *Any Questions*.[162] In an instructional tract written in 1975 for the CTS, Butler sought to find a balance between the 'sacrificial' and 'sacramental', utilising the language of the memorial banquet, but also stressing the 'real presence' as understood 'within the whole action and worship of the Mass' at the 'eucharistic altar and table'.[163] Nevertheless, a strongly articulated alternative opinion was voiced by theologically educated laymen such as Theophilis Stephen Gregory, who called upon his journalistic background to object eloquently to the abandonment of the Latin (in terms to be taken up from 1965 by the newly formed Latin Mass Society)[164] and remained a prominent correspondent in the Catholic press well into the 1970s.[165] Disparaging what he saw as the dry rationalism and cowardly compromises of the ARCIC statement, T. S. Gregory posed the provocative rhetorical question: 'When the priest (the real priest) lifts up the consecrated host and chalice, saying "This is the Lamb of God," is it the truth or a charade?'[166] Setting aside his unabashed and confrontational confessionalism, this Daventry correspondent was correct in identifying the heart of the issue as the changing understandings of the reality of, and ordinary Catholics' relationship to, the 'real presence' and related questions about the ways in which this could be accessed and evoked. The ways in which English Catholics interrogated and integrated these shifting understandings of the Eucharist was also reinforced through markedly transformed Eucharistic practices.

Voicing the understanding of a self-confessed 'ordinary layman' about the Eucharistic changes in the wake of the Second Vatican Council and the New Rite, Roger de Wever wrote in far-from-neutral tones to Cardinal Heenan, explaining:

> We used to hear about the sacrifice of the Mass, now it is the Eucharist. We used to be told that the bread and wine of the offering were about to be changed into the Body and Blood of Our Lord Jesus Christ. Now, the bread becomes the 'Bread of Life', the wine becomes, oh wonder!, a spiritual drink! How poor, how abysmally poor! A protestant clergyman can now, in conscience, offer the Roman Mass.[167]

Mr de Wever's letter doubtless received a sympathetic audience, although a response is not recorded in the archive, as a few years earlier Cardinal Heenan had written to Evelyn Waugh in revealing (but also consoling and placatory) terms: 'The Mass is no longer the Holy Sacrifice but the Meal at which the priest is the waiter. The bishop, I suppose is the head waiter and the Pope is the patron'.[168] However, other educated laity expressed countervailing frustration at clerical conservatism and 'extravagant reactions [which] accuse the new Mass of having abandoned the notion of sacrifice'.[169] Acknowledging some changes, but stressing a continuity in substance, the prolific author, convert and former politician Christopher Hollis[170] observed in 1974 that Roman Catholics were 'now no longer nearly so insistent on transubstantiation as they were', but thought this a shift in terminology – and its operation as a totalising explanatory metaphysic – rather than rupturing a continued recognition of Christ's 'real presence in the sacrament'.[171]

This movement towards the conceptualisation of the Holy Eucharist as a sacred meal or eschatological banquet was identifiable within numerous publications and lay practices through the 1970s, and a consequence of this shifting emphasis was also a re-interpretation of the host as 'spiritual food' which nourished, sustained and healed rather than as an untouchable object to be revered and worshipped from afar. This is well illustrated in the 'Q&A column' of Fr John Symon, writing for the *Catholic Herald* in 1968, who addressed a number of queries (and generated a sizable correspondence) on issues such as frequent communion, communion under 'both kinds' (i.e. reception of both bread and wine) and the relationship between communion and confession. Demonstrative of his liberal and reforming agenda, he pronounced that 'the Holy Eucharist' should be recognised 'as the most perfect means of participating at Mass and as the supreme encounter with Christ and our brethren'.[172] In answer to a layperson from Edinburgh's consternation at a 'shocking innovation', namely the proposed use of real bread within the mass, this liturgical 'agony-uncle' was unsympathetic:

> The bread for consecration should look as if it were intended to be eaten – it should not look altogether dissimilar from what we eat at the family table in our homes.[173]

This shifting theology, and its gradual impact on lay practice, was also noticed by other commentators, such as James O'Connell, who noted that the practice of regular weekly confession seemed to be falling into 'desuetude', to the consternation of some clergy. Rejecting assessments of a weakening of faith and religious decline, the eminent liturgical commentator diagnosed a 'growing consensus of the faithful as they recognise and resort to the healing power of the Eucharist'.[174] Echoing this shift in familial, generational terms, former nun and now lay pastoral assistant Judith, born in 1936, commented on contemporary practice:

> JE: My own nieces, none of them go to mass. They're not in irregular marriages but they never go to mass. But when they do go, they go to Holy Communion. Well, you wouldn't have done that pre-Vatican II, you'd have felt that you needed to go to confession, wouldn't you, if you'd missed mass for six months? (said while knocking the table for emphasis).[175]

By contrast, reception and full participation in the Eucharist – which was increasingly interpreted as 'communication in both kinds' – was increasingly seen as the best way of healing such estrangement and sustaining a nourishing connection with Christ and the Church. The trajectory of this development was laid down at the Council, when reception was linked to fuller participation in the mass and, whilst expressly retaining the principles of the Council of Trent on communion under one species, a greater range of occasions for reception under both kinds was also allowed.[176] Throughout the 1970s, these exceptions to the rule began to prove the norm, leading to the *General Instruction on the Roman Missal* which resonated with reforming liturgists like Father Harold Winstone (translator on the Liturgical Commission of England and Wales and Director of the National Liturgy Centre in Westminster), that:

> the bread and wine are consecrated not just to be adored, but to communicate Christ's life by being eaten and drunk by the faithful. Bread is for eating; wine is for drinking … The eucharist was to be a real commemorative meal, a banquet, a wedding feast celebrating Christ's espousal with his Church … and hence not just an eating – that would not constitute a banquet – but eating *and* drinking (original emphasis).[177]

The stress in this commentary on 'communicating' – an experiential, relational, and communal activity – is important to note. Accompanying these changes was also the increasing practice of reception of the host in the hand, linked by another member of the Liturgical Commission, Father Anthony Boylan, to the increasing lay integration of the theological implications of *Mystici Corporis Christi* and a newly articulated relationship with Christ:

> Christians today have a renewed awareness of their individual sacredness and realise that no part of their being is less sacred than other. Thus for many people to reach out in a gesture of wanting and gratefully receiving expresses deep Christian faith. … Upon reflection, receiving food into one's mouth from another's hand seems to many a gesture limited to the case of infants and the infirm. It is considered less becoming of an adult Christian – mature in faith.[178]

These changes to the mode of reception were part of a raft of changes to bodily movements and postures during the liturgy, beginning in 1964 with the incorporation of more active movement into the liturgy. This shifting between standing, kneeling and sitting in the liturgy was unfamiliar to most lay Catholics and initially disparaged as a 'bobbing up and down' during the mass without due reverence (i.e. through kneeling) at the time of consecration.[179] Reception of communion standing – rather than at the altar rail – and potentially from a 'lay minister of the eucharist' were modifications all flowing on from the 1970 New Rite. This led some people, resistant to the changes and fearful of their impact on reverence for the 'real presence', to compare the Eucharist procession to 'a queue for groceries, fish and chips, buses or any other earthly possession'.[180] Much of this anxiety was generated by the way in which such (unexplained) changes seemed to challenge long-held and habitually engrained practice. The layman Lawrence Hunt wrote to his pastor and soon-to-be head of the Liturgical Commission, to communicate his distress at rumours of new procedures disturbing ideas 'drilled into me since childhood'.[181] Mancunian Tony expressed similar reservations when moving to reception of communion in the hand:

> TC: The spiritual and, er, sacredness, if there is such a word, of the eucharist then. It held you in awe in relation to receiving the communion. And then, what you'd been bred with ... and then, changes all of a sudden and you think, well – 'I don't like this'. And that was my attitude when, er, it first came around. ...'Alright, it's OK now' but in the back of my mind it's still there, what we were bred – taught and bred like with, that only the priest could touch the host.[182]

Acknowledging the impact of these 'fresh shocks' to 'the poor old faithful', in a letter which also asked whether anything could be done for the Tridentine Mass 'non-cranks who would like a little peaceful co-existence for the old Mass', the reluctant reformer Cardinal Heenan mirrored the ambivalence of many laity. In a telling briefing to Archbishop Dwyer in 1970 he wrote:

> 1. Holy Communion in the hand: I don't want it, don't like it, but don't feel strongly about it. One or two places want to try it *ad experimentum* (a very convenient phrase!) ... Other hierarchies (German, Belgian, French, I think) have leave to permit it.[183]

However, not all the laity were as wary of change nor as unenthusiastic about the liturgical reforms. Writing to Cardinal Heenan as an aware and engaged layman, George Sommer reflected on the practice of 'communion in the hand' in Spain:

> Having given the matter some thought I have reached a personal conclusion that the new method is very beautiful. It seems to me somehow more intimate and committing and involving a high degree of voluntarily receiving Our Blessed Lord into oneself.

I also feel that the majority of us sin just as much with our hands as with our mouths so I would have no hesitation in accepting this new style.[184]

Strongly evident in this letter, and the new tropes by younger (or reformist) Catholics to articulate an intense, embodied and communal relationship to Christ which are explored below, was a prioritisation of faith as chosen, committed and personalised. At issue in these debates was a heightened negotiation of the relationship between tradition and development, the spiritual and the bodily, the sacred and the profane. Writing in strident terms in 1974 about the further 'desacralisation of the liturgy' through the decision to allow lay ministers of the Eucharist, the 'traditionalist' campaigner D. G. Galvin articulated many of these emerging tensions:

> [S]ince time immemorial, Catholics have been solemnly told that the Bread was so sacred that only the consecrated hands of the priest could touch it. Is it not inevitable that in time reverence for the actuality of the Real Presence in the Host, and for the priest himself as its one-time sacred dispenser, will diminish?[185]

A week later, the *Catholic Herald* printed a feisty response to this letter from Mrs M. E. Hodgkinson, a housebound sufferer from multiple sclerosis in Lancashire, who stood to benefit from increasing flexibility in distribution of the Eucharist by lay ministers supplementing the ministrations of over-stretched priests. Dismissing Gavin's arguments as 'balderdash', Mrs Hodgkinson observed that 'respect is more than genuflecting' and that 'humble recognition of Our Lord's Real Presence ... is increasing steadily even if expressed differently'.[186]

As the correspondence continued to rage, a letter from 'C.V.S.' drew the discussion back to communion in the hand, drawing upon historical examples and variant practices in churches such as St Peter's in Rome to maintain that 'although reverence should be expressed outwardly it need not be by rigid adherence to particular practices, many of which have never been constant or universal'.[187] Stressing attention to Christ rather than rubrics, the letter concluded:

> Shall we, like the Pharisees, pay more attention to outer show than to our inner state? Shall we, like Martha, be so busy about many things, in even Our Lord's service, that we allow ourselves to be distracted from thinking about Our Lord Himself?[188]

As this correspondent identified, through the utilisation of the biblical story of Mary and Martha, for many Catholics following the Second Vatican Council, an attentive, active and participatory sharing of this meal with Christ was understood as the most effective way for the people of God to establish and express their intimate relationship to their Saviour. As Mrs Hodgkinson and Christopher Hollis recognised, Christ's 'real presence' at the Eucharist was still acknowledged by most Catholics despite a reluctance now to delve into the theological intricacies of 'transubstantiation' and the movement away from certain stylised and ritualised practices of reverence. This fascinating shift in Eucharistic theology was coupled with a re-evaluation of the various Christological tropes employed by Catholics. These were similarly reconfigured to express an intensely personal, experiential yet corporate relationship with Jesus and the world-related actions that such a recognition compelled. From the earlier Christological analogies of the child of Nazareth, the suffering Saviour and the Sacred Heart emerged re-packaged representations of the incarnate, familial Christ as 'fully human', 'spouse' and 'friend of the poor' which the next section explores.

'Made in the likeness of Christ': Christ as humanitarian, bridegroom and comrade

In its synthesis of the theological trends and papal encyclicals *Mediator Dei* and *Mystici Corporis Christi*, the conciliar document *Lumen Gentium* (1964) provided a programmatic statement for a generation of Catholics negotiating the social tumult of the 1960s and seeking ethical answers to global issues. Articulating a more conscious and explicit emphasis on the Holy Spirit, and reinforcing the liturgical emphasis on 'active participation', the Council fathers pronounced:

> [B]y the communication of his Spirit, [Christ] constituted his sisters and brothers, gathered from all nations, as his own mystical body.
> In this body the life of Christ is communicated to believers, who by means of the sacraments in a mysterious but real way are made into the likeness of Christ. ... When we really participate in the body of the Lord through the breaking of the eucharistic bread, we are raised up to communion with him and among ourselves.[189]

Communicating the impetus of this theological restatement to a wider audience in 1972, the American Jesuit Francis Buckley translated these insights in terms attractive to a youthful, spiritually experimental audience:

> Christ as teacher is not so much a lecturer with blackboard, textbooks and fixed curriculum. He is more like a guru or Zen master, a man of God who reflects with us on his own life-style and helps us to understand the way he is and how we can be like him.[190]

Resonant with ideas such as 'the man for others' and 'worldly holiness' newly popularised through the Anglican Bishop of Woolwich's unexpected best-seller *Honest to God* (1963),[191] both these Catholic commentaries – one institutional and the other devotional – encapsulated the transformed understanding of the Christian believer's relationship to Christ through experience and action, including an active participation in the liturgy and interaction and experiential encounter at the communal meal (and beyond).

In the context of this now greatly enhanced emphasis on the liturgy as the pre-eminent Catholic religious practice, previously popular devotions were re-interpreted to stress their relationship to the mass and the Eucharist. For example, in tellingly faint praise, the Council affirmed these lay practices, so long as they 'cohere with the liturgy, in some way derive from it, and lead the people to it, inasmuch as the liturgy, by its nature, is far more important than they are'.[192] Such an impulse was manifest in devotional writing too; for example the Lancastrian solicitor (and part-time lay university chaplain) P. P. McCarthy took great efforts in his reflection on the rosary to link 'the first sorrowful mystery' to the offertory in the mass:

> From the pages of the Gospels Jesus [might] step out and walk and talk and play and suffer and rejoice with us, until we know him as a friend, so close to us in human experience, but so full of the wisdom and knowledge of God that inescapably he, as our brother, becomes our guide, our counsellor, our comforter in every circumstance of human life.[193]

This ideal of an intensely personal relationship, sustained by the Church and its liturgical practices, but also fostered through a newly appreciated emphasis on the scriptures,[194] was linked to a more 'this-worldly' spirituality or, as Father Patrick Fannon told a study conference of the Liverpool University Newman Association in 1968, to a theology in transition where 'The penitential spirituality had gone. People have gone 'liturgical' [and] we're more concerned with facing up to life in the world'.[195] Commentators such as Sister Mary Benedicta agreed, explaining to a slightly less theologically literate, avant-garde audience that the restless 'seeking [of] our own individual personalities' in the 1960s was really a 'searching for a more intimate experience of Christ ... [as] part and parcel of our daily life and not Someone way up there in the clouds'.[196] In terms reminiscent of Houselander, she spoke of Christ living and walking 'our streets and country roads', in 'hospitals, schools, shopping centres and financial markets', but most supremely identifiable in the Eucharist, in which 'we listen to his heart-beat and embrace him through reception of Holy Communion'.[197]

This understanding of Christ as accessible and 'truly human', as a fully realised, other-orientated human being, is one which Kevin, born in 1954 and director of the Trafford Park-based Centre for Church and Industry, embraces:

> KF: The best (image) I actually saw was of the Lord, was one I think (Fr) Joe Carter has somewhere in a frame, which is the Lord with a pint in his hand, stood at the bar, with a pint, drinking, the smiling Lord. Now, we forget that these are spiritual moments and I think ... that has to be seen. Now that's not being irreverent whatsoever. This is about the Christ that engages, in the real world. And that's why I'm so adamant about the Eucharist being part, central – I think it has far more significance.[198]

Slightly older fellow parishioner Peter, when asked whether Catholics' understandings of the Eucharist have changed, responded in a similarly reflective and intensely incarnational vein. Unlike Kevin who employed a communal gathering image, Peter melded a stress on the humanity of Christ to the crucifixion and the personal dimensions of faith:

> PK: I'm tempted to throw that one back at you and say 'Did people really understand the Eucharist then, and do we really understand the Eucharist now?' I have a faith that tells me the Eucharist is Jesus' body and blood. I can't prove that. I can't prove that transubstantiation has taken place. I believe it to be true, I believe it to be true because of the upbringing that I've had. But the understanding ... concept of the Eucharist – the notion of someone laying down his life for me. Phew. It's mind blowing.

I mean, I was thinking the other night, you know – that you actually think of a hand there, and 'I'll take a nail and drill that nail through that hand'. And that's just the start of it. And I'm thinking 'Not on my hand you won't'. It's superhuman – and then yet to say that Christ is superhuman is to demean the humanity of Christ ... The Eucharist therefore, I think, becomes a very personal thing, a personal communication to God.[199]

This personal communication and connection with God was also stressed by Mary, who was born after the Council, and who acknowledged that many of the children she teaches do not know anything about the 'Stations of the Cross' which remain part of her (and her daughters') annual preparation for Easter:

MH: I think because it's retelling the story, isn't it – the Passion? ... You can actually walk with Him, walk with Jesus and through the Passion. Starting off with the Last Supper and then like doing, Good Friday.[200]

As these various oral reflections illustrate, ranging across the theological spectrum and an age group whose adolescence or early adulthood straddled the decade of the Council, there is a marked and discernible priority given to an experiential, practical, active and embodied Christology. Strains of the older devotional forms and former Christological tropes may be present, as well as newer understandings of Christ as 'fully human', which are configured in ways which have contemporary relevance and make sense within people's own life stories.

This emphasis on 'experience', articulated by contemporary commentators and young clerics attuned to the 'signs of the times', was similarly noted by those keen to update theology and by those lamenting a passing worldview, concerned about a radical break from the traditional devotional styles and a more metaphysical Christology. Nevertheless, as is also evident from these oral history reflections on the crucifixion and the passion and the earlier discussion, this was not as marked a break with the past as the modernisers have sought to suggest. While the language of sacrifice and suffering became more muted in the latter decades of the century, it is possible to perceive marked similarities in the emphasis on a personal Saviour – explicitly embodied, intimately experienced and concerned with the welfare of the created order. Therefore, the changes so often discussed when speaking of the post-conciliar period relate more to the *manner* in which this encounter was mediated; part of the wider societal restlessness with all things 'traditional'. In a Catholic context, older devotions such as the rosary, benediction and Sacred Heart statues were interrogated, with a suspicion that these ritualistic forms and modes might be outdated, overly rigid or ecumenically unpalatable. Even the mass, which had attained an even greater significance in Catholic devotional life as the place of encounter with Christ, was subject to scrutiny in the emerging disinclination to rite and rote when an emphasis was placed on a personally determined, individually expressive and experiential faith. These tensions were well expressed in a 1968 pamphlet '*What are we doing at Mass?*' which in its title deliberately recalled and contested Father Martindale's liturgical classic and its continuing emphasis upon the priestly action. Within it, the theologian Nicholas Lash, then priest (now married and laicised Cambridge theologian), summarised these trends:

> An increasing number of people in England today do not see any purpose in organized acts of worship because, as they often put it, 'You do not have to go to church to worship God.' Which is perfectly true.[201]

He continued by also exploring a countervailing trend:

> There also seem to be an increasing number of people who are convinced that the celebration of the Eucharist together is the heart and centre of the life of the Christian people. Only a few years ago, it was quite normal for many devout Catholics, who regularly attended Mass, and whose depth of Christian faith showed itself in the quality of their Christian living, to be hardly concerned about what the priest was saying and doing at Mass ...
>
> Nowadays, we Catholics are making immense efforts ... and, for increasing numbers of Catholics, to take part in the Mass without going to Communion seems very odd indeed.[202]

In this juxtaposition, Lash encapsulated one of the central transitions in Catholic devotional life throughout the second half of the second century and a change at the most fundamental level related to the movement from structured prayer and mandated habits towards an emphasis on personal experience and authentic, chosen encounter.[203] It is within this framework of an increased emphasis on the centrality of mass, at a time when its form was being intensely negotiated, that the complexities of declining attendance numbers from the late 1960s should be interrogated.

This emerging imperative on an authentic, chosen engagement at church was also recognised by the bishops at the Council, who acknowledged that within an efficacious liturgy 'what [the people] think and feel must be at one with what they say'.[201] Across the denominational spectrum, liturgists and theologians in the 1960s and 1970s attempted to implement these new insights, advocating new liturgical translations and ritual experimentation as a means to address this desire for accessible, expressive and personally relevant communion services. Nevertheless, in a Catholic context there also remained an enduring, and sometimes conflicting, emphasis on the communal and corporate. As Mervyn Clive observed very early on in 1947, in reaction to this perceptible trend:

> The Catholic is not merely a self-contained unit to seek grace for himself out of this or that sacramental channel. He is not merely an imitator of Christ or a disciple of Christ, nor merely even a lover of Christ, but he is actually a cell of that very body which is Christ's.[205]

The liturgical confusion of the post-conciliar period and the excesses of some of the liturgical adaptations illustrate both priests' and parishioners' uncertainties about how to give due weight to the individually expressive and reflective alongside the active, corporate and therefore mandated elements of any ritual. As the noted commentator on Catholic spirituality Bernard Kelly observed two decades after the liturgical and devotional reforms:

> It would be unfortunate if the balance were to come down so heavily on the side of performing, or words and gestures and actions, as to leave little of inner silence ... a person who neglects to develop his personal prayer life will not be able to enter fully into the Liturgy; he will remain more or less a participant in the external rites without any deeper spiritual communication with God.[206]

Redeveloping the liturgy so that it was personally engaging as well as communally expressive posed many challenges for theologically astute liturgists as well as pastorally sensitive priests.[207] Priests and parish communities alike struggled with finding liturgical formats that communicated Catholics' relationship to a 'truly human' Christ and wondered whether the mass, or alternative forms of community (such as the pub or house gatherings) might aid this spiritual formation. Moreover, the increasing institutional recognition that the laity, as the people of God and members of his mystical body, had an imperative part to play in the make-up and mission of the Church posed other questions. These encompassed the ways in which believers' bodies were involved in this relationship with Christ, the presence of Christ within their bodily relationships with each other, and the ways in which Christ might be made present, both inside and outside conventional church settings.

Following on from this reconfigured Christological trope of Jesus as 'truly human' was an associated shift of emphasis in the ways in which this 'becoming like Christ' should also result in a greater authenticity (and sanctity) in Catholics' wider social relationships. As a starting point, the married state and love between husband and wife were reconfigured through a Christological lens. This incarnated, embodied relationship was re-examined as a model for the love of Christ for the believer and as an image of the Church. While the relationship between Christ and his Church has long been understood though the metaphor of marriage – with the Church known as the spouse of Christ – this analogy was developed through a romantic imaginative framework in the late nineteenth century and took on a particular pertinence through the valorisation of marriage generally in the post-war period. In Catholic circles, the re-appreciation of the importance of this sacrament was evidenced in *Lumen Gentium*, which praised the 'virtue of the sacrament of matrimony' in which married Christians 'both share in and symbolize the unity and fertile love between Christ and the Church'.[208] The family in this restatement of Catholic teaching was re-affirmed as 'the domestic church', and in lay Catholic writings from the 1940s onwards this link between the 'domestic' church and the 'institutional' church was explored.

Likening the nourishment and communion fostered in the family home to the sustenance given to the community gathered around the altar, Young Christian Workers (YCW) worker Ralph Russell stressed:

> Christ's sacrificial love ... overflows into the love of men and women for each other, and thus married love comes from the Mass ... Christ comes directly and gladly from the altar to their hearts, and they can be shown how the family table, with its source in sacrifice and love, is related to the Holy Table and the Sacred Banquet itself.[209]

This bodily encounter focused particularly on the Eucharist and the link between married love and Christ's sacrificial love, was also described in striking terms in a 1963 Catholic Marriage Advisory Council pamphlet:

You bring yourself to the altar with the priest; you become one with the oblation; you place your married life on the paten and in the chalice, consciously offering up your life to God in, with and through Christ … [and] you leave the Church saturated, impregnated with the reality of God's presence.[210]

As is evident in these commentaries, representative of a trend in Catholic writing on marriage and the mass from the late 1950s onwards, it is possible to see a re-conceptualised understanding of the 'real presence'. Within it, Christ remains *real-ly* present at the altar, but in a dynamic and active fashion rather than as an object of visual adoration. For example, whilst articulating contemporary concerns about divorce and contraception, but modulated through a newer register of the psychological health of the married relationship, Fr Alban Byron SJ wrote about 'Christ present and at work in the marriage as He is present and at work in the tabernacle'.[211] Drawing directly upon Pope Pius XII's theology of the Mystical Body, and the visceral, sensual imagery of devotion to the Sacred Heart and blood of Christ, he concluded of marriage:

> This is no isolated, paltry, personal adventure for two human beings, but part of an eternal fruitful enterprise. The couples are taken into and carried forward by the whole Body of Christ. They are placed in the full blood stream of the divine energy that vitalises the Body of Christ, and He Himself is at work in their union and in their love.[212]

Over the next twenty years, in gradual developments explored in the next chapter, the Catholic Church integrated some of these insights and gradually adapted its stance towards marriage (and sexuality within it). The scope of the changes and the intertwining of marriage with a newer Christology were well represented in a prayer for 'Growth in Family Love' penned by Monsignor Michael Buckley and Catholic educationalist Tony Castle in 1984:

> Lord, a healthy sexual relationship is so important in marriage that we want to thank you for ours. The priest, who prepared us for marriage, told us that the sacraments are a sign of your loving presence. Please help us not to forget that the sign of our sacrament, the sexual expression of our love, makes you present in our home. Please continue to enrich our lives and our family with your loving presence.[213]

Yet not all Catholics agreed with this profoundly embodied, 'this-worldly' interpretation of the sacraments of the Eucharist and marriage. *Private Eye* contributor Auberon Waugh, son of the convert novelist and himself a conservative polemist, denounced this new prayer book and the Catholic Church's attempts to try to catch up, 'wheezily', with the 'sex-obsessed sixties'.[211] A satirical lewd cartoon accompanying his tirade parodied the longstanding analogy of home and altar with an extreme representation of married love as a church-sanctioned and communal, public sacrament through depiction of a naked older couple making love on the altar surrounded by a priest, female religious and shocked laity.

Moreover, some Catholics were pained, for quite different reasons, by this increasingly strong emphasis on the Eucharist as the chief means of sustaining and deepening a relationship with Christ. For in valorising an ideal of Catholic marriage as mirroring the relationship between Christ and the Church, relationships non-conformant with this standard were implicitly denigrated. The bar on divorced and remarried Catholics receiving communion, the numbers of whom had grown in line with broader societal statistics, was highlighted in the reports of the Archdiocese of Birmingham and the Diocese of Salford for the National Pastoral Congress of 1980. The participating lay representatives in Birmingham flagged this issue as 'the most important aspect of the Church's teaching requiring modification', to acknowledge Christ's forgiveness and 'the possibility of Christ being reborn in someone's life through a new and loving relationship'.[215]

Reflecting on his experience in a Catholic school dealing with families in all their varieties (divorced, remarried and re-partnered, with children from previous marriages), Peter confirmed the importance of pastoral flexibility around this issue, drawing upon the model of a compassionate, human Jesus:

> PK: Well if you turn around and say 'Well, you're living over the brush, you can't have it (i.e. the sacraments), end of'; you've got a wall of hostility building up against the church. And I don't believe Jesus would have turned around and said 'Well, you're living over the brush, you can't do it'. You've got to think of Mary Magdalene. And what the reaction would have been to them.[216]

The implications of this re-orientated emphasis on the incarnation of Christ in relationships with others and the celebration of this encounter through the Eucharist also created tension in the area of 'mixed marriages', or marriages between a Catholic and a person of another faith (or none). Numbers of these were growing exponentially from the 1960s, as a consequence of greater social mobility. In the softening of denominational strictures and more frequent liturgical encounters encouraged by the ecumenical movement, the restriction of communion to the Catholic partner in a Christian marriage was a source of strong feeling and, over the decades, increasing lay disobedience. Examining these issues in a 1980 column on pressing contemporary concerns, the *Catholic Herald* serialised the struggles of a fictitious inter-faith family, the Bowmans. Illustrating the pain of separation at the communion table, as well as the newer stance of the church towards the public questioning of papal authority, daughter Susan challenged her mother on the issue of intercommunion:

> [W]e've grown to see that non-Catholics are lovely people who can put us to shame, and then when they want to come to Holy Communion with us, to say NO. … If they believe in His Real Presence, He will be changing their hearts and minds when he comes to them, and bringing them to unity … not just giving Himself as a reward for their having at long last got round to believing in things like infallibility.
>
> … Susan looked hard at me, 'Mum, it would make a lot of difference to you, wouldn't it, if Dad could join us when we go to Holy Communion?'
>
> 'Yes' I said simply. 'And to me,' said Susan. 'And I don't see why he shouldn't.'
>
> I'm not clear. There's the authority of the Church, but there's also Cardinal Newman's notion that Catholic truth is in the hearts and minds of the faithful. Well?[217]

This is a telling intergenerational exchange between a parent whose Catholic faith and religious practice had weathered but also adapted, and the questioning challenges of an adolescent searching for a thoughtful, integrated spirituality. In its discussion of ecumenism, intermarriage and intercommunion, papal authority and the conscience of the laity, backed by reference to Newman as an English Catholic proof text of orthodoxy, it illustrated many of the tensions in post-conciliar English Catholicism and the more existential questions of how a 'modern' Christian should nourish and sustain his or her relationship with Christ.

The implications of this subtle but decisive shift prioritising a greater appreciation of Christian identity not only challenged understandings of the nature of the 'domestic' church but also raised telling questions for the priesthood. Whilst bearing in mind that the 'lay apostolate' has a long history within the church, and that a growing appreciation of the people's share in the priesthood of Christ underpinned some 'Catholic Action' movements from the beginning of the twentieth century,[218] the Second Vatican Council overwhelmingly stressed, through *Lumen Gentium*, the essential part played by the laity in the life of the church and the various forms of priesthood (encompassing ordained ministry and a vocation to a holy lay life).[219] These theological tenets were 'translated' for Catholic teenagers in 1964 by Canon Drinkwater:

> In the priest, the people should see Christ the High Priest of humanity; in the people, the pastor should see Christ the Child, Christ the young Worker of Nazareth, Christ the Tempted, Christ the friendly Healer and Teacher, Christ the Sin-bearer, Christ the Sufferer, Christ the merciful Judge even of priests.[220]

This repackaging of 'new' and 'old' Christologies, whilst acknowledging Jesus as 'like us', was conjoined to a re-evaluated ecclesiology that expressly validated the contributions of the laity. The impact of changes to Eucharistic discipline and practice, such as the emphasis on the laity's part in the co-consecration of the elements and their eventual involvement in the distribution of Holy Communion led some, including the ever-critical correspondent D. G. Galvin, to disparage the work of '"progressive" and "Women's Lib" Catholics' leading to a diminution of reverence for the real presence in the host and, inevitably, for 'the priest himself'.[221] The Vatican was also fearful of this blurring of roles – an *Instruction* issued two years after the Council stressed the need for 'further explanation' of the ways in which ministerial priesthood 'differs from the common priesthood of the faithful in essence and not merely in degree'.[222] By 1980, Rome issued a strongly worded condemnation of this 'confusion of roles' and catalogued such 'falsification[s] of the Catholic Liturgy' which included 'indiscriminate shared recitation of the Eucharistic prayer, homilies by lay people, lay people distributing communion while the priest refrains ... abandonment of liturgical vestments, Eucharist celebrated outside church without need [and] lack of respect for the Blessed Sacrament'.[223] In Salford, Bishop Holland addressed these concerns in July 1980 through ruling that a 'Special Minister' cannot help himself/herself either from the altar or tabernacle as 'it must be clearly seen that the Holy Communion comes from the priest'.[224]

The 'Women's Lib' element, as it was disparagingly known in some circles, was another aspect of these emerging tensions. While there had always been strands of the Catholic tradition which acknowledged women's association with discipleship, particularly through Mary, who 'bore the Priest in her own womb as in a sanctuary',[225] in the post-conciliar (and second-wave feminist) context pressing questions were asked about women's status within, and contribution to, the work of the 'people of God'. In her emotionally sensitive reading of the gospels in 1946, Caryll Houselander presciently anticipated some of the later developments of feminist exegesis in drawing attention to the faith and love of a few devoted women, in the face of the apostles' doubt, which 'goes looking for Christ in the tomb, that believes in Him in all men, embalms him in sinners, trusts him as King, without trying to whittle down a single thorn in His Crown of Thorns'.[226] Moving from spiritual reflection to a plan for social activism, Ernest Graf OSB also wrote around the same time of the social apostolate of women who, through 'ardent love for Christ', strove to reproduce in their own lives the life of the Son of God on earth.[227]

In the years following the Council, stimulated by various social movements and growing feminist critique, this re-examination of the role of women in the church became more explicit and experimental. Addressing an audience of women disheartened by the inattention of their 'preoccupied breadwinner', Father Paul Brassell SJ held up to Catholic men and women in 1965 the perfect manhood of Christ: a 'man who is strong, but kind, heroic, but gentle, never abstracted, never self-centred, who knows the very secrets of her heart without her having to tell them'.[228] Reflecting something of the growing diversity of public and private roles filled by women and implicitly complicating the growing claims of Christianity's hostility to women, he contrasted pagan Rome with Christianity's foundations and opined:

> It was Christ who emancipated women. He came into this world with infinite pity and love for women. He owed His human nature, the instrument of our redemption, to a woman. He was always supremely kind, tender and loving in His treatment of women. ... That is why women, generous and brave, in His name and for His love, have taught little children, have nursed the sick, looked after cantankerous old men and women ... [and] flock to Christ in His tabernacle ... girls from their offices and factories, nurses from their hospitals, teachers from their classrooms, mothers and wives from their homes.[229]

Feminist analysis within and outside the church became more pronounced through the late 1960s,[230] with a 1966 survey of the World Union of

Catholic Women's Organisations presented to the Vatican as a 'cry of anguish'. It concluded:

> In essence Catholic women felt unable to play their full role in the Church. They were welcomed to repair vestments and help raise money, but little else. … women had been considered 'a low form of fringe life' until the Second Vatican Council.[231]

These sentiments reached a peak two years later in the controversy surrounding Pope Paul VI's ruling against artificial contraception, *Humanae Vitae*, when a number of women (and men) left the church, some never to return, in opposition to Rome's re-affirmed stance on birth control. Nevertheless things were also changing within the Church, as John Ryan (1921–2009), *Catholic Herald* cartoonist for forty years (and creator of the character 'Captain Pugwash'), humorously reflected, with a northern inflection (Figure 3.3).

Women's involvement in the liturgy as lay readers and the authors of bidding prayers, as well as within international lay forums (and as forthright female religious interrogating their vocations in line with the Conciliar Decree *Perfectae Caritatis* (1965)),[232] made women's ministry in the church more visible. So did their enhanced roles, a decade later, as Eucharistic ministers and altar girls in some progressive churches – though not for Mary, much to her disappointment.[233] Moreover, these debates were not just confined to Catholic circles. The Chair of the Laity Commission and Vice-President of the National Board of Catholic Women, Eleanor Barnes, generated considerable newspaper correspondence and comment when she speculated in a televised BBC debate about the Virgin Mary's place in the church, on women's vocation through baptism, and on Jesus' potential incarnation as a woman.[234] As a supportive correspondent, Mary Green from Sheffield, wrote in the wake of the telecast:

> If we agree with [those who argue] that only a male priest can represent or 'become' a male Redeemer, we must acknowledge the logical extension of [this] argument: it is impossible for a male Redeemer to represent a woman, and are women therefore unredeemed?[235]

The initiation of the campaign for the ordination of women within the Catholic Church, echoing developments within the Church of England, was the outcome of these pressures, leading to a definitive and dismissive statement by Pope Paul VI in 1976 on the question of women's admission

Gatherings at the family table 113

3.3 'Make Room Luv!', from *The John Ryan Ecclesiastical Fun Book* (Great Wakering: Mayhew-McCrimmon, 1973), n.p. [Reproduced with permission from the *Catholic Herald*, London, the estate of John Ryan (with thanks to Isabel Ryan) and The Bodleian Libraries, The University of Oxford, shelf mark 2706 e.547]

to the ministerial priesthood.[236] However, the issue had gained momentum not just from developments within wider British society and other Christian denominations, but also from the discussed re-conceptualisation of the Eucharist – moving from its understanding as a sacrifice of the High Priest on Calvary to the communal action of the people of God gathered to represent the sacred meal in the upper room. This explicit point was made by *Tablet* correspondent E. D. Turbin, writing in the month preceding the BBC broadcast:

> If the Eucharist is not 'sacred drama' but the worshipping Christian community in which there is neither male nor female, knowing and sharing Christ in the breaking of bread … it is difficult to see why a woman president should be an 'inappropriate sign'. There is no problem here if one believes that through baptism all share Christ's priesthood, which gives women equal title to preside with men.[237]

The question of married male clergy was an adjunct to this debate, with the argument made that the marital status (like the gender) of the priest should be irrelevant to the work of presiding at the altar at which the priest should be a 'sign' of Christ, emulating him in the love of Father and neighbour rather than through literal imitation (e.g. Jewishness, ethnicity, singleness etc.). In the wake of the resignation of many priests to marry, and the re-evaluation and reform of the charism of all religious orders at the direction of the Council,[238] these sacramental and ecclesiological changes were to send profound shock waves through the Catholic Church from the late 1960s and through the 1970s.

Writing in 1964 for English adolescents, and echoing his 1957 publication that opened this chapter, the prolific Canon Drinkwater prefaced his discussion of the Eucharist under the title 'the sacrament of comrades':

> This love of comrades – lifted up to supernatural level – is the main idea of Holy Communion: a unity of hearts, stronger than all differences of class or colour or education: genuine 'community' … Everything done in the Upper Room that night speaks of Comradeship: the washing of the disciples' feet, the promise of the Paraclete (which *means* 'comrade'), the prayer for the disciples. …
>
> People talk of the brotherhood of Man and it is a grand thing to work for – to rise above all class and colour prejudice, etc. – but remember that if men are all brothers it must mean they have one Father. Communion teaches that, and more than teaches: it gives men grace to live up to it.[239]

In this rather extraordinary devotional reflection, peppered with Christian socialist concepts and terminology, it is possible to discern a little-acknowledged strain of English Catholic social thought which was sympathetic to left-wing political concerns and seeking a rapprochement with the world. This eschatologically orientated impulse in post-war theology and social practice was reinforced by the Second Vatican Council,[240] through documents like *Lumen Gentium* which reappraised the Catholic Church's relationship with the modern world and the Christian's vocation to aid Christ in redeeming it.[241] The early twentieth-century French-initiated Jocist Movement, known as the YCW in Britain, was one of the chief pre-conciliar means for promoting a philosophy that integrated Christian life and progressive Catholic liturgy, through recognition that 'Christ was Himself a *Worker*' and therefore provided a model for 'prayer on the night-shift!'[242] YCW members, utilising the Jocist mantra of 'See, Judge, Act', were exhorted to take Christ with them into their workplaces and the layman William Rafferty wrote in 1957 about this mission linking docks and offices to the 'Altar and Table of God' as 'our spiritual Home and Power House where as God's Holy People [we] are united together with Christ our "Elder Brother"'.[243] Socialised within this movement, Kevin spoke of the Eucharist now with a broad social outreach:

> KF: I almost think that the Eucharist needs to happen at the school gate. Because that's where they are ... And having a liturgy, an appropriate liturgy in public – I've often wanted to do it in the middle of a factory. You know, this vision of the workbench being your altar. How many people see that? How many people do we really give that vision that their sink at home is their altar? That what the young mother does with her child, even if they're a single parent, that that care of that [child] is her altar? That very floor, that play mat where their child is, is their altar?[244]

This newer, social-justice orientated and eschatological spirituality rather than a 'devout pietism' was particularly necessary in the opinion of one of the Movement's chaplains in the 1950s to arm workers against the allure of Marxism and to counter the 'lurk[ing] ... unconscious Manichaeism' in the minds of many Catholics.[245] He therefore urged Christians to 'feel at ease in the world of nature, like a child in his father's home', and promoted the YCW as the means to recognise:

> God made the world for man, and man for Christ. ... It is not 'profane' as opposed to 'sacred': it is 'Christianisable' and our task is to make it Christian.[246]

More than a decade later, in tune with other 1960s social movements, such sentiments would decisively move into the mainstream of Catholic social teaching. The Council fathers placed before their people the model of 'Christ who worked as a carpenter and is always working with the Father for the salvation of all', explicitly pronouncing the 'apostolic holiness' of 'those who engage in work ... [and] through their labours perfect themselves, help their fellow citizens, and raise up all of society and creation itself to a better state'.[247] As signalled by this Constitution, which was developed (and sometimes also contradicted) by the papal encyclicals that followed, the emphasis had clearly shifted towards the recognition of the mission of the church as understood in terms of a 'realised eschatology' and the bringing into being, by Christians, of the kingdom that Christ inaugurated.[248]

From these often overlooked roots germinated the radical liberation theology movement that attained prominence following the 1968 Medellín Conference in Colombia of the Latin American Episcopal Council (CELAM). In its articulation of a 'preferential option for the poor' it shared much common ground with the idealism and activism of the protest movements of the 1960s and the growing influence of a general humanism concerned with the recognition and codification of human rights.[249] Catholics seeking to respond to this greater social awareness of poverty and hunger, warfare and racism, could draw upon the tradition of Christ the liberator, the poor Nazarene worker crucified by an unjust and oppressive authoritarian government but resistant and eventually triumphant.

The Catholic communist lawyer Peter Benenson called upon just such a model in his establishment of Amnesty International in England in 1961, as did Barbara Ward in the metamorphosis of the 'Sword of the Spirit' movement she co-founded into the Catholic Institute for International Relations.[250] These concerns also led Simon Blake OP, television presenter and prominent Campaign for Nuclear Disarmament (CND) activist, to make a call in 1970 for an 'unambiguous and clear condemnation of the killing of the innocent' in Vietnam:

> [H]as the Sermon on the Mount really no relevance to what is going on in our world? Is it intolerable and outrageous that I should work actively and therefore also politically for peace on earth?[251]

This Dominican's anti-establishment insights were tied by others back to the liturgy and the radical imagery of the Eucharist as an eschatological banquet which made 'demand[s] for the just distribution of the world's wealth', so that 'the desert has become a land of delights; a waste in which fifteen per cent of the people profit from seventy per cent of the available goods has become an Eden in which everyone has his fill'.[252] Strands within the countercultural movement also drew upon the currency of this radical Christology, such as the Christians participating in CND,[253] social activist movements[254] and anti-Vietnam protests, like that voiced by D. Hart writing in 1968 within the British underground newspaper *International Times*.[255] In an unexpectedly similar vein, in his 1966 Lenten Pastoral, the far from radical Bishop of Salford tied the proposals for a relaxation of the fasting laws on Fridays to solidarity with the poor through a common penance and sharing of the marks of Christ's crucified body, asking 'can we accept relaxation for ourselves and ignore the appeal of people condemned to perpetual fasting?'[256] The National Board of Catholic Women asked a similar question four years earlier through their Family Fast Day, thus inaugurating the Catholic Fund for Overseas Development (now CAFOD) in 1962.[257] This connection between the altar and the world was also, in the opinion of some Catholics, to be made tangible through the newly introduced bidding prayers. Responding in 1975 to a complaint in a *Tablet* opinion column about the 'anthropomorphic quality' of the prayers in some parishes, a letter from Peter Lane in Sussex rejected such criticism:

> The God whom we worship became a man in dirt and degradation. Any suggestion that the day-to-day affairs of men as shown in the bidding prayers have no place in the liturgy goes against the spirituality of the Offertory where we give 'the work of human hands' for Him to transform into His body.[258]

This continued a similar conversation a year earlier when Donald Nicholl generated a flurry of correspondence in contrasting:

> two men, one of whom accepts the same formation of belief as I do about the Body of Christ present at the altar. But this same man does not recognise the Body of Christ in the suffering of blacks in South Africa or the oppressed peasants of Brazil or the derelicts in London … [and] a second man who is very hazy about the manner of Christ's presence at the altar, but who recognises the Body of Christ in the suffering and oppressed by serving them all the days of his life … Which of those men believes in the real presence of Christ? Which of them recognises the Body of Christ?[259]

As Michael Williams, a Lecturer in Theology in Leeds, approvingly surmised from such correspondence and developments in contemporary, contextual theology, 'in recent years the regular mass-goer has been made only too aware that his Sunday-morning journey is not a retreat into a cosy private world. The changes in the liturgy do not allow him to forget the changes in society and in the Church'.[260]

In this chapter I have discussed the various ways in which English Catholics across the mid- to late-twentieth century understood their relationship with Christ as brother and have charted the shifting conceptions and constructions they utilised to imagine and embody this relationship – from Christ-child, suffering Saviour and Sacred Heart moving towards tropes emphasising Christ as a 'humanitarian', bridegroom and comrade. I have also explored many of the liturgical changes across the century, often associated with the Second Vatican Council but in reality beginning much earlier in the century through the reforming impulses of the liturgical movement which gradually worked their way into English Catholic theology and the lived religious practices of the laity. While acknowledging the impact of these changes to liturgical rote and rite on the habitual and embodied practices of English Catholics, I have urged attention to a little appreciated and more profound transformation during the period, namely the movement from an understanding of the Eucharist in predominantly sacrificial terms towards its appreciation as a sacred banquet and communal meal. It is this 're-orientation' of the altar which repositioned Catholic spirituality as the century progressed and required Catholics to re-conceptualise the ways in which they related to their brother Jesus, their fellow communicants, and the family gathered beyond their immediate, parochial meal table.

Despite the clearly marked signs of change this chapter has charted, both in the form of liturgy nourishing the spirituality of Catholics and the ways in which this was integrated and expressed, it also illustrates an overarching continuity in the substantive nature of the relationship between the Catholic believer and Christ which remained centred upon the mass and Holy Communion. A constant theme in Christology across the twentieth century was an emphasis upon an intensely incarnational, fleshy, presently-engaged and personally-accessible Saviour who, as Christ of the Sacred Heart or 'Chief Patron of CAFOD', was felt to empathise with the suffering and trials of the world and to be intimately active and involved in its redemption. As the *Times* religious correspondent (and *Tablet* contributor) Clifford Longley observed in 1979, in terms which resonated with those of fifty years earlier but were nonetheless reflective of very modern concerns:

> [T]urn Jesus into God, the great Christian temptation down the ages, and we can happily get on with the business in hand of spoiling the environment, selling arms to each other, torturing each other, and bombing each other into annihilation. Accept Jesus as our brother, and we are redeemed: we stand a chance, after all.[261]

Gatherings at the family table

The issues and concerns brought to these gatherings at the family table may have varied across the century, as did the language and rubrics in which the proceedings were conducted, but at a fundamental level English Catholics *before* and *after* the Council continued to view the Eucharist as a place of encounter with Christ, their Saviour and a model for right-living in the world. While a sacrificial, suffering and 'seen' Saviour had been the Eucharistic metaphor which Catholics employed, later in the twentieth century the Christ encountered at the Last Supper (and at Cana) invited Christians to break and share bread at a communal meal in imagery which resonated with a society craving community, solidarity and a proactive identity. As an example illustrating these elements of continuity and change, Pope John Paul II employed a fraternal metaphor when inviting the young people of England and Wales gathered in Ninian Park, Cardiff, in 1982 to reflect on the Eucharist:

> In prayer, united with Jesus – your brother, your friend, your Saviour, your God …
>
> Jesus becomes the model for our actions, for our lives … [and] through prayer you will have a part in salvation history as it unfolds in your generation.[262]

Whilst this part in salvation history should be realised in the first (and final) instance through reference to their Saviour (in unity with the Triune God), Catholics were also offered other, associated members of the 'household of faith', particularly the Virgin Mary, as a helpful mediator and model in their mission to a current generation. The next chapter explores the role of Mary in the familial and devotional lives of Catholics across the second half of the twentieth century.

Notes

1. Sheed, *Same*, 89.
2. Cordeiro, 'Liturgical', 188.
3. Common devotional saying – e.g. Fr Augustine O.F.M., *Ireland's Loyalty to the Mass* (London: Sands and Co., 1933), 208–9.
4. K. Aspden, 'Drinkwater, Francis Harold (1886–1982)' – www.oxforddnb.com/view/article/65569?docPos=2.
5. F. H. Drinkwater, *Going to Mass: the Eucharistic Drama and How to Take Part in It* (London: Catholic Truth Society, 1957), 4.
6. *Ibid*, 18.

7   Ibid.
8   S. Gilley, 'Knox, Ronald Arbuthnott (1888–1957)' www.oxforddnb.com/view/article/34358?docPos=1.
9   R. Knox, *The Creed in Slow Motion* (London: Sheed and Ward, 1949), 200.
10 R. Knox, 'The Mass in Slow Motion: VIII: Lavabo to Preface', *The Tablet*, 8 March 1947, 126 and *The Mass in Slow Motion* (London: Sheed and Ward, 1948).
11 W. Godfrey, *The Consecration of the World to the Immaculate Heart of Mary* (London: Catholic Truth Society, 1945), 3, 14–15.
12 Ibid.
13 M. Tindall, *The Beloved Son: A Child's Meditation on the Childhood of Christ* (London: Catholic Truth Society, 1955), 3.
14 'Q. Why is Jesus Christ truly man? A. Jesus Christ is truly man because He has the nature of man, having a body and soul like ours', *The Explanatory Catechism of Christian Doctrine* (London: Catholic Truth Society, 1921), 5.
15 F. H. Drinkwater, *Catechism Stories: A Teacher's Aid-book in Five Parts to Accompany the Abbreviated Catechism* (London: Burns and Oates, 1948), 34.
16 D. L. Greenstock, *Christopher's Talks to Catholic Parents* (London: Burns and Oates, 1951), 40.
17 Ibid, 42.
18 M. S. MacMahon, *Nazareth: A Book of Counsel and Prayer for the Married* (Dublin: Eason and Son, 1948), 214–15.
19 B. Jarrett, *The Catholic Mother* (London: Catholic Truth Society, 1943), 16.
20 Marguerite, 'WANTED – More *better* Catholics!', *Catholic Fireside*, 3 October, 1952, 223.
21 S. B. James, 'The Liturgy, Week by Week: Feast of the Holy Family', *Catholic Herald*, 5 January 1945, 4.
22 See Monsignor R. Knox, Obituary, *The Tablet*, 23 October 1954, 408; A. Harris, 'Houselander, Frances Caryll (1901–54)' www.oxforddnb.com/view/article/71620?&docPos=57.
23 C. Houselander, *The Passion of the Infant Christ* (London: Sheed and Ward, 1949), 22.
24 C. Houselander, 'Birth', reprinted in *A Rocking-Horse Catholic* (London: Sheed and Ward, 1960), 148.
25 Canon E. Masure, 'Mass: Sacramental Immolation', *Downside Review*, 65(201) (1947), 207 and MacMahon, *Nazareth*, 30–31.
26 G. Hurrell, *Talks on Mass and First Holy Communion* (London: Catholic Truth Society, 1946), 27.
27 Interview, Bernard, Recording STE 019 at 20.39–20.43.
28 Greenstock, *Talks*, 120.
29 G. Dyer, 'In the Octave of Corpus Christi', *The Tablet*, 10 June 1950, 459.
30 See P. M. Kane, '"She Offered Herself Up": The Victim Soul and Victim Spirituality in Catholicism', *Church History* 71(1) (2002), 116.
31 F. C. Houselander, *This War is the Passion* (London: Sheed and Ward, 1943), 1.
32 Ibid, 46–54.
33 J. Murphy, 'Omnipotentia Supplex: In Memory of a Gosport Night of Blitz', *The Tablet*, 5 November 1949, 295.

Gatherings at the family table 121

34 Bishop H. V. Marshall, 'Lent Pastoral 1955', 22 February 1955, 2. (Salford Diocesan Archive (hereafter SDA) Box 226).
35 *Ibid.*
36 Houselander, *War*, 57.
37 P. Winckworth, *The Way of War: a Meditation on the Stations of the Cross in Wartime* (London: Dacre Press, c.1944), n.p.
38 *Ibid*, final page.
39 Houselander, *Passion*, 110–11.
40 *Ibid*, 112.
41 D. Morgan, *The Sacred Heart of Jesus: The Visual Evolution of a Devotion* (Amsterdam: Amsterdam University Press, 2008).
42 For a history of the devotion in Britain, beginning in 1676 in Liverpool, see Morris and Gooch, *Down Your Aisles*, 14.
43 *Haurietis Aquas*, www.vatican.va/holy_father/pius_xii/encyclicals/documents/hf_p-xii_enc_15051956_haurietis-aquas_en.html, sections 107 and 109.
44 E.g. Anon, *The Sacred Heart and the Twentieth Century* (Birmingham, 1949).
45 *Haurietis Aquas*, s. 12.
46 See S. J. Boss, 'The Immaculate Heart of Mary: Visions for the World' in R. N. Swanson (ed.), *The Church and Mary: Studies in Church History* 39 (2004), 319–48.
47 P. Gay, 'The Manliness of Christ' in R. W. Davis and R. J. Helmstadter (eds.), *Religion and Irreligion in Victorian Society* (1992), 105.
48 See D. Morgan, *Visual Piety: A History and Theory of Popular Religious Images* (Berkeley: University of California Press, 1998), 97–124.
49 Medical Woman, A Girl, A Wife, '*Into their Company': A Book for a Modern Girl on Love and Marriage* (London: Burns, Oates and Washbourne, 1930), 77.
50 Interview, John, Recording STE 021 at 50.09–50.17.
51 In a Belgian context see T. Van Osselaer, '"From that Moment on, I was a Man!": Images of the Catholic Male in the Sacred Heart Devotion' in P. Pasture and J. Art (eds), *Gender and Christianity in Modern Europe: Beyond the Feminization Thesis* (Leuven: Leuven University Press, 2012), 121–36.
52 See 'Pastoral Letter' and *Ad Ven Clerum*, 25 November 1943, 8 (SDA 215 Marshall Papers).
53 Bishop Marshall, 'Written Note: Family Rosary Crusade', 1948/1951, 3 (SDA Box 211).
54 Interview, John at 50.22–50.30.
55 Houselander, *Rocking*, 32.
56 Interview, Mitzi, Recording STE 015 at 13.48–13.57.
57 Houselander, *Passion*, 19.
58 Hierarchy of England and Wales, 'Joint Pastoral Letter on the Sacred Heart', 6 (SDA Box 200, 200/235).
59 *Ibid.*
60 Houselander, *Passion*, 12.
61 G. Burns, 'The Sacred Heart and the Twentieth Century', *Clergy Review* 34 (1950), 23.
62 *Ibid*, 22.

63 On the emergence of the 'Divine Mercy', an alternative Christological devotion with a strong resemblance to the Sacred Heart, see Conclusion.
64 E.g. J. J. Coyne, 'Sacrifice and Sacrament', *Clergy Review* 38(1) (1953), 9.
65 F. H. Drinkwater, *Our Living Sacrifice: An Action Picture of the Holy Mass* (Dudley: Wellington Press, 1948), 11.
66 Archbishop of Liverpool, 'Devotion to the Sacred Heart: Think well on what it means', *The Catholic Gazette* 50(6) (1958), 127.
67 J. Chinnici, 'The Catholic Community at Prayer, 1926–1976' in O'Toole, *Habits*, 66.
68 T. Van Osselaer and A. Maurits, 'Heroic men and Christian ideals' in Y. M. Werner (ed.), *Christian Masculinity – Men and Religion in Northern Europe in the 19th and 20th Centuries* (Leuven: Leuven University Press, 2011), 63–94.
69 T. Corbishley, 'Cyril Charlie Martindale (1879–1963)' – www.oxforddnb.com/view/article/34911.
70 C. C. Martindale, *What is He doing at the Altar?* (London: Catholic Truth Society, 1931), 23.
71 C. C. Martindale, *The Mind of the Missal* (London: Sheed and Ward, 1929), 275 (fn).
72 H. McEvoy, *A New and Easy Way at Mass* (London: Catholic Truth Society, 1949), 1.
73 *Ibid*, 1–3.
74 Houselander, *Passion*, 123.
75 See G. Brown, 'Mass Performances: A Study of Eucharistic Ritual in Australian Catholic Culture 1900–1962' (PhD thesis, Department of History, University of Melbourne, 2003), 14.
76 *Mediator Dei* (1947), s. 131 – www.vatican.va/holy_father/pius_xii/encyclicals/documents/hf_p-xii_enc_20111947_mediator-dei_en.html.
77 Collected and reprinted in E. J. Mahoney, *Questions and Answers: The Sacraments* (London: Burns, Oates and Washbourne, 1946), 159.
78 Hurrell, *Talks*, 15.
79 I. Trethowan, *Christ in the Liturgy* (London: Sheed and Ward, 1952), 38.
80 E.g. F. M. Cabrol, *My Missal* (London: 1920); Stedman, *The Small Missal* (London: Catholic Truth Society, 1936) and *My Sunday Missal* (London: Burns and Oates, 1938).
81 J. D. Crichton, '1920–1940: The Dawn of the Liturgical Movement' in Crichton, *English*, 22 and Brown, 'Mass', 123.
82 Interview, Kathleen, Recording STE 011 at 6.39–7.06.
83 Bishop Marshall, 'Clergy Deanery Conference; *De Sacrificio Missae*', January 1944, Ad Clerum and Other Papers, 200/153 (SDA Box 200 Marshall Papers 1941–48).
84 G. MacGillivray, *An Introduction to the Mass* (London: Catholic Truth Society, 1950), 14–15.
85 Interview, Richard, Recording STE 010 at 5.22–6.21.
86 C. C. Martindale, 'Making Better Use of the Liturgy: Riches We are All Missing', *Catholic Herald*, 3 March 1945, 3.
87 C. R. A. Cuncliffe (ed.), *English in the Liturgy: A Symposium* (London: Burns and Oates, 1956).
88 'The Blessed Mutter of the Mass', *The Tablet*, throughout August 1953.
89 W. E. W. Crealock, 'The Liturgy and the People', *The Tablet*, 17 April 1953, 381.

90 T. Holland, 'Review: "The Work of Our Redemption"', *Catholic Gazette* 45(4) (1954), 89.
91 Bishop Marshall, 'Clergy Deanery Conference' (SDA Box 200 Marshall Papers 1941–48).
92 P. J. A. Nissen, 'Mobilizing the Catholic Masses through the Eucharist: The Practice of Communion from the Mid-19th Century to the Second Vatican Council' in C. Caspers, G. Lukken and G. Rouwhorst (eds), *Bread of Heaven: Customs and Practices Surrounding Holy Communion: Essays in the History of Liturgy and* Culture (Kampen: Kok Pharos, 1995), 145–64.
93 Interview, Peter, Recording STE 003, transcript page 3.
94 There was an expectation that Catholics should not receive communion when in a state of 'mortal sin', but 'scruples' about the distinctions between 'venial sins' and 'mortal sins' in practice meant that most of the laity would not communicate without preceding absolution. The connections between the Eucharist and Penance raise fascinating issues which merit substantial research in an English context, but which require separate and detailed treatment elsewhere.
95 An estimated 29% of the congregation received weekly in the US in 1963 – see O'Toole (ed.), *Habits*, 221.
96 Figures collated from mass returns suggest that the average Australian Catholic received around seven times a year in 1900, and that this had risen to a norm of 32 times per year in the 1950s (Brown, 'Mass', 107, 110).
97 E. Essex, 'Holy Communion and the Mass', *The Tablet*, 14 November 1953, 478–79.
98 *Mystici Corporis Christi* (1943), www.vatican.va/holy_father/pius_xii/encyclicals/documents/hf_p-xii_enc_29061943_mystici-corporis-christi_en.html, s. 4.
99 'The Real Presence of Christ in the Eucharist', *Catholic Encyclopedia* www.newadvent.org/cathen/05573a.htm.
100 *Mediator Dei* (1947), www.vatican.va/holy_father/pius_xii/encyclicals/documents/hf_p-xii_enc_20111947_mediator-dei_en.html, s. 68.
101 *Mediator Dei*, s. 70.
102 MacGillivray, *Introduction*, 9.
103 Interview, Kathleen at 29.46–30.11.
104 *Ibid*, at 32.17–32.46.
105 Interview, Tony, Recording STE 006 at 11.40–11.48.
106 Interview, Francis, Recording STE 016 at 7.11, 7.50–8.29.
107 *Ibid*, at 7.11–7.40.
108 H. Thurston, 'Benediction of the Blessed Sacrament', *The Catholic Encyclopedia* (New York, 1907), www.newadvent.org/cathen/02465b.htm; M. Rubin, *Corpus Christi: the Eucharist in Late Medieval Culture* (Cambridge: Cambridge University Press, 1991).
109 *Mediator Dei*, s. 32 and ss. 131–3 on benediction.
110 For background, see A. Taves, 'Context and Meaning: Roman Catholic Devotion to the Blessed Sacrament in Mid-Nineteenth-Century America', *Church History* 54(4) (1985), 482–95.
111 On the importance (and recollection) of the Latin hymns, see Interview, Kathleen at 2.30–2.37.

112 B. Huebsch, 'The Church on the Eve of Vatican II' in W. Madges and M. J. Daley (eds), *Vatican II: Forty Personal Stories* (Mystic, CT: Twenty-Third Publications, 2003), 47.
113 Interview, Tom, Recording STE 005 at 17.07–17.54.
114 The Taizé community is an ecumenical monastic order founded by Roger Louis Schutz-Marsauche drawing monks and pilgrims from across the world. Its extra-liturgical services centre on chanting and meditation.
115 Interview, Tony at 17.00–17.27.
116 Interview, Richard at 22.17–22.32.
117 Interview, Mary, Recording STE 007 at 32.45–33.03.
118 *Mediator Dei*, s. 133.
119 *Mystici Corporis Christi*, s. 19.
120 *Ibid*, s. 55.
121 *Ibid*, s. 81.
122 *Ibid*, s. 83.
123 *Christus Dominus*, s. 10 – www.papalencyclicals.net/Pius12/P12CHDOM.HTM.
124 J. C. Heenan, *Our Faith* (London: Thomas Nelson & Sons, 1956), 174.
125 C. Howell, 'The Liturgical Approach' in Cunliffe, *English*, 62.
126 *Ibid*, 63.
127 M. de la Bédoyère, *Living Christianity* (London: Burns and Oates, 1954), 118.
128 E. Masure, 'The Mass: The Sacred Immolation', *Downside Review* 65(201) (1947), 195–210; S. Moore, 'Towards a Eucharistic Definition of Sacrifice', *Downside Review* 69(218) (1951), 428–40 and H. F. Davis, 'The Mass as an Offering', *Downside Review* 70 (220) (1952), 119–34.
129 G. Hurrell, *The Saints and Us* (London: Sheed and Ward, 1948), 77.
130 Knox, *Creed*, 205.
131 J. Coventry, *The Breaking of Bread* (London: Sheed and Ward, 1950), 5.
132 C. Davis, 'The Real Presence', *Catholic Gazette* 50(11) (1958), 246.
133 C. Davis, 'What is the Eucharist?' *The Catholic Gazette* 50(1) (1958), 221.
134 N. K. Watson, 'Davis, Charles Alfred (1923–1999)' – www.oxforddnb.com/view/article/71960?docPos=3.
135 Tanner, *Decrees*, SC, s. 47, 830.
136 *Eucharisticum Mysterium*, s. 3 – www.adoremus.org/eucharisticummysterium.html.
137 *Ibid*, s. 10.
138 Latourelle, *Vatican II*, 351; D. Ryan, *The Catholic Parish: Institutional Discipline, Tribal Identity and Religious Development in the English Church* (London, 1996), 39.
139 F. H. Drinkwater, *Talking to Teenagers: Notes for Parents and Teachers* (London: Burns and Oates, 1964), 69–70.
140 M. Childs, 'The People's Mass', *The Catholic Gazette* 1(3) (1966–67), 8–9.
141 *Ibid*.
142 P. A. McGuinness, *A Gift from My Heavenly Father: First Communion Workbook* (London: Catholic Truth Society, 1981), 1.
143 Interview, Mary at 8.51–9.01.
144 *Ibid*, 9.08–10.29.
145 Interview, Peter at 11.52–12.39.

Gatherings at the family table

146 Interview, Patrick, Recording STE 015 at 26.55–27.00.
147 *Ibid*, 20.40–22.21.
148 R. J. Daly, 'Robert Bellarmine and Post-Tridentine Eucharistic Theology' in Bulman and Parrella, *From Trent to Vatican II*, 81. For a similar (but contemporaneous) assessment, from the Lecturer in Liturgical Studies at Heythrop College, see K. Donovan, 'The Changes in Mass – 2', *The Catholic Gazette* 61(3) (1970), 15–18.
149 P. Tihon, 'Theology of the Eucharistic Prayer' in L. Sheppard (ed.), *The New Liturgy* (London: Darton, Longman and Todd, 1970), 192–93; L. Sheppard, *Blueprint for Worship: An Interpretation of the Liturgical Constitution of Vatican II* (London: Darton, Longman and Todd, 1964), 53–69.
150 Interview, Kathleen at 17.15–17.38.
151 See A. Harris, '"The Prayer in the Syntax?": The Roman Missal, the Book of Common Prayer and Changes in Liturgical Language, 1945–80' in J. Garnett *et al.*, *Redefining Christian Britain: Post 1945 Perspectives* (London: SCM Press, 2007), 36–49.
152 D. Sheridan, Correspondence to Cardinal Heenan, 26th February 1969 (Archives of the Archbishop of Westminster (hereafter AAW) Heenan, HE1/L6(b) Litugy, Letters from Laity 1969–70).
153 *Ibid*.
154 A. Krynski, Correspondence to Cardinal Heenan, 3 February 1970 (AAW HE1/L6(b)).
155 *Ibid*.
156 See Harris, 'A Fresh Stripping of the Altars?'.
157 See M. Davies, *Cranmer's Godly Order: The Destruction of Catholicism through Liturgical Change* (Chumleigh: Augustine Publishing, 1976); *The Tridentine Mass* (1977); *The Roman Rite Destroyed* (1978); *Communion Under Both Kinds: An Ecumenical Surrender* (1980).
158 M. Bamford to Rev. E. Hill, OP, Letter, 8 February 1965 (Birmingham Archdiocese Archives (hereafter BAA) GPD/H/B2).
159 ARCIC, *Agreed Statement on Eucharistic Doctrine* (1971), s. 12 – www.anglicancommunion.org/ministry/ecumenical/dialogues/catholic/arcic/docs/eucharistic_doctrine1971.cfm.
160 *Ibid*, Note 2.
161 A. Allchin, *Eucharist and Unity: Thoughts on the ARCIC's Agreed Statement* (Oxford: SLG Press, 1972), 4.
162 D. A. Bellenger, 'Butler, Basil Edward (1902–1986)' – www.oxforddnb.com/view/article/39996.
163 B. C. Butler, *The Eucharist* (London: Catholic Truth Society, 1975), n.p.
164 A lay society dedicated to the preservation of the traditional Latin Mass (in its 1570 form) – see the letter from its Secretary, Mrs Iris Roper, 'The New Rite', *The Tablet*, 15 August 1970, 791 and C. Byrne, *A Guide to the Latin Mass Society: its Purpose and Functions* (London, 1997).
165 E.g. T. S. Gregory, 'The Language of the Mass', *The Tablet*, 15 February 1964, 191; 'The Languages of the Mass', *The Tablet*, 29 February 1964, 248.
166 T. S. Gregory, 'Pessimistic Ecumenism', *The Tablet*, 2 February 1974, 112.
167 Roger de Wever to Cardinal J. Heenan, Letter, 2 March 1970 (AAW HE1/L6(b)).

168 Letter from Cardinal Heenan to Evelyn Waugh, 28 August 1964, cited in J. Pearce, *Literary*, 49.
169 C. Hollis, 'Seven Ages', *The Tablet*, 2 March 1974, 196.
170 T. F. Burns, 'Hollis, (Maurice) Christopher (1902–1977)' www.oxforddnb.com/view/article/31248.
171 C. Hollis, 'Seven Ages', *The Tablet*, 2 March 1974, 196.
172 J. Symon, 'Question and Answer', *Catholic Herald*, 10 May 1968, 4.
173 *Ibid*.
174 J. O'Connell, 'New Approaches to Confession', *The Tablet*, 4 April 1970, 324. See also O'Toole (ed.), *Habits*, 184 and T. Koopmanschap, 'Transformations in Contemporary Roman Catholicism: A Case Study' (PhD thesis, University of Liverpool, 1978), 211.
175 Interview, Judith, Recording STE 009 at 41.06–41.20.
176 Tanner, *Decrees*, SC, s. 55, 831. See also *Ritus Communionis sub utraque specie* (7 March 1965); 'Eucharisticum Mysterium' (25 May 1967) and *Institutio Generalis* (Roman Missal, 3 April 1969, setting 14 fixed cases for reception of wine).
177 H. E. Winstone, *Communion under Both Kinds: Its Significance* (London: Catholic Truth Society, 1979), 8.
178 A. B. Boylan, *The Reception of Holy Communion in the Hand* (London: Catholic Truth Society, 1976), n.p.
179 C. Howell, 'Have you ever thought why you want to KNEEL when the proper attitude for a Christian at prayer is to STAND?', *The Universe and Catholic Times*, 11 December 1964, 6.
180 M. A. Mortimer to Cardinal J. Heenan, Letter, 4 June 1970 (AAW HE1/L6(b)).
181 L. V. Hunt to Archbishop G. P. Dwyer, May 1965 (BAA, GPD/H/B2 Liturgy: General 1964–5).
182 Interview, Tony at 12.50–14.45. Note also that the older generation of oral history interviewees, such as Joseph, Margaret and Nora, still receive communion on the tongue.
183 Cardinal J. Heenan to Bishop G. P. Dwyer, 28 February 1970 (BAA GPD/H/B5 Liturgy: General 1970–1).
184 G. Summer to Cardinal J. Heenan, 15 October 1970 (AAW HE1/L6(b)).
185 D. G. Galvin, 'Reasons for Decline in Reverence', *Catholic Herald*, 1 March 1974, 5.
186 M. E. Hodgkinson, Correspondence, *Catholic Herald*, 8 March 1974, 5.
187 'C.N.S.', Correspondence, *Catholic Herald*, 22 March 1974, 5.
188 *Ibid*.
189 Tanner, *Decrees*, LG, s. 7, 852–53.
190 F. J. Buckley, *"I Confess": the Sacrament of Penance Today* (Notre Dame: Ave Maria Press, 1972), 55.
191 J. A. T. Robinson, *Honest to God* (London: SCM Press, 1963), 101; M. Chapman, 'Theology in the Public Arena: the Case of South Bank Religion' in Garnett *et al*, *Redefining*, 92–105.
192 Tanner, *Decrees*, SC, s. 13, 824.
193 P. P. McCarthy, 'First Sorrowful Mystery' in A. F. Bullen, *The Rosary in Close-Up* (London: Geoffrey Chapman, 1962), 79.

194 Tanner, *Decrees, Dei Verbum*, 971–81.
195 K. Stephenson, 'People and Places', *Catholic Herald*, 10 May 1968, 10.
196 M. Benedicta, 'Personal Faith in Christ', *The Catholic Gazette* 61(12) (1970), 10.
197 *Ibid*.
198 Interview, Kevin, Recording STE 000, transcript page 9.
199 Interview, Peter at 16.10–17.25.
200 Interview, Mary at 30.31, 31.47–31.55.
201 N. L. A. Lash, *What are we doing at Mass?* (London: Catholic Truth Society, 1968), 1.
202 *Ibid*.
203 See O'Toole, *Habits*, 200 and E. Duffy, 'Rewriting the Liturgy' in Caldecott, *Beyond*, 107.
204 Tanner, *Decrees*, SC, s. 11, 823.
205 M. Clive, *Christ in Us: Some Thoughts on the Mystical Body of Christ* (London: Catholic Truth Society, 1947), 13.
206 B. J. Kelly, *Lay Spirituality: Its Theory and Practice* (London: Sheed and Ward, 1980), 35.
207 For the guidance of John Paul II on this issue, see *Dominicae Cenae* (1980), s. 10; www.vatican.va/holy_father/john_paul_ii/letters/documents/hf_jp-ii_let_24021980_dominicae-cenae_en.html.
208 Tanner, *Decrees*, LG, s. 11, 857–58.
209 R. Russell, 'The Theology of the Lay Apostolate – II', *New Life* 13(6) (1957), 216.
210 CMAC, *Beginning Your Marriage* (London: Catholic Marriage Advisory Council, 1963), 111.
211 A. Byron, 'Christian Marriage: A Great Sacrament', *Catholic Gazette* 55(10) (1964), 280–1.
212 *Ibid*.
213 M. Buckley and T. Castle, *The Treasury of the Holy Spirit* (London: Hodder and Stoughton, 1984), 170.
214 *Private Eye*, 16 November 1984, 25.
215 R. Thorp, 'National Pastoral Congress – Marriage and the Family', 1980, 3 (BAA GPD/S/N1/I). See also *Diocese of Salford Report, National Pastoral Congress* (Manchester, 1979) (SDA Pamphlet collection, no. B66).
216 Interview, Peter at 26.57–27.15.
217 'The Bowmans – A Family and their Faith: God loves Methodists too, doesn't He?', *The Catholic Herald*, 28 March 1980, 7.
218 Pereiro, 'Laity'.
219 Crichton, *English*, 31 and Tanner, *Decrees*, LG, s. 10, 857.
220 Drinkwater, *Talking*, 77.
221 D. G. Galvin, 'Reasons for Declining in Reverence', *Catholic Gazette*, 1 March 1974, 5.
222 *Eucharisticum Mysterium* (1967) s. 11, www.adoremus.org/eucharisticummysterium.html.
223 *Inaestimabile Donum* (1980) s. 4, www.adoremus.org/InaestimabileDonum.html.
224 Bishop Holland, Ad Clerum 8/80', 24 July 1980 (SDA Box 219).
225 A. Hadshar, 'Meditations in Lent V: From Crib to Cross', *The Tablet*, 21 March 1953, 237.
226 C. Houselander, 'Love and Suffering: The Tomb', *The Tablet*, 6 April 1946, 178.

227 E. Graf, 'Women's Work in the Apostolic Era', *The Clergy Review* 34 (1950), 88.
228 P. Brassell, 'The Dignity of Womanhood', *Catholic Gazette* 56(12) (1965), 343.
229 *Ibid.*
230 E.g. E. K. Taylor, 'Question Box: Was St Paul a Misogynist?', *Catholic Gazette* 56(8) (1965), 227.
231 See P. Nolan, 'Founder-member of the lay jet-set', *Catholic Herald*, 21 June 1974, 3.
232 Tanner, *Decrees*, PC, s. 1, 939. There is yet to be a full scholarly exploration of the effect of Vatican II on female religious life in Britain – in an American context see A. Koelingher, *The New Nuns: Racial Justice and Religious Reform in the 1960s* (Cambridge (MA): Harvard University Press, 2007) and C. G. Rogers, *Habits of Change: An Oral History of American Nuns* (Oxford: Oxford University Press, 2011).
233 See *Inaestimabile Donum*, 1980 s. 18. Mary discussed 'always wanting to be an altar girl' and a compensatory 'ringing the bells at communion', but was pleased that her girls could now be on the altar – see Interview, Mary at 34.38, 35.20–35.31.
234 M. Vincent, 'Convert who met TV Challenge', *Catholic Gazette*, 19 April, 1974, 3.
235 M. Green, Correspondence, *Catholic Gazette*, 19 April, 1974, 5.
236 *Declaration Inter Insigniores* – www.papalencyclicals.net/Paul06/p6interi.htm.
237 E. D. Turbin, 'The Ordination of Women', *The Tablet*, 16 March 1974, 273.
238 See Tanner, *Decrees*, PC (1965), 939–47.
239 Drinkwater, *Talking*, 150–2.
240 See P. Pasture, 'Christendom and the Legacy of the Sixties: Between the Secular City and the Age of Aquarius', *Revue d'Histoire Ecclesiastique* 99(1) (2004), 99.
241 Tanner, *Decrees*, LG, ss. 31–5, 875–8.
242 R. Russell, 'The Theology of the Lay Apostolate – I', *New Life* 13(5) (1957), 192–93.
243 W. Rafferty, 'Lay Life and the Liturgy', *New Life* 13(6) (1957), 206.
244 Interview, Kevin, transcript page 7.
245 E. Langdale, 'The Spirituality of Worker Leaders', *New Life* 4(1) (1950), 254.
246 *Ibid.*
247 Tanner, *Decrees*, LG, s. 41.4, 882.
248 E.g. *Populorum Progressio* (1967); *Octogesima advenines* (1971) and *Laborem Exercens* (1981).
249 T. G. McCarthy, *The Catholic Tradition: Before and After Vatican II, 1873–1993* (Chicago: Loyola University Press, 1994), 255; G. Rainer-Horn, *The Spirit of Vatican II: Western European Left Catholicism in the Long Sixties, 1959–1980* (Oxford: Oxford University Press, 2013).
250 M. Walsh, 'Ward, Barbara Mary (1914–81) – http://www.oxforddnb.com/view/article/31801?docPos=1 and J. Gartlan, *Barbara Ward: Her Life and Letters* (London: Continuum, 2010).
251 S. Blake O.P., 'Christians in Politics', *The Tablet*, 3 July 1970, 8.
252 J. Mosier, 'A Promise of Plenty: the Eucharist as Social Critique', *Downside Review*, 91(305) (1973), 305.
253 H. Nehring, 'The long, long night is over' in Garnett *et al*, *Redefining*, 138–47 and B. Kent, F. Williams and R. Gray, *Christians and Nuclear Disarmament* (London: Campaign for Nuclear Disarmament, 1977).

254 R. Clifford and N. Townson, 'The Church in Crisis: Catholic Activism and "1968"', *Cultural and Social History* 8(4) (2011), 531–50.
255 D. Hart, 'Jesus without Illusions' *International Times* 46 (1968), 14.
256 Bishop Thomas Holland, 'A Lenten Pastoral Letter', 11 February 1966, 1 (SDA Box 220).
257 Stanford, *Cardinal Hume*, 163.
258 P. A. Lane, 'Bidding Prayers', *The Tablet*, 15 March 1975, 264.
259 D. Nicholl, 'The Real Presence of Christ', *The Tablet*, 7 September 1974, 864.
260 M. Williams, 'The Eucharist, Church and the World', *Catholic Gazette* 64(10) (1973), 11.
261 C. Longley, 'Talking about God', *The Tablet*, 14/21 April 1979, 362.
262 E. Yarnold (ed.), *The Pope in Britain: Collected Homilies and Speeches* (Slough: St Paul Publications, 1982), 90.

Chapter 4

'A model for many homesteads'

Marian devotion, the Holy Family and Catholic conceptions of marriage and sexuality

Make a cross on your abdomen
When in Rome do like a Roman
Ave Maria, gee it's good to see ya...

The scene is familiar: Wembley Stadium, cold and blustery weather even in July, and the arena crowded to capacity. There is a cheer from the near 100,000 people gathered as the long-awaited and charismatic personality enters the arena and is welcomed over the loudspeaker by Mr Ted Kavanagh as 'that great international, that prolific goal scorer, who has brought his team to Wembley today'.[1] However, all is not quite as it seems. From the stadium's twin domes fly the Union Jack and the papal flag, the grandstand is adorned with the slogan 'The Family that Prays Together Stays Together' and the announcer, the chairman of this 'Rosary Crusade' and a Knight of St Gregory, continues:

> It is the ambition of every captain to bring his team to Wembley ... but the team that Fr Peyton has brought here to-day is the greatest team in the world – Family United.[2]

Resembling a football crowd, but drawn by explicitly spiritual preoccupations, this diverse congregation gathered on Sunday 27 July 1952 to hear the words of the charismatic Irish-American preacher Fr Patrick Peyton, advocating a return to family prayer and the reinforcement of traditional family values.

Exactly three decades later, another peripatetic Catholic figure would pack Wembley and preach a homily on Mary as an incomparable exemplar for right moral conduct and the stability and holiness of family life. However, despite the familiarity of Pope John Paul II's highly traditional message reasserting the indissolubility of marriage and condemning sexual permissiveness, the intervening years had witnessed many changes in the form and frequency of Marian devotional practice. The Polish pontiff used the distinctly modern language of personal dignity and human rights when speaking about contemporary marriage and family life, in an implicit recognition of the profound societal shifts in constructions of gender, marital relations and the role of sexuality between 1952 and 1982. If Father Peyton urged recourse to the rosary as 'a link that has the ability within it to tie, to unite, to bind your precious little family … to the Blessed Trinity',[3] Pope John Paul II's audience, in accordance with the movement charted in the last chapter, was exhorted to regular mass attendance as the most efficacious way to make God 'the living heart of your family life' and the home a 'school of prayer for both parents and children'.[4] Despite these clear changes in form, the substantive stress in Catholic teaching on the family, expressed by Father Peyton as the 'atom of civilization', and the chief means for the realisation of the kingdom, remained unchanged. The team gathered for the papal visit retained something of their identity as 'Family United', albeit a very differently 'configured' family and one which was compelled to encompass a great diversity of beliefs and practices within its midst. Moreover, whereas Father Peyton would seek to rally 'Mary's warriors', the English Catholics gathered to greet the Pope in 1982 had redefined themselves, through self-reflection and the lay-driven discussions of the 1980 National Pastoral Congress, as an 'Easter People'.

This chapter elucidates these shifts in Catholic spirituality and social identity in relation to the accompanying movements in gendered, societal and civic morality in the second half of the twentieth century. In contrast to a historiography which has taken at face value a 'golden age' for marriage for all Britons in the post-war period, it illustrates that Catholic attitudes in the 1940s and 1950s were not as homogeneous and uniformly conservative as often thought and that social attitudes in post-war Britain were similarly varied, but overwhelmingly cautious and resistant to wholesale, overnight revolution in the 1960s. It commences by examining the prevalence within post-war Catholic teaching of devotion to the Blessed Virgin Mary and her husband St Joseph, illustrating the ways in which this Holy Family served as an ideal and model for 'rightly-ordered' understandings of femininity, masculinity and the conjugal relationship. In ways that have been little appreciated to date, these understandings of marriage were also adaptive to, and constitutive of, broader theories of marriage and gendered relationships promoted by other marriage reformers and state agencies such as the National Marriage Guidance Council.

The second section examines an aspect of married life, namely attitudes to the role, function and purpose of sex, which underwent considerable transformation in the post-war period. It explores the ways in which, throughout the 1950s, there were considerable tensions within Catholic circles about the most appropriate means and methods of sex instruction, and a confusion of theologies of marriage in moving from a Marian-based model towards the explicitly sacramental model of the Body of Christ. This shift mirrored a broader transition from an understanding of sex in terms of sin and a central preoccupation within questions of salvation and moral standing, to a less metaphysical and more 'this-worldly' approach concerning itself with issues of over-population, the strain of unwanted pregnancies on married couples (and indirectly on society) and the integrity of loving relationships rather than spousal legalities. These issues surrounding the physical expression of 'married love' challenged the continuing usefulness of the 'Holy Family' as a model for Catholic marriage, underpinned as it was by less adaptable understandings of the nuclear family, gender roles and a continuing stress on procreation as the primary 'end' of marriage.

The final section of the chapter charts the transition from an institutionally promoted model of the 'Holy Family' towards Catholics' realisation and self-definition as an 'Easter People'. In the immediate post-conciliar period, the institutional promotion of Marian devotions went into abeyance, with an increased emphasis on Christological and liturgically focused prayer, as well as ecumenical collaborations. Evolving theologies of marriage sought to be responsive to both of these emerging impulses, as well as the broader societal premium on individual self-realisation in marriage. The re-emphasis upon Mary within Catholic teaching from the 1980s, at the personal behest of John Paul II, saw Mary harnessed by conservative and reactionary components of the church, as well as her co-option as a heroine for the poor and a champion of liberation theology. For Catholics educated earlier in the twentieth century, and those growing up in the wake of the Second Vatican Council, Mary remained 'Our Lady' and 'Our Mother', but the meanings and import attached to these terms, within both Catholic teaching and lay reception and practice, had shifted considerably.

The holy couple and marriage: Marian devotions, St Joseph and modern British home making

In a sermon delivered to the Catholics of northern England in 1945 that explicitly addressed issues such as the breakdown of family life and the spiritual priorities for post-war renewal, Bishop Marshall of Salford held before his flock a comprehensive model for familial relations:

> Catholic fathers can endeavour to follow the footsteps of St Joseph by the purity of their lives, by their vigilance and self-sacrifice. Catholic mothers can imitate the Mother of Jesus by their example, their modesty, their resignation and perfect faith. Catholic children can strive to be pious and obedient as the Child Jesus was. The whole family, father, mother and children, can unite daily in the service of God by family prayers. Thus Catholic homes can be preserved from the many dangers around them and, like the Holy Family, they can serve as models for many homesteads.[5]

One of the foremost instruments of this domestic piety advocated by episcopal leaders as well as by visiting priests within their high-tech pep-talks was the rosary, a widespread Catholic devotion comprised of fifteen decades (or collections) of prayers, namely ten Hail Marys, the Our Father and Doxology and concurrent meditation on specific events from the Gospel narrative. As both a meditative and a vocal prayer, believed to have been instituted by St Dominic in the thirteenth century and particularly commended to the faithful through numerous papal encyclicals after 1883, this physical, bodily form of Catholic piety was the stimulus for both theological tracts and spiritual ruminations, such as that written by a Dominican Tertiary in 1952 who described its 'unique excellence':

> While our fingers are occupied with the beads and our lips with words of praise and petition, our minds are directed to a fresh consideration of the main moments in the drama of Divine Love.[6]

It was something of this 'drama of Divine Love' which the so-called 'rosary priest', Father Peyton, sought to communicate in his four-month progress and public gatherings throughout England in 1952. Believing that he had been saved from life-threatening tuberculosis by the intercession of Mary, this globe-trotting and high-profile evangelist (whose cause for canonisation was opened in 2001)[7] dedicated his priesthood to spreading the practice of the rosary in thanksgiving, incorporating the co-operation of Christian Hollywood stars, and employing all modern means of travel and communication to promote his catch-phrase contention that 'The Family that Prays Together Stays Together'.[8] Lauded by headlines such as 'Thousands Flock to Hear Fr Peyton'[9] and '85,000 Throng at Birkenhead',[10] the Catholic press chronicled Peyton's exploits, including a gathering before a crowd of at least 30,000 in Hyde Park.[11] It was estimated that a total of one million English men and women in eight dioceses had personally 'heard the message that "the Family that prays together stays together"'.[12] This crusade, whose champion was commended to his UK compatriots as an 'Irish lad conquering the new world', was also designed to appeal to an indigenous English audience when likened by the Bishop of Lancaster to a holy 'rosary peddling' quest in the tradition of Malory's *Mort d'Arthur*.[13] The proceedings at Wembley encapsulated this mixture of faux-medieval nostalgia with modern-day evangelism and combative Catholicism in their dramatic mime re-enactments of scenes from the lives of Jesus and Mary, which in Catholic devotional tradition are grouped together as the fifteen Mysteries of the Rosary. From descriptions in newspaper reports, and a portion of the pageant preserved on newsreel,[14] crusade performances were reminiscent of medieval folk passion plays, ritually commemorating pre-Reformation 'merrie England' through the players' costumes, the incorporation of maypole festivities and their culmination in the creation of a 'living rosary' (the recitation of the prayer by the crowd while a statue of Mary was moved around a circle of beads patiently depicted by fifty-three groups of boys and girls clothed in white). In this performative enactment of incorporation into the Gospel drama, there was a ritualistic creation of a link between the sacral family and the families gathered. This analogy between the 'Holy Family' and 'ordinary Catholic families' was also stressed in contemporaneous written treatises, such as an article in the 1952 *Catholic Herald* which posed the rhetorical question 'why recite the rosary?' and answered in the following emphatic terms:

> BECAUSE it raises the family circle to a supernatural level. Not so much as earthly father, mother, son and daughter does the family pray, but rather as children of God, united in a higher family circle where God is Father and Mary Immaculate is Mother.[15]

These metaphysical understandings were more simply communicated to a youthful audience who, in the illustrations accompanying *My Rosary*

Book (1951) for example, were presented with the image of the rosary as a chain that linked the child believer to the heavenly court.[16] The symbolism of the rosary circlet and the tangible link it was believed to create in encompassing the Catholic home within the holy household was also well articulated by Caryll Houselander. Writing on the use of the rosary during the wartime, she extolled its benefits as:

> something ... *literally* to focus one's prayers, even just to hold in one's hands ... the one strengthening and comforting thing at times, just like finding your other's hand in the dark.[17]

Houselander's appreciation of the meditative, progressive and embodied dimensions of this traditional prayer echoed the contention of Father Peyton and other commentators,[18] who described the rosary as a 'school of religion with grades from kindergarten to heaven'.[19] Drawing upon the spiritual exercises of the church, but reproducing them in a simple and accessible ceremonial in the home, the gathering of father, mother and offspring round the hearth for family rosary was a common practice in many Catholic homes earlier in the twentieth century, which Peyton evoked in his crusade promotional poster.

Reflecting on their upbringing in Galway in the 1940s, before migrating to Manchester after the war to take up nursing, sisters Nora and Margaret (born in 1933 and 1935 respectively) recalled the nightly gatherings of parents, grandparents and multiple siblings for the family rosary, with the stern prohibition on going out, even to a 'dance or anything ... until the rosary was said'.[20] The practice continued in many Manchester homes well into the 1970s, but as Mitzi Smith reflected from the viewpoint of a 1960s childhood, the devotional necessities and theological intricacies of the daily discipline were not always appreciated by those involved:

> MS: [W]hen we were little in Longsight we used to live on a little avenue and we used to play out. And the door used to open and mum or dad used to shout 'rosary' down the street, and you'd be skipping with your friends. And they weren't Catholics, you know, on the road. And you used to sort of die a death! And they'd say 'Why do you have to keep going in and saying this? What is this "rosary"?' And actually, you didn't really know what it was. And then we all had to kneel down – we had little chairs I can remember – and we all knelt down facing a wall really with your

rosary, with your back to each other. And my dad had the first decade, then my mum, then my sister and then me.[21]

Whether communally recited by Catholics gathered to hear Father Peyton in Hyde Park, or begrudgingly participated in two decades later within a Longsight terrace, the practice of saying the rosary was a mark of denominational distinctiveness and a domestically apprehended piety. At the heart of this prayer, which linked the home to the divine household, was Mary, the human Mother of God, who in her believed intercessory powers was a potent exemplar for Catholics seeking to sanctify their own domestic lives through imitation of the Holy Family.

This 'school of faith', with its strong emphasis on Mary as mother and exemplar, was not however confined to familial prayer within the home but also encompassed a range of other colourful celebrations and communal devotions. Speaking of his mother's deep devotion to Mary and the routine of the family rosary in his Earlham home, fifty-four-year-old Tony reminisced about the strength of Marian devotion in 1950s parochial life and reflected that 'the family orientated round the fact that Mary was there'.[22] Enumerating the various Marian processions and crowning of Mary in May, weekly novenas and parish rosaries, he concluded that 'she did play a great part in Catholic life, did Mary. Certainly round here,'[23] which he clarified by speaking of the historic and longstanding devotion to Mary in Lancashire 'that's gone down through the families'.[24]

This intensely personalised acquaintance with and devotion to Mary is encapsulated in a story told by Francis, a generation older than Tony, who admitted that he 'had a crush on Our Lady more than anything else'.[25] He proceeded to describe an occasion when he was an altar boy at St Boniface's, Salford in the 1930s and had the 'great privilege' of unexpectedly crowning the statue of Our Lady during the May ceremony. Describing his ascent up the ladder behind the little girl designated as May Queen to protect her from falling, Francis recounted her fearful freezing-up at the crucial part of the ceremony, 'literally like the statue. She couldn't move, poor child'. He became emotional when describing his unexpected intervention (echoing his intervention at the Tabernacle in chapter three) and surreptitious crowning of the statue, giving rise to a lifelong devotion to Mary and an intense appreciation of her personal protection. This belief extended to her believed protection in the case of five serious motorbike accidents and a direct intervention, as a 'vocal warning', averting a deadly fall when a rung on a ladder broke whilst working.[26] Several generations later, Mitzi also had fond recollections of her role as 'cushion bearer' in the May Queen's entourage, conjecturing with adult eyes on the ways in which this parochial honour always seemed to go to the daughter of a 'big noise' in the parish, yet was a 'huge deal' that made her view Our Lady as 'somebody quite special' and as somebody 'you pray through, to Jesus through her'.[27]

Nevertheless, it should not be supposed that all English Catholics of a certain generation or strong Catholic background had an intense and personalised relationship with the Blessed Virgin Mary. When Joseph, now in his nineties, was asked whether he prayed to Mary, he flatly retorted, 'No. I say my prayers in church, that's all'.[28] Growing up of parents and grandparents born and bred in Manchester, Joseph's exposure to the rosary was merely within his Collyhurst parish and was not a feature of his home life, nor the way he raised his own children in the Catholic faith. A generation later, Tom remembered that while his Irish grandparents 'referred to Mary certainly quite a lot', he did not develop a devotion in his formative years growing up in post-war Trafford Park nor acquire extensive knowledge at the school or parish. Confessing, with some embarrassment, that 'the rosary … doesn't really mean a lot to me', he linked his Catholicism exclusively to the mass:

> TF: I, obviously I think about Mary but I … I never really, I never really relate to her, for some reason. Strange you should ask that, but no I don't… to be honest, I never even think about Mary … I go to worship God, you know.[29]

In his identification of the liturgy as the prime vehicle for his spirituality and doxology, Tom was representative of a trend, becoming stronger in the post-conciliar period, towards a more mass-centred Christology, focused outside the home and independent of the mediation of Mary. Gender as well as generational differences may also be a factor here. Nevertheless for some younger *female* Catholics such as Christine, who was born in 1959 to father Francis with his affection to Mary, devotion to Our Lady meant little and was merely 'part of the [Catholic] package'.[30] However, for very many other Catholics in mid-century Britain, both male and female, devotion to the Mother of God remained a salient part of their faith and adapted to wider and shifting social currents centred on the home and notions of a 'companionate' marriage.

First popularised as a concept upon the publication of Ben Lindsey and Wainwright Evans' sensational tract earlier in the century,[31] the growing currency in the post-war period of the 'powerful ideal' of the 'companionate marriage', with its attendant stresses on 'the importance of romantic love, sexual attraction and mutual interests', has been long recognised by historians of gender and the family.[32] Indeed, Janet Finch and Penny Summerfield have gone so far as to describe this model of marriage as 'the most distinctive feature of domestic life during the period'.[33] While historians of twentieth-century British history have developed this model to speak of a 'set of ideas' about marriage,[34] extended by Claire Langhamer's recent explorations of interwar courtship and adultery[35] and Szreter and Fisher's *Sex Before the Sexual Revolution*,[36] it is now possible to appreciate better the intricacies and shifting intellectual underpinnings of this increasing (yet precarious) emphasis upon companionship and individuality within the marriage institution. Yet the persistent and complex role of Christian discourse informing aspects of these ideals, ranging from the complementary but distinct roles of husbands and wives through to a conception of marriage as involving 'teamwork' and an implied breakdown in demarcated roles, is now being recognised.[37] In view of the clerical backgrounds of Herbert Gray[38] and David Mace,[39] founders of the National Marriage Guidance Council (NMAC) in 1938,[40] and the role of other religious commentators in public debates about regulation of the family life and sexuality,[41] the cursory attention to these intellectual and philosophical underpinnings conforms to the historiographical landscape outlined in chapter 2. Despite some developments, most revisionist histories continue to ignore the role of Catholicism in also shaping understandings of marriage during the period. In doing so, reformers drew upon distinctively Catholic conceptual resources which confirmed or complicated notions of companionate marriage being mainstreamed, and implicitly endorsed by the state, in funding the Catholic Marriage Advisory Council (CMAC) alongside the NMGC, in the late 1950s.[42]

Representative of the type of considerations involved in the increasingly heated discussions after the war of what 'partnership' and 'equality' in marriage might require, the Oxford Dominican Gerald Vann chided in 1952:

> [Y]ou hear a great deal nowadays about the equality of the sexes: there is a great danger here. If you are trying to defend women from the degradation

of being treated as a chattel ... then of course you are wholly right. ... But be careful: if by equality you mean an obliteration of the differences between the sexes you will end by destroying the integrity of both. For the whole idea and purpose of the difference is that the two together are complementary.[43]

Such an attempt to clarify the 'correct' Catholic perspective on the marriage partnership is illustrative of the increasing renegotiation of this relationship, and associated concepts of domesticity and familial harmony, throughout English society.[44] The tensions which this prescriptive tract sought to address may be gleaned from a 1945 Advent sermon of the Bishop of Salford, which traced the genealogy of the family from Adam and Eve through to the Christmas home in Nazareth, to admonish:

> The good Catholic mother must remember that her husband is the head of the home, and no matter how she may be provoked, she should not utter bitter words of reproach or disrespect in the presence of her children. The father has a right to expect reverence, obedience and love in his home, but he should take every precaution to render himself worthy of such veneration.[45]

Written within the context of traumatised men returning from the war, and women relinquishing the financial independence gained from war-work, the insistent tenor of this pastoral advice suggests a desire to reiterate norms in the face of an increasing instability in the Catholic, and indeed wider societal, understanding of 'the husband [as] the head, [and] the wife ... the heart of the home'.[46] Yet what emerged within the remainder of this pastoral instruction, delivered from all Manchester pulpits, was an increasingly complex understanding of the marital relationship in which:

> The Christian home ... should be a place where man and wife are united in mutual support and tender love. It should be a refuge in affliction, a shelter from the uncharitableness, the sorrows, and the quarrels of the world. Such a home can be found only where God is the acknowledged head of the home, and where husband and wife are permanently united in the service of each other.[47]

Although articulated within a distinctively Catholic rhetoric of the Holy Family, and drawing upon elements of the traditional theology of sacramental marriage, Bishop Marshall's description of the Christian home shared many of the characteristics of the companionate model of marriage circulating within mainstream non-Catholic culture, through its tacit endorsement of domestic co-operation and familial cohesion.[18] As an example of Catholic rhetoric about family stability, and expectations of fulfilment within marriage, encountered within countless marriage preparation pamphlets, his overly earnest prescription was articulated against the findings of the Royal Commission on Marriage and Divorce and fears about the 'divorce epidemic' which peaked at 60,000 marriage breakdowns in 1946–47.[49] In a collective submission to the Royal Commission, the Catholic Bishops of England and Wales disingenuously stated the 'simple point' that:

> it is historical fact that the attitude of people outside the Church has changed considerably during the last hundred years or so. It is not Catholics who have changed their ideas, but others.[50]

But, in fact, Catholic understandings and expectations of marriage were also changing, prompting both emphatic restatements of the traditional 'ends' of marriage, and a reactive reinterpretation of Catholic experiences of married life against the broader societal conceptions which Lesley Hall has explored in her newly revised history of sex, gender and social change in late twentieth-century Britain.[51]

Laity and clergy within the church were becoming proactive in responding to these trends, through the establishment of bodies such as the London-based CMAC initiated by Graham J. Graham-Green and his wife, whose work with London's bombed-out civilians impressed upon them the need for stable marriages to create a strong post-war society.[52] Commencing in 1946, branches of the CMAC were soon established throughout the country, spurring on other marriage-based initiatives such as the first Mancunian marriage guidance programme, set up at the Rusholme Church of the Holy Name in 1947.[53]

A spectrum of responses to these 'new patterns of family life' was made palpably clear in a memo written by the instigator of the innovative Mancunian marriage course, Fr Waterhouse. In his slightly self-serving and congratulatory report to his Bishop, this Jesuit priest commenced with a discussion of the 'well-meaning' but 'Protestant' agenda of the NMGC under its Presbyterian chairman, Herbert Gray, disparaging the 'tinge of hedonism' in its 'talk of "harmony" … about the happiness of partners and about the welfare of the nation, but not about pleasing God'.[54] He then denounced the CMAC, a rival to his parish-based programme, for 'following the fashion in social work instead of leading it'.[55] He was emphatic in his diagnosis that:

> the Catholic Marriage Advisory Council has cramped itself from the start by taking the non-Catholic Marriage Guidance Council as its model. It has merely baptised its principles and methods to get rid of the twin evils of contraceptive teaching and permission for divorce, but by not drawing its inspiration primarily from Catholic sources it has missed an opportunity to start some really constructive and positive work to restore family life on Catholic lines … [through] dedication to the Holy Family and St Thomas More, together with an appeal for prayers.[56]

This priestly polemic may be critiqued for its misapprehension of the continuing emphasis on marriage stability that was advocated by the NMGC, at least in the 1950s,[57] and for its overestimation of Catholic consensus on the 'evil' of contraception.[58] Nevertheless, this clerical commentator did identify the increasing realisation in Catholic circles that an appeal to a sacralised family life might yield 'constructive' and 'positive' models of marriage.

The creative and heterogeneous interpretations which arose from a sanctified understanding of married life, and its social consequences outside the home, were visually articulated in Tim Madden's long-running cartoon strip 'How's the family?' within the *Catholic Herald* newspaper. Gently parodying the quirks and absurdities of everyday domesticity within an archetypal Catholic family, the 1952 offerings showed 'Dad' helping with the after-dinner dishes and the tidying, actively involved in entertaining the children, and kneeling with his family by the hearth, under a portrait of Mary, in an unsuccessful attempt to enact Father Peyton's remedy for family disunity.[59] Drawing upon a distinctive arsenal of Catholic resources and heavenly personages to inform its vision of post-war reconstruction, English Catholic social teaching paralleled broader Christian thinking about the family as a microcosm of a well-ordered polis.[60] There was even an unexpected correspondence with the contemporaneous opinions of the secular pundits, such as the sexologist Eustace Chesser[61] who, despite markedly different objectives, concurred that 'the ideal marriage is an ideal community in miniature'.[62]

Outlining his agenda to provide a 'noviceship for marriage' in the Holy Name pre-nuptial course, Father Waterhouse identified his foremost objective as 'preparing [couples] adequately for the task of training the children who will be theirs later'.[63] This was founded in his conviction that:

> The family is the unit which God planned for society and the more we try to split it, the more we produce an unstable and unnatural social order in which not only is the State in difficulties but the Church herself cannot work effectively.[64]

Advocating 'preventatives' rather than palliatives, maternity and child welfare featured prominently in this Jesuit initiative, echoing a broader societal preoccupation in the post-war period with women's domestic roles and the appropriate socialisation of 'youth'.[65]

For Catholics, a powerful and longstanding emphasis on women's vocations as home makers and mothers could be articulated, and indeed extended, through appeal to the Virgin Mary, who was both a model and an intercessory aid for attainment of these ideals. In a representative pamphlet, recommending recourse to her in 'these times ... when there are many vexed questions about what is right and proper in a woman',[66] Reverend J. Nutt was at great pains to illustrate the continuing relevance of the Christian witness to the questions facing Catholics in 1948. Refracting controversies about the 'new women' and the glamorous housewife through the lens of Marian devotion, he addressed the wearing of make-up through an instructional analogy:

> Do not think within yourselves that times have changed so that it is sheer sentimentalism to put forward Mary as the ideal ... When Our Lady walked through the streets of Jerusalem, she met with all the varieties of women that are to be found in any modern city. With their airs and graces, their trinkets, their bleached hair, rouge and lipstick, they went mincing by the gentle maid ... Yesterday, to-day and the same for ever, she is the woman who finds favour in the sight of God, and also in the sight of men.[67]

Nutt's emphatic insistence on a particular understanding of Mary's femininity tapped into the increasing tensions about women's roles in wider British society and the need to provide a potent counter-image to dissuade Catholic women from adapting to these social mores. Numerous Catholic manuals for young women addressed the issue of make-up and the appropriate balance between attractiveness, fashionable dress and proper Catholic behaviour.[68]

In a similar vein, the Bishop of Salford, in a sermon to the Union of Catholic Mothers, had recourse to Mary as the one who offered 'the true norms and right ideals' of 'delicacy and modesty', allowing present-day youth to escape from the 'contagion' of the 'popular vision and corrupted public standards'.[69] However, in an article in the YCW magazine in 1948 on the formation of movement leaders, the chaplain Louis Hanlon advocated the need to make Our Lady relevant to the modern working girl, through reconstructing the 'vision in blue and white who blushes if she whistles or smokes a cigarette'. He insisted:

> [I]nstead of being something queer and abstract, [sanctity] becomes something tangible … The things God asked of her were human things, human joys and sorrows: to have a baby, love It, educate It and suffer because of It. He asked her to employ her body, hands, will and intelligence on quite normal human activities; to bend her back, to scrub the floor, to wash clothes, to look after a home.[70]

Within all these instructional commentaries, both Catholic and secular, there is an increasing recognition that the 'modern girl', against the foil of a 'Victorian' counterpart, should increasingly strive after a femininity that encompassed emotional maturity, self-expression and intellectual independence.

While some of these examples and instructional commentaries offered constraining and conservative conceptions of Catholic womanhood, other resources might also offer, paradoxically, a means for re-conceptualising models of femininity and domestic roles. In a bulletin to lay leaders of the 'Girls' YCW', its clerical editor urged 'working girls of the world' to abandon the stars of Hollywood and re-appreciate the 'Star of Heaven' who is like the reader in sharing 'all the worry that can come to any working-class girl and mother':

> Worry of a mother with nothing but a bit of straw for her new-born child. Worry of sudden evacuation, State control, looking for a house, unemployment, poverty and want.[71]

Anticipating trends in the post-conciliar period, the bulletin urged its female readers in 1948 to appreciate that as Mary:

> formed the body of Jesus within her, brought Him forth to the light of day, and trained Him up to perfect manhood, so her task is to form Christ within us, so that we may think like Christ, speak like Christ, and act like Christ.[72]

Advocating an equality of male and female discipleship, and also informed by leftist political principles, the Chair of the prominent feminist organisation St Joan's Alliance drew upon Catholic teaching to challenge gently traditional divisions of domestic labour. Responding to an ongoing correspondence in May 1952 within the *Catholic Herald* on the need for greater domestic training in Catholic schools, Phyllis Challoner stressed the desirability of moving the debate beyond practicalities to principle, and advanced:

> 'Home-making' is a wider thing than skill in domestic work, and we maintain that a training in accordance with their talents for both boys and girls, with a training of both equally in the whole subject of homemaking, will result in a comradeship in and out of the home that will solve more questions than how to satisfy a husband's pangs of hunger.[73]

At a time in which there was an extraordinary societal premium on women's maternity and housewifery,[74] these examples illustrate dimensions within Catholic teaching that could offer resources for dealing with the difficulties and stresses of domesticity. Marriage and household maintenance were sanctified and, through appeal to a holy ideal of 'Mary as 1950s Home maker', Catholic women were offered not only reassurance, but the means for potentially re-configuring their maternal roles.

There were also alternative models of femininity available within Catholic discourse with which to celebrate the single state and work outside the home. For example in his Catholic Truth Society (CTS) pamphlet, clearly indicating its audience by its title, *To Those Getting Married* (1946), Walter Jewell used the example of two girlfriends, one called to a religious order and the other to marriage, to celebrate the religious life as well as to elevate matrimony as a vocation and channel of God's grace.[75] This same theme was taken up by Bishop Marshall, addressing the many thousands of Mancunian Catholics gathered for the Whit walk in 1948. Remarking that 'the social position of women is, from the Christian point of view, very imperfectly set forth in the expression "Woman belongs in the home"', Bishop Marshall was an unlikely radical in urging the 'most emancipated woman of to-day' to realise the 'influence and freedom of action' offered through church history by women. Making reference to St Brigit, a saint of the early Irish church, he held before his audience the cult of a powerful religious woman, known for her independence of mind and her capable administration of a number of religious houses. Contending that 'never has the official church countenanced the "kitchen theory" of womanhood', he observed:

Luther wishes to confine her ambitions to wash-tubs and baby-linen; and the Koran quite takes it for granted that, outside marriage, she has neither value nor importance – the truth is that her own unique influence is intended to reach everywhere.[76]

Ecumenical and inter-religious scruples aside, this use of Catholic resources to support women's agency outside marriage, and beyond domestic confines, offered a sanctioned alternative to the overwhelming societal prioritisation upon marriage for those 'singled out' or in the 'shadow of marriage' after World War II.[77]

In addition to these shifting understandings of women's role as home makers, historians have long recognised the overwhelming emphasis in post-war welfare planning on a maternalist rhetoric[78] which sought to encourage women to move out of some areas of the labour market back into the home.[79] As the spokesman for an emerging social policy, which emphasised the scientific professionalism of good home making in a context of continued rationing, and the heroism of motherhood after their war-work, Field Marshal Sir William Slim utilised a home service broadcast in 1952 to praise women 'who set the standard in all the really important things – in truthfulness, honesty, decency, self-sacrifice and honour'. He went so far as to attest that 'the economy of the country was based on her shopping basket'.[80] Catholic mothers were equally exhorted to the appreciation that 'the hand that rocks the cradle not only rules but saves the world'.[81]

Clearly aware of the widespread influence of parenting manuals such as those of Bowlby[82] and Winnicott,[83] the Westminster Cathedral chaplain Michael Hollings,[84] writing in anticipation of the official 'Marian Year' of 1954, acknowledged that it was self-evident that Catholics relied on Mary, as Christ did, for 'a family must have a mother. It does not need modern psychology to tell us that'.[85] In his devotional reflections, he reminded his readers that:

> We should not forget Mary as a human mother. If we picture her as 'a queen most womanly', we must see her too with her back aching, her eyes tired, her fingers cracked with washing. We must see her in anxiety, in poverty, in aridity.[86]

Similarly seeking to make Mary 'everywoman', but moving beyond the arduous labour and trials of such maternity, a young Father Thomas Holland reflected before his elevation to the Salford episcopacy:

> Mary had all the rights of a mother over her Son. She had the joy of the Child's first smile, the delights of His first steps when He began to walk, the tender satisfaction of hearing His first uttered syllable ... the loving and intimate union of a mother suckling her child.[87]

This impulse in Catholic devotional and educational literature facilitated an intensely personalised relationship with Mary and the expression of a Catholic, Marian spirituality within everyday contexts. The ways in which the powerful relationship with Mary might be mapped onto familial models is well illustrated by Peter, responding to my question about the place of Marian devotion in his life:

> PK: There's a tale told about an old Irish woman who was in church one Sunday night and she was saying the rosary. And Jesus appeared to her and said 'Excuse me Bridie'. And she said 'Shush, I'm talking to your mother'. Now I think that sort of idea – I can see this in real life. If our boys want anything, they don't ask me. They ask their mother. ... But it's clear, to me at any rate, that you have the Trinity and above all others, then, there's Mary. No doubts whatsoever. The power behind the throne if you like. And the exemplar.[88]

While on the one hand offering women a potent role model and vicarious, deferential respect, the expectations born of comparison with this heavenly ideal might also be onerous. Exasperation with overly sentimentalised expectations of women, such as those outlined in the July 1951 edition of *Novena* under the heading 'Three Grades of Catholic Mothers', prompted correspondence from a Yorkshire woman asking for 'Grades A, B, C of Catholic Fathers' and 'Catholic Children', and another from Cheshire protesting: 'Three *grades* of Catholic Mothers! Makes us sound like eggs!'[89] Similarly, the strain that an increasing emphasis on women's primary responsibility for the family's emotional and psychological, as well as material, well-being could impose, is well articulated by an anonymous Catholic laywoman, who wrote about her prayers while 'resting on my knees, trying to pray and recover from a long day'. This self-titled 'Catholic Mother' intimately recounted her 'troubles' asking:

> Mary, what would you have done if there were electric toasters in your day and they didn't work and the toast was burned and the coffee wasn't good, and everyone left the house in a huff? Was St Joseph ever surly and short tempered

on an early morning after a late night? … Just give me the help I need to take things as they come, please, Mary.[90]

Despite her tiredness and frustrations, little alleviated by the assistance of newly available consumer appliances, 'Catholic Mother' nevertheless clearly derived personal satisfaction and unassailable authority within the household, not to mention an accessible emotional resource to enable her to fulfil her daily round. Within this worldview, maternal and household tasks were 'sanctified' and, in the words of another devotional pamphlet, 'the love of Heaven [brought] to the humblest homes of earth'.[91] For, as Father Greenstock reflected in his 1951 'Talks to Catholic Parents', motherhood was a 'public' role, best realised through its formation of children 'into the likeness of Christ',[92] which would create 'saints, not merely for the priesthood … but also in the workshop, the docks [and] the factories'.[93]

The Virgin Mary when re-visioned as a human mother could be made to respond to many of the temporal concerns of post-war society with its emphasis on an absorbing maternity and valorised domesticity. As these examples also illustrate, Mary's personal biography and a sanctified femininity might also complicate these models by offering to women ideals breaking the confines of the kitchen and reaching into the heavenly realm. The mutability, flexibility and potency of this maternal model continued in some Catholic circles well into the present. This is illustrated through a comparison of the aforementioned 'Catholic Mother' with a modern Mancunian mother, Mary. Born in Trafford Park in 1967 to Irish parents, and juggling parental responsibilities with employment duties, Mary (self-consciously) explains her devotion as vested in a shared maternity:

> MH: It's being a mother as well. I think she's (laughs). I think sometimes, (laughs), yeah, because I work full time as well and trying to balance being that and doing every – . I think sometimes – I mean, I do chat to her. Most days I'll have a chat with her and say 'You were a mother yourself, just…' (laughs). Cause you know what it's like – you've got that many balls in the air sometimes just trying to keep them all going, so yeah.[94]

When asked how 'having a chat to Our Lady' in 'bed or the bath' helped, Mary reflected:

MH: I suppose I've got that much going on sometimes I can always have a chat with her and say 'Ah, what do I do now?' And I've probably known what I should do, but after having the chat … I don't know. Maybe a couple of hours it becomes clear – 'Alright, well I sort it out, I prioritise, that needs to be done first, and that'. You know, work it like that.[95]

Whether as a sympathetic ear for domestic complaints, an aid to patience or a project manager assisting with prioritisation, devotion to Our Lady had the potential to elevate certain constructions of the feminine, enabling some women then (as now) to negotiate personal difficulties and to access the divine outside institutional constraints and clerical control.[96]

Paternity too was becoming increasingly contested in the post-war period, and the input of fathers in the creation of saints within the family and wider society more widely appreciated. Chiming with the recent reflections of John Tosh, Michael Roper,[97] Frank Mort,[98] Adrian Bingham,[99] and Martin Francis,[100] Lynn Segal observed that in the 1950s 'the man's place was *also* in the home', with men domesticated in the popular consciousness in the return from the battlefield to the bungalow.[101] The emergence of the welfare state model, with implications for understandings of the breadwinner's role and the family wage, meant that the roles of husbands and fathers and their involvement around the house were shifting. Conflict and anxiety resulted about a male identity that was more home-based, if not house-trained. After a shattering and brutal war, and a peace that brought acute housing shortages, employment dislocation, and the continuance of food rationing, men as well as women were unsure about their role in the household and anxious about their ability to provide for their families. Understandably, devotional practices that articulated a message of stable, robust masculinity, as well as a sentimental self-fulfilment to be found in the family, were designed to address a pressing contemporary need.

Exemplary of these trends were the rosary crusades of Father Peyton who, when addressing the crowds in 1952, endorsed a virile and self-consciously masculine Marian piety in which 'the family, in its proper character, [is] a little kingdom of God',[102] with 'the husband [as] God's representative'.[103] Reports of the crusades pointedly concentrated, for example, on the tenacious piety of father of five Charles Elliot, who walked thirty miles in the pouring rain to be present.[104] Much was also made of observations by the Hierarchy,[105] and indeed non-Catholic commentators such as the Anglican Rector Canon Bryan Green of Birmingham, who confessed himself 'very impressed by the number of men' at the rallies.[106] Peyton's promotional material gave prominence to photographs of the regimented thousands of male-only volunteers collecting rosary pledges in Newcastle,[107] and journalists spoke of the enormous presence of 'shirt-sleeved fathers – some pushing prams'.[108] Male spirituality was also highlighted in speaking of the effects of the crusade, through photos of the Durham miner clutching his rosary featured in the iconic *Picture Post* (Figure 4.1), reports celebrated an increasing number of boys carrying their rosary beads at school,[109] and the jubilant reception of news of Middlesbrough football star Wilf Mannion's conversion to Catholicism.[110]

The reaffirmation of male authority within the domestic sphere, and ostensibly over matters spiritual, was enshrined in devotions like the enthronement ceremonies of the Sacred Heart but also in the family rosary, which was advocated by laymen like Lawrence Rossiter to his male co-religionists as a 'ten minute' cure for paternal problems and the world's 'black paganism'.[111] In fact, for some Catholic men such as Nora's husband, leading the family rosary was a way of expressing fatherly care and a Catholic identity independent of church attendance:

4.1 A Durham miner (with Father Patrick Peyton) leading his family in the rosary, from 'Crusader for Prayer', *Picture Post*, 26 July 1952, 5. [Photo by Charles Hewitt, and reproduced with permission of Getty Images, London]

> NW: My husband was Catholic but he wasn't a wonderful Catholic. ... he would go, you know, for special occasions or when they were having First Communion ... But he would say the rosary with them and he'd always insist. We used to go to the bedroom and say it there. ... they'd all be upstairs and I had six children and, well, some of them didn't know, they'd hardly know their prayers, like the younger ones. But he'd always say the rosary, which was good. That was a good thing.[112]

These trends were counter to the dominant strain in the Catholic devotional literature which voiced the commonplace assessment that spiritually 'it is the woman who indisputably reigns',[113] and the numerous secular parenting manuals which evidenced a 'tendency to see successful childrearing in terms of constant mothering render[ing] the father relatively unimportant'.[114]

The 'legions of men' publicly participating in the huge processions to the Catholic shrine at Walsingham,[115] or to the little-known pre-Reformation shrine of Willesden for the Marian year in 1954,[116] illustrate the tensions apparent in the 1950s. On the one hand, these were proud and public male assertions of masculine power, strength and authority but in service and deference to Our Lady.[117] The 'true Catholic husband' was reminded to view his wife as 'a reflection of Mary of Nazareth' and as such to manifest devotion to both women by love, respect and 'never utter[ing] an unseemly word' in her presence.[118] Father of five Francis, who earlier confessed to having a 'crush' on Mary, linked this devotion to his understanding of marriage:

> AH: And Our Lady? You talk about praying the rosary – how important is Mary in your faith?
>
> FL: Well very much so actually, because of – every woman, to me all me life, has been on a pedestal. Because most of them are mothers you might say – except the single ones, that's understandable – but I've still got the greatest respect. And I've had it all my life. Every woman, irrespective of what people say about her ... You find your own views. I mean, I would say there's 80% of women have got two jobs, men I think they're only 5%. And that alone is an admiration that I have for women that, you know, they do it.[119]

Francis' reflections evince a perspective formulated in the pre-war period, and by the 1950s this 'admiration' for women was being reconfigured, alongside the role that husbands should play in a domestic setting. Far from a 'golden age' of marriage and complacent post-war consensus, this was a period of intense renegotiation of gendered roles.

As a way of providing further substance to these expectations of Catholic masculinity, beyond being a mere foil to Marian femininity, the Holy Family analogy proffered St Joseph as a model for the right behaviour of Catholic husbands and fathers. Priests composed prayers for 'family devotion to St Joseph', such as this illustrative example:

> St Joseph! Obtain for fathers courage to endure all that is demanded of them. Let them see in every wife and mother an image of Mary, the Mother of God, that they may show forth towards them the spirit of reverence and of chivalry. Give them fidelity to their married life, blessing to their labours and grace to guide those entrusted to their care.[120]

After extolling the sacrifices yet blessings of domestic life, this prayer then considered:

> the anxiety about daily food, the maintenance of home … [and] the spirit of the world … [which] bring worse danger to our children than did the dagger of Herod to the Holy Innocents.[121]

The prayer closed with a salutation to the 'Father of Christ esteemed' as a father 'to those Thy Foster son redeemed', whose intercession would aid fathers to 'stand out before their children as models of faithfulness to God and of strict fulfilment of duty'.[122] This somewhat unorthodox Trinitarian theology offered a construction of masculinity that was not only strong and stable, but also intimate and domestic. For, as Grace Hurrell reminded her youthful readers, St Joseph was 'the first person in what we call the "earthly trinity" of Nazareth' and as such had to mirror the love of God to Jesus, thereby teaching Catholics 'how very "homely" and easy to love God is'.[123]

Following on from speaking about his devotion to Mary, 'baby-boomer' and long-serving schoolteacher Peter spoke in revealing terms, vested in an internalised reading of the scriptures and an admiration of the conjugal fidelity of the foster father of Christ:

> PK: And I would go perhaps a little bit against everything else and put St Joseph up there as well. But then that's partly to do with the fact that … to take somebody as your wife knowing that they are carrying a child

and not knowing whose it was ... that's faith. Dear me. I don't have a faith like that. That is a quantum leap from the ordinary.[124]

In her writings, Caryll Houselander also concurred with this assessment, dismissing the 'grey-bearded statue' of Joseph as quite misrepresenting his true character as a just, strong man who trusted in God, accepted hardship and danger and renounced himself to protect the little and weak.[125] These examples illustrate the ways in which St Joseph was invoked as both a model of the 'good husband' and a 'provider', emulating 'the guardian of the Holy Family [who] could not fail them, say, through bodily indisposition, ... [as] the breadwinner for the Bread who had come down from Heaven'.[126] Portrayed within such literature as a stoic, silent type,[127] St Joseph's role as a model worker – to inspire the Catholic working class and to counter communist ideal types[128] – was endorsed through the establishment of his feast day on 1 May in 1955 by Pope Pius XII and explored through cartoons in the Catholic press paralleling carpentry with modern-day blue-collar jobs (Figure 4.2).

Within this period of a more ambiguous domesticity, the stress on duty and dependence was softened by added emphasis on the foster fatherhood of Joseph:

> Before He had sat in the midst of the doctors he sat on Joseph's knee and at it. And can we doubt that he was any more sparing with His questions than He was with those who were not likely to have the answers? Christ added to His experimental knowledge in the ordinary way. And surely in this case the mother did not occupy the whole scene.[129]

Writers of more psychologically influenced parenting manuals deplored those who diminished the father's role in the education of his children, and reconfigured Joseph as an inspiration to an involved paternity. Instructing fathers to patience and interest in schoolwork and conversation, and deploring the identification of fatherhood with discipline or to acting a fearful 'ogre', Father Greenstock assured his readers that 'many of the more difficult problems of adolescence would never arise at all if there existed more confidence between the child and father'.[130] This male educative and formative role also extended to setting an explicit example in religion to counter the insults of those who assert that 'religion is a thing for silly women and not meant for men'.[131] These exhortations to exemplary personal, social, religious and moral standards inevitably made

4.2 St Joseph the worker and May Day comrade, from the *Catholic Times*, 6 May 1955, 9. [Reproduced with permission from the *Universe and Catholic Times*, Manchester and the Bodleian Libraries, the University of Oxford, shelf mark N.11132 b.3]

explicit reference to restraint from excessive drinking,[132] a vice specifically targeted in Peyton's parables of marriages saved through the displacement of the pub by the routine of the evening rosary.[133] Peyton was not alone in articulating the clergy's blithe expectation that 'no father could [pray] … night after night and be a bad man'.[134]

These examples all demonstrate the concern of some Catholic educators to stress emphatically that, in his involvement in domestic life and spiritual socialisation especially within 'mixed marriages', 'the [Catholic] father is just as important as the mother in this matter'.[135] They also illustrate the increasing ambiguity within the period about gender relations and familial responsibilities. Discussing the considerable changes in contemporary married life and the renegotiation of relationships between husband and wife, the Royal Commission on Population (1949) attributed the loss of male status within the family and the end of 'unrestricted childbearing' to emerging models of marriage that stressed collaboration and concern for maternal health and well-being.[136] By the late 1950s, sociologists such as Young and Willmott, followed by Goldthorpe in the 1960s, were to reflect on the ways in which men from relatively affluent working-class backgrounds were increasingly actively involved in home life and parenting in a way that their fathers had not been.[137] These were, however, gradual shifts and transitions rather than precursors of a gendered revolution. As the 1957 lecture programme for a Manchester Marriage Training Course illustrated, amongst the talks for both spouses on the 'psychology of marriage' and 'budgeting', there were separate classes for men on 'painting and decorating' and 'handyman at home' whilst their fiancées attended Nurse Mrs M. Walsh's sessions on care of the infant.[138] Notably absent from this programme, but increasingly addressed in an emerging body of marriage preparation literature written by doctors and psychologists, as well as Catholic laypeople and pastorally orientated clergy, was information on the importance and function of sex within modern married relationships, which the next section surveys.

'Married Love': sexuality, sex education and contraception

When considering the marked changes and transformations in sexuality and birth control in English society over the twentieth century, Marie Stopes' best-selling book *Married Love* (1918) is usually cited as a harbinger of these trends,[139] characterised by its bold but poetic affirmation of the role of sex in creating and sustaining the perfect marriage: 'Together, united by the love bonds which hold them, they are a new and wondrous thing surpassing, and different from, the arithmetical sum of them both when separate'.[140] Two decades later, when his controversial marriage manual *Love without Fear* (1942) was unsuccessfully tried for obscenity, sexologist Dr Eustace Chesser articulated more explicitly the role of sex within an evolving ideology of companionate marriage relations.[141] Whether in agony aunt columns, titillating but condemnatory pieces in newspapers, or Gainsborough box-office hits like *The Wicked Lady* (1945) depicting sexually transgressive behaviour, the sexual knowledge of British men and women was increasing as the century progressed, as was their estimation of the importance of sexuality within married life.[142] However, as many historians have identified, freer discussion of sexual matters still refrained from exact physiological instructions for mutual sexual satisfaction and was premised on the monogamous marital relationship as the sanctioned site for such experimentation.[143] Government-endorsed initiatives such as the NMGC reflected this transition, discussing adultery and advocating 'scientific contraception, when used according to conscience within marriage', while framing its broader objectives in the language of 'spiritual, emotional and physical harmony ... achieved by unselfish love and self-discipline'.[144]

Although many historians of sexuality have tended to discuss the twentieth century with little reference to Christianity,[145] prominent exponents of reforms from the 1940s themselves advocated a closer integration of sexuality with spirituality.[146] For example, in his influential collection of essays on post-war reconstruction and social morality, the Protestant clergyman Edward Griffith critiqued the false dichotomy between sex and religion set up by 'certain exponents of religion' as well as the prevalent misinterpretation of 'sexual psychology' which views sex as 'the sum and be all of life, to the detriment of everything that pertains to the spiritual nature of man'.[147] Efforts to respond to such issues resulted in debates about school curricula, and the appropriate Christian approach to sex, which were not confined to clergymen or Christian theologians.[148] Ordinary Catholic laypeople and progressive pastors were engaged with these social changes and addressed the demand for increased sex education, with varying degrees of enthusiasm. Representative of the cautious but increasingly realistic approach adopted by some within the church was that of the Dominican Bede Jarrett who, in a speech to the Union of Catholic Mothers in 1943, addressed the changing attitudes to sex education:

> To many it comes as a shock that priests should now recommend Catholic children being taught the 'facts of life'. They contrast this present attitude of the priests with an older point of view which advocated the reverse, which was in favour of reticence, silence, and leaving children in ignorance of what life later really implied. But ... they ought certainly to recognise that it is demanded now since the world too is changed.[149]

Speaking of the impossibility of escaping 'the flaunting evidences of sex and sex appeal' within 'respectable magazines', 'ordinary books', and 'the "talkies"', Jarrett premised his conservative advocacy of limited sex instruction on the overarching imperative that 'children have to be educated to meet it'.[150] This issue was also prominently addressed a year later, in a 1944 Joint Pastoral of the Bishops of England and Wales on Sex Education within Schools. Contending that this information was best conveyed in a family setting rather than by the state (as proposed in a new Department of Education initiative) the bishops collectively advocated 'the removal of external temptations' and the 'determined inculcation of the practice of Christian virtue' rather than 'the imparting in public of fuller and more systematic knowledge of sex from the physiological or biological standpoint'.[151] However, in a tacit acknowledgment of the inroads made by social reformers and medical activists, the Pastoral closed by stating that while 'the supernatural Christian formation must always provide the foundation of the ideal education of youth', nevertheless 'the psychological aspect will doubtless have increasingly interesting contributions to offer'.[152] Whilst class-based sex education in schools was not yet condoned, there was recognition (in even the most conservative Catholic circles) that the insights of sexologists and psychologists could not be wholly discounted.[153]

The debate about the form of and forum for sexual instruction continued throughout the 1950s and 1960s, particularly centred on a distinction between 'sex education' and 'sex instruction' and the placing of biological and gynaecological detail within a moral framework. Writing in the early 1960s, one Catholic laywoman was strident in her advocacy of 'the intimacy of the family circle not the depersonalized and secular atmosphere of a class or lecture room' as the appropriate place for sexual instruction.[154] Yet a decade earlier, Aidan Pickering (a prominent commentator and biology lecturer at Ushaw College in Durham) advocated bolstering the infrequent parental teaching of sex education in the home, with sensitive collective classroom teaching, through a Catholic morality which 'envelops and sweetens the technical crudity'.[155]

The ways in which Catholic moral teaching was integrated within sex education manuals was slowly changing, responding to the greater knowledge and frankness in speaking about sexual matters in British society, and the integration (and interrogation) of these developments through a Catholic lens. Two publications by an anonymous female doctor, decades apart and differing in tone and content, are illustrative of the implications of this shifting stance within the Catholic community. The first, co-written in 1930 with a 'single young woman' and a 'married mother', as a manual for the 'modern girl whatever her walk of life', opened with a frank statement that:

> The truth about sex – that is, God's idea of sex – is not something to be told you in an emotional whisper … Sex is neither startling nor disgusting; it is perfectly simple because God made it. It only becomes complicated and repellent when men and women take it out of its setting in God's plan. Whether you go about the world and encounter all kinds of possible sources of temptation, or live a quiet and sheltered life, whether you become a nun, or live for some profession, or marry – you are a woman and a Catholic, and it is necessary for you to be quite clear about the answer to the question: 'What does the Catholic Faith teach about God's purpose when he made Woman?' Humbly facing the task, we hope this book will be able to give you the answer.[156]

Acknowledging the 'vitality' of the modern girl who drove motor cars, played sport as well as the piano, earned, and might now exercise public leadership as mayors, jurors or parliamentarians,[157] this commentary likened the sex instinct to the normal and natural desire for food,[158] and was forthright in acknowledging sexual desire in women. It suggested, for example, that sexual thoughts should be combated, depending on the temperament of the girl, by distracting daydreaming about the intricacies of domestic interiors or the relative merits of a Baby Austin or a Morris Minor.[159] Nevertheless, when speaking about sexual pleasure and intercourse within or outside marriage, this candour gave way to analogy and the contrast between an estimable 'tall sailing ship riding over the waves in windy weather' and the flailing of a drowning man.[160] Indicative of an increasing demand for practical as well as pastoral sexual instruction, its sequel published in 1939 by this same medically trained laywoman, included updated advice on manners, fashion and male companions but also confronted the issue of 'free love'. It was more candid in outlining physiological developments through menstruation and puberty and quite consciously employed the correct biological terms in its discussion of intercourse and pregnancy.[161]

Yet in many ways these more medically focused discussions of sexual maturation and physical intercourse differed from the vast majority of church authorised publications in the 1950s, which tended to rely upon 'Catholic' frameworks and resources to address the sexual formation of the young. Pamphlet writers such as Father Bede Jarrett urged recourse to Mary's biography in the teaching of biology, invoking a quintessentially Catholic prayer as containing, doubtless to the surprise of his readership, all the tools necessary for sexual instruction:

Catholic children say the word 'womb' in the 'Hail Mary' and should have some idea of the meaning of a word which they use several times each day. No matter how small a child is, it will be interested to know what is meant by 'the fruit of thy womb'; and it may be told at the same time that every baby is the fruit of its mother's womb.[162]

A similar stance was also reflected in Father Pickering's highly influential sex manual. This was sold in churches with a 'perforated section' to ensure purchase and use by parents only. Advocating recourse to Marian devotion and Catholic feast days to show how natural and good sex 'is to us Catholics',[163] and as an alternative to the explicit anatomy texts used within secular sex instruction,[164] Pickering flagged up the *Hail Mary*, the *Angelus*, and the Feasts of Our Lord and Our Lady, such as Christmas, the Annunciation, and the Immaculate Conception, as useful in speaking about pregnancy, the chronology of gestation and 'ordinary' conception.[165]

Within these post-war Catholic manuals, the role of the male in the act of conception and intercourse itself remained only obliquely referenced,[166] as men did not fit neatly within a Marian schema framed around the Immaculate Conception, the Virgin Birth and a divine parental actor.[167] Fears about male sexual desires and considerable consternation about (male) masturbation also underpinned this reticence and were expressly voiced by the English and Welsh Bishops in 1944 when discussing the father's role in instructing his son:

> Hence it is of the highest importance that a good father, while discussing with his son a matter so delicate, should be well on his guard and not descend to details, nor refer to the various ways in which this deadly hydra destroys with its poison so large a portion of the world; otherwise it may happen that, instead of extinguishing this fire, he unwittingly stirs or kindles it in the simple and tender heart of the child.[168]

Refraining from such highly emotive references, Father Pickering's 1950 instruction was more realistic in acknowledging the necessity of explaining God's plan for 'the marriage act' to boys, since 'the natural physical occurrences of erection and night-loss are pleasurable and therefore material for temptation', which if cast in purely negative and unexplained terms became 'an expanse of pleasure from which he is being excluded for some reason he cannot quite fathom'.[169] Other parenting manuals gave a particularly prominent role to fathers in this sexual instruction and the appropriate socialisation of boys, with numerous tacit references to masturbation or vigilance with those who manifested as 'book-worms'.[170] The message was given a more explicit and positive presentation in Pickering's 1957 pamphlet targeted specifically at young men. In a publication exhorting school leavers to steadiness in the faith and pride when derided for their Catholicism 'in the mill or the factory',[171] he lauded purity as 'a great and manly virtue, for it is the strong man who resists temptation' and recognises that 'your body is the Temple of the Holy Ghost; God is within you, and that thought helps you to respect your own body'.[172] Echoing the role models for masculinity discussed above, Father Pickering advocated recourse to Our Lady as a means of resisting (or displacing) temptation and realising self-control: 'In your night prayers say one Hail Mary to her for this grace, and the little ejaculation "Mother most pure, pray for us"'.[173] However, as Edward Griffith astutely observed in his observations on the infantile nature of many people's prayer life in mid-twentieth century Britain, whether this link between nightly prayers in bed and temptation to self-stimulation aided restraint or exacerbated difficulties, might be answered differently by a more psychologically aware pastor than a doctrinally orientated celibate.[174]

Many Catholic priests active in youth education in the post-war period were also moving to such conclusions. In his highly popular and frequently republished 'notes for parents and teachers', Canon Drinkwater's 1964 edition signalled something of a shift in liberal Catholic circles around issues of sex education and adolescence. In a section entitled 'On being fifteen', he assumed full knowledge of sex-developments and frankness in asking parents (or another trusted adult) for further information, and acknowledged the importance of this life-stage transition to adulthood.[175] Advocating the abandonment of 'sin' and guilt, particularly 'where sex-feelings come in',[176] towards an emphasis on responsibility and the formation of good character, Drinkwater's manual signalled the broader movement in the 1960s away from an understanding of the 'supernatural framework' for marriage and sexuality, premised on a naïvely framed Marian model, towards another that was more receptive of psychological insights.[177] This model was focused on Christ and stressed the importance of sex, procreative or otherwise, within the sacrament of marriage. This transformation was particularly centred on an explicit and more vociferous discussion about the purpose and 'ends of marriage', and increasing questions about the legitimacy of birth control, clearly present (though often unacknowledged) from the post-war period, and gathering momentum after the *Humanae Vitae* controversy in 1968.

While it has been argued that the 1939 *Growing Up* manual for girls written by 'A Catholic Women Doctor' shared many of the characteristics and terminology of similar publications by the secular marriage guidance and sex education movement, it clearly manifested a distinctive line of Catholic ethical teaching in its unequivocal determination that 'any man and woman who enters upon such an intimate bodily relationship together, without being married, are committing a moral sin'.[178]

This perspective enjoyed a near-universal official acceptance until well after the Second World War, and continued to be articulated in Barbara Dent's 1962 pamphlet for the CTS:

> There is a moral law regarding sex which is binding on all, including adolescent boys and girls. The use of sex, the deliberate indulgence of passion, the wilful stimulation of the senses, outside marriage, is sin. It is serious sin and it offends God. In fact, it is so serious, and it is so offensive to God, that it merits eternal punishment if the sinner does not repent and try to amend his way of life.[179]

Writing in the context of the rapidly growing sexual transformations in British society, and following in the wake of the *Lady Chatterley's Lover* trial and just before Philip Larkin's mythologised *annus mirabilis*, this Catholic laywoman was also forced to acknowledge these teachings as 'hard' and 'repugnant'.[180] Moreover, she explicitly acknowledged the 'sex urge' itself as 'good, wholesome, and natural'.[181]

Something of these conflicting messages, indicative of ethical perspectives in transition, might also be observed in a CMAC publication in 1963. Whilst continuing to speak of heaven and hell, the primary and secondary ends of marriage, traditional male and female roles and the 'home as a "little church"', *Beginning your Marriage* also included a 'profoundly modern' chapter on 'the marriage act' and described physical changes in the body during lovemaking, the curve of sexual excitement and information about the breaking of the hymen and sexual climax.[182] Within much of this literature, there remained a tacit reference to Marian models of purity and chastity, resulting in a particular emphasis on women as the guardians of these standards, who should exercise modesty in dress and behaviour 'to help the men they mix with to preserve self-control and live as good Catholics'.[183]

Yet neither was release from the 'double standard' and equality of sexual freedom always advocated by secular sex reformers. Chesser argued, on biologically essentialist grounds, that 'a woman's whole nature is fundamentally opposed to promiscuity'.[184] Mainstream, traditional Catholic teaching at least formally advocated sexual equality in its insistence upon virginal purity until marriage for *both* sexes, giving rise to counterbalancing commentaries addressed to men urging avoidance of 'occasions of sin', self-control and Christian ideals of 'chivalry and decency'.[185] In a modernised rendering of these imperatives by Canon Drinkwater in 1964, this 'right attitude towards girls' included recognising the 'difference between love and lust', valuing 'respect and companionship' and seeing women as 'human persons as you are', not just 'dolls' or 'judys'.[186] The practical implementation of these ideals, and the human difficulties they might pose, are neatly summarised by Francis when speaking about the motorbike ride on the first outing he took with the woman who was to become his wife, and the protracted courtship that followed:

FL: Kathleen told me about a fortnight after, she said 'I was ready for you, with my umbrella'! (both laugh)
AH: In case you tried anything?
FL: Yeah! (laughs) Well in them days you didn't, you had a very, very high respect for each other, you know. I mean sex or anything didn't even enter your mind whatsoever, even when you were courting, it didn't.[187]

Of course, for many Catholic men and women, sex did enter their minds, reflected for example in a 1959 compilation by the CMAC of written questions from school-leaving-age girls in an English convent school. Over half of this list of twenty questions for trained marriage guidance counsellors related to premarital sex and contraceptives, with the following typical of many Catholics' questions:

9. How far should one go in displaying affection towards a member of the opposite sex before marriage?
10. Should you allow your boyfriend to kiss you, and if so, to what extent? ...
16. How far should a girl allow her boyfriend to go in lovemaking, if they are intending to get married?[188]

Whilst the novelist David Lodge in his fictional rendering of 1960s London considered these relational wrestlings and spiritual calculations to be a distinctively Catholic and dying phenomenon, perhaps both

Catholic religious conformity in the early part of the twentieth century, as well as the contours of the 1960s 'permissive movement', have been overestimated. In a report presented by Christopher Brooks in 1965 at the CMAC's annual conference, the implications of the sociologist Michael Schofield's *Sexual Behaviour of Young People* (1965) survey for the organisation's educational strategies were considered in detail. Delegates would doubtless have been dismayed to hear that 'Catholic boys are seen to be neither more nor less experienced than the average (37% against 38%)'[189] and that 'there are few grounds for believing that Catholic teenagers in the mass differ much in behaviour and attitude from their non-Catholic fellows'.[190]

On the other hand, a few years later in 1971, Geoffrey Gorer also conducted a survey of English sexual proclivities, concluding that there were great regional differences in attitudes to sexuality, and that the nation remained 'a very chaste society' in which 26% of male respondents and 63% of females were virgins at marriage, with a further quarter of respondents marrying the person with whom they first had intercourse.[191] Leaving aside the perils of such statistics, particularly when addressing something as personal and private as sexual behaviour, it may still be safe to conclude that there was not as much 'swinging' in Britain in the sixties as has been commonly accepted by many historians.[192]

If Catholics' difficulties with the institutional church's teachings on premarital sex prior to the 1960s have been underestimated, so too have their tacit but often unvoiced circumventions of traditional teaching on artificial means of contraception. Catholic commentaries belligerently sought to convince their readership that contraception was an attack on true motherhood,[193] and a sin that deprived Catholic parents of the capacity to nurture their children's spirituality and socialise them through their holy example.[194] In mounting such arguments, church spokesmen sought to contrast spiritual nourishment with secular well-being. As Father George Dwyer (later Archbishop of Birmingham) acknowledged in his 1951 pamphlet for the CTS, birth control was a 'national habit' among non-Catholics in Britain, following its sanction by the Lambeth Conference in 1930, and that there was a 'standing temptation to Catholics' to opt for this solution despite knowledge that it was 'a grievous sin'.[195] Whilst sympathetic to the concerns of the 'good parent' who said "'I want to give my children more than a bare minimum ... I want my wife to have time to look after them properly, to bring them up well. She can't do it if there is a new baby every year'", self-control and personal sacrifice, through abstinence, remained the official church's (and Father Dwyer's) solution to family spacing and limitation.[196]

This traditional teaching seems to have been more acknowledged in the breach than in the practice,[197] as demonstrated by Mass Observation's 1949 report on the sexual attitudes of the British, dubbed 'Little Kinsey', after its more extensive and infamous US counterpart. Predictably, this report drew a strong link between churchgoing habits and disapproval of birth control, particularly marked in Catholic respondents, but also articulated by 36% of Church of England churchgoers.[198] The report was forthright in reporting that the most virulent opposition to birth control came from Catholic quarters, with an eighteen-year-old bank clerk denouncing it as a 'sin' and most others registering opposition purely on the grounds of conformity to church teaching.[199] Its extensive sample, however, surprisingly showed that 'almost half of the Catholics [surveyed] were in favour of birth control methods' and that 'these are by no means all renegade Catholics; about half of them had been to church within a week of answering our questions'.[200] The scale of this response would tend to indicate that some of those answering such a question may have been referring to the use of abstinence, the 'safe period' or *coitus interruptus* (which was not permissible according to strict church teaching). Nevertheless, the report provided examples of middle-aged Catholic women and men who even then conscientiously dissented from the church's teaching, on the grounds that it was a 'worse sin' to bring into the world 'unwanted babies',[201] and that consideration of the scale of maternal duties and money might make it a necessity.[202]

These findings seemed congruent with those issuing from the *Report of the Royal Commission on Population* (1949), which found that 46% of modern Catholic marriages (i.e. those undertaken from 1930–39) employed methods of birth control other than those sanctioned by the church.[203] Whilst Catholic commentators questioned the scale of the sample (394 Catholic women) and whether it was representative (i.e. taken from maternity wards in London and Glasgow), these findings did give church officials 'some cause for anxiety, if not alarm'.[204] Greater alarm, and considerable media publicity, and confessional controversy, was generated in 1963 when a Roman Catholic physician, Anne Biezanek, opened a birth control clinic in Wallesey (Merseyside) and the following year published a strident and internationally publicised justification of her decision subtitled 'A

Declaration of Faith'.[205] These briefly sketched but suggestive examples illustrate the need to situate these clearly changing Catholic attitudes to the permissibility of birth control, which exploded onto the public scene in the late 1960s, within a much longer historical trajectory.[206]

While half of the Catholics surveyed by Mass Observation in 1949 cited adherence to religious teaching as the definitive reason for non-use of contraceptive methods, a generation later the *Schofield Report* (1965) suggested that only 1% of its sample referenced religious reasons for non-use, despite Catholics making up 13.7% of those consulted. This led CMAC delegates ruminating on these findings to conclude that 'Catholic teaching against contraception has made little impression on our present-day teenagers'.[207] For some of those surveyed this might have signalled a loss of commitment to Catholicism as a whole, yet for other young (and practising) Catholics, this marked a renegotiation of ethics and morality, in line with the broader societal acceptance of scientific contraception. Correspondence columns and opinion pieces within the Catholic press were dominated by this issue, from the early 1960s onwards, and the pages of *The Tablet* were representative of the scope of the debate in middle-class circles. Such opinions included extensive discussion of the laity's attitude to 'the Pill',[208] personal reflections on the effectiveness of 'the rhythm method',[209] juridical arguments about natural law, reinterpretations of the church's current teaching on family planning[210] and the importance of these issues measured against other moral imperatives such as over-population and the nuclear threat.[211] Yet, as John Ryan and Paul Jennings humorously suggested in a cartoon in the *Catholic Herald* in 1968, perhaps the intensity of this debate and its theological intricacies were not uniformly debated by all English Catholics, particularly those of working-class origin (Figure 4.3).

These controversies and their interrogation by an increasingly educated Catholic audience, added to the growth in so-called 'mixed marriages' which raised pointed, ecumenical questions about Christian differences on contraception, made the English Hierarchy particularly keen for a conclusive resolution of the Catholic position. The Archbishop of Westminster, in an article in 1964 on 'Morality and the Pill', acknowledged 'the difficulties of the married state' but nevertheless advocated a hard line:

> Many husbands and wives are troubled in conscience. They know that the Church is an infallible guide in matters of faith and morals. But doubts are

'A model for many homesteads'

sown in their minds by imprudent statements questioning the competence of the Church in this particular question … But truth cannot contradict itself. The bishops feel bound to proclaim the unchanging nature of God's law.[212]

As it was, the Council did not specifically consider the issue of contraception, save in a short reference in *Gaudium et Spes* (1965) to responsible parenthood and planning.[213] Perhaps anticipating the intense divisiveness of this issue for the laity and conflicting interpretations even

Drawing it fine by John Ryan

"Encyclical? Bless you, I don't have time to read Encyclicals…"

4.3 Consternation about *Humanae Vitae*, from the *Catholic Herald*, 2 August 1968, 1.
[Reproduced with permission from the *Catholic Herald*, London, the estate of John Ryan (with thanks to Isabel Ryan) and the British Library Board, London, shelf mark bNPL j1966 (1968)]

amongst bishops, Pope Paul VI referred the matter to a specially convened commission of medical and theological experts, including married laity. The report of the commission, which developed a holistic and historical interpretation on the issue and situated biology within its human totality,[214] was leaked to the Catholic press, and precipitated widespread anticipation of a reinterpretation of Catholic teaching. Paul VI's ensuing encyclical, *Humanae Vitae* (1968), which rejected these findings and reiterated traditional Catholic teaching that contraceptive birth control was *intrinsece inhonestum*, therefore caused widespread shock internationally,[215] but particularly heated, confused and polarised debate in Britain.[216] This shock was not only because many Catholics had begun using contraceptives in anticipation of a revision of the encyclical *Casti Connubi* (1930), but also because the decision seemed flagrantly to disregard the expert advice of the official panel of theologians, medical practitioners and married couples, despite the increased emphasis on 'collegiality' promulgated by the Council.[217] On behalf of the English and Welsh Hierarchy, the Bishop of Salford urged deference to the Pope's judgement and the cessation of 'wrangling even among some of our own household',[218] but opposition came from prominent laypeople such as Lady Antonia Fraser, Rosemary Haughton, Graham Greene and members of the CMAC,[219] with some formulating a collective petition to Rome.[220] Clerical disquiet was also expressed from many quarters,[221] including by some Oxford Dominicans and prominent theologians from the London theological college, Corpus Christi,[222] until a decision by the English bishops later in the year to discipline priests who continued to critique the encyclical in public dampened dissent.[223] Further consideration of the intricacies of the debates which, in the assessment of Edward Stourton, represented 'a watershed with implications that went well beyond biology',[224] far exceeds the scope of this discussion. Nevertheless, for present purposes what emerged from these protracted and fraught discussions over many years was not only a sounding of broader issues such as the place of conscience, and the importance attached to papal authority by the modern Catholic,[225] but more particularly a reconsideration of the place of sex within the sacrament of marriage. This reconfiguration could no longer be contained within the bounds of the Holy Family model.

The strains which these debates about marriage and sexuality placed upon the earlier, Marian-inspired models of marriage and family life were well described in a letter from Bruce Stewart to *The Tablet* in 1964. Urging a consideration of the Christian experiences of the laity as opposed to disembodied discussions about natural law, he perceptively concluded:

> We patently suffer from an anomaly deep in the heart of the traditional Christian attitude to sexual matters: an anomaly that on the one hand can see to it that official night prayers conclude with the splendid versicle *beata viscera Mariae Virginis … et beatua ubera quae lactaverunt Christum Dominum* … – and on the other hand, allow Our Blessed Lady to be represented in so much side-altar art as unfavoured, prudish, and flat-chested.[226]

Whilst heightened by the societal changes of the sixties, this ambivalence had been presciently appreciated by Ronald Knox in 1949 when considering the creedal statement 'conceived of the Holy Ghost, born of the Virgin Mary'. Ventriloquising non-Catholic objections, and inchoate Catholic discomfort, he commenced by considering the Incarnation:

> [Y]ou Catholics are always telling us that marriage is a high and holy vocation, that there's nothing wrong about sex, sin only comes in when sex is used as it wasn't meant to be used; surely we should have felt much more certain of that if the Blessed Virgin had been really married to St. Joseph, and they had had a family just like other people? When it's put like that, the difficulty isn't quite so easy to answer.[227]

Knox's resort to traditional teaching to answer this question for his audience of convent schoolgirls would no longer satisfy theologically educated, leftist Catholic intellectuals in the 1960s. Brian Wicker, for example, was amongst those who called for a modern moral theology of sex,[228] and sex educator Reginald Trevett drew upon contemporary psychological resources to try to develop 'a solid doctrine of sexuality based on the facts of revelation and of science'.[229] Concerned laity, invoking common sense and conscience, echoed these calls in correspondence columns, exemplified by this strident letter from Tom Flynn:

> When my wife and I agreed to marry some years ago, we made the decision not for the purpose of procreation but because of love. We do not regard ourselves merely as two biological units designed to help continue the human race. Of course, we hoped that the result, the effect of our love would be children. But children come after the expression of love. … Even in the sweet yoke of marriage the cart should not come before the horse.[230]

Tentative precursors of this more holistic approach, which acknowledged the greater importance of sexual expression, whilst continuing to prioritise procreation, were emerging in the 1950s. This is evident in a Catholic Missionary Society publication authored by its leader (and later Archbishop of Westminster) who frankly acknowledged that 'sex is important. Nobody but a fool would doubt that'.[231] Nevertheless, in explaining the Catholic understanding of marriage as sacrament, and love as 'more than sexual intercourse', Father Heenan restated traditional Catholic teaching in identifying conception as the 'primary end' of marriage, with a secondary purpose 'so that a man and a woman can be united and satisfy the desires of love'.[232] Whilst consideration and reinterpretation of the 'ends' of marriage continued to occupy continental moral theologians in the interwar period, little advance could be made in view of Pope Pius XII's prohibition in 1944 on any re-conceptualisations,[233] and a persistent societal consensus that there are 'two purposes in marriage', namely the social, served by the 'creation of children', and the individual, through 'mutual enjoyment of the sex relationship'.[234]

Signs of an institutional shift were clearly signalled by 1964, when the bishops at the Second Vatican Council produced a restatement of the 'nobility of marriage and family life', free from discussion of primary and secondary ends, and described marriage as a covenantal partnership between free and equal individuals.[235] Contained, most tellingly, within a Constitution exploring the Christian's vocation to the transformation of the world, marriage was likened to the sacramental, embodied relationship between Christ and his church explored in chapter 3. Catholic commentaries stressed that marriage should be broadly modelled on 'the absolutely unique love between Christ and his Church' but otherwise should dispense with 'abstract ideals' or 'rigid rules' and instead focus on values, leaving 'the concrete realization of these values more and more to the creative responsibility of the couples themselves'.[236]

Exemplary of this transition from one moral framework to another is the parenting manual of Patrick Rorke SJ, *Through Parents to Christ* (1960), which was comparable to earlier commentaries in advocating sex education in the home, recourse to Our Lady as a model of piety (especially for boys) and a moralising condemnation of all forms of contraception. Yet in a section provocatively entitled 'Parents, do you understand sex?', this male celibate urged Catholics to acquire more than just 'facts' and move past guilt:

> Have you ever really thought this out together, and tried to see sex and marriage as God sees them? .... He designed the passion of sex and the act of union, and he wants married folk to use it, and blesses them for so doing. They are sanctified by the right use of sex ... [for] God is most intimately close to you when you are most closely together, making you two one.[237]

In the years that followed, Catholic devotional literature stressed that this right understanding of marriage and sex should be broadly modelled on the love and intimacy understood, theologically, to exist between Christ and his Church.

At the forefront of such re-articulations was the CMAC, which in 1963 produced a marriage manual employing biology and psychology as well as theology to urge Catholics to vest family sanctity in Christ, especially in the Eucharist and the mass, by bringing themselves to the altar, placing their married life on the paten and in the chalice, and leaving the church 'saturated, impregnated with the reality of God's presence'.[238] Two decades later, as a marker of the ways in which such approaches had been incorporated into the understandings of many lay Catholics, representatives at the 1980 National Pastoral Congress (NPC) promoted an 'understanding of sexual intercourse both as a life-giving act and as a communion of love and self to one's partner', stressing the need to see in sexual love a way in which a couple 'heal and sustain each other' and 'make Christ sacramentally present to each other'.[239]

Marian models of marriage and the family were utilised in the post-war period in an attempt to formulate a fruitful and updated theology of sexuality. Yet the tension contained in the Marian framework, expressed through contradictory theological impulses that stressed the Virgin Mary's asexuality, perpetual virginity, and her intercession as an aid to sinners in the battle for 'purity', rendered the 'Holy Family' an insufficiently flexible metaphor when negotiating the broad gendered and moral changes of the post-war period. Post-conciliar theologians and the progressive laity looked to new formulations of ecclesiology, and a Christ-centred eschatology, to replace Mary as a 'model for many homesteads'. Others sought to refashion a Marian theology that would again resonate with contemporary English Catholics.

From the 'Holy Family' to the 'Easter People': the NPC and modern family life

On 29 May 1982, Wembley Stadium was once again the setting for a large gathering of English Catholics, chosen by ballot to attend a mass presided over by John Paul II, on the occasion of the first visit of a pope to England and Wales since the Reformation. The sentiments expressed in his homily on human dignity and human rights had a currency in view of the Cold War arms race and the recent commencement of hostilities in the Falklands, but nevertheless echoed the Marian themes and familial metaphors encountered thirty years earlier:

> Man conquers space but is unsure about himself ... Our society needs to recover a sense of God's loving presence ... Let us learn this from Mary our Mother ... The world has largely lost its respect for human life from the moment of conception. It is weak in upholding the indissoluble unity of marriage. It fails to support the stability and holiness of family life. There is a crisis of truth and responsibility in human relationships. Selfishness abounds.[240]

In a subsequent gathering of 250,000 people at the Knavesmore racecourse in York centred on the theme of marriage, the pontiff underlined these preoccupations, denouncing divorce, abortion and the 'spread of a contraceptive and anti-life mentality'.[241] Making reference to his 1981 Apostolic Exhortation, *Familiaris Consortio*, John Paul II was also concerned to underline the 'positive aspects of family life today', namely 'greater attention to the quality of interpersonal relationships in marriage ... promoting the dignity of women, [and] to responsible procreation'.[242] In contrast to Father Peyton's vehement denunciations of the breakdown of family life, the pontiff was compassionate, but unyielding, in advising married people to draw from Christ's example 'the strength to bear Christian witness – at times very difficult – to the indissolubility of Christian marriage'.[243]

The substantial similarities in setting, rhetorical style and theological message of the papal and Peyton visits should not, however, obscure the broad transformations in the Catholic Church which profoundly affected the intention, interpretation and reception of the Pope's exhortations on Marian devotion and family life. John Paul II's promotion of Mary as a reference point for evaluating human dignity, and human rights, was a conscious attempt to reanimate the Marian cult, after considerable reinterpretation following the Council. In this final section, the ways in which Marian devotion was extricated from the 'Holy Family' model and re-modulated in an attempt to react to the changed needs and circumstances of Catholic life will be considered. This discussion also considers the 1980 NPC, and views this unprecedented gathering of clergy and laity to discuss the state of the Catholic Church in Britain as a bellwether of the opinions and concerns of a large (and fairly influential) section of the Catholic laity about marriage and family life. Through this lens, it is clear that the stance of English Catholics on 'mixed' marriages, divorce and contraception had shifted considerably over the post-war period. Paradoxically, they also continued to hold on to certain notions of a Christian family life that corresponded to earlier ideals articulated by Father Peyton. The diverse gathering of Catholics who the Pope addressed in his Pentecostal mass at Wembley employed differing constructions of Mary, and gave formulated personalised interpretations of the 'moral demands of Christian life' on which he, as Peyton, spoke. Yet, the centrality of the 'family of the faithful' to this refashioned vision of Catholic life and practice, and the eschatological vocation of the Christian to work for a fairer and more harmonious society, remained fundamental.

Undoubtedly one of the most surprising decisions of the Council,[214] the closely contested decision of the world's bishops to incorporate their pronouncements on Mary within the broader Constitution on the Church, had an important impact on theological interpretations and clerical encouragement of Marian devotions.[215] This decision marked the end of a tendency, often observable throughout this chapter, to consider the theology surrounding Mary ('Mariology') as discrete and isolated from doctrinal teaching on Christ, the Holy Spirit and the church.[216] The resulting 'decade without Mary' was implicitly acknowledged by Pope Paul VI in his 1974 Apostolic Exhortation *Marialis Cultus*. In this document he recognised that '[c]ertain practices of piety that not long ago seemed suitable for expressing the religious sentiments of individuals and of Christian communities seem today inadequate'.[217] Acknowledging that one of the chief difficulties then facing Catholics was 'the discrepancy existing between some aspects of this devotion and modern anthropological discoveries', Paul VI drew special attention to the 'picture of the Blessed Virgin presented in a certain type of devotional literature [which] cannot easily be reconciled with today's life-style, especially the way women live today'.[248] Theologians such as Karl Rahner contemporaneously sought to develop the Council's insights which removed Mary from the 'sacred family', and relocated her amongst the community of the faithful, as a model of perfect Christian and human discipleship.[249] Within this gradually emerging strand of Marian theology, the post-war proclamation of the Doctrine of the Assumption (1950) was re-interpreted, in ways that minimised its anti-materialist connotations and Cold War context, to celebrate Mary's 'bodily' redemption as an eschatological anticipation of the destiny of all Christians.[250] As an extension of these trends, liberation theologians drew upon post-conciliar scriptural developments in exegesis to recover the poor, working-class Nazarene woman Miriam as a model and inspiration for those in the third world trapped by poverty and structural powerlessness.[251]

From the perspective of many of the laity in England who had since the post-war period witnessed the disappearance of the 'Hail Mary' from the liturgical context, had lamented the removal of statues of 'Our Blessed Lady' from prominent positions near the altar, and had missed the month of May processions, rosary devotions and 'St Joseph the Worker' celebrations, these developments represented a clear rupture. Older Catholics such as Mrs E. M. Carey of Liverpool wrote to *The Universe* in 1974, prompted by Cardinal Heenan's response to *Marialis Cultus*, to ask the most pressing question: 'Where has the old devotion gone?'[252]

As a form of devotion considered quintessentially Catholic in the twentieth century, the rosary was a litmus test for many of the changing attitudes to Mary in the post-conciliar period. With the concentrated focus on the liturgy already explored, and an 'increased appreciation of the presence of the resurrected Christ as mediator, teacher and liberator', this left, in the words of one interpreter of Vatican II, 'little place for Mary as a relay station to Jesus'.[253] Commentators recommending the rosary to the generation socialised after the Council stressed the need for a 'well-meditated' rosary, and couched their arguments in terms that appealed to its scriptural basis (e.g. the Lukan Magnificat) and meditative qualities.[254] In a message to English and Welsh Catholics in 1974, Cardinal Heenan confirmed this trend, arguing that the re-naming of the Marian feast of Candlemas (which traditionally celebrated Mary's 'churching') to 'the Presentation of Our Lord' was not intended 'to displace Mary but to identify her even more closely with her Son'.[255] Clerical apologists such as Canon Richard Stewart, responding to an article by *Tablet* columnist

Terence Morris on the 'disuse' of the rosary, urged a reappraisal of the devotion as 'a prayer most suitable for us today, a Gospel prayer, a Christ-centred prayer – something far removed from those "crudest forms of Mariology" which Mr Morris sweepingly links with the old pattern of rosary, sermon and benediction'.[256] Mainstream, populist Catholic organs such as *The Universe* ran articles denouncing liberals who 'consider the Rosary outmoded and irrelevant in this surging, post-conciliar age', and pointed to growing Protestant interest in the practice, to reassure the readership in their continued devotions, despite the trend for extemporaneous prayer in 'this Space Age Church'.[257] Yet even highly conservative, traditional devotional journals like the *Catholic Fireside* felt compelled to cast their instructional pieces in inter-denominational terms, insisting that 'devotion to the Mother of the Lord is in accord with the deep desire and aims of the ecumenical movement'.[258]

In addition to these substantive concerns for a more Christ-centred, scriptural and ecumenical prayer, preoccupations in 1960s Britain around generational differentiation, new age spirituality and the premium placed on spontaneity and 'authenticity' were seen to militate against the rosary which was cast as monotonous, routinised, and part of the 'folk piety' of the older generation. Voicing these concerns in 1968, and seeking to assuage the misgivings of ordinary Northern Catholics, Father Richard Foley wrote:

> You meet Catholics nowadays (especially younger ones) who feel a little uneasy about Mary's status since Vatican II. … Are old-style Marian devotions consistent with today's mentality and mood? In particular, is the rosary suited to sophisticated, progressive, mature Catholics?[259]

While *The Universe* urged an appreciation of Marian devotions as appropriate to contemporary, post-conciliar Catholicism, the once-pietistic devotional journal *Novena* invoked Vatican II *peritus*, and the clerical endorsement of the Bishop of Middlesbrough, who spoke scathingly of a 'certain element in *avant garde* spirituality … that looks down its nose at the simplicities of traditional piety'.[260]

Writing in a 1970 article in the convert-orientated *Catholic Gazette*, the Jesuit Guy Brinkworth was even more combative in dismissing as 'theological Mary Quants' those 'vociferous, ubiquitous and self-appointed theological "whiz-kids" [who] are busy banishing our rosary as "meaningless mumbo jumbo" and "out of date"'.[261] Admitting, begrudgingly, that the rosary could easily become repetitive if merely recited rather than 'prayed', this former London schoolmaster commended the long history of the rosary, but also made recourse to the rosary's 'therapeutic' properties and the existence of comparable forms of 'metonomic contemplation' in other world religions to justify its re-discovery.[262] He concluded by drawing a link between 'patter and popular music', citing a 1969 sermon of Pope Paul VI who likened the repetitive lyrics and simple rhythms of popular music to saying a 'decade of the rosary', in an attempt to convince a younger generation of the essential place of Marian devotion within modern Catholicism.

For an older generation of Mancunian Catholics like Margaret and Nora, ingrained in the traditions of family rosary, such academic arguments were unnecessary and the rosary remains a daily component of their prayer life to this day. Among the generation reaching adulthood in the 1970s, however, these calls to renewal of the rosary and an insistence on its relevance, had mixed responses. Post-conciliar Catholic Mary continues to have regular 'chats' with Our Lady, but admits that she and her two daughters do not say the rosary regularly, save during October at their Catholic school.[263] Moreover, preceding Mitzi's humorous recounting of the family rosary interrupting her childhood games, her eighteen-year-old son Patrick confessed to having 'done the rosary less than ten times in my life really'. This was despite a recent trip to Lourdes on a youth pilgrimage, leading him to say: 'I don't think it's a thing that modern-day people my age do really, whereas it was a kind of norm for past generations'.[264] In speaking of the Virgin Mary, he explained that 'she's a woman first' and that he 'wouldn't really place her ... above any of the saints really', but concluded:

> PS: obviously if you have a Catholic faith, you're obviously devoted to Mary but not to the extent that past generations did. ... There's still an essential aspect of it, but not to the same extent.[265]

For a younger generation of English Catholics, the rosary and Mary's elevated status in the celestial family had given away to a more liturgically orientated, and Christocentric, Christianity.

Nevertheless, also present is a sense that Mary remains intensely important in her relationship to Christ, and some forms of Marian-related but transformed traditions, such as pilgrimage to Lourdes, continue to attract young Catholics. For some, like 72-year-old former Sister of

Charity and Catholic head teacher Judith, this post-conciliar questioning has itself facilitated the recent growth of a more personal relationship to Mary, whereas daily rosary with the religious community had left her unmoved. Explaining that, in her youth, Mary was 'a presence, someone who's always there without specifically paying attention to her' or 'somebody there up on a statue … with her blue veil and whatever', her contemporary reading of theologians like Teilhard de Chardin and Celtic spiritual writer John O'Donoghue had enabled her to see:

> JE: Mary, you know, holding Jesus on her knee. … supporting him and letting him grow as a baby … the human side of Mary … as a Jewish, just an ordinary Jewish woman. We forget that. Not that we forget that, I don't think it's even sunk in. Who did all the ordinary things.[266]

For Judith, as a single woman who spent many years in a highly regimented religious order, the earlier model of Mary as the Holy Mother of the Nazarene household did not resonate with her everyday life, nor offer theological, or spiritual resources, as it was able to do for some of her Catholic contemporaries. Moreover, despite the previously discussed attempts throughout the 1950s to render Mary as an 'ordinary Jewish woman', Judith felt alienated by the Marian devotions she encountered which celebrated the celestial Virgin on her pedestal. However, when understood as a corollary of a relationship to Christ, and cast into relief by the insights of liberation theology, and a world-focused eschatology, Marian devotion in a transformed guise might retain a place in the spiritual life of an 'Easter People', as the Catholics of England gathered at the NPC designated themselves.

Convened in Liverpool in early May 1980 and comprising 2,115 delegates representing parishes, church organisations and specific ethnic groups,[267] the NPC was opened by the Bishop of Liverpool who spoke to themes of renewal, Christian witness, and the social outreach required of an 'Easter People'.[268] This four-day conference was the culmination of extensive consultation papers, parochial study groups and official reports, and while intended as an opinion-gathering exercise, it also resulted in an unprecedented catechetical opportunity and means of adult apostolic formation.[269] As Bishop Holland explained to his flock in a 1979 Pastoral, in terms suggesting renewal and revival, and slightly reminiscent of the language used for the Rosary Crusade, the call to the Congress was:

> an S.O.S. ... [to] rally us sinners in the Catholic Church for a great occasion. ... What is it all about? Nothing less than the salvation of souls. Given the main theme, it could not be otherwise. The banner-head is 'Jesus Christ, the Way, the Truth and the Life'. We are publicly pledging ourselves – individually and as families, as parishes, deaneries, dioceses ... to one source of human happiness here and hereafter – the Man Jesus Christ.[270]

However, there were also marked differences between the NPC and Father Peyton's nationwide tour, not only in the priority given to lay perspectives but also, in the words of complaint by one priest, in the 'lack of reference to the Mother of God in the NPC literature'.[271] While this claim was contested by the clerical Congress organiser who produced examples of Marian prayers and hymns used at the liturgical celebrations,[272] the absence of extensive references to Our Lady or the Holy Family, particularly in the huge discussion topic of the 'Family and Society', was indeed marked. What featured instead, given the 'banner-head' theme of this gathering, was an intense focus on the parables, scripture references and resurrection-focused theology throughout.[273]

In prayers for the Congress' preparations distributed to all parishes in England and Wales, there was a traditional acknowledgment, reminiscent of those voiced by Peyton, that:

> The family has been called 'the domestic church', where people learn to love God and each other. Prayer together is the heart of the family life.[274]

Yet the remainder of the prayer continued in a distinctly modern register, acknowledging the fragility of modern family life:

> Father, you have called us to live together,
> As a single family,
> United by the ties of love,
> Sharing our tears and our laughter,
> Caring for one another and supporting one another.[275]

The emphasis within the remainder of the prayer was on the difficulties confronting families and the courage required of them, closing with the commendation of uniting these prayers 'to those of Our Lady as we say: "Hail Mary ..."'. The pamphlet concluded with the express statement that while intended as guidance, these prayers should not be prescriptive for 'each family, each group, learns to pray in its own way'.[276] This leaflet might be held to be symptomatic of the changes and continuities in Catholic spirituality when compared with the early 1950s. While there remained a stress on the sacredness of the family, and a passing nod to Mary, the emphasis had moved from anthropomorphic personification of the divine hierarchy, and exhortations to emulate the 'Holy Family', to a perspective that started with the particular Christian family, a more collaborative model of decision-making, and a recognition of spiritual needs beyond standard formula prayers.[277]

These themes were developed in preparations for, and presentations to, the Congress, with the Salford delegates reflecting on the corrosive effects of the 'pace of modern living' on family life and higher expectations through 'better educational opportunities'.[278] They went on to provide some 'practical suggestions' for addressing these pressures on families, spanning spiritual formation as well as socialisation:

1. The family should do things together, e.g. Mass, Confession, etc.
2. Families should discuss each other's problems.
3. Control TV input, censor books and papers.
4. Special care for elderly within the group.
5. The Church can help by fostering family feeling in the Parish.[279]

The National Report was less anecdotal and more analytical in the identification of materialism, affluence and the drive to long working hours as 'divisive of the family group' as well as the social climate, detailed as not eating together, the press, cinema and television, which were seen as counterproductive to many of the 'qualities needed for a stable Christian marriage'.[280] This reference to 'Christian marriage' was important, voiced in the context of a marked increase in so-called 'mixed marriages' by the 1980s,[281] and described by Hornsby-Smith as 'a major dissolution of the boundaries which for decades had safeguarded religious identity'.[282] The modification of canon law to make such marriages easier, most especially in removing the 'promises' to have children raised in 'the faith' from the non-Catholic party to the Catholic party, should be contextualised within a flourishing post-conciliar ecumenical context.[283] By 1979 when the Salford delegates reflected on such unions, it was clear that they were more concerned to draw a distinction between 'Christian marriage' and 'Civil marriage'.[284] Testimony to this shift, if compared to Father Waterhouse's 1947 Marriage initiative, was a publication of the CTS in

1979, in which Monsignor G. R. Leonard argued that 'help for marriages and families ought to be organised on an ecumenical basis' for 'we are not alone. There are Christians who share with us our sacramental vision of human love, marriage and family'.[285]

Within all of the pre-circulated discussion papers, and the recorded Congress discussions in one of its most controversial areas, 'Sector C: Marriage and Family', there was an explicit recognition by those 360 delegates specifically considering these issues that the projected 1950s 'ideal' of the family was no longer typical or feasible. For example, the key discussion paper provided a vignette of the typical English parish for focused reflection, and offered the description of a single mother parishioner bringing up a four-year-old on her own.[286] The example could equally have drawn upon another model prevalent in most congregations, namely that of remarried spouses with a combined family of children.

For some Catholics, there were ways of modernising and rehabilitating the previously prevalent 'Holy Family' ideal, as forty-year-old Mary, when asked whether Mary and her family provide a model for Catholics today, suggested:

> MH: I don't really know. Well, I mean, I suppose they were the family, the Holy Family. (long pause). I mean, obviously Mary lost Jesus at an early age and then like went with the other disciples. So I suppose in this day and age, yeah, there are a lot of blended families. The family's not just made up these days of just mum and dad and – [287]

The delegates from Salford in the 1979 preparations for the Congress also called for a more flexible understanding of the 'family', demurring:

> The Church is now in a great hurry to make the family supreme but, in doing so, it concentrated on a narrow concept of mother, father and children. The natural family includes cousins living away from home, maiden aunts and bachelor uncles, not to mention friends and acquaintances – these members of the church family seem to be forgotten at the moment.[288]

What these perspectives share is the recognition that the mid-century model of the stable and homogeneous 'nuclear' family was no longer socially tenable, and was, perhaps, an aberration from a broader understanding that had prevailed at the beginning of the twentieth century (and in earlier centuries) in Britain, and which persisted in many other places.[289] Nevertheless, what they also illustrate is the continuing recognition, in the words of the Final Report, that the family 'in its varied forms' is the 'basic community in society' and the 'universal experience of humanity... [with] a profound influence on spiritual and emotional growth'.[290] Moreover, the family was affirmed as the way in which 'most people are called to holiness of life' and the church to mission in the 'everyday world'.[291] While there had been a clear transformation in the forms and features of family life over the course of the century, the delegates gathered in 1980 to voice the opinions and perspectives of the practising laity in parishes throughout England and Wales articulated an understanding of the 'holiness of family life' which would be broadly consistent, in substance, with the papal exhortation two years later.

This broader correspondence should not, however, detract from the considerable diversity in interpretation and application of this continued valorisation of family life by the 1980s. Pope John Paul II's uncompromising homilies on modern morality and family instability were substantially different in tone from the commentaries of the NPC and the perspectives of many of those who took part in the papal visit, such as the 250,000 people gathered for mass in Heaton Park, Manchester on 31 May 1982.[292] Institutionally endorsed publications such as the CTS *Marriage and the Family* (1979) acknowledged that there was 'a distance between "theory" (hopes, expectations, the teaching of the Church) and the experience of family life exposed to "the wind of change"', and lamented this sense of isolation from the church which can be felt for 'the sincere Catholic'.[293] Similar sentiments were expressed by one of the foremost commentators in this area, the committed Catholic and practising psychiatrist Jack Dominian.[294] Writing on the 'deep awareness that marriage in the West is in the midst of a considerable transition',[295] his numerous publications throughout the 1970s discussed 'the New Morality', Freudian psychology, the goodness of sexuality and 'openness to children'. They advocated a liberal and non-judgemental perspective on these issues but one which was still faithful to church teachings.[296]

In a series of articles in 1979 entitled 'The Family Today', Dr Dominian began with an article on 'Permanency', identifying the modern arguments about 'the realisation of human potential' and 'fulfilment' and arguing that 'it is the task of Christianity to show that, since suffering is an essential part of any relationship, it is better to channel the energy and effort into achieving the desired result in a continuous relationship'.[297] Subsequent articles also demonstrated this combination of pastoral realism with an attempt to re-articulate a modern Christian ethos, particularly around divorce and remarriage, which had become major issues for the churches.[298]

Rising divorce rates after the Second World War, culminating in the Divorce Act (1969), and the greater tolerance of divorce in the Archbishop of Canterbury's report, *Putting Asunder* (1966), had created tensions for Catholics unable themselves to adhere to the church's traditional insistence on the indissolubility of marriage.[299] The lay delegates preparing for the NPC in Birmingham articulated the strong feelings of many within the parishes in identifying the needs of divorced Catholics as an area for modification, and reform, in Catholic teaching and practice.[300] Starkly contrasting with the attitudes of the Catholic bishops at the Royal Commission on Marriage and Divorce in 1952, and the uncompromising position of many writers attacking the 'selfishness of the divorce courts'[301] and the devastation to children,[302] the NPC urged compassion towards the one in three marriages in Britain that now ended in separation and divorce:

> The church needs to find ways both of witnessing to the life-long and exclusive commitment of Christian marriage and yet showing understanding and giving aid to those involved in such marital breakdown, including those who have entered into stable second marriages.[303]

This call for a re-modelled church teaching which would acknowledge the complex realities of married life whilst upholding the Christian ideal signals well the shift manifested in much of the Catholic press and marriage-related commentaries away from a soteriological approach, based on duty, law and understandings of 'sin'. The newer theological emphasis, which emphasised 'the presence of Christ in marriage',[304] was one that took greater account of the increasing cultural priority on the experiential, psychological and self-expressive aspects of human relationships.

This tension between the letter and the spirit of the law was most clearly manifest in the debates on sexuality and contraception at the NPC and subsequently in the Catholic press. In an article published in anticipation of the Congress, 'When Law and Love Conflict', Clifford Longley described the situation in Britain regarding the 'laws of marriage':

> There does appear to be a shift taking place in attitudes towards these legal requirements. ... One was either an observant Catholic or an ex-Catholic and the very expression 'lapsed' carried the overtones of outsider-ness, of

no-longer-belongingness. But recent and reliable surveys into the Roman Catholic population for this country show a significant minority who wish to go on regarding themselves as 'Catholics' even if they do not obey some or all, of the rules.[305]

Delegates from the Diocese of Salford preparing for the Liverpool gathering adhered strictly to the discussion paper's questions and in the absence of an official mandate refrained from an official report on the matter of contraception.[306] However, those from the Archdiocese of Birmingham explicitly acknowledged that 'despite the lack of any question touching explicitly on birth control this came up frequently ... as a source of problems in marriage' (original emphasis).[307] The lay representatives called for 'more clarity' and a 'more positive approach in the Church's teaching', recognising the role of 'conscience'.[308] Citing results from questionnaires in two Birmingham parishes which reported that the church's teaching was unrealistic and disregarded medical, social and financial considerations, the area of strongest support for the church's teachings (77%) was from the 55+ age group, showing a clear generational split.

This perspective was reflected in the NPC's report, which called for a fundamental re-examination of the church's teaching on marriage, sexuality and contraception, drawing a distinction between authentic official instruction and infallible teaching, challenging 'the teaching Church ... [to] take notice of the insights of married Christians into the meaning of their life-long sexual relationships'.[309] It called for a fundamental re-examination of the guidance on marriage, on sexuality and on contraception', with an openness to 'change and development'[310] and, in a previous section on 'the role of sexuality in marriage', stressed that 'intercourse can be a life-giving act between the couple even when, as in the vast majority of occasions, it does not produce a new life'.[311]

Responses to the NPC were mixed in the Catholic press. *The Tablet's* editorial welcomed the delegates' call for 'change or development – to our minds the words in this context are virtually synonymous', and recognised that 'such issues are strong meat, not for children'.[312] It concluded by commending the way in which these controversial issues were discussed 'in the atmosphere of respectful, serious honesty and mutual trust created by the hierarchy's own initial invitation'.[313] The *Catholic Herald* was also complimentary in citing the Congress as an example of the growth and maturity of the laity in voicing honest dissent and caring criticism,[314] with the Congress' special correspondent stressing the diversity of the gathering which 'really did turn out to be a genuine cross-section of people and not the unrepresentative group of middle-class activists that some had predicted'.[315]

However, a quite divergent stance emerged from the strongly conservative, mostly northern and older, mass-going readership of *The Universe* which, in advance of the Congress, conducted a 'ballot of issues' to which 3,500 persons responded. These responses expressed concern about the revised liturgy, support for traditional devotions such as benediction and the rosary, and a strongly disapproving stance on abortion, euthanasia and birth control.[316] This 'alternative' litmus test of lay opinion, and the subsequent coverage of the Congress, drew some strong criticism for its 'partial and sceptical' stance that had 'seriously misrepresented the proceedings'.[317] Yet other correspondents wrote despairing of the gap between the NPC's findings and papal teaching,[318] and *The Universe*'s columnists continued to question whether the Congress Report represented the *'sensus fidelium'*, or the true faith of the laity.[319] Whilst *The Universe*'s editor in personal correspondence took pains to praise the sincerity and diligence of the delegates in tackling 'the sometimes difficult subjects on the agenda',[320] the newspaper continued to assert the substantial 'disagreement between our readers and the Congress ... on contraception' and their vote against change to the church's teaching 'by 2,532 to 732'.[321]

Given that *The Universe* has remained the Catholic newspaper of choice for the Mancunian Catholics interviewed for this book, while they manifest a diversity of perspectives on issues of marriage, sexuality and contraception even now, perhaps this popular poll, and the editorial stance on the NPC, was more reflective of an older generational cohort than distinctions based on class or locality. In any event, by presenting the NPC's sentiments in favour of development of church teaching on contraception to the Synod on the Family in Rome in 1981, the Archbishop of Westminster, Cardinal Hume, and Archbishop Worlock of Liverpool, found themselves in the vanguard of progressive Catholic opinion. Both members of the Hierarchy were at pains to distinguish the theological difficulties of 'good, conscientious and faithful sons and daughters of the Church' about the use of contraception[322] from the 'new morality' epitomised in the British *annus mirabilis* of 1967 which legalised abortion, homosexual acts between consenting adults, and the provision of birth control advice through the NHS.[323] Rather, as the theologian John Burgess recognised, the sexuality debate had become 'the vehicle for getting at the most basic questions of faith', not just the role of conscience and papal authority within the Catholic Church but, more importantly, 'what it means to be human before God'.[321] Such concerns underpinned the papal reference in the gathering at Wembley to 'the crisis of truth and responsibility in human relationships', and the recovery of a 'sense of God's loving presence' giving rise to the concentration on a Christian anthropology later in his papacy.[325] For the Catholics gathered in Liverpool in 1980 for the largest lay-constituted conference ever held in Britain, their deliberations and collective discussions led them to conclude that Christ's presence was affirmed within lifelong marital and sexual relationships, in addition to, and independent of, a loving and creative act of conception. It was their contention that the church discipline appropriate for an 'Easter People' should look rather to the spirit than to the letter of the law, as did its founder and Saviour.

Alongside the increasing recognition of the married relationship as something prior to, and separate from, parenthood, the ever growing proportion of 'working mothers' across class backgrounds (as part of an international trend) who sought fulfilment and remuneration outside the home and beyond their roles as mothers challenged the mid-century emphasis on Mary predominantly as 'handmaiden and mother', fulfilled exclusively by her home-based maternity.[326] In the socially tumultuous interwar years,[327] many publications articulated a greater cognisance of 'girls … longings for careers and independence after marriage', yet others used the example of Mrs Jellaby in *Bleak House* as a salutary warning to those who ignored their families and instead called for a 'Christian feminism that regards marriage and having children as a great career in itself'.[328]

By the middle of the century, with the broader re-valorisation of maternity and childbearing, instructional commentaries were less apologetic and more insistent that 'any wise mother will sacrifice any career of her own for the sake of her children … Others who have not her ties will do the public work in her place, but no one else can do her mothering for her'.[329] With the pressure in certain sectors of the post-war welfare state requiring women's labour, and the growing levels of affluence and consumption, the Catholic media began to address the issue of working women, across all strata of society, coming home from the workplace tired, jaded and 'unfitted for the job for which they became mothers'.[330] Addressing the frequently voiced arguments of women who worked to provide more for their children, these writers insisted emphatically: 'YOUR CHILDREN DO NOT WANT THESE THINGS: THEY WANT YOU' (original emphasis).[331] Instructional morality stories like 'Sauce for the Goose' painted a picture of the domestic disharmony resulting from an insecure male breadwinner and the materialistic, impatient desires for vacuum cleaners or refrigerators at the expense of the 'children's welfare'.[332]

In a similar vein, Margaret Saville's 1962 article 'Danger – Wives at Work' generated a fierce and heated correspondence in the *Catholic Herald*,[333] with some women welcoming her clarion call[334] and others dismissing this 'ill-informed and offensive article'.[335] Economic imperatives, rather than strong feminist principles, tended to be the ground on which these issues were debated, and, by 1980, 62% of English married women were working (though half of this figure was in part-time employment).[336]

The ideological perspective of English Catholics towards this trend was quite varied, in keeping with a broad diversity of opinions within wider British society.[337] Editorials in the Catholic press discussed the Equal Opportunities Commission's findings that 22% of all working women would like to stay home if they could,[338] whereas the historically conservative, 'family-oriented', Union of Catholic Mothers caused some controversy in 1980 in making a public statement that 'working mums are here to stay' and 'women's liberation' had much work to do in addressing the 'second shift' that mothers do at home.[339] Congress preparations elicited the dimensions of these conflicting opinions, with the Birmingham laity reporting 'two differing points of view', but 'urging the Church to come to terms with reality' and to 'act supportively' rather than 'making such mothers feel guilty'.[340] The Salford report, compiled by Fr Duggan SJ of the Holy Name parish, similarly reported 'diverse opinions', particularly about the stresses that existed in the family,[341] but was more cautious in reporting that 'the general consensus was not against married women's working, provided their families did not suffer as a result' and that such work was not just for 'luxuries'.[342] The NPC itself sought to straddle these two positions in recognising economic necessity, loneliness or the desire for a higher standard of living as 'good and acceptable reasons' for women going out to work. It called for the ending of discrimination against women by employers, whilst also advocating 'more emphasis … on the positive contribution to human well-being performed by women who devote themselves to home-making'.[343]

These complex issues were also increasingly combined with discussions specifically on women's status and power in society and the church, and informed by the broader cultural and intellectual inroads made by second-wave feminism by the late 1970s.[344] While not the most hotly debated issue at the Congress, there was a frank acknowledgment of 'a serious lack of balance in the Church between the sexes because the Church was led, organised and largely planned by men'.[345] To this end, the NPC made a recommendation for the church to provide more extensive roles, and enable women to become more fully involved, beyond their restriction to 'traditional "domestic" jobs like church cleaning and preparing first communion breakfasts'.[346] This identification of women, in church as at home, with the domestic, and the challenges to this model posed experientially by 'working mothers' and intellectually by the demands of second-wave feminism, also led to a dissolution of the 'holy homestead' model and Mary as the perfect 1950s housewife. As Kevin observed, from a present-focused perspective:

> KF: So those traditional devotions in that way appealed to a particular … unless you adapt it in a way that people understand it will not have the cultural significance that it had then. My mum would have been at home having the twins, myself, the kids – short periods at work – nevertheless the focus was the home. Now you've got a double mortgage to survive, so you've got double incomes. Where's Mary in all that? That's an interesting one – maybe I'll think about it. Where's Mary in all that?[347]

This task of reappraising Marian devotion and the ways in which it might provide a model of faith and strength to contemporary Christians, unbundled from past inter-denominational controversies or constraining understandings of women's role in the family and the church, has been an agenda for the final two decades of the twentieth century.

Devotion to St Joseph as part of the 'holy homestead' model was in a similar state of transition towards the latter part of the twentieth century. Though at the apogee of its institutional endorsement when the spouse of Mary was included by Pope John XXIII in the Roman Canon, and invoked in the litany of saints in the opening and closing speeches of the Second Vatican Council, these were somewhat forced and overly earnest institutional promotions of a saint worthy of greater veneration.[348] By the time of the NPC, the nexus between St Joseph and a re-conceived Catholic fatherhood was no longer evident, and the sole reference to 'St Joseph the Worker' was in the delegates' (non-enacted) proposal to upgrade his liturgical feast day to 'emphasise the importance of the world of work.'[349] Part of the explanation for the diminishing prominence of this devotion lies with the post-conciliar trend towards a more masculine, robust liturgical Christology previously described, and evidenced in a 1960 *Catholic Gazette* article which called upon fathers to lead their family to the altar rails and thus reclaim their vocations as head of the family and leader of the home.[350] By the 1980s, the anti-communist and celebratory 'working class' dimensions of the devotion had ceased to resonate with many Catholics, concerned about the Cold War nuclear superpowers (but not communist ideology) and now aspirational in their middle class identification.

Perhaps the most important explanation for St Joseph's devotional disappearance was also the marked instability in understandings of fatherhood. This was related to women's increasing capacities as supplementary breadwinners and also to a greater psychological appreciation of the role and importance of fatherhood by both women and men. Something of this transition may be appreciated in the 1970s editions of *Novena* which had moved from addressing an almost exclusively female audience to including articles on DIY and male fashion,[351] challenging correspondence on reappraising masculinity and femininity,[352] and a letter from a father to St Gerard, previously known as 'the Mother's Saint' to ask for readers' prayers for his collapsed marriage and a reunion with his pregnant wife.[353] An article in the 1970 June edition addressed to male readers provided tips on 'How to Keep your Wife Happy' and counselled that something more than 'the modern panaceas of a fatter pay packet or a better adjusted physical love' might be required.[354] It went on to advise that:

> Most wives don't particularly want their husbands to help with all the small chores of nappy changing, feeding babies with sieved food, or pushing the pram in the park. But once the children get to walking age, then the husband is a very necessary part of family life.
> It is very difficult for a wife to bring up children on her own.[355]

Some influential Catholic spokespeople, such as the President of the Laity Commission, went even further:

> Society and the Church has tended to assume that being a wife and mother comes naturally. Fatherhood was seen as a desirable adjunct to the satisfactions of being the breadwinner. The pressures of living in a technological age, and the insights of modern knowledge, make it clear that parental responsibilities

and marital relationships are deeply important to both men and women, and demand a great deal more than blind instinctive reaction.[356]

Devotion to St Joseph, less developed and less multi-faceted than its Marian counterpart, was not flexible enough to be mobilised for adapting constructions of fatherhood and masculinity, the sharing of domestic responsibilities or as a foil for the female 'wage packet' provider.[357] For, as Mary laughingly suggested, when speaking of her 'chats' with Mary and asked about her devotion to St Joseph:

> MH: I think he's, I suppose, I wouldn't – I mean I know Joseph but I would pray to Our Lady. I wouldn't think of Joseph, I suppose he's like (laughs) … I mean, he's the husband isn't he? It tends to be the woman that does most of it. I know that's not right, but…[358]

Despite concerted institutional efforts to reanimate devotion to St Joseph as both a worker and devoted father with the 'Christ child on his knee', this interviewee articulated clearly the social and spiritual difficulties encountered in the promotion of his cult. Despite a brief resurgence, St Joseph remained a residual identity dependent upon, and deferential to, longer-standing Marian narratives. Rapid social change and feminist critique had concentrated attention upon the transformation of models of marriage, motherhood and gendered employment, but by the 1980s, and even today as Mary hints, constructions of masculinity and fatherhood remain in transition.[359] Writing in 1980 in *The Universe* on issues to be addressed at the forthcoming NPC, the Catholic Conservative MP for Bath, Chris Patten, highlighted the little appreciated family issues of concern to his constituency as fathers' difficulties with custody, divorce settlements and issues of fair access to their children.[360] As was acknowledged in a publication compiled collectively from working papers for the 1981 Synod on the Family, the Canon Law Society of Great Britain and Ireland and the Archdiocese of Liverpool's preparations for the NPC:

> there is a need to think hard about the role of the father in the family and how to help him to fulfil that responsibility. He is overlooked in current schemes, and he often feels increasingly insecure, especially about the proper exercise of authority in the family.[361]

The Catholics in England who wholeheartedly welcomed the historic visit of the Pope to England in 1982 and heeded his message that 'the future of your society, the future of humanity, passes by way of the family',[362] entertained profoundly altered understandings of private and collective prayer, family life and their relationship with religious authority to those of their parents and grandparents gathered for the rosary rallies and the other public Marian professions of the faith in the 1950s. This re-conception involved a movement away from the use of the Blessed Virgin Mary and her husband, St Joseph, as a 'model for many homesteads' towards a more Christologically underpinned but also psychologically informed and existential, experientially grounded understanding of marriage, family life and gender relations. Moreover, while Catholics at the end of the twentieth century continued to acknowledge the importance of Mary, suspicion about the 'outdated' nature of the rosary, debates about 'working mothers' and increasing recognition of women's marginalisation within the church led to the erosion of the mid-century emphasis on Mary's holy maternity and home making skills. For a younger generation following the Second Vatican Council, Mary remained 'Our Lady' and 'Our Mother', but the meaning and import attached to these terms had shifted considerably.

The fulcrum for all these transitions were debates initiated in the postwar period but bursting onto the public scene with the *Humanae Vitae* crisis in 1968, around sexuality and contraception and the broader transition away from an understanding of sex in terms of sin and purity, duty and self-discipline. What emerged amongst a newer generation of practising Catholics in the post-conciliar period was a more overtly embodied, incarnational approach which acknowledged the integrity (and sacramentality) of loving relationships over doctrinal legalities, and redefined marriage, parenthood and work without reference to the previously dominant Marian model. Having considered the profound changes in understandings of the liturgy and the Eucharist, and the repositioning of Mary, 'first of the saints' within church teaching and Catholic devotional life, the next chapter will consider 'the communion of the saints' and shifting constructions of virtue within English Catholic and civic society.

Notes

1   'Magnificent and Moving Pageant at Wembley', *Catholic Times*, 1 August 1952, 12.
2   *Ibid.*

3   *MovieTone Newsreel* 'Family Rosary Hyde Park Story 57475' www.movietone.com/ N_POPUP_Player.cfm?action=playVideo&assetno=73988 (free site registration required for access).
4   Yarnold, *Pope*, 35.
5   Bishop Marshall, 'An Advent Pastoral Letter on the Christian Family', 19 November 1945, 8 (SDA, Box 226).
6   Dominican Tertiary, *Simple Rosary Meditations* (London: Burns and Oates, 1951), 2.
7   See www.fatherpeyton.org/cause-for-sainthood.html.
8   P. J. Peyton, *The Ear of God* (London: Burns and Oates, 1954), 136.
9   'Thousands Flock to Hear Fr Peyton', *Catholic Times*, 9 May 1952, 1, 12.
10 '85,000 Throng Rally in Birkenhead', *Catholic Times*, 6 June 1952, 3.
11 'Cardinal's Call to Family Prayer: 30,000 at Rally', *Daily Telegraph and Morning Post*, 7 July 1952, 5; 'Return to Family Prayer Urged: Pope's Letter Read at Rally', *Manchester Guardian*, 28 July 1952, 2; cf. 'Family Rosary Preached in Hyde Park: Crowd of 100,000 hears Fr Peyton', *Catholic Times*, 11 July 1952, 1, 12.
12 'Rosary Crusade Sweeps to Climax', *Catholic Times*, 18 July 1952, 1.
13 Bishop T. Flynn, 'Foreward' in Peyton, *Ear*, vii.
14 *MovieTone Newsreel* 'Family Rosary Crusade' Story 57578' www.movietone.com/ N_POPUP_Player.cfm?action=playVideo&assetno=96758 (free site registration required for access).
15 'Why Recite the Rosary' *The Catholic Times*, 11 July 1952, 7.
16 Dominican Sisters, *My Rosary Book* (London: Catholic Truth Society, 1944), n.p.
17 In M. Ward, *The Splendour of the Rosary* (London: Sheed and Ward, 1946), 20.
18 M. Dominic, *A Rosary Chain* (Oxford: Blackfriars Publications, 1947); E. Quinn, 'Mass or Elite?', *The Clergy Review* (1952) 37(12), 726–31.
19 Peyton, *Ear*, 108.
20 Interview, Margaret and Nora, Recording STE 022 at 16.47–16.53. See also Peter, who recalled the '8 o'clock' routine of family rosary at his grandparents' house', at 58.58–59.36.
21 Interview, Mitzi at 9.54–10.31.
22 Interview, Tony at 20.25.
23 *Ibid*, 21.12–22.25.
24 *Ibid*, 23.11–23.42.
25 Interview, Francis at 36.50–36.52.
26 *Ibid*, 36.53–38.15.
27 Interview, Mitzi at 11.33–11.58.
28 Interview, Joseph, Recording STE 023 at 19.34–19.39.
29 Interview, Tom at 26.49–27.40.
30 Interview, Christine, Recording STE 017 at 20.28–20.30.
31 B. B. Lindsey and W. Evans, *The Companionate Marriage* (London: Brentano's Ltd, 1928).
32 Davidoff, *Family Story*, 190.
33 J. Finch and P. Summerfield, 'Social Reconstruction and the Emergence of Companionate Marriage, 1945–59' in D. Clark (ed.), *Marriage, Domestic Life and Social Change: Writings for Jacqueline Burgoyne (1944–88)* (London: Routledge, 1991), 7.

34 *Ibid.* See also A. Giddens, *The Transformation of Intimacy: Sexuality, Love and Eroticism in Modern Societies* (Cambridge: Polity Press, 1992).

35 C. Langhamer, 'Love, Selfhood and Authenticity in Post-War Britain', *Cultural and Social History* 9(2) (2012), 277–97; 'Love and Courtship in Mid-Twentieth Century England', *Historical Journal*, 50(1) (2007), 173–96; 'Adultery in Post-War England', *History Workshop Journal* 62(1), 86–115.

36 36 S. Szreter and K. Fisher, *Sex Before the Sexual Revolution: Intimate Life in England 1918–1963* (Cambridge: Cambridge University Press, 2010).

37 S. Morgan, '"Wild Oats or Acorns?" Social Purity, Sexual Politics and the Response on the Late-Victorian Church', *Journal of Religious History* 31(2) (2007), 151–68.

38 A. Harris, 'Gray, Arthur Herbert (1868–1956)' – www.oxforddnb.com/view/article/102454?&docPos=45.

39 A. Harris, 'Mace, David Robert (1907–1990)' – www.oxforddnb.com/view/article/101176?&docPos=76.

40 See J. Lewis, 'Public Institution and Private Relationship: Marriage and Marriage Guidance, 1920–1968', *Twentieth Century British History* 1(3) (1990), 233–63 with passing reference to these religious influences.

41 Grimley, 'Law, Morality and Secularisation'; T. Jones, *Sexual Politics in the Church of England, 1857–1959* (Oxford: Oxford University Press, 2012).

42 J. Lewis, D. Clark and D. H. J. Morgan, *'Whom God hath Joined Together': The Work of Marriage Guidance* (London: Routledge, 1992).

43 G. Vann, *Eve and the Gryphon* (London: Blackfriars, 1952), 29.

44 C. Langhamer, 'The Meanings of Home in Postwar Britain', *Journal of Contemporary History* 40(2) (2005), 341–62.

45 Bishop Marshall, 'An Advent Pastoral Letter on the Christian Family', 19 November 1945, 4 (SDA Box 226).

46 MacMahon, *Nazareth*, 7.

47 Marshall, 'Advent Pastoral', 3 (SDA Box 226).

48 Finch, 'Companionate Marriage', 7; M. Richards and B. J. Elliot, 'Sex and Marriage in the 1960s and 1970s' in Clark, *Marriage*, 33–34 and on 'Christian mutualism', M. Collins, *Modern Love: An Intimate History of Men and Women in Twentieth-Century Britain* (London: Atlantic Books, 2003).

49 R. McKibbin, *Classes and Cultures: England 1918–1951* (Oxford: Oxford University Press, 2000), 303; M. Abbott, *Family Affairs: A History of the Family in 20th Century England* (London: Routledge, 2003), 110–12.

50 'Divorce Wrecks Nation's Family Life: Bishops Issue a Grave Warning', *Catholic Times*, 4 July 1953, 6.

51 L. Hall, *Sex, Gender and Social Change in Britain since 1880* (2nd edition, London: Palgrave, 2012).

52 Lewis, *Whom God*, 71; A. Harris, 'Love Divine and Love Sublime: The Catholic Marriage Advisory Council, the Marriage Guidance Movement and the State' in A. Harris and T. Jones (eds), *Love and Romance in Britain, 1918–1970* (London: Palgrave, 2014), Chapter 8.

53 Marshall, 'An Advent Pastoral Letter', 6 (SDA Box 226).

54 H. Waterhouse SJ to G. A. Beck, 'Some Notes on Marriage Guidance', 2 June 1947, 1 (SDA Box 186, Catholic Societies, Folder No 8 CMAC).
55 *Ibid*, 2, 5.
56 *Ibid*, 2.
57 E.g. D. Mace, *Marriage: The Art of Lasting Happiness* (London: Hodder and Stoughton, 1952).
58 L. Stanley, *Sex Surveyed, 1949–1994: From Mass Observation's 'Little Kinsey' to the National Survey and the Hite Reports* (London: Taylor and Francis, 1995), 98–9.
59 T. Madden, *How's the Family? Cartoons in the Catholic Herald* (London: Burns and Oates, 1965), n.p.
60 E. g. J. Fitzsimons, 'The Family and the Nation: Reflections on some Recent Statistics', *The Tablet*, 8 September, 1951, 152–53; Bishop of Southwell, 'Faith and Freedom' *Sunday Times*, 3 August 1952, 6.
61 L. Hall, 'Chesser, Eustace (formerly Isaac Chesarkie) (1902–73)' – www.oxforddnb.com/view/article/40923?docPos=2.
62 E. Chesser, *Marriage and Freedom* (London: Rich and Cowan Medical Publications, 1946), 15, 144.
63 Waterhouse, 'Some Notes on Marriage Guidance', 5 (SDA Box 186, Folder 8 CMAC).
64 *Ibid*, 3.
65 E.g. D. Riley, *War in the Nursery: Theories of the Child and Mother* (London: Virago, 1983) and C. Steedman, *Landscape for a Good Woman* (London: Virago, 1986).
66 J. A. P. Nutt, *Talks for the Month of May* (London: Burns and Oates, 1948), 14.
67 *Ibid*.
68 E.g. Catholic Woman Doctor, *Growing Up: A Book for Girls* (London: Catholic Truth Society, 1939), 35, 40–43. See also C. Wildman, 'Religious Selfhoods and the City in Inter-war Manchester', *Urban History* 38(1) (2011), 122 and S. Todd, 'Flappers and Factory Lads: Youth and Youth Culture in Interwar Britain', *History Compass* 4(4) (2006), 714–30.
69 Bishop Marshall, 'Sermon Notes – Union of Catholic Mothers', c.1946, 1 (SDA File 021).
70 L. Hanlon, 'Our Lady and the Formation of Leaders', *New Life* 1(5) (1948), 99–100.
71 Young Christian Workers Archives (hereafter YCW), File: Occasional Publications ('Girl Mother', May 1948, *YCW Girl Leaders' Bulletin and Campaign Programme*, 2).
72 *Ibid*.
73 P. C. Challoner, 'Domestic Science: Homemaking', *Catholic Herald*, 23 May 1952, 2.
74 P. Summerfield, 'Women in Britain since 1945: Companionate Marriage and the Double Burden' in J. Obelkevich and P. Catterall (eds), *Understanding Post-war British Society* (London: Routledge, 1994), 60–2.
75 W. Jewell, *To Those Getting Married* (London: Catholic Truth Society, 1946), 2.
76 Bishop Marshall, 'The Authorised Official Programme of the Catholic ANNUAL Procession', 1948, 5 (SDA, File Box 200, 200/236).
77 K. Holden, *The Shadow of Marriage: Singleness in England, 1914–60* (Manchester: Manchester University Press, 2007); V. Nicholson, *Singled Out: How Two Million Women Survived Without Men After the First World War* (London: Penguin, 2008).

78 G. Bock and P. Thane, *Maternity and Gender Policies: Women and the Rise of the European Welfare States, 1880–1950s* (London: Routledge, 1991); S. Pedersen, *Family, Dependence and the Origins of the Welfare State, Britain and France 1914–45* (Cambridge: Cambridge University Press, 1993).
79 P. Summerfield, *Reconstructing Women's Wartime Lives: Discourse and Subjectivity in Oral Histories of the Second World War* (Manchester: Manchester University Press, 1998).
80 W. Slim, *Courage and Other Broadcasts* (London: Cassell, 1957), 57–63.
81 M.E. Yates, 'The Catholic Mother in the Modern World', *The Catholic Times*, 1 October 1954, 7.
82 J. Bowlby, *Childcare and the Growth of Love* (London: Penguin, 1953).
83 D. W. Winnicott, *The Child and the Outside World: Studies in Developing Relationships* (London: Tavistock, 1957).
84 J. Ferguson, 'Hollings, Michael Richard (1921–1997)' – http://www.oxforddnb.com/view/article/65225.
85 M. Hollings, 'Every Year a Marian Year', *The Tablet*, 5 December 1953, 539.
86 *Ibid.*
87 T. Holland, 'Everyman's Mariology: Mother of God', *The Catholic Gazette*, 45(2) (1954), 39.
88 Interview, Peter at 29.46–31.04.
89 Letters to the Editor, *Novena*, October 1951, 146.
90 'Catholic Mother', 'Talking to Mary', *The Catholic Times*, 18 July 1952, 7.
91 R. J. Roche, *Mother Most Amiable* (Dublin: Irish Rosary, n.d.), 7.
92 Greenstock, *Christopher's*, 59.
93 *Ibid*, xi.
94 Interview, Mary at 16.20–16.45.
95 *Ibid*, 16.53–17.20.
96 A. Hermkens, W. Jansen and C. Notermans (eds), *Moved by Mary: The Power of Pilgrimage in the Modern World* (Farnham: Ashgate, 2009).
97 J. Tosh and M. Roper, *Manful Assertions: Masculinities in Britain since 1800* (London: Routledge, 1991).
98 F. Mort, 'Symbolic Fathers and Sons in Post-war Britain', *Journal of British Studies* 38(3) (1999), 353–84.
99 A. Bingham, *Gender, Modernity and the Popular Press in Inter-War Britain* (Oxford: Clarendon, 2004).
100 M. Francis, 'The Domestication of the Male? Recent Research on Nineteenth and Twentieth-century British Masculinity', *Historical Journal* 45 (2002), 637–52.
101 L. Segal, 'Look Back in Anger: Men in the Fifties' in R. Chapman and J. Rutherford (eds), *Male Order: Unwrapping Masculinity* (London: Lawrence and Wishart, 1988), 68–96.
102 Peyton, *Ear*, 112.
103 'Famous Football Ground Scene of Rosary Rally', *Catholic Times*, 20 June 1952, 12.
104 '35,000 at Another Great Rosary Rally', *Catholic Times*, 16 May 1952, 1.
105 E.g. Auxiliary Bishop of Birmingham, Bishop Bright – 'This is a man's Crusade yet one not confined to Catholic families only' – 'Wembley Plans Growing for Crusade', *Catholic Herald*, 6 June 1952, 6.

106 'One of the Greatest Religious Crusades', 1952, 17 (Archives Holy Cross Family Ministries (hereafter AHCFM) File: 01-13-02-04-00 Lancaster).
107 P. Grant, 'Record of the Family Rosary Crusade', 1952, 12 (AHCFM File: 01-13-03-04-00 Durham).
108 'Rosary Crusade Rings Capital', *Catholic Herald*, 11 July 1952, 1.
109 Grant, 'Record', 18–19 (AHCFM File: 01-13-03-04-00 Durham).
110 'One of the Greatest Religious Crusades', 13 (AHCFM File: 01-13-02-04-00 Lancaster).
111 L. Rossiter, 'Rosary Solves Father's Problems', *Catholic Times*, 4 July 1952, 7.
112 Interview, Nora at 54.12–54.58.
113 Vann, *Eve*, 30.
114 Finch, 'Companionate', 12.
115 E.g. 'Our Lady of Walsingham: Impressions of a Pilgrim', *The Tablet*, 24 July 1948, 56.
116 See 'Coronation of Our Lady of Willesden', 3 October 1954, 1–2 and 'The Coronation of Our Lady of Willesden – Report', Mgr Derek Worlock, 26 July 1954 (AAW, Griffin, Coronation of Our Lady of Willesden Rally, 3 October 1954); 'At Wembley', *The Tablet*, 9 October, 1954, 345.
117 On the interconnections between Marian devotions (and pilgrimage processions) and expressions of Catholic masculinity, see K. Massam, 'The Blue Army and the Cold War: Anti-Communist Devotion to the Blessed Virgin Mary in Australia', *Australian Historical Studies* 24(96) (1991), 420–8.
118 Bishop Marshall, 'Christian Marriage and the Christian Home: A Lenten Pastoral Letter', 29 January 1940, 9 (SDA, Box 215).
119 Interview, Francis at 16.49–17.37.
120 MacMahon, *Nazareth*, 249.
121 *Ibid.*
122 *Ibid*, 250.
123 Hurrell, *Saints*, 40.
124 Interview, Peter at 31.05–31.32. Also M. Joseph, 'I Think of Joseph ... A Christmas Meditation for Husbands and Fathers', *Novena*, December 1968, 17–19.
125 Houselander, *Passion*, 101.
126 M. Oliver, *Fair as the Moon: Mary, Purest of Creatures* (Dublin: M. H. Gill and Son, 1949), 98.
127 See Peyton, *Ear*, 48 and Nutt, *Talks*, 55.
128 See Bishop Holland, 'Prayer for those in Industry', 2 May 1968 (SDA, Box 220, 12/68).
129 Oliver, *Fair*, 98.
130 Greenstock, *Christopher's*, 114.
131 *Ibid*, 115.
132 *Ibid*, 117.
133 Grant, 'Record', 33 (AHCFM File: 01-13-03-04-00 Durham).
134 Quotes from Father Peyton's Speeches, 1951, 1 (AHCFM, File: 01-13-02-02-00 Lancaster).
135 Greenstock, *Christopher's*, 16.

136 Royal Commission on Population, *Family Limitation and its Influence on Human Fertility during the Past Fifty Years, Volume 1* (London: HMSO 1949–54), 40–41, 137–51 and 220.
137 See M. Young and P. Willmott, *Family and Kinship in East London* (London: Routledge and Kegan Paul, 1957), 10; 13–15; J. Goldthorpe, D. Lockwood, F. Bechhofer and J. Platt, *The Affluent Worker in the Class Structure* (London: Cambridge University Press, 1969), 104–05.
138 'Holy Name Marriage Training Course 1956–7', n.p. (SDA Box 24 CMAC 1946–76).
139 L. Hall, 'Stopes, Marie Charlotte Carmichael (1880–1958)' – www.oxforddnb.com/view/article/36323.
140 M. C. Stopes, *Married Love: A New Contribution to the Solution of Sex Difficulties* (ed. R. McKibbin, Oxford: Oxford University Press, 2004), 108–09. The book sold over 750,000 copies between 1918 and 1931. For a discussion of Stopes and the reception of her book, particularly by married men, see L. A. Hall, *Hidden Anxieties: Male Sexuality, 1900–1950* (Cambridge: Polity, 1991).
141 E.g. E. Slater and M. Woodside, *Patterns of Marriage: A Study of Marriage Relationships in the Urban Working Classes* (London: Cassell, 1951), 174. Contrast G. Gorer, *Exploring English Character* (London: Cresset Press, 1955), 132–33.
142 S. Brooke, *Sexual Politics: Sexuality, Family Planning and the British Left from the 1880s to the Present Day* (Oxford: Oxford University Press, 2011); cf. H. Cook, 'Emotion, Bodies, Sexuality and Sex Education in Edwardian England', *Historical Journal* 55(2) (2012), 475–95.
143 McKibbin, *Marie Stopes*, xlvii, xlix and l.
144 'National Marriage Guidance Council: General Principles and Aims', n.d. (SDA Box 24).
145 S. Szreter, *Fertility, Class and Gender in Britain, 1860–1940* (Cambridge: Cambridge University Press, 1996), 564–5, 568–71; C. Waters, 'Sexology' in H. G. Cocks and M. Houlbrook (eds), *Palgrave Advances in the Modern History of Sexuality* (Basingstoke: Palgrave 2006), 41–63. Cf. Jones, *Sexual Politics*.
146 H. Gray, *Men, Women and God: a Discussion of Sex Questions from the Christian Point of View* (London: SCM Press, 1923). Cf Cook, *Long*, 343.
147 See E. Griffith (ed.), *The Road to Maturity* (London: Victor Gollancz, 1944), 9, 16, 225.
148 McLeod, *Religious Crisis*, 28.
149 Jarrett, *Catholic Mother*, 18.
150 *Ibid*, 19.
151 Joint Pastoral, reprinted in J. Leycester King, *Sex Enlightenment and the Catholic* (London: Burns, Oates and Washbourne, 1944), 54.
152 *Ibid*, 58.
153 See A. DeRogatis, 'What Would Jesus Do? Sexuality and Salvation in Protestant Evangelical Sex Manuals, 1950s to the Present', *Church History* 74(1) (2005), 97–137.
154 B. Dent, *Sex in Adolescence* (London: Catholic Truth Society, 1962).
155 A. Pickering, 'Religious Instruction and Purity', *Clergy Review* 36(12) (1951), 348–57.
156 Medical Woman, *Into their Company*, xxi–xxii.
157 *Ibid*, xiv, xvii.
158 *Ibid*, 2.

159 *Ibid*, 20–1.
160 *Ibid*, 14.
161 Catholic Woman, *Growing* 2, 7, 10, 14. See also Catholic Mother, *Preparing our Daughters for Life* (London: Catholic Truth Society, 1942), 16.
162 Jarrett, *Catholic Mother*, 10.
163 A. Pickering, *Sex-Instruction in the Home* (London: Catholic Truth Society, 1950), 7.
164 *Ibid*, 5.
165 *Ibid*, 14.
166 *Ibid*, 13.
167 *Ibid*, 18.
168 'Joint Pastoral' in King, *Sex*, 56.
169 Pickering, 'Religious Instruction and Purity', 352.
170 Greenstock, *Christopher's*, 232; B. Jarrett, *Purity* (London: Catholic Truth Society, 1929), 23; C. C. Martindale, *The Difficult Commandment: Notes on Self-Control Especially for Young Men* (London: Manresa Press, 1931).
171 A. Pickering, *From Boy to Man* (London: Catholic Truth Society, 1957), 17.
172 *Ibid*, 21.
173 *Ibid*, 23.
174 Griffith, *Road*, 33.
175 Drinkwater, *Talking*, 78–82.
176 *Ibid*, 142–6.
177 See H. M. Dresden-Coenders, *The Psychology of Sex Instruction: An Educational Study* (London: Sheed and Ward, 1963), 18, 96–102.
178 Catholic, *Growing Up*, 9. On similar perspectives across a Christian spectrum, see T. Evans and P. Thane, *Sinners? Scroungers? Saints?: Unmarried Motherhood in Twentieth-Century England* (Oxford: Oxford University Press, 2012).
179 Dent, *Sex*, 7.
180 *Ibid*.
181 *Ibid*, 8.
182 CMAC, *Beginning your Marriage* (London: Catholic Marriage Advisory Council, 1963), 16, 26, 31–2, 80–95.
183 Catholic, *Growing Up*, 35; P. Rorke, *Through Parents to Christ* (Billinge: Birchley Hall Press, 1960), 40.
184 Chesser, *Marriage*, 58.
185 Catholic, *Growing Up*, 34–5.
186 Drinkwater, *Talking*, 159.
187 Interview, Francis at 32.13–32.35.
188 'Written Questions from girls aged 16–17 years in an English convent school', 1959 (SDA Box 24).
189 Brooks, 'CMAC Educational Work and the Schofield Report', Annual Conference Report 1965, 5 (SDA Box 24).
190 *Ibid*, 7.
191 G. Gorer, *Sex and Marriage in England Today: A Study of the Views and Experience of the Under-45s* (London: Nelson, 1971), 30.

192 M. G. Schofield, *The Sexual Behaviour of Young People* (London: Longmans, 1965), 248; Marwick, *Sixties*, 74–80; Szreter and Fisher, *Sex*, 113–64, and 386–7 for an earlier period.
193 Jarrett, *Catholic*, 4–5.
194 Rorke, *Through*, 3.
195 G. P. Dwyer, *Birth Control* (London: Catholic Truth Society, 1951), 3.
196 *Ibid*, 13.
197 See C. C. Martindale, *The Cup of Christ* (London: Sheed and Ward, 1930), 60 acknowledging (probably mostly middle-class) use of artificial contraception.
198 Stanley, *Sex*, 98; K. Fisher, *Birth Control*, 150–3, 156.
199 Stanley, *Sex*, 100.
200 *Ibid*, 98.
201 *Ibid*, 99–100.
202 *Ibid*.
203 Royal Commission on Population, *Family Limitation*, 82.
204 H. Sutherland, *Control of Life* (London: Burns, Oates and Washbourne, 1951), 197.
205 A. Biezanek, *All Things New: A Declaration of Faith* (London: Pan, 1964).
206 See A. Harris, '"The writings of querulous women": Contraception, Conscience and Clerical Authority in 1960s Britain' (forthcoming).
207 Brooks, 'CMAC', 4 (SDA Box 24).
208 Femina, 'What Women Think about the Pill', *The Tablet*, 23 May 1964, 586–7; C. Derrick, 'What do the Laity Think?', *The Tablet*, 10 April 1965, 415.
209 Catholic Mother, 'When Rhythm Doesn't Work', *The Tablet*, 10 April 1965, 417.
210 'Morals, Marriage and the Pill', *The Tablet*, 16 May 1964, 543–4; 'Nailing Up Theses', *The Tablet*, 20 March 1965, 312–13.
211 C. Clark, 'Population and Prosperity: The Essential Role of Increasing Numbers', *The Tablet*, 14 July 1962, 662–63 and H. L. Kirkley, 'OXFAM and Family Planning', *The Tablet*, 20 February 1965, 218; Leslie, 'Christianity and the Bomb', *The Tablet*, 19 May 1962, 481.
212 J. C. Heenan, 'Morality and the Pill: The Third Session of the Council', *The Tablet*, 9 May, 1964, 529–30.
213 Tanner, *Decrees*, GS ss. 50 and 51,1103–04.
214 Hastings, *Modern*, 231.
215 'UK Reaction Most Intense', *Catholic Herald*, 23 August 1968, 2.
216 For a snapshot of conflicting views in the *Catholic Herald* see 'Not the Last Word', *Catholic Herald*, 2 August 1968, 4; N. St John-Stevas, 'The Real Issue Facing Us Today', *Catholic Herald*, 9 August 1968, 5; F. P. Smith, '"Pope" Norman Questioned', *Catholic Herald*, 23 August 1968, 5.
217 McLeod, *Religious*, 192.
218 'Bishops Urge People to Back Encyclical', *Catholic Herald*, 9 August 1968, 2; Bishop T. Holland, *Ad Clerum*, 22 October, 1968 (SDA 219).
219 'Cardinal Gives Reason for Statement: "Pastoral Task"', *Catholic Herald*, 4 October 1968, 1.
220 'Birth Control Debate Grows', *Catholic Herald*, 2 August 1968, 1; P. Harris, A. Hastings, J. Horgan, L. Keane and R. Nowell, *On Human Life: An Examination of* Humanae Vitae

(London: Burns and Oates, 1968). Cf. Fr G. McKell, 'Novena Opinion Poll', *Novena*, October 1968, 12–14; Lady Lothian, 'The Six Reasons Why I agree with the Holy Father', *Novena*, October 1968, 15–16.
221 Fr B. Passman, 'Authority's the Issue', *Catholic Herald*, 16 August 1968, 5.
222 V. A. McClelland, 'John Carmel Heenan, The Second Vatican Council and the Rise and Fall of an English *Lumen Vitae*' in A. Seery (ed.), *Essays in Tribute to J. Valentine Rice, 1935–2006* (Dublin: Lilliput Press, 2010), 69–97.
223 'Pain at Any Price', *Catholic Herald*, 1 November 1968, 4.
224 Stourton, *Absolute Truth*, xxiv.
225 E.g. Kenny, *Goodbye*, 242 – 'the Pill did more than control fertility: it sowed sedition; it evangelized for autonomy'.
226 B. Stewart, 'The Council Debate on Marriage', *The Tablet*, 28 November 1964, 1352.
227 Knox, *Creed*, 67–68.
228 B. Wicker, 'Keep Left for the Church – Part II', *Blackfriars* 44 (517–18) (1963), 317–25.
229 R. Trevett, *The Tree of Life: Sexuality and the Growth of Personality* (London: Geoffrey Chapman, 1963), 124.
230 T. Flynn, Letter, *The Tablet*, 5 December 1964, 1384–5.
231 J. C. Heenan, *Why Marry?: A CTS Torch Pamphlet* (London: Catholic Truth Society, 1950), 18.
232 *Ibid*; Dwyer, *Birth Control*, 8; M. Robins, *Boy Meets Girl* (London: Catholic Truth Society, 1959), 12.
233 E. P. Ennis, 'The Ends of Marriage', *Clergy Review* 37(5) (1952), 270–81.
234 Griffith, *Road*, 204.
235 Tanner, *Decrees*, GS ss. 47–9, 1100–02.
236 S. E. Kutz, 'Conscience and Contraception' in T. D. Roberts (ed.), *Contraception and Holiness: The Catholic Predicament* (London: Collins, 1965), 49.
237 Rorke, *Through*, 26.
238 CMAC, *Beginning*, 111.
239 NPC, *Liverpool 1980: Official Report of the National Pastoral Congress* (Slough: St Pauls Publications, 1981), 351.
240 'A Charismatic Visit', *The Tablet*, 5th June 1982, 568–69.
241 Yarnold, *Pope*, 31.
242 *Ibid*.
243 *Ibid*, 32.
244 Alberigo and Komonchak, *History*, 481.
245 Tanner, *Decrees*, LG, 891–8.
246 De Fiores, 'Mary', 471.
247 *Marialis Cultus*, Introduction, s. 5 –www.vatican.va/holy_father/paul_vi/apost_ exhortations/documents/hf_p-vi_exh_19740202_marialis-cultus_en.html.
248 *Ibid*, s. 34.
249 K. Rahner, *Mary Mother of the Lord* (London: Catholic Book Club, 1963), 37.
250 G. Greene, 'Our Lady and Her Assumption: "The Only Figure of Perfect Human Love"', *The Tablet*, 3 February 1951, 88–9.

251 L. Boff, *The Maternal Face of God: The Feminine and Its Religious Expressions* (San Francisco: HarperRow, 1987) (original Portuguese edition 1979).
252 E. M. Carey, 'Where has the old devotion gone?', *Universe*, 24 May 1974, 4.
253 McCarthy, *Catholic Tradition*, 367.
254 G. Brinkworth, 'Roses for the Rose', *Catholic Gazette* 61(8) (1970), 24 and Bishop A. Clark, 'Marialis Cultus: Pope Paul's Apostolic Exhortation', *The Tablet*, 6 April 1974, 354.
255 'Let Mary Brighten Our Lives Again…', *The Universe*, 10 May 1974, 25.
256 R. L. Stewart, 'Marialis Cultus', *The Tablet*, 22 February 1975, 183–4 and T. Morris, 'Periscope: Signs of Faith', *The Tablet*, 25 January 1975, 74.
257 F. Johnston, 'Now it's the Ecumenical Rosary', *Universe*, 11 October 1974, 6.
258 T. Cranny, 'Mary the Mother of Unity', *Catholic Fireside*, 13 January 1978, 27.
259 R. Foley, 'Mary: What Vatican II Really Said', *The Universe*, 3 May 1968, 3.
260 'Editorial', *Novena*, May 1970, 7.
261 G. Brinkworth, 'Renewal and the Rosary', *Catholic Gazette* 61(7) (1970), 17.
262 *Ibid*.
263 Interview, Mary at 28.09–28.20.
264 Interview, Patrick at 8.35–8.44.
265 *Ibid*, 8.54–9.40.
266 Interview, Judith at 45.36, 47.07–47.33.
267 For detailed lists of Delegates, Session Chairs and Representative Organisations, see Liverpool Diocesan Archives (LDA), S6 XXXIII A/2; A/15; D/18.
268 Homily of D. Worlock, Archbishop of Liverpool, 2 May 1980 in NPC, *Liverpool*, 105–07.
269 NPC, *Liverpool*, 7.
270 Bishop Holland, 'Pastoral, 25 February 1979', 1 (SDA Box 219).
271 J. Ware, 'Don't Leave out Our Lady', *Universe*, 25 April 1980, 9.
272 T. Shepherd, 'Letter', *Universe*, 2 May 1980, 14.
273 NPC, *Liverpool*, 23.
274 NPC, *Roman Catholic Church, England NPC Discussion Papers* (Liverpool, 1979); loose pamphlet: 'Evening Prayers for the Family at Whitsuntide'.
275 *Ibid*.
276 *Ibid*.
277 Kelly, *Lay*, 105.
278 *Diocese of Salford Report: NPC*, 1979, 1 (SDA, Pamphlet Collection B66).
279 *Ibid*.
280 NPC, *Liverpool*, 66.
281 Coman, *Catholics*, 100, who states that over 55% of marriages were 'mixed' by the mid-1970s. See also Hornsby-Smith, *Catholics in England*, 94: 1930–59 (30%), 1960s (47%) and 1970s (67%).
282 Hornsby Smith, 'Recent', 128.
283 Pope Paul VI, *Motu Proprio: Matrimonia Mixta* (1970) – www.vatican.va/holy_father/paul_vi/motu_proprio/documents/hf_p-vi_motu-proprio_19700331_matrimonia-mixta_en.html.

284 *Salford NPC Report*, 2 (SDA, Pamphlet Collection B66), cf. 'Diocesan Reports', *Liverpool*, 68 regarding the 'suspicion and concern' mixed marriages still elicited.
285 G. R. Leonard, *Marriage and the Family* (London: Catholic Truth Society, 1979), 42–3.
286 NPC, *Liverpool*, 22.
287 Interview, Mary at 18.39–19.11.
288 *Salford NPC Report*, 3 ((SDA, Pamphlet Collection B66).
289 Delap et al., *Politics*, Introduction.
290 NPC, *Liverpool*, 350 (s. 100).
291 *Ibid*, s. 101.
292 C. Longley, 'Contraception: How many will heed the Pope?', *The Times*, 7 May 1982, 10; Hornsby-Smith, *Roman Catholic Beliefs*, 119–39.
293 Leonard, *Marriage*, 12.
294 J. Dominian, *Being Jack Dominian: Reflections of Marriage, Sex and Love* (London: Society for Promoting Christian Knowledge, 2007).
295 J. Dominian, 'Five Minutes with the Pope: On problems of Family and Marriage', *The Tablet*, 20 February 1982, 176.
296 'The Church and the Sexual Revolution', *The Tablet*, 24 October, 1970, 1022–23 (and subsequent issues); J. Dominian, *Christian Marriage: The Challenge of Change* (London: Darton, Longman and Todd, 1968).
297 'The Family Today: Permanency', *The Tablet*, 21 June 1979, 697.
298 'Faithfulness', *The Tablet*, 4 August 1979, 745–6 (and subsequent issues).
299 See J. Lewis and P. Wallis, 'Fault, Breakdown and the Church of England's Involvement in the 1969 Divorce Reform,' *Twentieth Century Britain History* 11 (2000), 308–32 and McLeod, *Religious*, 225–6.
300 'National Pastoral Congress – Marriage and the Family', R. Thorp, 1980, 3 (BAA, GPD/S/N1/I).
301 J. A. Brieg, 'Rosary your Secret Weapon', *Catholic Times*, 11 July 1952, 7.
302 Houselander, *Passion*, 39; Vann, 'Moral Dilemmas: 1 The Muddled Marriage', *Blackfriars*, 34 (1953), 374–80.
303 Pratt, *Easter People*, 21. See also *Congress Report: The Principle Documents of the 1980 National Pastoral Congress of England and Wales* (London: Catholic Truth Society, 1980), 20–25.
304 NPC, *Liverpool*, 165.
305 C. Longley, 'When Law and Love Conflict', *The Tablet*, 30 June 1979, 618.
306 *Salford NPC Report*, 1–5 (SDA, Pamphlet Collection B66).
307 Thorp, 'NPC, 3 (BAA, GPD/S/N1/I).
308 *Ibid*.
309 Pratt, *Becoming*, 21.
310 NPC, *Liverpool*, 170.
311 *Ibid*, 168.
312 'Lessons from Liverpool', *The Tablet*, 17 May 1980, 471.
313 *Ibid*.
314 F. Gumley, 'The Herald Says', 2 May 1980, 1; cf. D. G. Galvin, 'Beware the Radicals at the Congress', *Catholic Herald*, 30 May 1980, 4. See also K. Saunders and P. Stanford, *Catholics and Sex: From Purity to Perdition* (London: Heinemann, 1992).

315 J. Carey, 'And they went their several ways rejoicing', *Catholic Herald*, 16 May 1980, 3.
316 'Congress 1980', *The Universe*, 2 May 1980, 1, 4, 18–19.
317 D. J. Smith, 'Sounding the Laity's Opinion' and '35 Delegates Sign Protest', *Universe*, 6 June 1980, 9.
318 H. Gallagher, 'A Snub to the Pope's Teaching', *The Universe*, 23 May 1980, 7.
319 B. Harrington, 'And now the Big Summing-Up', *The Universe*, 16 May 1980, 11.
320 C. Monckton, Letter, *Universe*, 20 May 1980, 16.
321 'The End of the Beginning', *The Universe*, 9 May 1980, 14.
322 P. Hebblethwaite, 'The Pope on the Family', *The Tablet*, 9 January 1982, 29.
323 I. Machin, 'British Churches and Moral Change in the 1960s' in W. M. Jacob and N. Yates, *Crown and Mitre* (Woodbridge: Boydell Press, 1993), 226.
324 Cited in Ellis, *Serpent*, 63.
325 E.g. *Familiaris Consortio* (1981) – www.vatican.va/holy_father/john_paul_ii/apost_exhortations/documents/hf_jp-ii_exh_19811122_familiaris-consortio_en.html.
326 T. Kelly and A. Kelly, 'Our Lady of Perpetual Help, Gender Roles, and the Decline of Devotional Catholicism', *Journal of Social History* 32(1) (1998), 5–26.
327 S. Todd, *Young Women, Work and Family in England, 1918–1950* (Oxford: Oxford University Press, 2005); A. Bingham, '"An Era of Domesticity"? Histories of Women and Gender in Interwar Britain', *Cultural and Social History* 1(2) (2004), 225–33.
328 Medical Woman, '*Into their Company*', 61; S. Wilkinson, 'Mother's Apostolate', *New Life* 14(6) (1958), 187–91.
329 Jarrett, *Catholic*, 22.
330 Rorke, *Through*, 10.
331 *Ibid.*
332 I. Ross, 'Sauce for the Goose', *The Harvest* 73(5) (1961), 84–6.
333 M. Saville, 'Danger – Wives at Work', *Catholic Herald*, 23 March 1962, 9.
334 P. Duffy, 'Wives and Work', *Catholic Herald*, 19 April 1962, 2.
335 See the correspondence, *Catholic Herald*, 6 April, 1962, 2.
336 McLeod, *Religious*, 173, who estimates married women in paid employment rising from 26% (1951), to 35% (1961) to 47% (1971). Note however that in 1951, as 1981, only 30% of all adult women worked full-time – P. Summerfield, 'Women', 62–3.
337 See M. Wandor (ed.), *The Body Politic: Writings from the Women's Liberation Movement in Britain 1969–1971* (London: Stage 1, 1972), 124–30, 138–45.
338 'The Working Mother's Dilemma', *The Tablet*, 5 May 1979, 423.
339 'Women's View: Working mums …' *Universe*, 18 April 1980, 19.
340 Thorp, 'NPC', 1980, 3 (BAA GPD/S/N1/I).
341 *Salford NPC Report*, 2 (SDA, Pamphlet Collection B66).
342 *Ibid*, 5–6.
343 NPC, *Liverpool*, 239.
344 E.g. M. Borg, 'Women's View: Is the Church unjust to Women?', *The Universe*, 11 April 1980, 15; A. Murphy, '"Five Minutes with the Pope" (22): Women's status in the Church', *The Tablet*, 8 May 1982, 452. For a discussion of Christianity and Second Wave Feminism, see McLeod, *Religious*, 175–82.
345 Pratt, *Becoming*, 14.

346 *Ibid*, and the recommendations encompassing education, administration, roles in worship and consideration of issues surrounding women's ordination – *Liverpool 1980*, 151–4.
347 Interview, Kevin, transcript page 11.
348 R. L. Smith, 'Letter: St Joseph', *The Tablet*, 20 June 1964, 702; Kelly, *Lay*, 160, 178.
349 See NPC, *Liverpool*, 53, 241, 257.
350 M. Gallon, 'Three Wishes for 1966: For Men, For Families, For All', *Catholic Gazette*, 57(1) (1966), 3–4.
351 I. Mort, 'Man and Home', *Novena*, April 1970, 22–3.
352 Miss E. M. T. Hunter, 'Incredulous Laughter', *Novena*, May 1970, 6; Dr K. Walsh Brennan, 'Marriage and the "Ring of Truth"', *Novena*, March 1970, 8–10.
353 Anon, 'Thank you St Gerard', *Novena*, April 1970, 19.
354 M. Bingham, 'How to Keep your Wife Happy', *Novena*, June 1970, 18.
355 *Ibid*, 19. Also M. V. Mullally, *Catholic Motherhood: A Unique Chance to Co-operate with God* (London: Catholic Truth Society, 1974), 3.
356 E. Barnes, 'Women in Society and the Church', *New Life*, 29(6) (1973), 14.
357 J. Oger, *The Sacrament of Partnership* (London: Catholic Truth Society, 1971), 19–20.
358 Interview, Mary at 17.55–18.12.
359 M. Francis, 'A Flight from Commitment? Domesticity, Adventure and the Masculine Imaginary in Britain after the Second World War', *Gender and History*, 19(1) (2007), 163–85; J. Brannen and A. Nilsen, 'From Fatherhood to Fathering: Transmission and Change among British Fathers in Four-Generation Families', *Sociology* 40(2) (2006), 335–52.
360 C. Patten, 'What about the Family?', *The Universe*, 21 March 1980, 19.
361 Leonard, *Marriage and the Family*, 40.
362 Editor, 'A Charismatic Visit', *The Tablet*, 5 June 1982, 574.

Chapter 5

'Plaster saints' or 'spiritual friends'?
St Thérèse of Lisieux, St Bernadette Soubirous and the Forty Martyrs

> *Light a votive candle,*
> *Listen and the band'll*
> *Play you the Vatican Rag.*

In a theatrical play written in 1948 to commemorate the fiftieth anniversary of St Thérèse's death from consumption in a French Carmelite convent, Gilbert Cesbron provided the following stage directions for his opening scene – A gathering of an Intellectual Society in an old convent with its cloister in ruins from war-time bombing save for:

> a brand new statue of St Thérèse of Lisieux (the model to be found in all religious art shops), pink, vapid, smiling, nauseating. At the foot of the statue is a bed of beautiful flowers.[1]

Further authorial directions called for the curtain to open on the scene of a lively gathering and the 'hum' of an indistinct discussion, from which should emerge 'words current in literary and intellectual circles at the time ... [for example] ideology, surrealism, existentialism, bottleneck, freedom of speech, neurosis, distribution, collectivism, relativity'.[2] With the scene thus set, the opening act began with a friendly but fiery confrontation between an 'intellectual' and the resident 'priest', with the former denouncing:

> This little cardboard saint, this character out of a children's prize book, made to order for the century. Woolworth, theme songs, marshmallows, novels for housemaids, films with happy endings ... Automatic cure-dispenser, drop a shilling in the slot, light a candle, and there you are![3]

His clerical interlocutor agreed with this characterisation of St Thérèse as a modern saint to 'this century of rogues, racketeers and people who know all the answers',[4] but built up a contrastingly positive image sustained by her autobiography, *The Story of a Soul*. This book, with its themes of 'envy, secrecy, incomprehension, despair, darkness, temptation – blood ... Silence!', could appeal to all including 'the butcher's boy or the mechanic's assistant'.[5] This dramatic juxtaposition of the clash between faith and reason, religiosity and modernity, models of holiness and the gendered nature of piety provided the premise for the reconsideration of *The Story of a Soul* by the fictive intellectual circle on stage, as a way of retelling the familiar life story of Thérèse Martin to a twentieth-century theatre-going public.

This was not, however, merely a recitation of biographical events in the fashion of previous hagiographies but also a modern recasting of the meaning of sanctity. Similar remodulations were also taking place within the vast literary, cultural and artistic outpourings commemorating the canonisation of another popular saint of the twentieth century, St Bernadette Soubirous. In a comparable fashion, Sister Mary Francis' play, *Smallest of All* (1958), was written to commemorate the centenary of the believed apparitions of the Virgin Mary to Bernadette in Lourdes, and painted a picture of a vivacious, stubborn and sharp-witted seer with a complex, contradictory personality[6] who resisted the twentieth-century trappings of success ('money, praise, fame') for spiritual fulfilment and sanctifying suffering.[7]

These two plays, written within a decade of each other and addressed to very similar audiences, encapsulate well the thematic considerations and devotional preoccupations of this chapter. The interwar period witnessed a prodigious output of pamphlets and devotional literature that retold the familiar stories of St Thérèse and her 'shower of roses' and sought to explain the happenings at Lourdes and the account of the French peasant girl who 'saw a lady'. Such novels, newspaper articles, pious instructionals and theological treatises continued to be published after the Second World War, but a distinctive shift is observable in these hagiographies. The saints, previously seen as exemplary character models of obedience and sacrifice, are portrayed in accounts that placed a greater premium on their historicity and personality, and the situation of their trials and sufferings appear within a more explicitly psychological framework.

The continuing tensions placed upon pre-existing models of holiness are also starkly illuminated by consideration of the cause for the canonisation of forty English and Welsh men and women, both laity and clergy, who were martyred during the Reformation. Commencing as an official cause through petition to the Vatican in 1960, and culminating in the canonisation ceremony at St Peter's on 25 October 1970, an analysis of this process illuminates the spectrum of opinion within the English church on the place of the 'communion of saints' within the devotional life of the laity. Moreover, the ambiguous and hesitant response to the cause illustrates the imperative, as the century progressed, to emphasise models of sanctity that resonated in personal, experiential, 'this-worldly' and active terms. This movement in lay religiosity, and the need to 'update' the presentation of saintly witness, seemed to be appreciated by the church hierarchy itself. On a visitation to Lisieux in 1980, Pope John Paul II emphatically stressed:

> Saints never grow old. They never become figures of the past, men and women of 'yesterday'. On the contrary, they are always men and women of the future, witnesses of the world to come.[13]

For some English Catholics as the century progressed, 'lighting a votive candle' was no longer as efficacious in creating a connection with the communion of saints or conveying an image 'of the world to come'. For others, however, including many young people, the pulling of a *voiture* conveying an elderly, sick or disabled pilgrim up the steep streets of a Pyrenean village remained an efficacious and 'devotional' action of service and sacrifice, articulating an experiential spirituality which grappled with suffering and its meaning. For yet others, the vivid picture of an everyday spirituality, and a soul in psychological torment, encountered through the pages of Thérèse's autobiography, remained a model which continued to speak to the needs of contemporary Catholics and their disorientation within modern society.

For most practising English Catholics, the 'steps' they used to express their Catholic identity remained the movements of and responses to the liturgy and a prayer life centred on Christ and the Father. However, where a sense of fellowship with the heavenly family was adapted in ways that were compatible with a post-conciliar reappreciation of the God-man, Jesus, and an emphasis upon the historical and universal, this chapter demonstrates that English Catholics remained encouraged and inspired by the saintly lives of those who had gone before them.

Endeavouring to elucidate for a working-class readership the abstract metaphysics of the 'communion of saints', the doctrinal intricacies of indulgences and the conception of the church as 'militant, suffering and triumphant', Canon Arendzen used a weekly column within the popular *Catholic Times* in 1956 to explain:

> All the children of Christ's kingdom form one family in which each member is in touch with all, thus creating one household and one home of which God is the Father Almighty and all are brethren in Christ Jesus, whether here on earth being tried, or after death being purified or finally in heaven glorified. … We should therefore not limit our invocations to saints in the calendar. We may have parents, brothers, sisters, friends already in heaven. We should speak to them.[9]

Attempting the same feat some six years earlier, Monsignor Knox explained question 102 of the Penny Catechism, and the prayer in the Canon of the Mass, by pithily observing:

> The Church is divided into three large bits; part of it is on earth, part of it is in heaven, part of it is in Purgatory. The Church in heaven is all Saints. The Church in Purgatory is All Souls. The Church on earth is all sorts.[10]

Irrespective of the extent of their theological grasp of this complicated conception of a church transcending historical time and space, English Catholics retained an emotional and intuitive understanding of this teaching well into the 1960s.

The way in which 42-year-old Mitzi reflected on early childhood memories of a popular devotional practice on All Souls Day, described as 'the communion of saints', illustrates this:

> MS: [During the mass you] pray for people who've gone before you … there's one day in the year when you can move people from Purgatory to Heaven, that's what we were taught. And if you say one Our Father, Hail Mary and the Glory Be, that makes one person. And in my mind they used to literally come out of a gate – you know, as a child you could see it – they came from a gate and went into heaven. … And we used to do it as many times as we could before the time we had to be home. So that we could get these people to jump out of Purgatory (both laugh). So you have this vision of those people up there, definitely.[11]

Perhaps most telling of the fading of this form of ecclesiology (and notions of sin, hell and purgatory) is the retort of Mitzi's 18-year-old son, Patrick, to this tale of playful childhood piety that it 'Sounds a bit *crazy*'.[12] This reaction might be explained initially by his own socialisation in the Catholic Church of the 1990s, which has tended to emphasise the experiential, the eschatological and a 'this-worldly' ethic. However, this is not merely a question of generation and upbringing, but also of gender and temperament. For a young male with an intellectualised and studied theological belief, this spiritual landscape seems foreign. But for most Catholics throughout a good proportion of the twentieth century, this vision of an accessible celestial realm, and a community of souls with whom the believer had a personal relationship, continued. There were saints for all occasions. For example Kevin's father, who was constantly travelling in the post-war years through his occupation as a bus driver, found devotion to the popular 'patron saint of travellers, St Christopher'.[13] The Catholic press in the 1950s reinforced this understanding of a customised relationship between the believer and the saints, with the *Catholic Times* offering colouring competitions on the life of St Antony,[14] cartoons depicting the trials of the Reformation martyr, Blessed Robert Southwell,[15] and a weekly 'Saint of the week' column. Detailed lives of the saints remained perennially popular, with one of the most successful being Father Martindale's acclaimed BBC broadcasts on holy men throughout the centuries. This was followed up by a book of the series[16] and a supplementary volume, nearly two decades later, on female saintly exemplars.[17] Explaining the difference between the British public's admiration for a heroic figure or historical thinker and a Catholic's 'moulding of their lives' on the model of St Francis, St Teresa or St Ignatius, Martindale reflected:

> Saints were, and *are*, real and living persons, with whom millions of other living people hold they can get into vital contact, and certainly do manage their lives on that assumption. And, they consider, experience bears them out. The thing succeeds.[18]

Kathleen, born in Trafford Park in 1923, and living and working in the industrial park for her whole life (save for a brief sojourn in Stretford during the Blitz), would certainly concur with this assessment. While admitting devotional attachments to St Jude and Our Lady, St Antony remains her personal favourite, reinforced by her lifelong membership of the church of the same name and a familial incarnation in the form of a devoted nephew. When asked how the saint of Padua, to whom she 'prays a lot', helps, she light-heartedly responded:

KF: Oh. St Antony – I don't know. I shouldn't say it but sometimes at the match when we're getting beat I say 'Please St Antony, find us a goal!' (both laugh) Sometimes he does. Sometimes he does, and I say 'Thank you St Antony!' It's awful isn't it? Bringing religion into (a Manchester United game). ...

AH: And through the years, other than the goals in football, has he been a living person in your life? The way you would pray to him – in the middle of the day would you talk to him?

KF: Yeah. Yeah. If I lose anything, I'd say 'St Antony, help me find it', you know. Sometimes he does, sometimes he does. Sometimes you find it a couple of days later, but you find it.[19]

This is a friendship premised on accessibility and an everyday efficacy, with Margaret attributing the location of lost books as recompense for a Novena to St Jude.[20] Her sister Nora goes further in thanking the 'patron saint of lost causes', petitioned through daily prayer, for the emotional and mental recovery of her bereaved daughter.[21] For both women, this devotion to the saints has strong familial resonances and miraculous connotations. Margaret referred to their mother's devotion to St Anne and to their intensely religious grandmother:

MR: Every Saturday night she used to light three little candles, my gran. Put them on the floor in the bedroom. And that was the Divine, what do – you know the three – Father, Son and the Holy Ghost, you know. And she always did that for the martyrs. And there was a story that went that there was a flood and it poured into all the houses, and the three candles were left lit.[22]

For these women, now amongst an older generation of Mancunian Catholics, this was a lively and intensely personal relationship that has been sustained over the years, frequently with a familial orientation, and usually invoked for domestic application.

Amongst the panoply of saints whose friendship could be sustaining and whose intercession could be called upon in times of distress and need, English Catholics had two particular favourites, in addition to St Francis of Assisi.[23] As the twentieth century progressed, the 'lives' of two female religious – Saint Thérèse of Lisieux and St Bernadette of Lourdes – became 'sites' for exploring and negotiating troubling issues relating to 'modernity', such as the relationships between faith, rationality, suffering and psychology. But before considering the religious cults attaching to these very modern saints, and the transformations discernible in their presentation over the course of the twentieth century, a brief biographical explanation of both women and their historical setting is necessary.

Models of sanctity: Thérèse, Bernadette and an evolving hagiography

In an eclectic but perceptive comparative study of Thérèse of Lisieux and Teresa of Avila, Vita Sackville-West observed of the former: 'her very modernity, her closeness to us in date, makes the material legacy of St Thérèse so multiple, so personal, so detailed'.[24] This is indeed true and, whilst this Carmelite nun was unknown in her life, within a decade of her early death in 1897 her life story had quickly attained international renown. Born Marie-Françoise-Thérèse Martin in 1873, this youngest child of devout Catholic parents grew up in relative material comfort with four sisters in the Normandy towns of Alençon and Lisieux. Upon the death of her mother from breast cancer in 1877, Thérèse was raised by her sisters Pauline and Marie, in a close-knit and pious environment, until both older sisters left for the strict and enclosed Carmelite convent in Lisieux (in 1882 and 1886 respectively). Following petition of the church authorities, including an audience with Pope Leo XIII, the traditional age threshold of twenty-one years for entry into the cloistered religious life was waived and Thérèse was given leave by the Bishop of Bayeux to enter the convent in 1888. Here she remained for nine years, observing the rule of the order in her prayer life, housekeeping tasks and some duties in the instruction of the convent's novices. This austere and relatively uneventful life was broken by the onset of tuberculosis in 1896 and, between this time and her death in 1897, she was instructed by the Prioress (her sister Pauline, Mother Agnes of Jesus) to write the three documents which have been published as her posthumous autobiography *The Story of a Soul*. Over half of the material within this unique biography relates to reflections about Thérèse's childhood, and the Martin family home, and the remainder is an outline of her approach to the spiritual life. This is known as the 'little way', which she described as 'the way of spiritual childhood', the way of 'trust and absolute self-surrender', offering to God 'the flowers of little sacrifices'.[25] These writings were circulated on Thérèse's death in lieu of an obituary. This was deemed fortuitous by one religious contemporary who wondered what the Mother Superior could write of a young nun that 'had never done anything worth speaking about'.[26] From the original 2,000 copies circulated to Carmelite convents, the fame and popularity of the autobiography spread, and the convent started to receive not only requests for copies, but also letters recounting spiritual favours, or 'roses', granted by the intercession of Thérèse. These numbered over 500 per day by 1914 and, by the time of her canonisation on 17 May 1925, there were over thirty-five translations of the work, 30 million pictures and photographs, and 17 million relics circulating throughout the Catholic world.[27] On 19 October 1997, Pope John Paul II declared her one of the thirty-three Doctors of the Universal Church. Thérèse was only the third woman to join this august company of saints who have been highlighted for their contributions to the theological or doctrinal development of the church.

In marked contrast to the rich personal detail and vast material legacy for the life of Thérèse Martin, Bernadette Soubirous has been called 'the most hidden of saints'.[28] Remembered as a visionary, but displaced by the accounts of the apparitions of the Virgin Mary, Bernadette is best known for her accidental establishment of a place of pilgrimage, bringing with it mass tourism and a reputation for healing. Born Marie-Bernarde Soubirous on 7 January 1844 in Lourdes, Bernadette was the eldest of six surviving children. Her father, a miller, and her mother, a laundress, saw their economic fortunes reduced during her childhood and struggled with unemployment, the discomforts of a large family living in a single room (a former prison cell) and the effects of extreme poverty. Bernadette's childhood was punctuated by illness (including cholera and chronic asthma), which disrupted her schooling but did not prevent her working for periods of time as a shepherdess for her aunt in the nearby village of Bartrès. On 11 February 1858, when fourteen years old, Bernadette went with her sister and a friend to gather firewood at the foot of a hill called Massabielle. Separated from the others, she had the first of eighteen visions (visible only to her) of a young girl about her own age and height, wearing a white robe and veil with a blue girdle, a golden rose on each foot, and a rosary hung from one arm.[29] The story of the visions divided opinion amongst her family, the townspeople, and civic and clerical authorities. The identity of the lady also remained mysterious until the seventeenth vision, with Bernadette calling her simply 'the lady' or '*Aquerò*' (which is Gascon Occitan for 'that'). Numerous visions focused on the need for prayer and penance and, during the ninth visitation, Bernadette was given instructions to drink from the spring which flowed under the rock, and to eat the plants which grew freely there. Her digging and ingestion of mud, and surrounding weeds, provoked ridicule but from the muddy patch a spring later began to flow, which was soon reported to have healing properties. In the thirteenth vision, the 'lady' requested the building of a chapel and the establishment of processions. Weeks later, on 25 March 1858 (the feast of the Annunciation) she reportedly gave her name to Bernadette with the phrase 'I am the Immaculate Conception'. Upon the cessation of the visions, Bernadette sought to withdraw from the public gaze, attending the hospice school run by the Sisters of Charity where she learned to read and write. She later joined the convent of this same order in Nevers at the age of twenty-two. There she worked as an assistant in the infirmary, and a sacristan, contracting tuberculosis and dying at the age of thirty-five on 16 April 1879. From the first certified cures of Louis Bouriette – a man blinded in an accident who recovered his sight – and a young child saved from a form of consumptive wasting disease, there have been sixty-seven cures 'verified' by the Lourdes Medical Bureau, through scientific and medical examinations, as 'inexplicable'. Bernadette's body was exhumed in 1909 in the processes of preparation for her beatification and was found to be 'incorrupt', namely preserved from decomposition. It is now displayed, with a wax coating over her face and hands, in a gold and glass reliquary at the convent in Nevers. Bernadette was canonised on 8 December 1933 and designated as the patron saint of sick persons, the family and those in poverty.

Near-contemporaries and canonised within eight years of each other, St Thérèse and St Bernadette were household names for English Catholics and two of the most popular models of Catholic femininity. Both were frail and celibate religious women who modelled a 'good death' in conformity with a popular trope of nineteenth-century romantic literature, and suffered their early demise from that most prevalent disease of the century, tuberculosis.[30] There were marked differences, however, in their class backgrounds and educational opportunities. Thérèse had an idyllic childhood, a solid education and left written records of her reflections and spiritual relationships. This could not be more different from the deprived and poorly educated Bernadette, who was illiterate at the time of the apparitions and, from all accounts, had a very superficial knowledge even of forms of prayers and the catechism. Nevertheless, from these biographical accounts, in their original iterations, certain similarities

'Plaster saints' or 'spiritual friends'?

emerge in the casting of these modern saints as models of virtue. These include an emphasis on innocence and childhood, the place of suffering, and the relationship between materiality and the miraculous. As the following survey of hagiographical literature illustrates, the presentation and performance of these virtues across the twentieth century illuminates the increasing complexities of sanctity as the century progressed.

In the Bull of Canonisation of St Thérèse of the Child Jesus and the Holy Face (*Vehementer exultamus hodie*, 17 May 1925), Pius XI stated:

> Today, faithful flock of Christ, the Church offers a new and most noble model of virtue for all of you to contemplate unceasingly. ... Without going beyond the common order of things, in her way of life she followed out and fulfilled her vocation with such alacrity, generosity and constancy that she reached a heroic degree of virtue. In our own day, when men seek so passionately after temporal goods, the young maiden lived in our midst practising in all simplicity and devotedness the Christian virtues ... May her example strengthen in virtue and lead to a more perfect life, not only the cloistered souls but those living in the world.[31]

This description of Thérèse's sanctity was extended by, and amplified within, the vast and enduringly popular literature on this 'great little Saint'. Publisher Burns and Oates, in an advertisement in 1948, acknowledged the steady sales and demands for reprints,[32] and key to this success was the presentation of the saint as sweet, childlike, obedient and tragic, which had mass appeal to a reading public with a penchant for romance, and saccharine tales of innocence and domesticity. Holy cards, devotional pamphlets and the ubiquitous church statues presented an image of a passive, smiling and obedient religious woman, clasping a crucifix and a bunch of roses to her heart. This interpretation of the Saint of Lisieux is perhaps representatively depicted by the Missionary of the Sacred Heart, Father M. D. Forrest, who in *The Fragrance of the Little Flower* (1934) described:

> the hidden little Carmelite nun whom Providence has now placed before the entire world on a holy pedestal with a halo around her brows on which gleams in heavenly letters the word CONFIDENCE! ... Hers was not merely unbounded confidence in God; twas the sweet, imperturbable, unshakable confidence of a little child reposing tranquilly on the arms of an affectionate, smiling Father.[33]

Benedict Williamson in his writings on St Thérèse invoked a similar image of 'our beloved Mistress', exhorting devotees to reference her model in their nightly examination of conscience and thus ask 'Have I been pure, chaste, modest ... sweet, gracious, gentle ... as generous, as self-sacrificing and self-forgetting as a disciple of S. Thérèse ought to be?'[34] Some publications in the decades following expressed discomfort with this model, and sought to distance their accounts from 'the endless *kitsch* surrounding the figure of Thérèse' and the 'shut-in, perfumed air' of *The Story of a Soul*.[35] Tracts appealing particularly to a theologically literate middle class of the 'sophisticated [who] still deplore the serenely smiling face of the statue', worked to distance themselves from the 'roses and air of sentimentality which clings to the cultus'.[36] Yet within most biographies, sustained by well-cited examples from the autobiography such as her description of herself as a 'little ball', or 'plaything' for the Child Jesus,[37] and the likening of her 'little way' to an elevator to heaven, powered by the arms of Christ,[38] the overwhelming imagery was of a simple, trusting and childlike sanctity which the faithful were encouraged to emulate. This was deemed a particularly adaptable model for young Catholics, with numerous books for children drawing upon the tantrums and misadventures of Thérèse in her youth to teach schoolchildren,[39] and particularly young girls,[40] that 'saints were not holy as holy from the moment they are born. They have to try very hard to become saints'.[41] Expanding explicitly on the 'Holy Family' model, such authors proposed 'as a model for every Christian family the home of little Thérèse',[42] and Louis and Zélie Martin (née Guérin) were proffered as a 'vivid portrayal of a Christian marriage',[43] leading to their beatification on 19 October 2008. Within such appeals to childlike simplicity, trust and obedience, Catholics were offered an emotionally charged, familially inflected alternative to worldly sophistication, jaded anxiety and intellectual scepticism. The 'Little Flower', an instantly recognisable celebrity disseminated through photographs, relics and her internationally best-selling writings, had been transformed in the fifty years after her death, as Sophia Deboick has impressively charted,[44] from a historical person, into a modern, commercially-packaged ideal.

A similar process of transformation was taking place in the presentation of another 'saint of our own times', St Bernadette. Laywomen such as Frances Parkinson Keyes sought in the image of the childlike, rural and unsophisticated 'sublime shepherdess'[45] a master key for her narration. Others, however, such as the English Jesuit Father R. H.

Steuart, drew upon a sentimental but also strong image of 'this poor little half-starved, ailing, defenceless child, standing up to the alternate threats and cajolery, the menaces and flattery of civil and ecclesiastical authorities'.[16] These themes of (seemingly) worldly weakness, and an embattled truth prevailing, were best encapsulated in one of the most influential portrayals of St Bernadette for a generation of Catholics in England, and around the world.

Released in the United States two days after Christmas at the height of the Second World War, popular Academy Award-winning film *The Song of Bernadette* (1943) had a screenplay written by George Seaton and was based on a successful book by Franz Werfel. Werfel was a Jewish Czech émigré, novelist and playwright who had fled to France with his family in 1938, and escaped detection by the Nazis through hiding at the pilgrimage place of Lourdes, sheltered by local families and the religious who staffed the shrine. As an act of thanksgiving for this deliverance when later safely in the United States, Werfel wrote the story of Bernadette, which he called 'a novel but not a fictive work'.[17] This literary *ex voto* spent thirteen weeks at the top of *The New York Times* best-seller list, sold millions of copies and drew both criticism and acclaim as Werfel was declared 'a religious spokesman for our time'.[18] The film, made shortly before his death in 1945, was equally successful and featured a little-known Jennifer Jones as the innocent and artless saint, ridiculed for her simplicity but triumphant through her strong-willed, determined and sincere piety. Reinforced by the striking promotional posters produced by Norman Rockwell, the film depicted a 'heartfelt but not saccharine [portrait of] an adolescent faith [providing] a contrast to the eroticised screen females that the Hollywood studio system was then promoting, such as Joan Crawford, Marlene Dietrich and Mae West'.[19]

The film also had a huge impact in Britain, with the première at the New Gallery Cinema arranged by the Earl of Clarendon and Mrs Gordon Moore as a fund-raiser for the Toc H War Services Fund,[50] attended by the great and the good, including the King and Queen of Yugoslavia. Not all commentators were entranced by Jennifer Jones' 'wide-eyed candour and innocence', nor by the quality of the 'trivial' and 'facetious' dialogue between believers, the anti-clerical party and the local politicians.[51] The public, though, seemed to love it.

John, a teenager at the time of the film's release, attributed his fervent devotion to St Bernadette to the impact of Werfel's story:

JM: I've read a lot about St Bernadette, you know. I've seen the film – have you ever seen that film?

AH: 'Song of Bernadette'?

JM: Yes, 'Song of Bernadette'. What a lovely film. I've got it on tape and now and again I watch it. But I've read the book first before I ever saw the film. (AH: Yeah) And I love the book too. She's my favourite saint.

AH: Why is she your favourite – other than this family connection [i.e. a family grave in Mosstown dedicated to Our Lady of Lourdes, of which he had earlier spoken]?

JM: Well, you know, just reading the book and – I've not been to Lourdes, but I'd love to go to Lourdes. I've been to other places.[52]

Fellow Mancunian Kevin, born a decade after the film's release, recalled screenings, and the incorporation of the saint into the school curriculum, well into the 1960s:

KF: Saint Bernadette was a key (saint) ... because of Lourdes. And also the film. And the film made a big mark. The film was shown, it was seen. You saw it. And that in itself was important. I think it was even shown in the parish hall once. Someone managed to get a big projector and it was shown in the parish hall. But again that was just reinforcement – Saint Bernadette, Saint Bernadette at school was referred to on many occasions.[53]

Also, it seems that the appeal of St Bernadette and her tale of childhood innocence, courage, and the limitations of scientific rationality, appealed beyond Catholic circles. The film's opening titles made an appeal to those of any faith with the premise: 'to those who believe, no explanation is necessary. To those who do not believe, no explanation is possible'. Given Werfel's Jewish background, the British Jewish community supported the film and even some years after its release *The Jewish Chronicle*, on 28 May 1948, carried a large advertisement for this 'film of great beauty and emotional quality [which] returns to the West End'.[54] This general re-release, at a central London cinema, indicated that the film's popularity remained strong long after the immediate hype of its Oscar triumph.

Catholic educators themselves recognised the catechetical and missiological opportunities of the large number of religious films doing well at the box office in the 1940s, including the much-loved *The Bells of St Mary's* and *Going my Way* (starring Bing Crosby as an affable singing priest). Freda

Lockhart, writing in 1948 for a Catholic Film Society conference, reflected on the appeal of 'the sentimental view of [Catholicism] embodied in what I believe Maritain calls "*l'art rue St Suplice*"' and advised that the ecclesiastical authorities should harness the 'vast power' of this 'potent ally'.[55] *The Song of Bernadette* clearly fell within this category, offering a picturesque and compelling portrayal of Catholic femininity, and supernatural piety, which chimed with the needs of a war-time generation engaged in a quite different battle of ideologies, but seeking reassuring reminders of a simpler, familial and communal age of certainty.

An appeal to the 'ordinariness' of both saints was also a dominant strain within the laudatory hagiographies composed to celebrate the lives of these two French girls. Presented with an everyday and attainable picture of sanctity, rather than a daunting image of self-mortification, ascetic terrors and supernatural ecstasies, a Catholic laywoman conjectured that 'we, who are average persons ... can pattern our lives after [theirs]: at least, in some small degree, in purpose, in purity, and in resourcefulness, and in faith'.[56] St Thérèse was the more malleable in this respect, with both lay devotees and clerical sponsors stressing her exemplary habits of informal prayer, humility and small and inconspicuous acts which required 'no special training, nor calls for a life removed from the daily business of the world'.[57] Intimately acquainted with her familial relationships and life-stages through the autobiography, a wide section of the Catholic laity identified with Thérèse and thought of her as 'one of us', and 'the child of an ideal Catholic family, the product of an ideal Catholic education, the model of a nun'.[58]

This interpretation did, of course, require some suppression of the elements of her biography relating to her comfortable middle-class childhood and cloistered, celibate religious life. This was tackled directly within gushing, romanticised biographies, such as that of Frances Keyes, who asserted that the example offered by Thérèse transcended the particularity of her circumstances:

> We do not need to feel that because she was a Carmelite nun and we are housewives or artisans, typists or teachers, social leaders or politicians, that this makes any difference either; her basic principles are applicable to every walk of life.[59]

Others such as Vita Sackville-West also deemed her an 'imitable saint', 'expressing the daily need of ordinary folk' with the simplicity and audacity of her call to do ordinary things extraordinarily well.[60] Unsurprisingly, clerical biographers emphasised the role of her religious vocation in fostering an appreciation of her own imperfections and providing a context for an austere simplicity, with biblical parallels:

> Her life in Carmel was a continual Nazareth: this is her great appeal. She beckons us along a way we all can travel: she has lit up the ordinary drudgery of the everyday with supernatural glory.[61]

Attempts were made to present Bernadette's biographies in a broadly similar fashion, conjuring an image of an ordinary, unimportant and impoverished folk girl representative of a simple but pious laity. But the hazy details of her life before the visitations of 'the lady', and afterwards in the convent of Nevers, could pose problems for widespread identification with the saint, as Father Steuart SJ acknowledged:

> [A]t first sight (and perhaps even increasingly with further acquaintance) her life presents itself to us as so remarkably devoid of the features demonstrably common to all the other saints known to us that it is a real difficulty to associate her with them.[62]

In recounting the story of the peasant girl of the Pyrénées whose character remained more opaque because so sparsely recorded in written form, devotional writers tended to conflate elements of her biography with the nun of Lisieux. For this reason, novels on Bernadette's life, and accounts of the shrine of Lourdes, were characterised by tales of her quest for smallness and obscurity. These included her rebuke to crowds who sought to touch her or claim pieces of her garments as relics, and the sale of holy cards of her for a penny, which she laughingly dismissed as 'all I am worth'. Perhaps the best known example of her self-defined 'littleness' was her response to the Mother Superior's questions about the Marian visions and the dangers of vainglory attached to being so chosen. In response, Bernadette is said to have likened herself to a broom, which is of utility for a time when sweeping, but otherwise relegated to its place in the corner.[63] This led the Dominican pamphleteer Bede Lebbe to conclude that 'fifteen or twenty years before the time of St Thérèse of Lisieux, [Bernadette] had initiated, without noticing it, the "little way" of spiritual childhood ... confidence and abandon, and piety with a candid glance which goes straight to God and permits her a certain familiarity regarding the things of God'.[64] Others likened St Bernadette to St Thérèse in her miracle-working potential: 'St Theresa has spent her heaven doing good upon earth, just as she promised. Might not St Bernadette do the same if we troubled to ask her?'[65] Finally, the analogy was also, occasionally, reversed and coupled with Christological resonances, as within the Dominican Henry Petitot's tract which urged all 'learned men – psychologists, historians, philosophers and theologians – to drink of the spring of living water which has been dug and disclosed by the saint of Lisieux'.[66]

What seems to emerge from these and countless other devotional pamphlets discussing St Bernadette and St Thérèse was a profound awareness of the modern context within which their devotional cults were operating, and an increased sensibility towards, and anxiety about, the effects of democratisation and class relations. As a saint for 'ordinary people', St Thérèse was held to have 'guided us away from the bewildering complexity, the difficult intellectualism, the mutiplied divisions ... of many so-called spiritual books', and thus, according to Cardinal Bourne of Westminster, 'has banished mathematics from our faith'.[67] Sheila Kaye-Smith's study of sanctity in 1952, couched in language disparaging of the contemporary society, drew similar conclusions about St Thérèse's mass appeal:

> She comes with a special message for an age that badly needs inspiration. It is an age that has lost its aristocracy, its kings, its geniuses, its great men. It is an age of mass production, of mediocrity, of democracy, the rank and file, the common man. ... Thérèse's call is to the average man, who in our day exists for the first time as a real person instead of a statistical calculation. She calls even him to be a saint.[68]

It was not just as an exemplar that St Thérèse resonated with ordinary Catholics of all different classes. The 'Little Flower' was also believed to be an equally indiscriminate intercessor. It was reported that millions of French soldiers during the First World War wore Thérèsean medals as a form of protection on the battlefield, and afterwards sent accounts of the 'roses' they had been granted in thanksgiving to Lisieux, the collation of which accelerated the canonisation process.[69]

By 1965, couched as an instructional devotional tale recounting the struggles of a large working-class family to find accommodation (and thereby vindicate its non-contraceptive choices), the *Catholic Fireside* published a long story about the mysterious workings of the Little Flower. In this saccharine but compelling work of fiction, the intention of the elderly landowner Mr Hadley to sell his large house to 'the right kind of people' was inverted, so that family values rather than affluence carried the day. A shared devotion to 'the girl from Lisieux', only acknowledged at the conclusion of the tale, enabled this crossing of class barriers and an everyday miracle, in the form of long-sought after accommodation. Mother of seven Connie is led to conclude: 'We may not be upper crust, but we do have friends in high places'.[70]

English Catholics, male and female, working-class or establishment, were offered such solace in the multi-faceted, mutable saintly symbols of Thérèse and Bernadette. These were, to use Barbara Corrado Pope's phrase, 'heroines without heroics',[71] practising an unsensational sanctity and therefore one which could 'be imitated by the great multitude of men and women who lead a hidden life full of work on this earth and are destined to remain forever unknown'.[72] As these early hagiographies illustrate, this emphasis upon the ordinary English Catholic's emulation of their exemplary conduct, which included equanimity in the face of suffering, was premised on a soteriological spirituality. By following in the footsteps of Bernadette, or practising Thérèse's 'little way' in their everyday life, the average Catholic might ameliorate his or her immediate context but, more importantly, could also be confident of his or her inheritance of a celestial home.

A fundamental aspect of this soteriological impetus was an overarching emphasis on suffering and its redemptive functions, most starkly illustrated in the biographies of Bernadette who was told by the 'lady' during the third apparition (18 February 1858), 'I do not promise to make you happy in this world but in the other'. Her life story was characterised by pain and trial, encompassing poverty and illness, the unwanted and demanding attentions of church and secular authorities as well as shrine devotees. Additionally she endured the austerities and personality difficulties encountered in the convent, and the sufferings of a painful death.

Constant emotional and physical sufferings, albeit of a slightly different order, were amply conveyed through *The Story of a Soul*, with loss and abandonment a constant theme.[73] Starting with the early death of Thérèse's mother, this pattern continued with the sorrow (and mental breakdown) precipitated by the departure of Pauline for the convent, followed by Céline, and finally the mental deterioration and death of her beloved father. To these personal losses could be added the trials and hardships of the convent, requiring patience to cope with the annoyances of communal life, such as cantankerous older nuns, distractions during prayer and unintentional wettings whilst doing the laundry.[71] These sufferings culminated in Thérèse's account of her stoic struggle with the onset of tuberculosis and her protracted, wasting death. Devotional writers such as Abbé André Combes and Vernon Johnson commended Thérèse's journey as a 'story of the transfiguration of suffering through a simple correspondence with grace [which] will have its message for everyone who reads it, for we all have to suffer'.[75] This description resonated with the constant presentation of the saint of Lisieux, perhaps best exemplified by Father M. D. Forrest, who eschewed academic analysis for poetic eulogy:

> St Thérèse drank deeply and constantly of the chalice of Gethsemane, and yet to this heroic maiden whose heart was aflame with love for her Divine Spouse the bitter potion contained in that chalice seemed a supernatural nectar.[76]

Similar assessments were made of St Bernadette by Canon J. I. Lane who, in a children's book, wrote about her hard life, 'full of suffering', and concluded that 'just as Our Lord had to carry His wooden cross to Calvary, so Bernadette had to bear crosses of a different kind'.[77] In an earlier publication he outlined these sufferings more fulsomely, particularly 'the dissection of her soul':

> She was tried beyond endurance by friend and foe, ecclesiastical and lay, in the myriad of attempts to get from her own lips the story of what she had seen, and in the cross-questioning which always followed. She knew no peace in the street, where she was looked at as if she were a wild beast, as she said herself ... Who could have been surprised had she lost her simplicity, her candour, above all her patience?[78]

The heroic dimensions of this story were, however, sustained by Bernadette's retention of patience and the constancy of her claim that 'I saw her'. Nowhere is this better exemplified than in the moving presentation of the purifying and reparative efficacy of suffering within *The Song of Bernadette*. This film, and the earlier novel, impressed upon a generation of Catholics that trials, hardship and physical and emotional pain were central accompaniments of faith. In a more theological vein, and in terms virtually identical with those used of Thérèse, Bernadette's 'passion narrative' was likened to that of Jesus:

> Her sufferings were a chalice of which she drank deeply. Her whole existence may be described as one long martyrdom, nailed with her Master to the Cross.[79]

Whilst the incarnational, Christological dimensions of Bernadette's sanctity were occasionally explored,[80] much more common was the situation of her service and sacrifice within a Marian analogy. In a number of publications in 1958 to commemorate the centenary of the apparitions, Bernadette was depicted as a partial 'mirror of Our Lady'; as a handmaid to the divine plan, but one who was more than a passive instrument of revelation.[81] In a contemporaneous article in the Redemptorist publication *Novena*, Father Anthony Pathé attributed Bernadette's canonisation not to the apparitions or 'the wonders of Lourdes' but to her 'imitation in her own life of what she had seen of the beauty and goodness of Mary, expecially her humility'.[82] In an echo of the Magnificat, which was slightly transgressive of Trinitarian orthodoxy, and illustrative of a highly-elevated Mariology, Father Pathé concluded that 'Our Lady regarded the humility of *her* handmaid'.[83]

Similar themes of poverty and humility were stressed in more left-leaning publications, such as the appeal to St Bernadette as a model for YCW girls, despite St Thérèse's formal (if little utilised) occupation of the title of patron saint:

> [S]he may not be wearing shawl and sabots, but they keep meeting her in the Movement, a young girl from a poor family, very simply trying to model her life on Mary's pattern. She may see no visions, and get no help from miracles, but her vocation is very much like that of Bernadette.[84]

Redolent of themes and preoccupations explored in the previous chapter, the flexibility of pre-conciliar Marian theology allowed it to be woven through Bernadette's well known life story. Moreover, this juxtaposition was implicit in countless visual representations of Bernadette, who on holy cards, staged photos and celluloid was depicted in her head shawl and prayerful demeanour as a smaller, replica Mary of Nazareth.

Despite these attempts to present her as an ordinary woman made saintly through her life of humility and simplicity, for many English Catholics like Helen, born in Manchester in 1965, it was her contact with the divine and her communication with the Virgin Mary alone which made the Pyrenean peasant girl holy: 'Yeah, 'cause obviously she appeared – Our Lady appeared to St Bernadette'.[85]

If the mental and physical sufferings, humility, and supposedly miraculous happenings of Bernadette's life seemed beyond the experience and actual emulation of many ordinary Catholics born in relatively comfortable and urban circumstances, the 'absence of extraordinary mortifications' within Thérèse's life and her own avoidance of, as she put it, 'the macerations of the saints' seemed to offer a more promising model.[86] In the assessment of Barry Ulanov, a jazz critic and American Professor of English literature, 'the greatness of Thérèse's little way is that there is no misery too small to be accommodated by it, nor any distress too large to be comprehended by it'.[87] Mastery of weaknesses, restraint of harsh words, good cheer and humble acceptance of irritations, were offered as universally available, almost democratic, avenues towards saintliness.[88] Recapitulating themes explored in chapter 3, writers drew upon Thérèse's writings and a popular Christological understanding of the 'mystical body' to flesh out the implications of this embrace of suffering and the aspiration to sanctity. In the numerous allusions to Christ as husband and lover throughout her autobiography, illustrated in her words of rapture on her communion day ('How sweet was the first kiss of Jesus to my soul')[89] or the 'wedding invitation' she wrote for the novices on her consecration to the religious life,[90] devotion to Jesus was understood in this extreme use of the marital metaphor. Taking this cue, the former Anglican, then Catholic chaplain at the University of Oxford, Vernon Johnson, used highly erotic and charged language when narrating her life, for example likening her reported final words and death to an act of physical consummation:

> Never was St Teresa more safely in her Father's embrace than when, after eighteen years of continual physical suffering and unrelieved spiritual desolation, she said making an act of love in the dark: 'Oh – I love Him – My God, I – love – Thee'.[91]

Within this framework, suffering was conceived as a means of union between herself and her Saviour, emulating the inseparability of love and suffering 'focused to a point upon the Cross'.[92] Therefore the pains, crosses and afflictions of life were not to be enjoyed in themselves, but nevertheless 'endured gladly ... because they liken us to Him we love. *Love makes likeness.* The lover's one desire is to be like the beloved'.[93] Perhaps conscious of a degree of displacement in clerical commentaries celebrating the religious life, and undoubtedly aware of the jarring nature of such language to a lay and secular audience, the Redemptorist John Carr tackled directly the issue of sacrificing and selfless love with a swipe at 'modern' and immoral society:

> In our age … in a society where the word 'lover' has but one meaning and where the 'lover' has usurped the theatre, the kinema [sic] and the bookstall … in a society whose judges are overworked in hearing the 'love' stories of its divorce courts; in this society, in this civilisation, in this age we read another love-story, so instinct with essential love, so fair and sweet with the fine flower of it, as to make the lover of romance look a cheap when he is not a hideous counterfeit.[94]

In this exhortation to a modern world to recognise 'true' love and recant of its 'proud consciousness of its enlightenment' and self-sufficiency, Father Carr was juxtaposing Christological love and sacrifice with a 'materialist' world, that 'practically reckons without its Maker', and was dismissive of the miraculous.[95]

In this call for a sanctity addressed to the concerns of the age, Father Carr was reiterating the preoccupations of the papacy and the English Hierarchy who looked to these modern saints for a cure to society's profoundly modern 'illnesses'. Within an English context, Cardinal Griffin of Westminster (1943–56) advocated devotion to St Thérèse as 'the best antidote to present-day paganism and materialism'.[96] Similarly Ronald Knox identified Bernadette's message as addressing the 'spirit of materialism', with the capacity to 'deliver us from that captivity of thought; to make us forget the idols of our prosperity, and learn afresh the meaning of suffering and the thirst for God'.[97] In her simple and unshakeable public witness to faith and the supernatural, and particularly in the presentation of her 'triumph' against highly educated and sophisticated opposition, Bernadette was proposed as a counter to 'twentieth-century' doubt and secularism:

> What Bernadette's example demands – and receives – is the emulation of stubborn silence against mockery and unbelief … As Bernadette said to one scoffer, 'I have to tell you what I saw; but I don't have to make you believe it'.[98]

This victory of the 'little person' against powerful forces armed with the most unlikely of weapons had a long biblical history, but was given a distinctive twentieth-century presentation in the shadow of world war, rapid scientific and technological advances, systematic genocide, and global ideological systems. In an article written five years after the Second World War and at the height of Cold War anxiety, Bernard Prentis ruminated:

Was there ever an age like ours in the explicit exploitation of hate? Class is called upon to hate class, party to hate party, nation to hate nation. ... All souls are little souls in the sense in which the saint applied it to herself but most of us are indeed little souls, little because we have little will-power, little understanding, own little, do little, count little in the mass parts, mass movements, mass terrors which stalk workshop, street and home. ... Unless the little souls seek perfection in the little things all is lost.[99]

The universalising strains of this exhortation to 'an age when the stand by the hero, the martyr ... has passed'[100] sought to reassure English Catholics that firm adherence to their faith, even if sometimes inarticulately expressed, and the daily practice of virtue, even in the face of widespread 'social disintegration', could collectively transform society. Whether expressed as adoption of the 'little way', or recognition of 'the Lady's' call for 'penance', Thérèse and Bernadette were explicitly mobilised within the instructional literature against the chief concerns of the century. For earlier commentators who had not yet moved on from the terminology used to contest the Victorian 'crisis of faith', this was identified as 'purblind Rationalism and the many other "isms" that follow in its train, of which spiritualism and modern Buddhism are not the least'.[101] Later commentators, living through the Spanish Civil War, the regime of Stalin and escalating Korean hostilities, were more specific about the 'ism' to be addressed, contesting the alternative utopian appeal of communism,[102] and its 'specious claim that it has come into the world to bring happiness to the poor and the suffering and the oppressed'.[103]

It was just such preoccupations which underpinned the emphasis in these devotional writings upon an everyday sanctity and spirituality designed to appeal to the working classes, and characterised as requiring a tenacious, 'masculine' strength of will despite the folksy and floral packaging. Biographers created in the life stories of Bernadette and Thérèse a mechanism for countering secularism, and affirming the continued operation of the miraculous. This prompted a more cautious and theologically liberal clergyman, in one of the most widely read biographies of Bernadette, to renounce the tendency to use 'Lourdes as a sort of machine for proving the supernatural' and cautiously to limit the explanatory powers of science in respect of the healing of bodies and souls at this site.[104] Others, however, including one of St Thérèse's most influential and prolific biographers, employed more creative and experimental analogies:

Thérèse offers to students who have split the atom ... the example of a human being who 'drew in' her human possibilities to their least dimensions, who reduced the problem of sanctity to the atomic notion of a complete and simple cleaving to the will of God. ... she is the saint of the atomic age ... Her voice deserves greater attention than even that of Einstein; for hers is not the echo of the fear of evil, but the will to do good.[105]

Whilst often expressed in quite different registers, some defensive and others unabashedly modern and expressive, the earliest hagiographies of St Bernadette and St Thérèse exhibited common themes centred upon the simplicity (and childlike) nature of their faith and trust in God, the efficacy of suffering as a means of sanctification, and the need for a form of Catholicism and saintly virtue to stand against many of the developments of contemporary society. Far from 'plaster saints', these roughly contemporaneous French women provided dynamic 'sites' for the projection and performance of multiple understandings of sanctity, class-concerns and gendered identities. The discernible shifts in emphasis in the biographies of these saintly women as the twentieth century progressed, which prioritised the need to historicise and authenticate their lived experiences and personal psychologies, illustrate key shifts in the presentation and enactment of forms of morality, virtue and identity for English Catholics, as this chapter now explains.

From sentimental and edifying hagiographies to historical and psychological portraits

Promoting itself as 'new to the Catholic public' in being 'neither a blind panegyric, nor a work of devotion' but written with the 'detached, objective and impartial spirit of a historian',[106] Etienne Robo's *Two Portraits of St Teresa of Lisieux* (1957) was perhaps the most controversial and striking example of a discernibly different phase in the hagiographies published from the middle of the century. Within this self-consciously revisionist work, the French-born parish priest of Farnham engaged with the literary presentation and pictorial legend of St Thérèse, complete with an appendix on 'neurosis', and a detailed discussion of the released photographs of Thérèse and their 'authenticity'. The portrait that emerged from his account was of a flawed and psychologically frail humanity, and the 'unexpected use' Thérèse made of these resources 'as the means of reaching sanctity'.[107]

Two years later, in 1959, Ida Friederike Gorres published her equally provocative biography, reflecting on recent attempts to search beneath:

> the rosy, saccharine glaze of sentimental bad taste and moralism … to show Thérèse in as strong as possible contrast to that sort of 'distortion' … as a psychological problem, a misunderstood woman of great importance, a repressed artistic nature, and so on.[108]

She concluded, presciently from her mid-century vantage point, that 'this trend is still growing'[109] and it has, in fact, continued well into the twenty-first century, with a clutch of reinterpretations following Thérèse's elevation to the status of female 'Doctor of the Church'. At play within these more recent biographies of St Thérèse, and to a lesser extent those of St Bernadette, is the intense (re)prioritisation of these saints as historical persons, authentic personalities and individual psychic entities, rather than (merely) two-dimensional, instructive moral exemplars.

The increasing emphasis upon the 'historical' and the 'patristic' in the theological and devotional life of the church as the twentieth century progressed has been discussed more fully when considering the liturgy. It also took a very specific form in respect of the biographies of St Thérèse and St Bernadette. Comparing both saints, and commentating on the task of the biographer, Frances Keyes remarked that:

> We do not have to grope far into the shadowed past to reach them. It is still possible to talk, freely and frankly, with persons who knew them in the flesh, and who give our own impressions of them substance and vitality. They seem real no less than close, and this, to the average woman who seeks to understand them, is of supreme importance.[110]

This notion of the laity's identification with the saint was an interpretative emphasis also found within the earlier biographies, but it was now expressed in a register of 'historicity' and invoked as a guarantor of explicability and authenticity. This trend may also be discerned in B. G. Sandhurst's publication in 1953 of the translated testimonies of the men and women of Lourdes who had 'seen' the young girl who herself 'saw the Lady'. In an introduction to the volume by the longstanding English authority on the saint, C. C. Martindale SJ contended that the alleged miraculous occurrences at the shrine did not speak for themselves, for 'without knowledge of the *history* of an event, I cannot understand the event itself' (original emphasis).[111]

Around the same time, the Dominican Bede Lebbe's *The Soul of Saint Bernadette* was emphatic in its aim to counter the historical inaccuracies of *The Song of Bernadette* and dwelt on assertions concerning the legitimacy of its sources, from the first-hand testimonies of Cros, the detailed enquiries of 1878–79, and the account of an anonymous religious of Nevers.[112] In his volume for the centenary of the apparitions, the professional historian Hugh Ross Williamson acknowledged this difficulty in moving away from partisanship and the perils of fiction to create an account of Bernadette's life beyond the 'outlines of an eager piety ... and the caricatures of sceptics like Zola'.[113] This trend reached its most comprehensive and scholarly apogee in René Laurentin's *Bernadette of Lourdes: A Life Based on Authenticated Documents* (1979),[114] and his published volumes of testimonies and letters remain the definitive starting-point for more recent discussions of the saint and the apparitions at Lourdes.[115]

This revisionist, unabashedly historicist, fashion was even more marked, however, in the biographies of St Thérèse following the release of the original French manuscript of *The Story of a Soul* in 1956. Previous translations of the memoir had been made from the manuscript released from the convent on Thérèse's death, which had been substantially rewritten by the Reverend Mother Agnes of Jesus (Thérèse's sister, Pauline) with an eye to the conventions of literary expression, and the expectations of a good Carmelite. Upon Pauline's death in 1951 a new, 'original' and unmodified manuscript emerged, and much was made of the identification of over 5,000 amendments within a text previously thought to give access to the 'authentic' voice of the saint. The revised character portraits of Robo and Gorres were only the first to engage with the new text, and other biographers were at pains to present a stark contrast between previous 'distortions' of an inaccurate manuscript, burdened by now unfashionable and sugary prose and clichés. Biographers such as J. Beevers compared the older descriptions of Thérèse as like 'looking at her through a steamy window', whereas now 'both steam and glass have gone and we can see, clear and bright, a most engaging character and a great saint'.[116] The terms of this rehabilitation encompassed a movement away from the concept of 'spiritual childhood', towards the recognition of Thérèse as a sophisticated theological writer, ecclesiastical revolutionary and a tormented but defiant soul.

One of the readily identifiable strands within this new theological re-reading of St Thérèse was the prominence of a this-worldly, active emphasis that reworked the 'everyday' and 'accessible' spirituality identified in the earlier works. For Jean Guitton, this was the recently-appreciated recognition of Thérèse's revolutionary genius: 'instead of seeing sanctity as an ascent *to* heaven *from* earth, [she] thought that heaven should be able to see the *missionary work* entrusted to us being continued on earth'.[117] Dominican Bernard Bro also identified the need to 'refurbish the statue' or 'regild the picture' so that intellectuals might understand what 'the people' had always intuited, namely that a cloistered nun might yet have something relevant to say to our struggle for a better world.[118] Drawing upon *Lumen Gentium*, and fleshing out her message for 'the deprived, the lost, the hopeless, the crushed [and] the poor all over the world',[119] Father Bro reflected:

> In her very simple, very direct sort of life, Thérèse made the same reversal of priorities as the Second Vatican Council was later to make, the emphasis falling rather on the way you live than the way you think. She believed that God appears in the events of everyday, a God present and saying to each individual 'Are you willing?'[120]

The re-drawing of this saint in post-conciliar language continued with Michael Hollings's biography, written after his service as Chaplain at Oxford (1959–70) when undertaking challenging pastoral work in the poor and mixed-ethnic communities of Southall and Bayswater. For this author, 'when so many feel powerless, so many are deprived of their rights, of their voice, of their human dignity and liberty', Thérèse's witness of:

> Placing herself utterly in the hand of God, waiting on his mercy, even when he himself is silent ... all this puts before us an example which is simple, but if lived out, has all the elements of heroism.[121]

Subsequent biographies have continued this 'translation', likening Thérèse's advocacy of littleness to the 'option for the poor' central within liberation theology,[122] and her contemporary theological relevance as her recognition of 'the unity of the sacred and the secular'.[123] Despite these obvious shifts in language and presentational emphasis from the earlier lives of Thérèse, there remained an enduring emphasis upon an imitable, simple and countercultural sanctity, expressed now in terms accessible to a new generation of the faithful.

The most recent extension of this tendency to rewrite Thérèse's life through the lens of a younger generation's cultural and spiritual preoccupations may be seen in the prevalent revisionist biographies written from an expressly feminist perspective. The presentation of Thérèse Martin as a feisty female and independent thinker began with the tentative suggestions in Father Bro's 1979 biography that she represented a 'jolt' to a church struggling with 'the theory of women's rights'.[121] Whilst the more recent biographies fall outside the scope of this consideration, it is worth noting that this trend has continued. For example the 2001 biography by Monica Furlong offers to twenty-first-century readers a Thérèse who was a 'model for power, endurance and resourcefulness of women' negotiating a patriarchal institution.[125] The desire for priesthood, and missiological self-expression described in the autobiography[126] has been mobilised to contest the restriction of the office of priest to men. Kathryn Harrison's contribution on Thérèse in a 'Famous Lives' series, alongside volumes on Proust, Mao, Mozart and Warhol, depicts a woman known as the 'Little Flower' but more appropriately recognised as 'the Little Nettle'. As she puts it, those who 'look beyond the smile to the doctrine will find themselves stung and provoked'.[127] Finally, feminist theologians initially repelled by her presentation in early years[128] have returned to examine the 'theology' in *The Story of a Soul* and have reappraised her focus on the scriptures, her advocacy of a 'priesthood of the laity' and her intensely Christological and incarnational theology. In terms that, perhaps surprisingly, confirm John Paul II's decision to elevate St Thérèse to a Doctor of the Church, recent secular and Catholic-feminist writers have been led to the assessment that 'with good reason Thérèse has been called "the saint of the Council", its prophet and forerunner'.[129] Biographical portraits highlighting her naïvety, obedience, advocacy of suffering and celestial efficacy have been replaced by depictions of a new saint for a new age, as the unanticipated popularity of the recent tour of Thérèse's relics to England in 2009 disclosed to a puzzled secular media.[130]

Other predominant 'secular' preoccupations of the post-war period are also encountered in the more recent biographies of Thérèse Martin, and those rarer modern character studies of Bernadette Soubirous. Despite Pope Pius XII's ambivalence towards psychoanalysis well into the late 1950s (particularly those influenced by a Freudian focus on biology and deterministic drives)[131] the 'new gospel of psychology' had begun to penetrate into the mainstream cultural *Zeitgeist* by the 1950s and was becoming the most common form of knowledge and practice to describe the 'Self'.[132] However, recent intellectual histories of twentieth-century Britain now contend that it is 'difficult to accept without serious qualification the idea that the period saw either a new pre-eminence of the psychological over other influences in thinking about the self or a fundamental disjuncture'.[133] Recognising the fundamental congruence between both science and religion in 'addressing the "big questions" about human nature' – for example human welfare and happiness, sources of and remedies for mental distress, and a professional caste charged with 'cure of souls' – these writers on the relationship between psychologists and churchmen in Britain have identified a 'substantial convergence and congruence of interests between them within the prevailing cultural climate and considerable overlap in membership'.[134] Whilst Freudianism and some strains of psychoanalysis remained an area of contestation, and marked differentiation, for much of the century,[135] recent historical studies have suggested that both popular and academic psychology until the 1950s had a common orientation towards the practical and the spiritual.[136] The conclusion of much of this recent, innovative and closely-textured analysis of the intellectual culture of British society during the twentieth century has been the recognition that, at least until the 1950s:

> Psychology provided a bridge between tradition and modernity, a source for the re-articulation and full realization, rather than the end, of a subjectivity realized in service, character and values, and in the self's relation to the social and the spiritual.[137]

This same shift is discernible in the biographies of Thérèse and Bernadette, which focused on the saints' psyches, critiquing the relationship between religious experience and hysteria, the interplay between doubt and belief, and the compatibility of religion with an adult, fully individuated and self-realised personality. In the case of Bernadette, these enquiries initially, and inevitably, focused on the apparitions and, in the early but much reprinted biography by Martindale, the author disclaimed a 'duty to dissect the psychology of Bernadette'.[138] He went on to cite Dr Bertin's 1906 medical study, and dismissed the possibility of hallucination (as there were 'none of the psychical pre-requisites'), and autosuggestion (as 'they had no psychic preface or sequel').[139] The historically driven biographies of the 1970s built upon these cues, grappling with the lack of information available to discuss Bernadette's 'interior axis'[140] and considering the psychological effects of her 'visual and auditory experience'.[141] Perhaps because of the paucity of material to sustain such an enquiry, the most effective psychological exploration of Bernadette was in fictionalised, dramatic form in John Kerr's play, *Mistress of Novices* (1973). Exploring the antipathy between Bernadette and Mother Marie-Thérèse Vauzou that had been briefly touched upon in *The Song of Bernadette*, Kerr's dramatisation of the later, adult years of Bernadette's life in the convent of Nevers was a psychological exploration of modern scepticism, the limitations of science, jealousy, pride, doubt and human frailty.[142]

Thérèse was also given modernised and psychologised treatment in John Tavener's opera, *Thérèse* (1979). In a musical performance which premiered at the Royal Opera House in Covent Garden, and was full of dramatic musical extremes and symbolic darkness, the despair of the fields of Flanders, German concentration camps and suggestions of atomic annihilation were made to mirror Thérèse's autobiographical accounts of her 'passion', namely the loss of her faith in the final days of her illness.[143] A puzzled and unsympathetic reviewer observed that 'most of the action is in her mind, outside time and place', with Freudian identifications of Christ with her father and explorations of psychic breakdown and a 'descent to Hell' contributing to the making of the saint.[144]

From the late 1950s, biographers had begun to grapple explicitly with the 'psychology' of Thérèse, observing her 'compelling search for the solution to the problem of existence' along the lines of the existentialists,[145] and drawing parallels with Baudelaire, Camus and Sartre to highlight her struggles with doubt and an early death.[146] This was nothing less than, in the assessment of Bro, a 'democratizing of the "dark night of the soul"',[147] and in this respect justified her addition to the company of those 'three other giants dominating modern thought', Marx, Nietzsche and Freud.[148] These biographies presented Thérèse as a model of Christian life and experience, struggling with abandonment and depression, and striving for authenticity and self-realisation. Self-knowledge and self-acceptance, rather than the language of sin, of pliant suffering or soteriological expectation, illustrated the shifted terrain for the narration and exploration of sanctity as the century progressed.[149]

These transformations in interpretative frame are well illustrated by comparing the spirituality and devotions towards the saints manifested within one Mancunian family across the generations. Beginning with a childhood tale of a Sacred Heart statue accidentally dislodged from its prominent place on the piano by the family cat and then lovingly repaired, Francis proudly recounted his longstanding hobby of making, mending and repainting statues of various devotional personages, now numbering into the many hundreds. In the course of this conversation, Francis reflected on his recent 'acquaintance' with St Thérèse, after 'painting her' three years ago for a local parish and at the request of his current parish priest. When asked why St Thérèse was appealing to Catholics, he explained:

> FL: Well, again, human nature comes into it, I think. If you pray to her and you get your intention, I think that helps you again – 'Oh, she must be listening'. And then you feel sometimes that it takes a while for your prayer to get through, and you've got to be content. There's millions of people in the world and they can't get everybody at once. You have to sort of take your turn, get in the queue, like they do with the telephone. Get in the queue, and eventually it comes back down to you.
>
> AH: Do you think you always get what you want, with your intentions?
>
> FL: Well, in general yeah. But in general I don't ask too much, because we've been told, or it's in your teaching that, you don't tempt God too much. Occasionally I tempt and say 'Oh, I could do with winning bingo tonight, I'll give you half!' (laughs).[150]

A generational contemporary of Kathleen, whose relationship with St Antony was similarly expressed, Francis narrates a personal relationship with the saint focused on intercessory aid, material engagement (centred on statues and votive candles) and understood sometimes in contractual terms. This may be contrasted with the account of his daughter, Christine, who nonetheless also narrated an intensely incarnational faith, initially stimulated by a picture of St Thérèse on a calendar which made a deep impression on her as a twelve-year-old girl: 'as soon as I saw her she just jumped out at me, like somebody had touched you basically'.[151] Now forty-nine, following her return to the church and faith after a protracted absence, and a crisis in her personal life, she described her relationship to the saint:

> CW: But if you read stories about her you just feel so close to her, 'cause she had such a struggle. And I think a lot of people have the same struggle. They try to be good but obviously a lot of selfishness can come into it. And if you read her stories (pause) – 'cause she wasn't a wonderful

person, like most people think saints are wonderful from when they were born. Course we're all human beings, we've all got the same failings. But to try and overcome these failings is what she did. Even if it was in a very small, hidden way. And I keep thinking: 'I'm not that bad to a certain degree'.[152]

For Christine, this is an intensely integrated relationship and one in which the psychological trials and traits of Thérèse Martin are patterned onto the contours of her own life. Her reflections, especially centred on dealing with her marital breakdown, mental illness and economic struggles, echoed the intentions and reflections of many English Catholics (from a variety of generational backgrounds) who availed themselves of the recent 'reverse pilgrimage' of Thérèse's relics throughout England.[153] Not for them was the portrait of a 'pink, vapid, smiling, nauseating' girl-saint which Cesbron parodied and then reconstructed within his mid-century play.

Not all English Catholics, of course, have undertaken this reflective act of constructing a relationship with the saints and re-framing their cloying, dated and sometimes puerile depictions. Here again considerations not only of generation, but also of temperament, taste, socialisation and, in some cases, gender, are at play in deciding whether to add a favourite saint to the family portraiture. For some, such as eighteen-year-old Patrick, the saints are accepted as a theological concept, but have never assumed an active presence in his Catholic life:

> PS: No, you think of, I think of the saints just as 'the saints'. Not as individuals ... I just think of them as a – (AH: conglomerate?) Yeah. A bundle of saints.[154]

Yet for another generational contemporary, eighteen-year-old Sinead from Burnley, there is one amongst the celestial multitude to whom she has a great devotion and feels she owes a debt of thanks. Plagued by health issues since birth, Sinead recounts the strongly personalised and internalised story of her grandmother's novenas to Padre Pio when she was hospitalised as a newborn, and her 'miraculous' recovery when a relic of the stigmatic's clothing was placed beside her in the prenatal incubator.[155]

In the case of Saint Bernadette, such acts of personalisation and intellectual rehabilitation have been more limited, for the historical excavations of biographers have yielded sparse resources to re-package her as an adult woman, with a sophisticated theological message and a complex psychological landscape.[156] This has led sixty-one-year-old university lecturer Richard to observe curtly 'the idea that you have this little girl that has a message from a Lady and she has this secret thing, just, oh no. Complete anathema to me'.[157] Yet for many people an (implicit) connection with St Bernadette, and an experience of the wider communion of saints, has been made personal, tangible and psychologically transformative through the place of pilgrimage that she inaugurated (as Ruth Harris has masterfully explored).[158] Its continued (and increasing) popularity, especially with the young, which the present author has tracked, shows its personal relevance today.[159]

Changing constructions of the communion of saints: the canonisation of the Forty Martyrs

Writing in *The Catholic Gazette* on the occasion of the canonisation of the forty martyrs on 25 October 1970, the Jesuit postulator of the cause, Philip Caraman, anecdotally reminded his English and mostly convert readership:

> They are not cardboard figures from stained glass-windows, these martyrs of ours. They are men of our own blood, of our own speech, of our town tricks of manner and thought. St Thomas More, with his hearty jokes on the scaffold, John Kemble, smoking his last pipe – could they be anybody but Englishmen?
>
> And surely, if they have not forgotten, among the delights of eternity, the soft outlines and the close hedgerows and the little hills of the land that gave them birth, they will expect to see in us, their successors, something of that hourly intimacy with heaven which ruled their lives.[160]

This theme of an appropriate and accessible model of Christian holiness for Englishmen (and women it could be added, given the canonisation of Margaret Clitherow, Anne Line and Margaret Ward) was taken up by 'a lady from Liverpool' attending the ceremony in Rome with 10,000 others,[161] who observed 'At least it means … that we will have some saints in heaven who understand English'.[162] 'And Welsh', added papal reporter, and at that time Jesuit priest, Peter Hebblethwaite, before acknowledging her point that 'the communion of saints became almost palpable in these martyrs'.[163] To these qualifications could have been added the specification of 'northern', for amongst the forty canonised for their opposition to the Reformation were 'seven Lancastrian martyrs', to whom a particularly fervent and popular devotion attached.[164]

Yet how important was this canonisation to the Catholics throughout England in 1970? Did these newly canonised saints assume proportions and personalities beyond mere 'cardboard figures'? In describing in lavish detail the ceremonies that were part of the festivities of Rome, such as the flower bearers' risqué mini-skirts (redeemed by veils) and the presence of an Anglican representative of the Archbishop of Canterbury, Hebblethwaite went on to add:

> As the martyrs represented a cross-section of English society of their day, so the pilgrims were a cross-section of English Catholic life in 1970. There was even the odd reluctant intellectual swallowing his scruples in the collective emotion.[165]

This reference to the presence of the 'odd intellectual' directly poses the question of how widespread devotion to the forty martyrs was among English Catholics of different classes, temperaments, and localities, and whether the timing of the canonisation created consternation in particular quarters of the Catholic community. Concerns about the popularity of the cult, and the ecumenical challenges posed by the canonisation, were addressed by the Archbishop of Westminster in a Pastoral letter.[166] Referring to the articulated misgivings of the Archbishop of Canterbury about the canonisation, and those Christians (including Catholics) who 'feared that the memory of what the Martyrs suffered for the faith might rekindle the fires of religious controversy', Cardinal Heenan referred to the Pope's overruling of this objection, and Rome's acknowledgment of Protestant heroism during this time of religious tumult.[167] Even more problematic was the so-called 'challenge to the imagination of the modern world', which his counterpart in Salford, Bishop Holland, unabashedly raised.[168]

These three aspects of the canonisation – its popularity, ecumenical palatability and perceived connection of martyrdom with 'modern-day concerns' – will be considered in the final part of this chapter, as a case study for the consideration of the place of the cult of the saints within the faith lives and devotional practices of latter twentieth-century English Catholics.

Following the opening of the cause for canonisation in 1960 by Pope John XXIII, in response to a petition from the Hierarchy of England and Wales, the Bishop of Salford wrote a letter to the Catholic schoolchildren of his diocese:

> It is not enough, however, to know about the martyrs. We must love them and we must pray to them. We must also encourage other people to know about them and to have devotion to them. ... Above all be proud of the heroic example they showed in their lives and in their deaths. Be proud of the faith which you hold to-day, the same Catholic faith which they held, and in defence of which they were ready to give their lives.[169]

Recalling events such as the unveiling of a statue for the English martyrs in 1952, when 15,000 Liverpudlians joined 35,000 others in a silent march,[170] and the popularity of the cult surrounding the Jesuit Edmund Arrowsmith whose 'holy hand' was kept in a reliquary in Ashton-in-Makerfield,[171] there was some foundation in 1960 for Father Caraman's nevertheless overly-exuberant assessment of:

> an astonishing revival of the faith ... nothing hysterical, nothing forced in the devotion. There is no pressure, no mass drilling. The response is spontaneous, widespread and deep-felt.[172]

In an attempt to tap this perceived popularity, a number of public rallies were held, such as the Martyrs' Exhibition at Stonyhurst in 1963, attended by 5,000 people,[173] and a Martyrs' Mass at Belle Vue in 1965, at which Archbishop Beck (having been translated from the Salford to the Liverpool diocese) told the crowd that 'nowhere else in England was the cause of the martyrs so dear to the hearts of the people because so many of the martyrs were Lancashire folk'.[174]

This sense of a historic, enduring and native 'English' Catholicism was articulated in the oral testimony of Yorkshire-born Mancunian Judith:

> AH: In 1970 they canonised the Forty Martyrs (JE: Yes). Do you recall if that was important?
> JE: Oh yes. Oh yes. I was very, very annoyed that I couldn't go to the canonisation. Because of my – I mean there is a venerable Thomas Atkinson, [and] my mother's maiden name is Atkinson. We've never actually proved that he, that we are directly connected with him but one of my great aunts always used to say that he was ... I came across

> one piece of paper where it would be my great grandfather about five times back, or six times back, was fined in 1722 for no, refusing to take the oath. So the line goes right back there. So when the English martyrs … – oh, yes, I was very proud of that.[175]

While not all Catholics could, of course, claim a familial connection to the martyrs, nor the familiarity that Judith readily acknowledged,[176] the empirical testaments of recusant history, and claims to 'authenticity' established through the excavation of the past, were common strategies used in furtherance of the cause. The Jesuit files at Farm Street, London – the administrative centre for the pursuit of the canonisation, known as the Office of Vice Postulation (OVP) – are full of copies of manuscripts and historical materials, painstakingly gathered in a positivist historical vein, to establish exact dates, facts and biographical details of the forty men and women put forward to Rome. Illustrative of these efforts are materials relating to the careful authentication of the skull of 'the martyr monk of Manchester', Ambrose Barlow, including a letter based on a comparison of x-rays of the head to an authentic portrait, to conclude that:

> a formidable case can nevertheless be made out on purely historical grounds that the relic is indeed Bd. Ambrose Barlow. The new anatomical findings strengthen this beyond anything that could have been hoped for two years ago.[177]

Given the longstanding public devotion to the relic,[178] and its permanent location in the Bishop's House at Wardley Hall, Manchester, public contributions were successfully sought for a 'more elaborate casket for public devotion'.[179]

It was also realised that this appeal to 'an antiquarian's interest in the past' might not be palatable to 'the ordinary Catholic [for whom] it is impossible … to remember even the main facts about the Forty'.[180] For these English (and Welsh) Catholics, many of whom might also self-identify as first, second or third generation Irish Catholics, the promoters of the cause attempted to create a heroic, inspiring hagiography.

Writing on the Lancastrian layman John Rigby, Father Forshaw painted a picture of a man of strong physique, 'who was conscious when his heart was being pulled out', and who preserved his chastity, even in a 'lusty age', thereby earning the endorsement:

> For sheer manliness … we could look very far before finding a more worthy example for today.[181]

'Plaster saints' or 'spiritual friends'? 237

This appeal to the violent and the visceral was collectively endorsed by the Diocesan Representatives' Committee, to which Father Whatmore advocated the circulation of medals and badges to schoolchildren, but especially 'pictures of the Martyrs, particularly of their executions. They make a very great impression on boys and on the whole a valuable impression'.[182] Perhaps it was just such sentiments that prompted the General Postulation committee in 1963 to commission Mrs Daphne Pollen to paint a collective illustration of the forty martyrs, with the Tower of London, gallows at Tyburn, and a makeshift altar, centre-stage (Figure 5.1). Within her historically inflected re-visioning of this group of diverse saints, virtue is presented in romanticised and typologised terms, with demure Margaret Clitherow in the foreground, aristocratic Philip Howard with his hound, and surrounding ranks of male sanctity spanning priesthood, scholarship (with Edmund Campion clasping a book) and the virile martyrdom of teacher Richard Gwyn with hat and quill.

A similar theme was advocated in notes circulated to the clergy for 'Short Sermons on the English and Welsh Martyrs' at the very beginning of the cause. Stressing the ties of 'blood, environment and nationality', as well as 'spiritual inheritance', and advocating a degree of artistic licence in extending this to 'their jokes ... their interest in sport', priests were advised of their applicability and relevance to English Catholics.

In a section on 'martyrs and heroism', the clergy were advised to draw upon the 'great age of English "heroes"', e.g. sea-captains' but to contrast their desire for fame, or wealth, or power, with the 'true courage of the martyrs' who:

> had true manliness, reflecting Christ's courage in his suffering, uttering the truth fearlessly in front of his judges, praying for his enemies. It is the same story with all the martyrs, including women.[183]

Evidenced in the developments in the historiography of St Thérèse of Lisieux, the lauding of 'heroics' on a grand scale and a hagiography without individuality, personality or an engagement with the subject's psychology (particularly in dealing with the now unpalatable appeal to suffering) could not hope to generate, or even stimulate, much devotion amongst the uninformed.

As sixty-five-year-old Tony reflected, speaking of his own acquaintance with the seven Lancastrian martyrs through localised devotion to St

238   *Faith in the family*

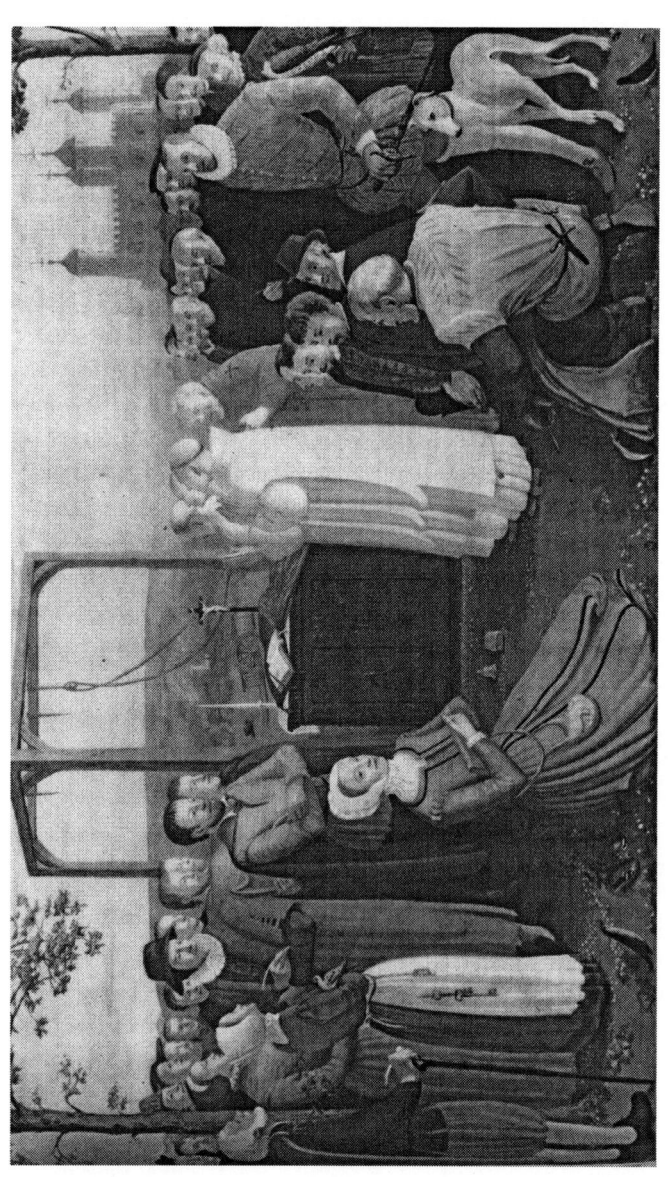

5.1 Commissioned painting of the Forty Martyrs by Daphne Pollen, from the *Universe and Catholic Times*, 10 July 1964, 1 [Reproduced with permission from the Governors of Stonyhurst College, Lancashire, *Universe and Catholic Times*, Manchester and The Bodleian Libraries, The University of Oxford, shelf mark N.11132 a.3]

Ambrose Barlow in Didsbury, and their names used for 'house groupings' at his school:

> TC: I think it would have been better if they'd just said St so-and-so and St so-and-so rather than just (a) block, because forty is a lot to (laughs) comprehend. ... So I think if they had condensed it a little bit they might have ... well people might have appreciated it a bit more.[184]

By 1963 the diocesan representatives themselves were beginning to recognise that, even on the more sanguine assessment of Fr Caraman SJ, devotion 'is stronger in some parts of the country than others'. As Monsignor Reynolds bluntly articulated, 'the country as a whole has not shown sufficient devotion to the Forty Martyrs ... [and] as a whole there is still much indifference'.[185] This assessment was definitively confirmed, in a devastating report in 1966 to the Hierarchy of England and Wales, by James Walsh SJ while reflecting on his first year as sole Vice-Postulator of the cause. In disarmingly direct and unequivocal terms, he wrote of the 'unpalatable truth of dwindling devotion' and the attitudes of the Catholic laity 'ranging from minority support to majority indifference'.[186] In his opening gambit, he charted the difficulties confronted in fulfilling his brief:

> In many quarters, it has become the fashion to see devotion to the saints as démodé; the cult of the Martyrs as a sign of the state of siege, and the Cause as inopportune to the ecumenical movement.[187]

Cataloguing hostility particularly amongst educated Catholics and tepid clerical support, he acknowledged:

> Northern Catholics naturally tend to be more Martyr-conscious, but on the whole the truth is that the Forty Martyrs have lost their mystique in the modern world.
>
> I have no faith in attempts at promotion through gimmicks or contrived 'revivalism'. The problem is to show the relevance of the cult to reality in this day and age; for the sense of historical drama which once was a feature of devotion to the Martyrs had faded and dwindled. We live in an almost uniquely sceptical time, with pop-heroes and TV images for our demigods.[188]

While revisionist biographers were striving, often successfully, to make St Thérèse into a psychologised, anti-authoritarian and theologically-sophisticated role model, tapping into modern-day spiritual propensities for an immanentist, everyday religiosity, this was a much harder feat to accomplish for forty individuals of varied background and with sparse biographical materials. As a 'bunch of saints', it was difficult to create a personal relationship, unless it already pre-existed for reasons of familial identification or an accident of locality, with a saintly collective. These difficulties were compounded by the clear tensions posed by the promotion of the cause to the welcome and newly emerging ecumenical movement, which was popular amongst the clergy and the educated laity, particularly in urban centres like London, in the years immediately following the Council.[189]

Illustrative of the traditional presentation of the forty martyrs to Catholics of England and Wales is Father Greenstock's *Talks to Catholic Parents* (1951) that advised:

> [M]ake sure at the same time that your children never take the Mass for granted. Tell them stories of the English Martyrs during the days of persecution and so make them see that this, which we offer now in comparative ease and comfort, is the same as that for which they gave their lives so cheerfully.[190]

This link between the martyrs and the mass had been traditionally mobilised in the presentation of a highly defensive, triumphalist and 'ghetto-style' Catholicism, which J. A. Fletcher took great delight in disparaging in the correspondence columns of *The Tablet* when discussing the 'ecumenism' of a widely circulating CTS pamphlet and its analysis of the 'regrettable' (but excusable) Protestant martyrdoms under Mary who was 'at least … engaged in suppressing error, whereas her father was suppressing truth'.[191] These lines of interpretation were further hardened in some quarters, when the connection between the martyrs, the mass and their 'Reformation resistance' were used as exemplars for those contesting the changes to the liturgy following the Second Vatican Council.[192] Devotion to the martyrs was, for example, advocated by Latin Mass Society members such as Roger de Weaver, who in correspondence to Cardinal Heenan in 1970 vowed to 'read my Tridentine Mass in my beloved Roman Missal' on the model of 'the Blessed English martyrs who generously gave their lives rather than forego the very Mass which has now been thrown into the ecumenical hotpot'.[193]

Astutely aware of the political sensitivities, and difficult rhetorical strategies for contesting such perceptions, Bishop Beck of Salford wrote to Bishop Dwyer of Birmingham in 1963 to discuss 'the rumour which seems to be growing that there will be opposition in Rome to the completion of the Cause of the 40 English and Welsh martyrs on the grounds that their canonisation might be injurious to the ecumenical movement'.[194] By 1965, in view of the growing momentum of the Council and interdenominational rapprochement, the Hierarchy was unable to ignore these sensitivities or the widespread objections to the isolationist and triumphalist tone of prevailing promotional strategies. On Martyrs Sunday in 1965, the OVP issued a provocative and proactive manifesto entitled 'The Forty Martyrs and Christian Unity', which acknowledged:

> [T]here have been some misgivings about the Cause in some quarters. Some have feared that the Cause may serve only to emphasise the very divisions we now seek to heal, cause offence to our separated brethren, and injure the sense of fellowship which, over the past few years, has marvellously grown.
>
> In truth, however, it is quite otherwise … it was precisely the 40 Martyrs who, in the act of dying for love of truth, first uttered this prayer for forgiveness, first expressed their love of the separated brethren, and first prayed that all should be one again.
>
> By doing so they anticipated the ecumenical movement by 400 years and sowed the seeds for all that is happening today.[195]

This statement was coupled with the institution of an annual ecumenical pilgrimage to the Protestant Martyrs' Memorial in Smithfield, led by Father Tigar SJ, and which in 1970 was seen as an important counterpoint to ecumenical objections to the canonisation.[196] Whilst *The Universe* with its readership of northern, working-class Catholics took this as a sign that the cause was 'nearing its climax',[197] and printed letters from the official lay spokesperson for the cause which drew parallels between the martyr-priests and post-conciliar empowerment of the laity through community-based churches,[198] the readership of *The Tablet* was engaged in a protracted correspondence about the mass, the martyrs and the meaning of ecumenism.

The correspondence was initially sparked by a Miss Joan Eland who bluntly contended that, whilst not 'want[ing] to drag up old bitterness', it was clear that 'the martyrs died for the conversion of England, apprehended while saying the Mass in Latin' and for 'the one true faith'.[199] Wary of such adverse publicity, Father James Walsh SJ answered this correspondence in terms that reiterated the *Manifesto*, defining ecumenism with reference to the Conciliar document as 'the restoration of unity among all Christians'. Father Walsh then drew subtle examples from the 'unity in the papacy', as opposed to the primacy of Peter, and 'convergence on the central doctrine of the Eucharist', rather than the Latin mass. Resorting to emotive imagery, and admitting a degree of casuistic reasoning, the OVP acknowledged:

> [T]he interaction of insistence on purity of doctrine with the ecumenical dialogue is a subtle business... There is about ecumenism a climate of open-mindedness which was hardly uppermost in the Martyr's mind as the hurdle jerked him to Tyburn and his captors promised him freedom in return for his apostasy.[200]

Subsequent correspondents were less unequivocal about the 'subtleties', and laywoman Margaret FitzHerbert asked:

> Who is he trying to fool? Anyone who had read the lives and utterances of the martyrs knows that, rightly or wrongly, they regarded Protestantism as the enemy and themselves as soldiers in the fight against it. ... it is disingenuous to suggest that the martyrs died for ecumenism or for anything other than their Catholic faith.[201]

Her liberal, pragmatic approach unexpectedly corresponded with that of a traditionalist clergyman, who similarly saw Father Walsh's letter as 'unhelpful' and 'strange history',[202] for the martyrs were:

> not forerunners of the Abbé Portal or Fr. Küng. ... They were reactionary enough to die for that denomination against which the gates of hell have not prevailed, either before or after 1962.[203]

Preaching at a mass in Liverpool before the canonisation, Cardinal Willebrands, President of the Pontifical Council for Promoting Christian Unity, acknowledged that 'we perform impossible contortions if we try to see such attitudes as ecumenical in any sense we could now give the term'.[204] Instead, he advocated an interpretation that saw the martyrs as modelling 'the virtues of the apostle – constancy, courage [and] utter dedication to the truth'.[205]

This was an approach far more likely to resonate with an educated audience in a wider, post-1968 context, which was attuned to the articulation of protest in terms of heroic individualism and anti-authoritarianism through, for example, Robert Bolt's *A Man for all Seasons*, a popular play (and later film) celebrating Sir Thomas More as a model of conscience and 'civic rights'.[206] The success of such recasting in the case of post-conciliar Christological writings, or recent biographies of St Thérèse, has already been explored, and, writing on the eve of the canonisation for a Mancunian audience, Father Allen also acknowledged this more recent tendency:

> to treat the martyrs as demonstrators for civil rights. It is said they died 'for conscience'. Broadly speaking they did. But that was not uppermost in their minds when they stood in the dock.[207]

These reasons were, on Father Allen's more reactionary and defensive assessment, 'the Mass' and the 'Christian truth', which he saw as uniting Catholics and Protestants now in an ecumenical enterprise as enemies of humanism, secularism and materialism. The Bull of Canonisation issued by Pope Paul VI also employed such language, strongly endorsing the martyrs as 'examples of that loyal integrity which rejects false compromises in matters held as sacred and is not afraid to declare its own convictions' to counter the growing 'materialism and naturalism' of contemporary society.[208] In the investigatory processes into the miracles required for the canonisation, these oppositional juxtapositions of faith with 'materialism', and religiosity against 'naturalism', and 'secularism', were also in evidence.

At the request of the promoters of the cause when it opened in 1960, accounts of favours and cures flowed into the OVP, and were published in their weekly *Bulletin* (of unknown circulation numbers) for the elucidation of the faithful, and the stimulation of further accounts. In these initial years, the relics of the martyrs seemed to be particularly effective in granting many of these petitions. An example is the case of 'J. A. O'C', whose granddaughter was severely ill with leukaemia, and who was discharged from hospital following a blood transfusion and a blessing with a relic of Blessed John Southworth.[209] The relic of Blessed Edmund Arrowsmith, used to bless 'M.R's' husband diagnosed as 'dying of cancer' and given the prognosis of 'three weeks of intense pain', answered the family's prayers 'in a very special way' in ensuring his peaceful and gentle death the next day.[210] Both favours indicate the inter-meshing of belief and science in procuring, in their different ways, an outcome pleasing and acceptable to the faithful.

Summarising the wealth of information forwarded to the Office of Vice Postulation throughout 1960, a report to the Hierarchy stated that over 5,000 petitions had been forwarded in response to the Tridua of Prayer in Westminster and Salford, and observed that, 'not all the letters by any means were for the cure of illnesses'. It noted that some begged for spiritual strength, others 'as at Lourdes, ask only for courage and grace to bear their suffering', and there were also some letters that 'even non-Catholics have written, impressed by the faith of their friends, asking for prayers'.[211] The report concluded that 'the majority of the petitions has been from families', and that many were written 'in calm resignation, adding the clause "if it be God's will"'.[212]

These conclusions seem to summarise well the breadth and variety of petitions and thanksgivings recounted in the *Bulletins* over the decade 1960–1970, with the first three listed in a 1962 edition including:

1. S. R for success in a very difficult examination (Sr Regis, SW1)
2. T. D. for the preservation of a marriage, which was in danger of breaking up (Fr. T. Dunphy)
3. P. P. for the cure of arthritis in his right hand, which prevented him from writing legibly (P. Phelan).[213]

As this example illustrated, the ordinary, everyday and contemporary concerns of a cross-section of English Catholics were brought to the attention of the forty martyrs and, for some, there was an answer to their petition.

Analysis of the archives across the decade of investigation shows that the concerns and troubles of family members, and the difficulties of modern family life, made frequent appearances in these lists. The efficacy of the forty martyrs in solving and supporting family troubles was well illustrated in a letter in 1963, from a father of six:

> My wife became so sick mentally that she made two attempts at suicide. The psychiatrist said that he could do nothing for her unless she entered a mental hospital for treatment, perhaps for a period of two years. Her going to hospital would have meant the break-up of our family, so the children and I said a decade of the rosary every night for their Mum to the Forty Martyrs.
>
> A crisis came one evening in our home. My wife was so bad I was going to call the police, the children were crying and there was no adult in the house to help me ... In desperation I asked the Forty Martyrs to help me, especially Margaret Clitherow. After a short while my wife quietened down, and became

so well that I went off to my night work. She has never had occasion to visit a psychiatrist since.[214]

The invocation of Margaret Clitherow, the convert wife of a Yorkshire butcher who refused to plead recusancy to save her children from testifying, could be seen as a particularly apposite choice in this case of a threat to the stability of the family unit, and the exhaustion of the alternative avenues of conventional psychiatry. For this Catholic husband and father, the cult of the saints was believed to have answered needs which science alone could not address.

The circumvention of traditional medical advice, coupled with a dogged adherence to church teachings, namely medical recommendations of abortion, caesarean section and sterilisation, were also central to the case of Mrs Walsh of Eccles, Lancashire, in 1961. The invocation of the forty martyrs by herself, her husband and family during a difficult ninth pregnancy, compounded by extreme diabetes, and a heart condition, was thought to have resulted in the safe delivery of the child, and the cessation of these other symptoms on the birth of the child, 'Leo Ignatius'.[215] Enquiries from the OVP, following a statement from the husband and wife, produced non-committal, somewhat negative comments from the Catholic gynaecologist[216] and the following, exasperated response from the parish priest:

> The Walshes are an amazing family with limitless faith. I very much agree that she was extraordinarily fortunate in getting away with the last lot and that it was an answer to prayer.
>
> If the Forty Martyrs were responsible, I hope they repeat their good work, because Mrs Walsh frightens me to death every year lest her husband be left with a house full of children.[217]

While crediting the family's subjective belief in the power of prayer and efficacious intervention, also implicit in Father McGinnell's response is clear discomfort. Tacit within his response is a disinclination to discount less supernatural explanations, and unarticulated alternative remedies, some within and others transgressing church teaching, which might circumvent the need for such a 'miracle'. In this example, from 'client', medical practitioner and priest, is present a spectrum of Catholic responses to saintly intercession and devotional efficacy.

Whilst this case illustrates the tensions sometimes highlighted between faith and medicine, and the differing interpretations of believer, medical professional and pastor, other accounts of healings and favours indicated a co-operative, harmonious collaboration and holistic interpretation across such frameworks. One of the most illustrative was a letter from Dr Jes Alwyn who wrote to Father Walsh on 2 January 1968 about his patient, Mrs Jean Shuker, who had been trying to conceive for ten years, and who haemorrhaged from six weeks until twenty weeks during pregnancy:

> From the night that I first saw her, until in fact she was confined, I prayed that the 40 Martyrs would intercede on behalf of this woman.
>
> In my experience I have never seen a pregnant patient lose so much blood over such a prolonged interval and retain a viable pregnancy. I am loath to label this patient's case as miraculous but it is certainly extraordinary and I attribute her good fortune more to prayer and the 40 Martyrs than my medical expertise. By the way this patient is not a Catholic but she herself regards her good fortune as miraculous.[218]

In response to a letter from the OVP asking for the clinical reports, Dr Alwyn went on to write:

> I think it is reasonable to say that we have become spiritually rather sophisticated and that almost certainly 20 years ago Mrs Shuker's case would be considered a miracle, but I quite agree with you that it is more than impressive as an extraordinary favour. ... Although she was given, I think, conscientious care the success of her pregnancy, in my opinion, cannot be attributed to this alone.[219]

Dr Alwyn found an audience receptive to his cautious, but open-minded, perspective at Farm Street, as Father Walsh was similarly aware of the changed 'spirituality' of the contemporary Catholic and the difficulties in differentiating the 'miraculous' from the 'extraordinary' at a time of rapid medical advances.

Towards the conclusion of his 1966 report mentioned earlier on the 'State of the Cause', Father Walsh discussed the progress made by the OVP towards documenting the necessary two miracles for the canonisation. Observing that 'the case of Mrs Matthewman (Salford) is already well known to your Lordships', he then catalogued the other contenders, including a boy in Brentwood diocese who had recovered from cancer but whose doctors were not 'co-operative' in assisting enquiries, and the recovery of a five-year-old Preston boy from seemingly irreparable brain damage, which was 'await[ing] further medical evidence'.[220] These difficulties led him to observe that to meet the criteria of 'a miracle' – that is, an irreversible and permanent recovery inexplicable by reason or medicine – the 'severe criteria of modern science are increasingly hard to meet'.[221] He wondered whether it might be better to pursue a new, theological approach to enquiries, interrogating the relationship between the 'providential' and the 'miraculous'.[222]

Eventually the cause did establish its 'miracle', marked by the determination of the Medical Council of the Sacred Congregation of Rites on 30 July 1969, that the cure of a young mother affected with a malignant tumour (fibrosarcoma) in the left scapular, Mrs Matthewman of Blackburn, was 'gradual, perfect, constant and unaccountable on the natural plane'.[223] This miracle was deemed sufficient to prove the cause for the canonisation of the forty, leading the Vatican to dispense with the documentation surrounding the second example.

Tuberculosis had been the disease dominating the efforts of the medical profession, and the concerns of the public, at the turn of the twentieth century when St Thérèse and St Bernadette had been canonised and this disease was central to the cures and 'flowers' recounted to establish their intercessory efforts. It therefore seemed only appropriate, towards the twentieth century's conclusion, that cancer, and the quest for a cure, which in its initial stages had involved a visit to Lourdes when Mrs Matthewman was pregnant with her third child, were seen to be within the purview of the saintly forty.

In a letter to the *Catholic Herald* reflecting on the ongoing cause for the canonisation of the forty martyrs during 1968, M. Russell from Upminster reflected:

> How many of our youngsters are interested in keeping Sunday holy by reading 'The lives of the Saints', yet I believe many of them are doing more good with their time by practical help in the various projects directed at the poor and aged.
>
> By all means let us remember these holy people, let the story of their lives be written for our example, but why spend large sums of money to call them officially 'Saint'?[224]

As this chapter has illustrated, the perspective articulated by this Catholic from Essex was shared by many, but by no means all, of his co-religionists as the twentieth century progressed. In the commonly circulating re-tellings of the lives of St Bernadette and St Thérèse, there was a demonstrable movement away from the pious instructional hagiographies produced at the beginning of the century, towards claimed 'biographical histories' of these women, interpreting their lives and times chiefly through the lens of psychology. Through this process, English Catholics were provided with an inspirational model 'like' them, despite potential differences in class, gender, nationality and marital status.

In the narration of the lived religious lives and spiritual experiences of these women, Catholics in the latter half of the twentieth century were supplied with universal exemplars which, conformant to the trends in Christology and Mariology already explored, modelled religious authenticity, the witness of conscience, and an eschatological engagement with everyday concerns and wider injustices. Similar perspectives were articulated by the recently retired head teacher Peter who admitted that, 'I think in general our devotion to the saints has waned somewhat',[225] but went on to observe that:

> PK: the ones that (remain popular) have still got some modernity about them, if you like, rather than the ascetics and the brains of the past. ... Thérèse of Lisieux. A holy person, a very holy person. Bernadette Soubirous we can put in the same bracket as well. Can you aspire to that kind of holiness, or should you be looking at, say, people who had – and I don't mean this to be disrespectful to them – *real* lives. ... practical – (like) Maximilian Kolbe. Do we need to bring our saints right up to date, or do as we've done for centuries?[226]

This concern with 'real' lives, and the ways in which modern medicine and clinical psychology have increasingly emerged as rival but sometimes complementary for interrogating these saints and associated 'miracles', also frame the interpretation of the pilgrimage sites connected with these saints which I have explored elsewhere.[227] To this day, one hundred and fifty years after the apparitions to Bernadette, this famous shrine in the Pyrénées remains a place where English Catholics, in their tens of thousands, annually go to remember their 'holy people' (St Bernadette, the Virgin Mary and all the saints), but more importantly to emulate saintly behaviour, through the development of a personally expressive spirituality, and an active devotion in the care and service of other pilgrims.

While some saints have gained or retained their appeal through clerical presentation or lay-led apprehension of their resonance with contemporary concerns and embodiment of an incarnational and inspirational spirituality, others have receded from the devotional scene. Speaking of the culture of devotion to the saints, Richard recounted a surprising appeal to 'St Antony' by a Hindu work colleague and then reflected:

> RD: But that's sort of superstitious really, isn't it? It's not really a devotion. I think when you think about, when you say 'Pray to St Anthony', 'cause you've lost something, what you're actually doing is you stop, because you do the panic bit, right. So you're like 'Where is it? What have I done with it?' and you actually stop, say for that short time, and you think 'Now, I remember what I did …'
>
> AH: That's really interesting, that's really interesting.
>
> RD: (laughs) But it doesn't say much about the devotion to St Anthony, does it? (laughs)
>
> AH: Well, it does say something about the way –
>
> RD: Superstitious.
>
> AH: Well, Catholicism has always had a folk element …
>
> RD: Superstitious. (laughs)[228]

But elsewhere in the course of this interview, Richard was surprisingly open to the reality and operation of the metaphysical and confessed a strong belief in the broader conception of the 'communion of saints'. Rooted in the sense that he had inherited from his grandmother a type of gift as a 'medium' – an aptitude that he found 'strange', 'frightening' and 'had never really pursued' – Richard contended that 'the idea that people die and they've no connection with them once they've died or something, I'd disagree with. Because I've found you do'.[229] As a highly educated and theologically astute male, from a mixed Catholic background, Richard's experiences and perceptions vary from others considered in this chapter, and indicate that, in this extra-liturgical, 'optional', 'customisable' area of Catholic devotional life, there remains a wide scope for the interplay of personality, temperament and socialisation.

The example of the forty martyrs explored in this chapter illustrates this complex constellation of issues. For while the movement to 'historicise' Saints Bernadette and Thérèse made them adaptable, universal and timeless, this same attempt in the case of the English martyrs conjured a recusant 'English' past and nostalgia for an older-style, defensive church. This presentation did not wholly resonate with a 1970s English Catholicism that was ethnically mixed, ecumenically engaged and focused on social activism. Nevertheless, for some people towards the end of the twentieth century, such as the grateful father of six whose wife had regained her mental health, or the non-Catholic woman who survived a life-threatening pregnancy, the saints remained indispensable spiritual friends who, whether engaged through votive candles or heartfelt prayer, remained available for imitation and intercession.

Notes

1. G. Cesbron, *No Plaster Saint: A Play about St Thérèse of Lisieux* (London: Hollis and Carter, 1948), 1.
2. *Ibid*, 2.
3. *Ibid*, 6.
4. *Ibid*.
5. *Ibid*, 10.
6. M. Francis, *Smallest of All: A Play in Three Acts. For Our Lady of Lourdes on the Hundredth Anniversary of Her Coming* (London: Samuel French, 1958), 77.
7. *Ibid*, 74–6.
8. Cited in E. McCaffrey, *Heart of Love: Saint Thérèse of Lisieux* (Dublin: Veritas, 1998), 17.
9. Canon Arendzen, 'Members of God's own family', *Catholic Times*, 23 November 1956, 9.
10. Knox, *Creed*, 197.
11. Interview, Mitzi at 27.30–28.19.
12. Interview, Patrick at 28.23–28.26.
13. Interview, Kevin, transcript page 14.
14. 'Young People's Corner: St Anthony the Great', *Catholic Times*, 22 September 1950, 8.
15. Blessed Robert Southwell, *Catholic Times*, 20 July 1956, 8.
16. C. C. Martindale SJ, *What are the Saints? Fifteen Chapters in Sanctity* (London: Sheed and Ward, 1932).
17. C. C. Martindale SJ, *The Queen's Daughters: A Study of Women-Saints* (London: Sheed and Ward, 1951).
18. Martindale, *Saints?*, 15.
19. Interview, Kathleen at 22.18–22.52; 26.19–26.44.
20. Interview, Margaret at 47.09–47.28.
21. Interview, Nora at 26.18–26.38.
22. Interview, Margaret at 7.09–7.35.
23. Saint Francis was another highly popular saint – see M. Heimann, 'St Francis and Modern English Sentiment' in S. Ditchfield (ed.), *Christianity and Community in the West: Essays for John Bossy* (Aldershot: Ashgate, 2001), 278–93.
24. V. Sackville-West, *The Eagle and the Dove: A Study in Contrasts, St Teresa of Avila, St Thérèse of Lisieux* (London: Michael Joseph, 1943), 116.
25. T. Martin, *The Story of a Soul: A New Translation* (Brewster: Paraclete Press, 2006), 210–25.

26 J. Carr, *Truly a Lover: Some Reflections on Saint Teresa of Lisieux* (London: Sands and Co, 1925), 17.
27 B. Corrado Pope. 'A Heroine without Heroics: The Little Flower of Jesus and Her Times', *Church History* 51(1) (1988), 50.
28 R. Laurentin, *Bernadette of Lourdes: A Life Based on Authenticated Documents* (London: Darton, Longman and Todd, 1979), 4.
29 D. A. Foley, *Apparitions of Mary: Their Meaning in History* (London: Catholic Truth Society, 2000), 33.
30 T. Taylor, *Bernadette of Lourdes: Her Life, Death and Visions* (London: Burns and Oates, 2003), 178–9.
31 See T. N. Taylor, *Saint Thérèse of Lisieux, The Little Flower of Jesus* (London: Burns, Oates and Washbourne, 1927), 279–89.
32 Advertisement, 'St Thérèse', *The Tablet*, 18 September 1948, 184.
33 M. D. Forrest, *The Fragrance of the Little Flower* (Dublin: Burns, Oates and Washbourne, 1934), 31–2.
34 B. Williamson, *St Thérèse and the Faithful: A Book for Those Living in the World* (London: Burns, Oates and Washbourne, 1935), 62.
35 I. F. Gorres, *The Hidden Face: A Study of St Thérèse of Lisieux* (London: Burns and Oates, 1959), 7.
36 J. B. Morton, *St Thérèse of Lisieux: the Making of a Saint* (London: Burns and Oates, 1954), 6.
37 Martin, *Story of a Soul*, 153–4.
38 *Ibid*, 230.
39 J. Beevers, *St Thérèse of the Child Jesus* (London: St. Paul Publications, 1960), 10–12.
40 M. Doran, *The Little Flower: A Religious Drama in Three Acts* (London: Samuel French, 1928).
41 J. Bate, *St Thérèse of Lisieux for Children* (London: Catholic Truth Society, 1960), 5.
42 B. Williamson, *The Sure Way of St Thérèse of Lisieux* (London: Kegan Paul, 1928), 208.
43 Most famously S. J. Piat, *The Story of a Family: The Home of the Little Flower* (Dublin: M.H. Gill and Son, 1947), x.
44 For a groundbreaking, sustained study of the material (and commercial) development of this cult, see S. Deboick, 'Image, Authenticity and the Cult of Saint Thérèse of Lisieux, 1897–1959' (Unpublished PhD thesis, University of Liverpool, 2011) and 'The Creation of a Modern Saint' in P. Clarke and T. Claydon (eds), *Saints and Sanctity* (Woodbridge: Suffolk, 2011), 376–89.
45 F. Parkinson Keyes, *The Sublime Shepherdess* (London: Burns, Oates and Washbourne, 1941).
46 R. H. Steuart, *Diversity in Holiness* (London: Sheed and Ward, 1936), 174.
47 F. Werfel, *The Song of Bernadette* (New York: Viking, 1942), 6.
48 See J. T. Frederick, 'Franz Werfel and the Song of Bernadette', *College English* 4(6) (1943), 339.
49 P. M. Kane, 'Jews and Catholics Converge: *The Song of Bernadette (1943)*' in C. McDannell (ed.), *Catholics at the Movies* (Oxford: Oxford University Press, 2008), 85.

50 'The Song of Bernadette', *The Times*, 6 March 1944, 6.
51 'New Gallery: "The Song of Bernadette"', *The Times*, 28 March 1944, 2.
52 Interview, John at 31.18–31.55.
53 Interview, Kevin, transcript page 15.
54 'The Song of Bernadette', *Jewish Chronicle*, 28 May 1948, 18.
55 F. B. Lockhart, 'Catholics and the Cinema: The Conference of the Catholic Film Society', *The Tablet*, 28 August 1948, 136.
56 F. Parkinson Keyes, *St Teresa of Lisieux* (London: Eyre and Spottiswoode, 1950), 180.
57 Morton, *Thérèse*, 95.
58 Gorres, *Hidden*, 6.
59 Keyes, *Teresa*, 180.
60 Sackville-West, *Eagle*, 140.
61 V. Johnson, 'St Teresa and Her Mission' in V. Johnson (ed.), *The Mission of a Saint* (London: Burns, Oates and Washbourne, 1947), 20.
62 Steuart, *Diversity*, 167.
63 J. I. Lane, *St Bernadette and the Apparitions at Lourdes: Told for Children* (London: Burns, Oates and Washbourne, 1937), 67.
64 B. Lebbe, *The Soul of Bernadette* (Tralee: Kerryman Ltd, 1946), 72.
65 B. G. Sandhurst, *We Saw Her* (London: Green and Co, 1953), 212.
66 H. Petitot, *Saint Teresa of Lisieux: A Spiritual Renascence* (London: Burns, Oates and Washbourne, 1927), xxv.
67 P. Liagre, *A Retreat with St Thérèse* (London: Douglas Organ, 1947), 10.
68 S. Kaye-Smith, *Quartet in Heaven* (London: Cassell & Co, 1952), 217.
69 F. Lang, *Smiles of God: The Flowers of St Thérèse of Lisieux* (London: Burns and Oates, 2003), 157.
70 G. Vianney, 'The Right Kind of People: Sometimes it seems you can never do the right thing', *Catholic Fireside*, 9 August 1968, 83–5.
71 Pope, 'Heroine', 46.
72 M. M. Philipon, *The Message of Thérèse of Lisieux* (London: Burns, Oates and Washbourne, 1950), 42.
73 For a discussion of the central role of suffering and the cult of 'mystical substitution' in the cult of St Thérèse, see R. D. E. Burton, *Holy Tears, Holy Blood: Women, Catholicism and the Culture of Suffering in France, 1840–1970* (Ithaca: Cornell University Press, 2004), 20–61; Kane, 'She Offered', 107ff.
74 Martin, *Story of a Soul*, 281–5.
75 V. Johnson, 'Introduction' in A. Combes, *St Thérèse and Suffering* (Dublin: M. H. Gill and Son, 1951), viii.
76 Forrest, *Fragrance*, 14.
77 Lane, *Bernadette*, 65.
78 Lane, *This Way to Lourdes: A Handbook for Pilgrims* (London: Burns, Oates and Washbourne, 1933), 20.
79 M. Trouncer, *A Grain of Wheat: The Story of St Bernadette of Lourdes* (London: Hutchinson and Co, 1958), 232–3.
80 See Keyes, *Sublime*, 191; A. Ravier, *Bernadette* (London: Collins, 1978), Preface.

81 H. R. Williamson, *The Challenge of Lourdes* (London: Burns and Oates, 1958), 97; R. Knox, *Captive Flames: A Collection of Panegyrics* (London: Burns and Oates, 1940), 128–9 who compares her to Moses.
82 J. Pathé, 'Lourdes — and the saint who was put back in the corner', *Novena* 8(6) (1958), 184.
83 *Ibid.*
84 R. Bogan, 'The Call of Bernadette', *New Life* 14(3) (1958), 62.
85 Interview, Helen, Recording STE 018 at 24.48–24.54.
86 Philipon, *Message*, 27.
87 B. Ulanov, *The Making of a Modern Saint* (London: Jonathan Cape, 1967), 10.
88 Williamson, *Sure*, 32.
89 Martin, *Story of a Soul*, 77.
90 Martin, *Story of a Soul*, 187–9.
91 Johnson, 'St Teresa', 21.
92 V. Johnson, *Spiritual Childhood: A Study of St Teresa's Teaching* (London: Sheed and Ward, 1953), v.
93 Williamson, *Sure*, 16–17.
94 Carr, *Truly*, 16.
95 *Ibid.*
96 Cited in Johnson, *Mission*, Foreward.
97 Knox, *Captive*, 132.
98 Ulanov, *Making*, 7.
99 B. Prentis, 'The Phenomenon of Saint Teresa', *The Catholic Herald*, 28 April 1950, 6.
100 *Ibid.*
101 Williamson, *Sure*, 237.
102 Carmelite Nun, *Our Eternal Vocation* (Glasgow: Sands and Co, 1949), 12, 205.
103 Morton, *Thérèse*, 2.
104 C. C. Martindale, *Bernadette of Lourdes* (London: Catholic Truth Society, 1924), 61 (and 1934, 1943 reprints).
105 A. Combes, *St Thérèse and Her Mission: The Basic Principles of Theresian Spirituality* (Dublin: M. H. Gill and Co, 1956), 21.
106 E. Robo, *Two Portraits of St Teresa of Lisieux* (London: Sands and Co, 1957), 9.
107 *Ibid*, 238.
108 Gorres, *Hidden*, 14.
109 *Ibid.*
110 Keyes, *Sublime*, 13.
111 C. C. Martindale, 'Introduction' in Sandhurst, *We Saw*, xvi.
112 Lebbe, *Soul*, viii.
113 H. R. Williamson, *Challenge*, xii.
114 Laurentin, *Bernadette*.
115 E.g. T. Taylor, '"So Many Extraordinary Things to Tell": Letters from Lourdes, 1858', *Journal of Ecclesiastical History*, 46(3) (1995), 457–81.
116 Beevers, *St Thérèse*, 72.
117 J. Guitton, *The Spiritual Genius of St Thérèse* (London: Geoffrey Chapman, 1958), 8.

118 B. Bro, *The Little Way: The Spirituality of St Thérèse of Lisieux* (London: Darton Longman and Todd, 1979), 4.
119 *Ibid*, 16.
120 *Ibid*, 20.
121 M. Hollings, *Thérèse of Lisieux* (London: Collins, 1981), 50.
122 McCaffrey, *Heart*, 78.
123 E. Mary, *Saint Thérèse of Lisieux: Her Relevance for Today* (Oxford: SLG Press, 1997), 17.
124 Bro, *Little*, 14.
125 M. Furlong, *Thérèse of Lisieux* (London: Darton Longman and Todd, 2001), 134.
126 Martin, *Story of a Soul*, 159, 169, 214, 286.
127 K. Harrison, *Saint Thérèse of Lisieux* (London: Weidenfeld and Nicolson, 2003), 2.
128 J. Wolski Conn, 'Far From Spiritual Childhood', *Spiritus: A Journal of Christian Spirituality* 6(1) (2006), 68–89.
129 McCaffrey, *Heart*, 77; H. U. von Balthasar, *Thérèse of Lisieux: The Story of a Mission* (London: Sheed and Ward, 1953).
130 See A. Harris, 'Bone Idol? British Catholics and Devotion to St Thérèse of Lisieux' in Christie *et al*, *The Sixties*, 429–52.
131 B. Ziemann, 'The Gospel of Psychology: Therapeutic Concepts and the Scientification of Pastoral Care in the West German Catholic Church, 1950–1980', *Central European History* 39 (2006), 82.
132 E.g. N. Rose, *Governing the Soul: The Shaping of the Private Self* (London: Routledge, 1989).
133 M. Thomson, *Psychological Subjects: Identity, Culture and Health in Twentieth-Century Britain* (Oxford: Oxford University Press, 2006), 5.
134 G. Richards, 'Psychology and the Churches in Britain 1919–39: Symptoms of Conversion', *History of the Human Sciences* 13(2) (2000), 58.
135 On the stance of the difference schools of British psychology to religion see Richards, 'Psychology', 62.
136 M. Thomson, 'The popular, the practical and the professional: psychological identities in Britain 1901–1950' in G. C. Bunn, A. D. Loview and G. D. Richards (eds), *Psychology in Britain: Historical Essays and Personal Reflections* (Leicester, 2001), 131.
137 Thomson, *Psychological*, 13.
138 Martindale, *Bernadette*, 2.
139 *Ibid*, 59–60.
140 Laurentin, *Bernadette*, chapter 14.
141 Ravier, *Bernadette*, 10.
142 J. Kerr, *Mistress of Novices: A Play* (London: Samuel French, 1973), 35.
143 J. Tavener and G. McLarnon, *Thérèse: An Opera in One Act* (London: Chester Music, 1979).
144 W. Dean, 'Opera: Thérèse', *Musical Times*, 120 (1641 Baroque Music) (November 1979), 932–3.
145 Combes, *Thérèse*, 21.
146 Guitton, *Spiritual*, 9.
147 Bro, *Little*, 14.
148 *Ibid*, 14; K. Stern, 'St Thérèse of Lisieux' in C. B. Luce (ed.), *Saints for Now* (London: Sheed and Ward, 1952), 261–77.

149 E.g. P. C. Vitz and C. P. Lynch, 'Thérèse of Lisieux: From the Perspective of Attachment Theory and Separation Anxiety', *International Journal for the Psychology of Religion* 17(1) (2007), 61–80; T. R. Nevin, *Thérèse of Lisieux: God's Gentle Warrior* (Oxford: Oxford University Press, 2006).
150 Interview, Francis at 43.30–44.30.
151 Interview, Christine at 21.03–21.17.
152 *Ibid*, at 21.48–22.24.
153 Harris, 'Bone Idol.'
154 Interview, Patrick at 32.19–32.43.
155 Interview, AH with SD, 27 July 2006, Lourdes (handwritten notes).
156 See Taylor, *Bernadette of Lourdes*, 317.
157 Interview, Richard at 41.44–41.54.
158 R. Harris, *Lourdes: Body and Spirit in the Secular Age* (London: Penguin, 2000).
159 A. Harris, '"A place to grow spiritually and socially": the experiences of young pilgrims to Lourdes' in S. Collins-Mayo and B. P. Dandelion (eds), *Religion and Youth* (Aldershot: Ashgate, 2010), 149–58.
160 P. Caraman, 'Forty Saints', *Catholic Gazette* 61(10) (1970), 10–11.
161 'Canonization of the Martyrs: Arrangements in Rome', *The Tablet*, 17 October 1970, 1010.
162 P. Hebblethwaite, 'St Peter's: A Day to Remember', *The Tablet*, 31 October 1970, 1047.
163 *Ibid*.
164 These seven martyrs are: Saints John Almond, Edmund Arrowsmith, Ambrose Barlow, John Plessington, John Rigby, John Southworth and John Wall. See P. Caraman, *Seven Lancashire Martyrs* (London: OVP, 1960).
165 Hebblethwaite, 'St Peter's', 1048.
166 'The Canonisation: Cardinal Heenan's Address', *The Tablet*, 31 October 1970, 1061.
167 'Cardinal Heenan's Trinity Pastoral Letter', *The Tablet*, 23 May 1970, 510.
168 Bishop T. Holland, 'My Dear People', *The Harvest* 4(3) (1970), 9.
169 Bishop G. Beck, 'Ad Ven Clerum', 7 July 1960 (SDA Box 220).
170 'Men will March in Silence…', *The Universe*, 25 April 1952, 1.
171 See for example reports of 1,500 to 2,000 people venerating the relic after a High Mass for Christ the King and the Forty Martyrs – OVP, '*BULLETIN* No. 42, 4 November 1960' (BAA AP/M6, Folder 3).
172 P. Caraman, *The Forty Martyrs* (London: OVP, 1960), 16.
173 OVP, '*BULLETIN* No. 83, 12 July 1963' (BAA AP/M7).
174 H. St. John, '6,000 Petition the Pope', *The Universe and Catholic Times*, 16 July 1965, 1.
175 Interview, Judith at 57.03–57.55.
176 She also spoke about a lack of knowledge of the English martyrs amongst her history group within the parish of St Antony's – Interview, Judith at 58.03–58.12.
177 Letter from J. E. Rambler to Father Walsh SJ, n.d. (ABSI, Box 3 'B'). See also D. J. Stoner, *Blessed Ambrose Barlow* (London: Longmans, 1961).
178 Catholic Truth Society, 'Tercentenary of the Martyrdom of Blessed Ambrose Barlow OSB', 10 September 1941 (SDA Box 200–200/57).

179 Bishop G. Beck, *Ad Ven Clerum*, 12 September 1961 (SDA Box 220).
180 B. Forshaw, '"All is but one death": Blessed John Rigby, Layman', *Westminster Cathedral Chronicle*, n.d. (ABSI Cause of the English Martyrs, Box 32, 'R').
181 *Ibid.*
182 OVP, 'Minutes of the Meeting of Diocesan Representatives', 6 April 1960 (BAA AP/M6).
183 OVP, 'Notes for Short Sermons on the English and Welsh Martyrs', c. 1960 (BAA AP/M6).
184 Interview, Tony at 35.15–35.55.
185 OVP, 'Minutes of the Diocesan Representatives Meeting', 24 April 1963 (BAA AP/M7).
186 J. Walsh, 'Vice-Postulator's Report to the Hierarchy of England and Wales on the State of the Cause of the Forty Martyrs', 1966 (BAA GPD/P/A1).
187 *Ibid.*
188 *Ibid.*
189 See also A. Atherstone, 'The Canonisation of the Forty English Martyrs: An Ecumenical Dilemma', *Recusant History* 30(4) (2011), 573–87.
190 Greenstock, *Talks*, 127.
191 J. A. Fletcher, 'The Martyrs and Ecumenism', *The Tablet*, 16 October 1965, 1160–61.
192 H. R. Williamson, *The Modern Mass: A Reversion to the Reforms of Cranmer* (Devon: Britons, 1969).
193 R. de Weaver (Oulton Broad) to Cardinal J. Heenan, 2 March 1970 (AAW Heenan, HE1/L6(b)).
194 Letter, Bishop Beck to Archbishop Dwyer, 'The Cause of the 40 Martyrs and the Ecumenical Movement', 9 April 1963 (BAA AP/M7).
195 OVP, 'The Forty Martyrs and Christian Unity: A Manifesto for Martyrs' Sunday 1965' (BAA AP/M7).
196 'The Message of Martyrdom', *The Tablet*, 17 January 1970, 50–1.
197 'Forty Martyrs Nearing Climax', *The Universe and Catholic Times*, 9 July 1965, 1.
198 H. Kay, 'Ecumenism and the "40"', *The Universe and Catholic Times*, 2 July 1965, 8.
199 J. Eland, 'The Martyrs and Ecumenism', *The Tablet*, 14 August 1965, 915.
200 J. Walsh, 'The Martyrs and Ecumenism', *The Tablet*, 21 August 1965, 939–40.
201 M. FitzHerbert, 'The Martyrs and Ecumenism', *The Tablet*, 4 September 1965, 985.
202 H. E. G. Rope, 'The Martyrs and Ecumenism', *The Tablet*, 11 September 1965, 1012–13.
203 H.E.G. Rope, 'The Martyrs and Ecumenism', *The Tablet*, 2 October 1965, 1098.
204 'Ecumenism and Martyrdom: Cardinal Willebrands at Liverpool', *The Tablet*, 24 January 1970, 93–4.
205 *Ibid.*
206 'Men for All Seasons', *The Tablet*, 24 October 1970, 1017–78.
207 J. Allen, 'The Forty Martyrs', *The Harvest* 4(3) (1970), 20.
208 Pope Paul VI, 'Martyrs into Saints', *The Tablet*, 23 May 1970, 509.
209 OVP, '*BULLETIN* No. 5, 10 June 1960', 1 (BAA AP/M6 Folder 3).
210 *Ibid.*

211 OVP, *BULLETIN* No. 26, 2 December 1960', 1 (BAA AP/M6, Folder 3).
212 *Ibid.*
213 OVP, *'BULLETIN* No. 72, 16 November 1962', 1 (ABSI, Filing Cabinet (FC) 34, Drawer 3, 'Lists of Favours and Petitions').
214 OVP, *'BULLETIN* No. 77, 17 May 1963', 1 (BAA AP/M7).
215 Statement of J. Walsh, 'Walsingham' (Eccles) to J. Walsh SJ, 9 November 1961 (ABSI Box 108 63A EWM – Cures).
216 Letter, Dr Richards to J. Walsh SJ, 11 October 1961 (ABSI Box 108 63A EWM – Cures).
217 Letter, J. L. McGinnell to J. Walsh SJ, 15 November 1961 (ABSI Box 108 63A EWM – Cures).
218 Letter, J. Alwyn to J. Walsh SJ, 2 January 1968 (ABSI, FC 34, Drawer 3).
219 Letter, J. Alwyn to J. Walsh SJ, 1 March 1968 (ABSI, FC 34, Drawer 3).
220 Walsh, 'Vice-Postulator's Report', 1966 (BAA GPD/P/A1).
221 *Ibid.*
222 *Ibid.*
223 P. Molinari, 'Canonization of 40 English and Welsh Martyrs', *L'Osservatore Romano*, 29 October 1970, 6. For a full, anecdotal discussion of this case, by Mrs Joan Matthewman's journalist brother, see W. Keenan, 'Medicine and a Modern Miracle', *Catholic Medical Quarterly* (1974) XXVI(2)(182), 66–74.
224 M. Russell, 'Why spend on saint-making?', *Catholic Herald*, 10 May 1968, 5.
225 Interview, Peter at 31.41–31.49.
226 *Ibid*, 32.51–36.09.
227 See A. Harris, 'Lourdes and Holistic Spirituality: Contemporary Catholicism, the Therapeutic and Religious Thermalism', 14(1) (2013) *Culture and Religion* (doi:/10.1080/14755610.2012.756411).
228 Interview, Richard at 27.02–27.54.
229 *Ibid*, 34.10–35.45.

Chapter 6

Conclusion

Hymns ancient and modern

On 27 May 1982, a group of Mancunian schoolchildren were interviewed about the forthcoming visit of the Pope to Heaton Park. When asked about their school activities to prepare for the visit, they recounted putting up pictures, writing prayers (when not interrupted by football practice!) and learning a 'very nice' song, adding 'we learnt it from a record'. The interviewer enquired whether the young boys and girls could sing it for him, and they confidently began:

> Welcome John Paul;
> It comes from one and all.
> Your love for mankind,
> Is in our hearts to find,
> With your help we can all set it free.
>
> When you reach out your hand,
> Bringing joy to this land.
> With love as our guide
> Every heart fills with pride …
> Show the world how to forgive.[1]

Three days later, Piccadilly radio station broadcast through the night a live show from Heaton Park, Manchester, setting the scene for the papal visit, ahead of the 9am open-air mass on 31 May. Interspersing interviews with some of the 250,000 Lancastrian Catholics beginning to gather, spoken segments were mixed with an 'appropriate play list' that included Boney M ('By the rivers of Babylon'); Abba ('Fernando'), John Denver ('You fill up my senses') and Simon and Garfunkel ('Sound of Silence'). Amongst the cast of characters interviewed by Mike Sweeney (a self-confessed Catholic but not 'dead dead religious' as he put it) was Kath, who had come with twenty-six relatives, as it was a 'family event',[2] and

Barbara and Finoula from Warrington, who spoke about their church-going faith and extemporaneous use of bin bags to keep warm.[3] An interview with teenager Mick, from Cheetham Hill, prompted consideration of why people had come. In answer to the interviewer's question of whether he was religious, the young man said 'not really', in contrast to his dad 'who likes to go to church a lot', but that he nevertheless really 'wanted to see the Pope'.[1] In contrast, two young Anglican men from Bolton, who unabashedly declared a strong faith in 'Jesus Christ as [our] personal Saviour', gave their reasons for coming as to witness to the need for a 'more united faith' and as a counter to Protestant protests about the papal visit, because 'he is a world religious leader'.[5]

One of the highlights of the overnight broadcast was an interview with Father Kevin O'Conner,[6] who spoke about the months of choir rehearsals in preparation for the mass in a simulated outdoor setting at the scoreboard end of Old Trafford Park. Choirmaster O'Conner spoke of the difficulties of negotiating four-part settings for ordinary parishioners who had never really sung in harmony before, and the outdoor performance acoustics for his choir of 3,179 people. While admitting that twenty-five well-amplified voices 'would have sufficed', the decision to involve over 300 parish choirs from throughout the diocese was prompted by a recognition that 'the pope's visit is a pastoral visit for all the people, and he's very anxious that he's involved with the maximum number of people in the North West'. Renditions of 'Come down O love divine' to the tune composed by Ralph Vaughan Williams in the early twentieth century, and 'I am the bread of life', a more recent composition by Suzanne Toolan in 1971, followed. This was a foretaste of the liturgical settings used in the Papal Mass the following day. With its mixture of hymns old and new, from both the Catholic and Church of England traditions, in this open-air mass twelve men were ordained to the priesthood before a vast crowd (though not as numerous as the overly-optimistic estimate of one million).[7] As a further sign of the vastly changed ecumenical and inter-religious setting that surrounded this visit, an hour before this mass Pope John Paul II had met the Chief Rabbi of the United Kingdom, Sir Immanuel Jakobovits, at the Convent of the Sisters of Nazareth in Manchester.

In moving from its opening, with the *Vatican Rag* to this account of *'Welcome John Paul'* (coupled with Boney M), this book has explored from a historical perspective, and using the framework of lived religious experience, many of the issues encapsulated in these contemporaneous, archived, oral history interviews. These reflections have been situated against the backdrop of an academic literature discussing the 'secularisation' of British society and the continuing salience of Catholic identity amidst the widespread economic, social and cultural changes of the postwar period. Touching upon issues of family cohesiveness, the socialisation of the young in the faith, liturgical adaptations, ecumenical and inter-faith rapprochement, and a 'cultural Catholicism' that might not be 'dead dead religious' or manifested by 'going to church a lot', the reflections of these ordinary Mancunian Catholics illustrate the shifts, both at an institutional level and amongst the laity, in the *modes of expression* and *agreed forms for mediation* of a Catholic identity towards the end of the century.

In these concluding remarks, I will tease out some of the tangled and interwoven threads of continuity and change, as well as the contradictory and countervailing trends that have been examined in this study of the spirituality and popular religiosity of Catholics in England from 1945 to 1982. The Pope's 'Paradoxical People'[8] gathered in Heaton Park (and earlier in the month at Wembley Stadium), presented a markedly different *tableau vivant* to those assembled to celebrate the Restoration of the Catholic Hierarchy of England and Wales in 1950 and singing 'God bless our Pope', as recounted in chapter 2. Nevertheless, in their refrain 'Welcome John Paul', and the recognition of this as a 'very sociable' 'family event' – which could encompass an all-embracing definition of the church family manifested in the witness of this 'world religious leader' and 'man of peace' – there remained an articulation of the 'family of faith' though in a different key, tempo and register. These old and new tunes, centred around the marked and manifold changes in British society over three decades, and shifts in the understandings of, and emphasis upon, traditional devotional forms. At root, they turn on the overarching premium now placed on an experiential, self-authenticating and efficacious lived religious practice which might dispense (or sometimes dovetail) with institutional expression and hierarchical, clerical determination. These changes were generated by forces both within and beyond the church, allowing Catholics now to 'evince disobedience to and disagreement with ... the church as an institution ... yet continue in apparently happy and untroubled identification with their faith'.[9] While there had been a little-appreciated spectrum of opinion within the Catholic Church on matters doctrinal and moral prior to the Second Vatican Council, the changed cultural setting of late twentieth-century Britain allowed for greater acknowledgment and articulation of this diversity of opinion and practice, and the reconfiguration of a Catholic identity accordingly.

*

Writing in *The Tablet* in 1970 prognosticating what 'the church in 1984' would be like, layman J. M. Cameron reflected on the Council and wrote of the passing of a certain presented 'unity of culture' and form of practice 'tied to ecclesiastical observance, to a closely-knit family structure, [and] to an attitude towards marriage, divorce and sexual morality … within which, not unhappily, Catholics lived'.[10] Counter to Orwell's literary predictions of social dystopia in this future year, Cameron viewed Catholic culture as an 'earthen vessel' and wrote about the challenge for a 'church in the world' to find 'new vessels' for the old wine of the gospel message. He presciently forecast a 'fall in Catholic numbers' but also a 'degree of self-consciousness' amongst those who remained in the pews, leading to a 'praying Church and understanding Church' in dialogue with the outside world and comfortable with plurality.[11] This book has explored just such transitions and transformations, describing the English Catholic Church 'in motion' and its own reappraisal of itself (in the terms of the Council) as a 'pilgrim people' on the move.

Not all components of the English Catholic Church were prepared for, or accepting of, these cultural adaptations and modulations of the old message through newer means. Resistance to the replacement of the traditional liturgical language with the vernacular, or the use of some components of the cult of the saints to shore up a metaphysical and anti-modernist position, are just two examples of this tendency. But 'development', and re-interpretations of 'tradition', have also been a constant (if little-appreciated) feature of popular Catholicism across two millennia. This study has argued that what changed in the twenty-five years after the Second World War was the degree to which this development or 'historicity' was self-consciously acknowledged, and yet related to elements of continuity and consistency. An intensely incarnational, experiential and familial-focused religiosity runs through this period of profound transition and experimentation. This is a form of Christian language, expressed through an English Catholic 'dialect', that has continued to be used by individuals and communities from the middle of the twentieth century onwards to articulate a form of cultural identity within the changed context of an increasingly ethnically, religiously, socially and morally plural Britain.

For some their vocabulary had not changed greatly from that learnt in their childhood earlier in the century, whereas others, including many of those younger Catholics gathered in Heaton Park, had modulated their language through contemporary cultural forms, personal conscience, ecumenical commitments and inter-religious sensitivities. Others still sought to adopt a Christian identity as a form of radical, counter-cultural identification, conjuring a Christ-radical of CND, or liberation theology, commitments. For others still, a defensive, oppositional identity, insisted upon strict adherence to all Vatican teachings as a marker of Catholic identity, except in their preference for the then-illicit Tridentine mass. As all these heterogeneous strands of 'post-conciliar' Catholicism illustrate, particularly in their integration with, or reaction to, contemporary British society, this was not a context in which 'God is dead' but, rather, intensely debated. The gospel story, as retold in civic parks (or in churches, pilgrimage places and domestic practices) and as represented on mainstream radio and television, as well as through more conventional forms of catechesis, still had the currency and force to challenge some, to comfort others, and to incite curiosity, in equal measure to condemnation, from yet other quarters.

This study has concentrated on three key and inter-related devotional changes within the lived religious landscape of Catholics in England, namely Christology (expressed in the mass and the Eucharist), Mariology (manifest through the rosary and devotion to the Holy Family) and the cult of saints (particularly devotion to St Thérèse of Lisieux, St Bernadette and the Forty Martyrs). It has sought to understand the changes in devotional *form* and theological *emphasis* in these areas from the perspective of the popular spirituality, devotional intensity and scripted religiosity of ordinary English Catholics, across three generations, and encompassing the theological spectrum. This methodology has advocated a shifting of analytical focus from a preoccupation with form, and a catalogue of changes, towards an approach that identifies and interrogates the religious experiences and attitudes they embodied. However, while acknowledging unexpected devotional continuities in elements of the liturgy, Marian devotions and the cult of saints, this book has clearly argued that there *was* a shifting accent in the theology and popular piety in this reception period around, and after, the Council. This is broadly understood as a move from a soteriological approach, centred on sin and salvation, towards an eschatological emphasis on the realisation of the 'kingdom' as present in the world and as manifest in the relationships between God and the created order, which could encompass all humanity as well as Catholics.

Chapter 3 tested this assessment against an examination of the Catholic liturgical and extra-liturgical, Christological and Eucharistic devotions from 1945 until the time of the papal visit. It argued that while the scale of the impact on the laity of the changes to the language, rite and rote of the mass should not be underestimated, there was also a more substantial and unrecognised shift discernible in the Eucharistic theology of the Catholic Church. This transformation from a 'sacrifice-focused' theology towards one reconceived as a 'gathering at the family table' was inaugurated by the early twentieth-century liturgical movement, and extended by the Second Vatican Council, paving the way for an ecumenical 'every-man' Jesus as conjured in the catechetical lessons of Mary on sacralised 'fish and chips' and Coke. The overwhelming constant across these liturgical and theological transformations nevertheless remained an emphasis on an incarnational, fraternal and accessible Saviour, linking together constructions of Christ as the Sacred Heart with the radically compassionate Christ who was 'truly man', a loving bridegroom and an advocate of human rights to counter social injustice.

Moving beyond the period considered by this discussion, and into the distinctly new era of John Paul II's extended papacy and the more radically 'reforming' pontificate of Benedict XVI,[12] there are contemporary signals of marked changes within the present-day Catholic Church which may modify this golden thread of continuity across the twentieth century. As Patrick Pasture has described this trend, this is presented as a 'revival' or a 'reversal', 'a search for new boundaries and new hierarchies, new certainties and new religiosities'.[13] An important part of this new phase encompasses the reanimation of 'old' and emotive issues surrounding habitual language, bodily posture, and Latin translation, raised by *Liturgiam Authenticam* (2001) and the implementation of the new English Translation of the Order of the Mass in English Catholic parishes from September 2011.[14] To this should be added the greater sanction given to use of the Tridentine Rite in *Summorum Pontificum* (2007),[15] prompted in part by English Catholics through the so-called 'Agatha Christie' indult in 1971. This was a petition signed by the famous crime novelist and other Catholic and non-Catholic notables such as Kenneth Clark, F. R.

Leavis, Cecil Day-Lewis and Iris Murdoch and which was extended to the universal church in 1984. This encouragement of liturgical diversity takes a variety of forms, across an impossibly broad theological spectrum, including sanctions for the Jewish-derived Eucharistic banquets of the growing missionary Neo-Catechumenate movement,[16] through to recognition of a vaguely-defined 'Anglican patrimony' with the inauguration of the Anglican Ordinariate in full communion with Rome.[17]

Underpinning all these liturgical changes, which Benedict XVI has described as a 'springboard for a renewal and a deepening of Eucharistic devotion all over the English-speaking world', is an emphatic re-assertion of a transcendent and exclusive, other-worldly and divine Christology signalled in *Dominus Iesus* (2000)[18] and *Sacramentum Caritatis* (2008).[19] These recent Vatican pronouncements on the liturgy, the Eucharist and the relationship between Christians – often grouped under the term 'the New Evangelisation' – should be set within a broader, twenty-first century context of press-fuelled fears about Islam and 'post-secularism', the impact of globalisation, and the widespread spiritual and identity 'seeking' which seem to be key preoccupations for Western Europeans in this new millennium.

Marian devotions and reverence for St Joseph in the context of the Holy Family were the focus of chapter 4. This chapter explored the ways in which the mother and foster father of Christ functioned as flexible ideals and models for Catholic mothers and fathers, who were also subject to broader societal injunctions about femininity, masculinity and their conjugal relationships in post-war Britain. It argued that through the transitions of the 1960s, and an intense focus on sexuality within the married relationship, a more adaptable model for marriage was sought in Christological terms, leading Marian devotions to slip (for a time) out of the institutional frame. By the late 1970s, efforts were under way to reinterpret and repackage Mariology, in terms that resonated with gender roles and social expectations towards the end of the twentieth century, and yet could also be integrated with 'older' devotional forms like the rosary. This trend continued in a heightened, emphatic and zealous form throughout John Paul II's pontificate, and his intense personal devotion to Mary was shared by many of the ordinary laity within the worldwide church.[20] The promotion of Marian shrines and piety under his leadership (such as his frequent pilgrimages to Lourdes and Fatima), the inauguration of the controversial apparitions at Medjugorje in 1981 which have been coupled to conservative Catholic teachings (on birth control, AIDS and abortion), and the emergence of the Anglican-Catholic (ARCIC, 2005) agreed statement on the Blessed Virgin Mary as 'a pattern of hope and grace'[21] show considerable efforts – across class and generational spectrums, as well as theological orientations – to re-establish and indeed re-inscribe the place of the mother of Jesus in the life of the church.

Chapter 5 examined the shifting hagiographical traditions surrounding St Thérèse of Lisieux and St Bernadette Soubirous, as two prominent examples of a changing Catholic engagement with the 'communion of saints'. It argued that there was a movement from the presentation of these saints as exemplary, childlike character models of obedience, suffering and sacrifice towards accounts that placed a greater premium on each saint's historicity and personality, within an explicitly psychological framework. Through exploring the devotional cults attached to both saints and attempts to reanimate devotion to the forty martyrs, it argued that the saints and devotional practices that continued to resonate were those whose life stories (and devotional places) were adaptable and flexible enough to prioritise an experiential and eschatological spirituality.

There was a raft of popular new additions to the ranks of sanctity under Pope John Paul II, ranging from the selfless sacrifice of Maximilian Kolbe in a Nazi concentration camp, who was canonised in 1982, and the beatification of humanitarian worker Mother Teresa in 2003, through to the Italian stigmatic Padre Pio in 2002.[22] Perhaps most telling is the rehabilitation of the visions and writings of the Polish religious Mary Faustina Kowalska when she was canonised in 2000, whose painted image of 'Christ of the Divine Mercy' may be seen as a twenty-first century evolution from 'Sacred Heart' devotion (with its Cold War connotations), complete with novena prayers on rosaries and the institution of 3pm as an 'Hour of Mercy' which recalls the older practice of the Angelus. As a new devotion particularly active on the internet, and through the establishment of a vast pilgrimage shrine in Kraków, it commands devotion to tens of millions worldwide.[23] With an emphasis on the 'experiential' and 'eschatological', which need not displace the mystical and metaphysical, it is fair to say that devotion to the saints remains a vibrant, prominent (but often perplexing) dimension of contemporary Catholic spirituality.[24] The relics tour of St Thérèse of Lisieux throughout England and Wales in 2009, which was visited by over 300,000 people throughout the country,[25] with congregations comprised of older Catholic men and women but also a markedly younger cohort, including Catholics who had arrived in Britain over the last ten or twenty years, is a recent example.

Another of the central themes explored throughout these pages has been the emergence of a concept of the self conceived as a 'personality', constructed chiefly through a psychological framework and prioritising 'experience' as the key component in this process of identity construction and spiritual expression. Through this lens, it has been argued that English Catholicism should be viewed alongside a redefined concept of 'spirituality' in the latter half of the twentieth century, chiefly one which was responsive to the societal premium placed on 'authenticity', customised self-expression, and the questioning of traditional structures and externalised, imposed authority.

As the various chapters have demonstrated, this has involved for many Catholics a reprioritisation of the demands of conscience, and an interrogation of the relationship between the believer, church hierarchies and papal authorities. This is well illustrated in the reflections of Mancunian mother and son Mitzi and Patrick, who contrasted the position of an earlier generation with their own understandings of the Catholic Church:

> MS: Nobody questioned. I think people probably did question in their own private surroundings, but not in school or not in an open discussion in church or anything like that. I think it was a little bit – you couldn't question really. You weren't kind of allowed to question. Whereas now the young people are allowed to question, which is much better. It's more open, much better.
> PS: I think it is, definitely.
> AH: It's almost the only way with the current environment…
> MS: Yeah, that's right. Otherwise they're going to lose lots of young people, aren't they? Mind you there's still a lot of things that you would question about the Catholic Church. Like Patrick was saying, you kind of make it your own. And you might not agree with that and you might not say it to everybody you meet but you keep that personally to yourself. And then you just get along with being – trying to be a good Catholic.
> AH: You sit with the contradictions?
> PS: Yeah, that's right. I sometimes think there's a bit of a difference between the Church, the Church in Rome and the Church as in the people.[26]

Highlighted in this oral history interview, and indeed a constant preoccupation throughout this study with its focus on belief and lived religious experience, are the complexities encountered in dealing with the relationship between belief, institutional affiliation, and religious practice across the second half of the twentieth century. Also central to the textured patterns, which the analysis throughout has sought to acknowledge, is the interplay of related and qualifying categories such as gender, generation and class. Through engaging with and examining the devotional preferences of English Catholics of different generations, with diverse understandings of the role of their faith in identity formation and expression, the differences attributable to these multifaceted 'lived religious experiences' and personal subjectivities have been highlighted. Sometimes the interviewees themselves have stressed these contrasts within their own network of social and familial relationships. Margaret, for example, spoke of the 'really high-class questions' about Catholicism asked by her son, now an American Professor, for which she had no answer, and little purchase, in view of her own self-confessed 'simple' and unquestioning approach to belief.[27]

Shifts in spirituality, emotional needs and institutional commitments through the life-cycle are yet other themes that have emerged. Peter recounted his children's challenge to 'an institution that seems to come up with rules and regulations that they don't understand or don't agree with'.[28] Nevertheless, he went on to recount his children's own acknowledgement that 'Catholic Christianity is still where their roots are', with this ethical commitment prompting one son to charitable activities and his youngest child to confess that 'he intends to die a [practising] Catholic'.[29] Tom and Richard also spoke about their children, who self-identified as Catholic whilst not regularly attending church,[30] with Tom's children returning to institutional practice on the birth of their own children.[31]

Considerations of the life-cycle, and changes in an individual's devotional preferences over time, were also articulated by ninety-one-year-old Joseph, who candidly observed:

> JE: You go to church more. As you get older, you understand it more. That's the main thing. As a 'littlun' you didn't know much about it. You wanted to go and play football or something else, you know. Being honest. You wanted to dash out and play with your pals. Same as if your mother said 'Wash the pots', you'd make an excuse to dash out on. Get away. But course as you get older you don't do that. You concentrate on it more.[32]

As these snapshots and the more integrated oral history extracts explored throughout illustrate, rich and dense pictures of belief, religious practice and English Catholic identities emerge from these life stories. These complexities defy simple characterisation or categorisation, and certainly belie statistically derived efforts to reduce religiosity to regular church attendance, or mere doctrinal orthodoxy.

Through examining Catholic conceptions and constructions of the 'celestial family', this book has shown the changing spiritualties and social identities of earthly English Catholic families, and the ways in which they articulated, expressed and performed their faith and religious convictions as the twentieth century progressed. It has argued that there have been substantial changes in the ways in which this 'household of faith' has been defined and enacted. The close-knit structures which regulated kinship ties, and maintained relationships across neighbourhoods, schools and church organisations, have reacted to, and adapted under, the dramatic and far-reaching social, cultural and economic developments of the century. English Catholics' conceptions of themselves within society, and their expectations in relation to their religious beliefs and identities, have also been transformed. As the preceding chapters have illustrated, this greater self-consciousness and self-confidence, mirrored by the broader social priority on personality, self-realisation and self-expression, has led many to reprioritise the insights of experience and the demands of conscience, which in many instances has required an interrogation of the relationship between the believer, church hierarchies and papal authority. Nevertheless, this book argues that a sense of a distinctive Catholic culture, and one articulated in familial vocabulary – albeit reconceived in much wider and more flexible terms – persists.[33]

During the period from 1945 until the papal visit to Britain in the early 1980s, this English Catholic 'household of faith' increasingly embraced experimentation and adaptation, felt confident in its dialogue with the outside world, and began to respond to the challenges of cultural, ethnic and religious pluralism. It was this redefined and reconceived 'household of faith' which gathered in Heaton Park – or engaged with the suite of papal events broadcast on television and radio – in May 1982. Attentive to the marked changes and complexities in the performed register, the broader cultural landscape and the 'religious' language manifest in this extended papal pilgrimage, this gathering, along with the other Catholic devotions and spiritual practices considered here, manifested a broad continuity of expression, vision and performance. This was a form of 're-membering', which enabled an affirmative answer to Frank Sheed's provocative question in 1968, *Is it the same Church?*

Notes

1 North West Sound Archive (hereafter NWSA), 'Children Talking, 27 May 1982', 1982.7364 at 1.20–2.33. Author unknown.
2 NWSA, 'Pope Visit (ROT) 10" NAB', 1983.1438 at 8.27–10.12.
3 *Ibid*, 32.00–57.
4 *Ibid*, 33.00–33.55.
5 *Ibid*, 40.48–42.25.
6 NWSA, 'Pope's Visit 4', 1983.1487, at 26.58–32.10.
7 'A Charismatic Visit', *The Tablet*, 5 June 1982, 568. See also Holland, *For Better and For Worse*, 266–8 for an intimate account of the papal visit, and reference to St Ambrose Barlow O.S.B and the other Lancashire Martyrs within the homily.
8 See Hornsby-Smith, *Catholic Beliefs*, 119–39.
9 *Ibid*, 139.
10 J. M. Cameron, 'The Church in 1984', *The Tablet*, 12 December 1970, 1199.
11 *Ibid*, 1200.
12 See J. L. Allen, *Pope Benedict XVI: A Biography of Joseph Ratzinger* (London: Continuum, 2005).
13 P. Pasture, 'Religious Globalisation in Post-war Europe: Spiritual Connections and Interactions', *Archiv für Sozialgeschichte* 51 (2011), 71.
14 www.catholicherald.co.uk/news/2011/01/18/new-mass-translation-to-be-used-in-parishes-from-september/ and P. Endean SJ, 'Liturgist: "I'm at a loss with the new Missal"', 21 November 2011 – www.thetablet.co.uk/blogs/206/17.
15 www.vatican.va/holy_father/benedict_xvi/letters/2007/documents/hf_ben-xvi_let_20070707_lettera-vescovi_en.html.
16 E. Curti, 'Who are the Neo-Cats?', *The Tablet*, 6 January 2001, 6 – www.thetablet.co.uk/article/6528.
17 www.vatican.va/holy_father/benedict_xvi/apost_constitutions/documents/hf_ben-xvi_apc_20091104_anglicanorum-coetibus_en.html.
18 www.vatican.va/roman_curia/congregations/cfaith/documents/rc_con_cfaith_doc_20000806_dominus-iesus_en.html.
19 www.vatican.va/holy_father/benedict_xvi/apost_exhortations/documents/hf_ben-xvi_exh_20070222_sacramentum-caritatis_en.html.
20 A. Nachef, *Mary's Pope: John Paul II, Mary and the Church Since Vatican II* (London: Sheed and Ward, 2000).
21 www.vatican.va/roman_curia/pontifical_councils/chrstuni/angl-comm-docs/rc_pc_chrstuni_doc_20050516_mary-grace-hope-christ_en.html; A. Harris and H. Harris, 'A Marian Pilgrimage: Reflections and Questions about ARCIC's *Mary: Grace and Hope in Christ*', *Ecclesiology* 2(3) (2006), 339–56.

22 M. Walsh, 'John Paul II and His Canonizations' in P. Clarke and T. Claydon (eds), *Saints and Sanctity* (Woodbridge: Suffolk, 2011), 415–37.
23 J. Garnett and A. Harris, 'Canvassing the Faithful: Image, Agency and the Lived Religiosity of Devotion to the Divine Mercy', *Annual Review of the Sociology of Religion* 4(2013) (forthcoming).
24 L. S. Cunningham, *A Brief History of Saints* (Oxford: Oxford University Press, 2005), 102–26 and A. Harris, 'Undying Devotions: Catholic Symbolism after Vatican II', *The Tablet*, 15 December 2012, 10–11.
25 A. Harris, 'Bone Idol?', 429; S. Ryan, 'Resilient Religion: Popular Piety Today', *The Furrow* 56(3) (2005), 131–41.
26 Interview, Mitzi & Patrick at 17.08–18.02.
27 Interview, Margaret at 43.05–43.17.
28 Interview, Peter at 20.24–20.33.
29 *Ibid*, at 20.4–21.12.
30 Interview, Richard at 8.20–8.35.
31 Interview, Tom at 21.26–21.40.
32 Interview, Joseph at 12.19–12.54.
33 For similar arguments on the evolution of Catholicism in Italy and Spain, see E. Pace, 'Religion as Communication: The Changing Shape of Catholicism in Europe' in Ammerman (ed.), *Everyday*, 37–49.

Appendix
Oral history interviews

Nineteen oral history interviews in 2007 were drawn from two parishes, in distinct and contrasting locations, in the Diocese of Salford.

Parishes

St Anne's parish church, Crumpsall
Located in the north of Manchester, Crumpsall had been transformed at the end of the nineteenth century from a rural village into a working-class suburb caught up in industrialised urban sprawl. It is now characterised by a diverse multicultural community and relatively inexpensive rental accommodation. The existing parish church replaced an older structure built in the 1950s and there remains a large local parish school.

St Antony's parish church, Trafford Park
Trafford Park was built on the Manchester Ship Canal at the turn of the twentieth century, within the world's first industrial park, and was inhabited by many of the employees of the nearby factories and warehouses, including Westinghouse, Hovis and Kellogg. St Antony's 'tin hut mission church' was built for the workers in 1904 and is still in use today. As industry declined in the second half of the twentieth century, and with the drive towards slum clearances in the 1960s, Trafford Park has become purely industrial and St Antony's has changed from a parish church to a commuter, 'gathered community'. Nevertheless, as an adjunct of its longstanding mission to the working classes, a 'Centre for Church and Industry' was founded on the old primary school site in 1979.

Interviewees

Bernard
Interview at St Anne's, Crumpsall on 15/09/07, STE 019
Born in Liverpool in 1967, the youngest of four children, Bernard comes from a strong Catholic background and his uncle is a priest in the Archdiocese of Liverpool. He works selling and installing sound systems, very often within church buildings, and met his wife Helen when installing a sound system at her place of work. He moved to Manchester in 1993 when they married, and he is now an active member of St Anne's parish – co-ordinating a social group with Helen some years ago, and currently organising the Eucharistic Ministry programme in the parish. He and the family keep up to date with Catholic and diocesan news via various websites.

Christine
Interview at St Anne's, Crumpsall on 15/09/07, STE 017
The middle child of Francis and Kathleen L., Christine was born in Crumpsall in 1959 and was baptised, made her first communion, and was confirmed and married in St Anne's parish church. She married young and drifted away from the church, and regular mass attendance, in late adolescence. Her marriage ended after seventeen years and she found support and comfort in her family and, gradually, within the church to which she returned. She now regularly attends St Francis' parish church, near Gorton Monastery, and has served as a Eucharistic minister. She is also involved in the pro-life movement, regularly reading the *Pro-Life Times*, and has a strong devotion to St Thérèse of Lisieux. She works as a medical laboratory assistant.

Francis
Interview at St Anne's, Crumpsall on 15/09/07, STE 016
Born in Eccles, Salford in 1928, Francis was the second child of seven children and on the death of his uncle and aunt very suddenly, the family moved to Lower Broughton to take care of their two orphaned girls. His local parish was St Boniface's church, where he served on the altar from age seven until married at twenty-six to Kathleen by his brother, Father Joseph. Leaving school at fourteen, Francis had a good and stable job with a heating and ventilating firm, travelling with his work for thirty-five of

the forty-three years he was employed by the company. In his 'retirement' he attends daily mass at St Anne's church, helps to maintain the premises, and is an essential mainstay of the community. He regularly reads *The Universe*.

Helen
Interview at St Anne's, Crumpsall on 15/09/07, STE 018
Helen was born in Manchester to Irish parents in 1965, and moved with her parents, two brothers and a sister to Crumpsall when just a young baby. She attended the local parish school, received her first communion and confirmation in St Anne's church, and some years later she and Bernard were also married here. They have two children, Joseph (then 11 years) and Anastasia (then 7 years). Both children attend the parish primary school and volunteer as altar servers in the parish. Helen balances household responsibilities with part-time work as a teaching assistant at a local high school.

John
Interview at St Anne's, Crumpsall on 16/09/07, STE 021
John was one of seven children born into an English Catholic family (with some Irish heritage generations back) in 1930 in Ancoats. His father died young in 1937 and, as the second youngest child, he and his brother were raised by their mother alone and evacuated to Longridge, Preston during the Blitz. In 1942, John and his brother re-joined their mother and relocated to Gorton, where he remained throughout adolescence, and for a further ten years following his marriage in 1955. In 1965, John, his wife and young family emigrated to Australia, but returned in 1967 to Cheetham Hill before finally settling in Crumpsall. During his working life, he was employed as an electrician and telephone engineer, and his wife Joan worked as a secretary. He has been a member of St Anne's church since 1972, serving as a Eucharistic minister, reading daily at mass and, since 2007, has undertaken catechetical work with young children. Both John and Joan read *The Universe*.

Joseph
Interview at St Anne's, Crumpsall on 17/09/07, STE 023
Joseph was born of English working-class stock in Collyhurst, Manchester in 1917, worshipping at St Patrick's church before moving in adolescence

to St Monica's where the parish priest was Father Marshall, later Bishop of Salford. When Joseph married in the 1950s he moved to Crumpsall and has remained there ever since, with his two children attending the parish and local school when young. After a stint away during the Second World War, he returned to Manchester and worked for forty years as a postman. His association with St Anne's parish now stretches over fifty years – he enjoys the sense of community, the chats with a 'cuppa' after mass and, while over ninety, continues to serve on the altar at mass and welcome people on entering the church.

Judith
Interview at St Antony's, Trafford Park on 17/08/07, STE 009
Judith was born on a farm in North Yorkshire in 1936, the daughter of an Anglican father but with strong Catholic, recusant links through her maternal side back to the Venerable Tom Atkinson. After boarding at a Sisters of Charity secondary school, she joined the Order in 1954 and taught in a succession of schools in Manchester, Dundee and St Helen's, rising to headship positions. She left the Order in 1987 and took up a full-time role in the parish of St Antony's, helping to co-ordinate the liturgy, run a scripture and church history group for lay parishioners and to assist with administrative work in the parish. She regularly reads *The Tablet* and enjoys the theological writings and spiritual reflections of John O'Donoghue and Daniel O'Leary.

Kathleen
Interview at St Antony's, Trafford Park on 17/08/07, STE 011
Born the third of six children to Northern Irish immigrant parents in Trafford Park in 1923, Kathleen has been part of St Antony's parish for the entirety of her life – going to school and living and working in the Industrial Park (at Hills' aircraft factory) save for a brief sojourn in Stretford during the Blitz. She is an avid supporter of Manchester United, a committed member of the parish, and has a strong devotion to St Antony and St Jude. She never married and reads *The Universe* now and again.

Kathleen L.
Interview at St Anne's, Crumpsall on 15/09/07, STE 017
Like her husband Francis, Kathleen was born in Salford in the inter-war years (1927) and was raised by her maternal grandmother, as her mother

died when she was six weeks old. She worked as a full-time mother, raising three children. She has recently 'made the acquaintance' of St Anne and is working on improving her prayer life through meditation and spiritual reading, such as the writings of John Paul II. She has read *The Universe* for many years and attends daily mass at St Anne's church.

Kevin
Interview at St Antony's, Trafford Park on 07/08/07, STE 000 and STE 001
Kevin was born in 1954 in Old Trafford (St Alphonsus' parish) and raised within a traditional Irish-Catholic, working-class family. Both parents emigrated from Ireland, his father working as a local bus driver and his mother combining raising a family with employment as a 'dinner lady' at a local school. Moving from teenage involvement in the Young Christian Workers' movement (YCW), Kevin's studies in the brewing industry and strong involvement in the trade union movement prepared him for his current role as Director of the Centre for Church and Industry. Established in 1979 in collaboration with his old school chaplain Canon Jo, then priest at St Antony's, the Centre was built on the old site of the St Antony's primary school and is situated in the middle of Trafford Park Industrial Estate. He studied theology and Catholic Social Teaching at Plater College, Oxford and reads *The Tablet*, the *Catholic Herald* and *The Universe*. He is married to Elizabeth, whom he met through the YCW, and they have three grown children.

Mary
Interview at St Antony's, Trafford Park on 17/08/07, STE 007
Born in Trafford Park in 1967 to Irish immigrant parents, Mary and her family were moved by the 'compulsory purchase order' clearing housing from the Industrial Park to nearby Stretford. Despite the shift, Mary continued to cycle back to St Antony's church every Sunday for mass and to participate in the very strong Young Christian Workers' group, given the headquarters were located in Salford. She has continued to come to the parish ever since, bringing her two daughters (then aged 17 and 14) who serve as altar girls. Mary is also a Eucharistic minister and part of the sacramental preparation programme for first communion in the parish and at St Hugh's, Stretford. In addition to her family responsibilities, she works part-time.

Margaret
Interview at St Anne's, Crumpsall on 17/09/07, STE 022
The younger sister of Nora, Margaret was born in 1935 and migrated in 1951 (two years ahead of her sister) to Manchester to take up a nursing position. She met her husband, an Irishman and underground pipe layer, at an Irish dance and they were married for forty-three years, until his death just before Christmas in 2005. She has two sons and the youngest, Seamus, is a university lecturer in Ohio. Both she and her sister help out in the parish by cleaning the church, and do 'a wonderful job with the brasses'. She has read *The Universe* for many years.

Mitzi
Interview at St Antony's, Trafford Park on 17/08/07, STE 015
Mitzi was born in 1956, the second of four children. Her parents were Irish post-war migrants who emigrated seeking work, met at an Irish dance in Manchester, and then settled in Longsight. When Mitzi was 11, the family moved out of Manchester to Sale and, after a stint in Gatley when first married in 1985, she has now returned to Sale. She commutes into Manchester regularly given her role as deputy head and Year 6 teacher at a large Catholic primary school in Wythenshawe. She has attended mass at St Antony's church for the last decade and she and her children (her husband is not a Catholic) are drawn here by the pastoral leadership and sense of community in the parish. She often reads *The Universe*, as did her parents, who also subscribed to *The Catholic Messenger* and were sent *Ireland's Own* from relatives remaining in the Republic.

Nora
Interview at St Anne's, Crumpsall on 17/09/07, STE 022
Nora was born in Galway, Ireland in 1933, the second child (but eldest surviving) of devout Catholic parents. She followed her younger sister Margaret over to Crumpsall, Manchester in 1953 for nursing work and there she met and married William (a Belfast-born Catholic three years her senior) who worked as a joiner. They had six children and she returned to nursing work when her youngest child started secondary school. She is blessed with many grandchildren, some close by in Manchester and others living in Melbourne. She reads *The Universe* and her parents read the *Far East Messenger*.

Patrick
Interview at St Antony's, Trafford Park on 17/08/07, STE 015
Patrick, the youngest of Mitzi's three children, was born in Sale in 1990. He attends St Ambrose's College (a Catholic all-boys' school) where he is in the upper sixth and plans to study religion and philosophy through to A-level. Following in the footsteps of his older sisters, he made a pilgrimage to Lourdes in 2007, helping the elderly and sick pilgrims and carrying the Diocese of Shrewsbury banner in one of the torchlight processions. He also does volunteer work in the summer in Romania and enjoys reading, football and politics (youth cabinet). He hopes to read history at university when he leaves school.

Peter
Interview at St Antony's, Trafford Park on 07/08/07, STE 003
Peter was born in 1944 in Fairfield into what he describes as 'a Manchester family with Irish stock' – the link to Ireland traced through his great-grandparents. He taught for forty-two years, initially training in maths, moving into literacy and special needs, before taking on leadership positions in schools. In his retirement, he is a school governor and magistrate. Peter's connection with some of the parishioners of St Antony's church and its long-time parish priest Father Jo was forged in 1974 when he took up the deputy headship of St Alphonsus', Old Trafford. He has two grown sons and his wife, also a committed member of the parish, has just retired from her role as a special needs teacher. Peter regularly reads *The Universe*, the *Catholic Times*, *The Tablet*, *The Crusader* and *The Catena*.

Richard
Interview at St Antony's, Trafford Park on 17/08/07, STE 010
Richard was born in Trafford Park in 1947, shortly after his twin brother, and was raised a Catholic within a mixed background. His mother was brought up in Trafford Park within St Cuthbert's Church of England parish by an Orangeman father, but converted to Catholicism upon her marriage. In contrast, Richard's father was the son of a foundry worker in the nearby Westinghouse factory, with Irish/American parentage and through this an Irish Republican Brotherhood lineage. He has just retired from a position as Senior Lecturer in Electronics at Manchester Metropolitan University. Richard's connection with St Antony's church

extends over sixty years – his two children were raised in the parish, and he continues to play an active part, providing music at each Sunday mass and helping to organise the centenary commemorations in 2004.

Tom
Interview at St Antony's, Trafford Park on 07/08/07, STE 005
Tom was born of English parentage in Trafford Park in 1946, an only child raised mostly by his mother from the age of seven onwards following the death of his father from injuries suffered in the Royal Navy. His connection with the parish and the local area stretches back to these childhood days, and has been further cemented by working in the Centre for Church and Industry since 2000 and as a magistrate. He and his wife are strongly involved in the parish community, as readers and Eucharistic ministers, and their three children and grandchildren also worshipped at St Antony's church when young. He occasionally reads *The Universe*.

Tony
Interview at St Antony's, Trafford Park on 07/08/07, STE 006
The son of a steelworker from Warrington, Tony was born in 1943 in Irlam and was a stalwart of St Teresa's parish church there, where he served as an altar boy well into his twenties. He met his wife, Anne, in the parish and they adopted a child, Ruth, from the Catholic Rescue Society. The family became involved in St Antony's church around 1976 or 1977, initially due to the flexibility of mass times but over the years they have come to value the sense of spiritual community. He regularly reads *The Universe*.

Select bibliography

Manuscripts and archival materials

Archives of the Archbishop of Westminster (AAW)
Griffin, Coronation of Our Lady of Willesden, Coronation of Our Lady of Willesden Rally, 3 Oct 1954
Heenan, HE1/L6(a) Liturgy, Letters from Laity 1964–8
Heenan, HE1/L6(b) Liturgy, Letters from the Laity 1969–70
Heenan, HE1/E7(b) English and Welsh Martyrs, Cause of, 1970

Archives Holy Cross Family Ministries (AHCFM)
Crusades: Lancaster 01-13-01-00-00, 01-13-02-04-00
Crusades: Birmingham 01-13-01-03-00
Crusades: Durham 01-13-03-04-00
Crusades: London 01-13-03-04-00
Crusades: Newcastle 01-13-04-04-00

Archivum Britannicum Societatis Iesu (ABSI)
Cause of the English Martyrs, Box 2 ('A'); Box 3 ('B'); Box 30 ('P'); Box 32 ('R'); Box 34 ('S'); Box 38 ('W') [7 Lancastrian martyrs]
Cause of the English Martyrs, Box 111 62A Mrs Matthewman Cure
Cause of the English Martyrs, Box 105 63A 'Programme of Fr. Tighe's Coach Pilgrimage to the shrines of England and Wales ... Canonization Booklet etc.'
Cause of the English Martyrs, Box 108 63A EWM – Cures
Cause of the English Martyrs, Filing Cabinet 34
Drawer 3, 'Lists of Favours and Petitions'; 'Circulars – Salford'
Drawer 4, Liverpool Cure, Mr C. M. Coyne

Birmingham Archdiocese Archives (BAA)
BAA AP/M6 Cause of the English and Welsh Martyrs 1955–62 Folders 1–4
BAA AP/M7 English and Welsh Martyrs, 1963–65

BAA GPD/F3/71 (Archbishop George Dwyer) Sermons
BAA GPD/H/B2–5 Liturgy: General 1964–71
BAA GPD/H/C6 National Liturgical Commission
BAA GPD/P/A1 Cause of the English and Welsh Martyrs 1965–71
BAA GPD/S/L11 Lourdes 1966–78
BAA GPD/S/M2 Catholic Marriage Advisory Council 1965–81
BAA GPD/S/N1/I National Pastoral Congress

Liverpool Diocesan Archives (LDA)
LDA S6 XXIX A/59 (Discussion Papers)
LDA S6 XXXIII A/1–A/57; B/4–64; D/18 (NPC)
LDA S6 XXXVI A6–9; B/2–37 9 (NPC Press Releases)
LDA S6 XXXVIII A/15 Sector 'C' Reports
LDA S6 XXXVIII A/21–2 Correspondence
LDA S6 XXXVIII A/23 Criticisms in Press, Apos. Delegate, Minority Report

North West Sound Archive (NWSA)
1982.6345 Monsignor John Allen, September 1981
1982.7252 Out and About, 10 May 1982
1982.7330 Father Gerard Neath, 1982
1982.7364 Children Talking, 27 May 1982
1982.7384 Meeting, 31 May 1982
1982.7387 Nazareth House, 31 May 1982
1982.8295 Papal 21/1/82
1983.1487 Pope's Visit (4)
1983.1438 Pope Visit (ROT) 10" NAB

Salford Diocesan Archives (SDA)
Marshall Papers (1939–55): Boxes 021, 120, 200, 204, 211, 215, 220, 226 (Sermons, Pastorals, Ad Clerum and Personal Notes)
Beck Papers (1955–64): Box 220 [Marshall-Beck-Holland]
Holland Papers (1964–83): Box 219; Box 220 [Marshall-Beck-Holland]
Catholic Marriage Advisory Council 1946–76: Box 24
Catholic Societies: Box 186
Diocesan Pilgrimage Lourdes 1949–79: Box 197
Pamphlet Collection B66.

Young Christian Workers (YCW)
File: 4.1–4.2 Young Worker Newspaper 1949–60s and 1980s *New World Magazine*
File: Christian Workers Priests' Bulletin
File: Occasional Publications

Select bibliography

File: Young Worker Magazines 1938–58
File: *New Life* files, 1945–80

Frequently cited primary sources

Karen Armstrong, *Through the Narrow Gate: A Nun's Story* (London: Flamingo, 1995).
Beevers, John, *St Thérèse of the Child Jesus* (London: St. Paul Publications, 1960).
Boylan, Anthony B., *The Reception of Holy Communion in the Hand* (London: Catholic Truth Society, 1977).
Bro, Bernard, *The Little Way: The Spirituality of St Thérèse of Lisieux* (London: Darton, Longman and Todd, 1979).
Bullen, Anthony F., *The Rosary in Close-Up* (London: Geoffrey Chapman, 1962).
Butler, B. Christopher, *The Eucharist* (London: Catholic Truth Society, 1975).
Caraman, Philip, *Seven Lancashire Martyrs* (London: Office of the Vice Postulate, 1960).
Carr, John, *Truly a Lover: Some Reflections on Saint Teresa of Lisieux* (London: Sands and Co, 1925).
Catholicism To-Day: Letters to the Editor (London: Times, 1949).
Catholic Mother, *Preparing our Daughters for Life* (London: Catholic Truth Society, 1942).
Catholic Woman Doctor, *Growing Up: A Book for Girls* (London: Catholic Truth Society, 1939).
Cesbron, Gilbert, *No Plaster Saint: A Play about St Thérèse of Lisieux* (London: Hollis and Carter, 1948).
CMAC, *Beginning Your Marriage* (London: Catholic Marriage Advisory Council, 1963).
Combes, André, *St Thérèse and Suffering* (Dublin: M. H. Gill and Son, 1951).
Davis, Charles, *Liturgy and Doctrine: The Doctrinal Basis of the Liturgical Movement* (London, 1960).
———, *A Question of Conscience* (London: Hodder and Stoughton, 1967).
Dent, Barbara, *Sex in Adolescence* (London: Catholic Truth Society, 1962).
Drinkwater, Francis Harold, *Catechism Stories: A Teacher's Aid-book in Five Parts to Accompany the Abbreviated Catechism* (London: Burns and Oates, 1948).
———, *Our Living Sacrifice: An Action Picture of the Holy Mass* (Dudley: Wellington, 1948).
———, *Going to Mass: the Eucharistic Drama and How to Take Part in It* (London: Catholic Truth Society, 1957).
———, *Talking to Teenagers: Notes for Parents and Teachers* (London: Burns and Oates, 1964).
Dwyer, George Patrick, *Birth Control* (London: Catholic Truth Society, 1951).

Forrest, Michael D., *The Fragrance of the Little Flower* (Dublin: Burns, Oates and Washbourne, 1936).
Gorres, Ida Friederike, *The Hidden Face: A Study of St Thérèse of Lisieux* (London: Burns and Oates, 1959).
Greenstock, David L., *Christopher's Talks to Catholic Parents* (London: Burns and Oates, 1951).
Guitton, Jean, *The Spiritual Genius of St Thérèse* (London: Geoffrey Chapman, 1958).
Heenan, John Carmel, *Why Marry?: A CTS Torch Pamphlet* (London: Catholic Truth Society, 1950).
———, *Not the Whole Truth: An Autobiography* (London: Hodder and Stoughton, 1971).
Holland, Thomas, *For Better and For Worse: Memoirs of Thomas Holland* (Salford: Salford Diocesan Catholic Children's Rescue Society, 1989).
Hornsby-Smith, Michael, *Reflections on a Catholic Life* (Peterborough: Fastprint, 2010).
Houselander, F. Caryll, *This War is the Passion* (London: Sheed and Ward, 1943).
———, *The Passion of the Infant Christ* (London: Sheed and Ward, 1949).
———, 'Birth', reprinted in *A Rocking-Horse Catholic* (London: Sheed and Ward, 1960).
Hurrell, Grace, *The Church's Play* (London: Sheed and Ward, 1945).
———, *Talks on Mass and First Holy Communion* (London: Catholic Truth Society, 1946).
———, *The Saints and Us* (London: Sheed and Ward, 1948).
Jarrett, Bede, *The Catholic Mother* (London: Catholic Truth Society, 1943).
Jewell, Walter, *To Those Getting Married* (London: Catholic Truth Society, 1946).
Johnson, Vernon, 'St Teresa and Her Mission' in Vernon Johnson (ed.), *The Mission of a Saint* (London: Burns, Oates and Washbourne, 1947).
Kelly, Bernard J., *Lay Spirituality: Its Theory and Practice* (London: Sheed and Ward, 1980).
Kenny, Anthony, *A Path from Rome: An Autobiography* (Oxford: Oxford University Press, 1986).
Keyes, F. Parkinson, *The Sublime Shepherdess* (London: Burns, Oates and Washbourne, 1941).
———, *St Teresa of Lisieux* (London: Eyre & Spottiswoode, 1950).
King, J. Leycester, *Sex Enlightenment and the Catholic* (London: Burns, Oates and Washbourne, 1944).
Knox, Ronald, *Captive Flames: A Collection of Panegyrics* (London: Burns and Oates, 1940).
———, *The Mass in Slow Motion* (London: Sheed and Ward, 1948).
———, *The Creed in Slow Motion* (London: Sheed and Ward, 1949).

Lane, John Irving, *St Bernadette and the Apparitions at Lourdes: Told for Children* (London: Burns, Oates and Washbourne, 1937).
Lash, Nicholas, *What are we doing at Mass?* (London: Catholic Truth Society, 1968).
Lebbe, Bede, *The Soul of Bernadette* (Tralee: Kerryman Ltd., 1946).
Leonard, George, *Marriage and the Family* (London: Catholic Truth Society, 1979).
MacGillivray, George, *An Introduction to the Mass* (London: Catholic Truth Society, 1950).
MacMahon, Matthew S., *Nazareth: A Book of Counsel and Prayer for the Married* (Dublin: Eason and Son, 1948).
Madden, Tim, *How's the Family? Cartoons in the Catholic Herald* (London: Burns and Oates, 1965).
Martin, Thérèse, *The Story of a Soul: A New Translation* (Brewster: Paraclete Press, 2006).
Martindale, Cyril Charlie, *Bernadette of Lourdes* (London: Catholic Truth Society, 1924).
———, *The Mind of the Missal* (London: Sheed and Ward, 1929).
———, *The Cup of Christ* (London: Sheed and Ward, 1930).
———, *The Difficult Commandment: Notes on Self-Control Especially for Young Men* (London: Manresa Press, 1931).
———, *What is He doing at the Altar?* (London: Catholic Truth Society, 1931).
———, *What are the Saints? Fifteen Chapters in Sanctity* (London: Sheed and Ward, 1932).
———, 'Introduction' in B. G. Sandhurst, *We Saw Her* (London: Green and Co, 1953).
McCaffrey, Eugene, *Heart of Love: Saint Thérèse of Lisieux* (Dublin: Veritas, 1998).
McEvoy, Hubert, *A New and Easy Way at Mass* (London: Catholic Truth Society, 1949).
Medical Woman, A Girl, A Wife, *'Into their Company': A Book for a Modern Girl on Love and Marriage* (London: Burns, Oates and Washbourne, 1930).
Morton, John Bingham, *St Thérèse of Lisieux: The Making of a Saint* (London: Burns and Oates, 1954).
Nutt, J. A. P., *Talks for the Month of May* (London: Burns and Oates, 1948).
Oliver, Fr Michael, *Fair as the Moon: Mary, Purest of Creatures* (Dublin: M. H. Gill and Son, 1949).
Peyton, Patrick J., *The Ear of God* (London: Burns and Oates, 1954).
Philipon, Marie Michel, *The Message of Thérèse of Lisieux* (London: Burns, Oates and Washbourne, 1950).
Pickering, Aidan, *Sex-Instruction in the Home* (London: Catholic Truth Society, 1950).
———, *From Boy to Man* (London: Catholic Truth Society, 1957).
Ravier, André, *Bernadette* (London: Collins, 1978).
Robins, Michael, *Boy Meets Girl* (London: Catholic Truth Society, 1959).

Robo, Etienne, *Two Portraits of St Teresa of Lisieux* (London: Sands and Co, 1957).
Rorke, Patrick, *Through Parents to Christ* (Billinge: Birchley Hall Press, 1960).
Sackville-West, Vita, *The Eagle and the Dove: A Study in Contrasts. St Teresa of Avila. St Thérèse of Lisieux* (London: Michael Joseph, 1943).
Sheed, Frank, *Is it the Same Church?* (London: Sheed and Ward, 1968).
Steuart, Robert H., *Diversity in Holiness* (London: Sheed and Ward, 1936).
Taylor, Thérèse, *Bernadette of Lourdes: Her Life, Death and Visions* (London: Burns and Oates, 2003).
Tindall, Mary, *The Beloved Son: A Child's Meditation on the Childhood of Christ* (London: Catholic Truth Society, 1955).
Ulanov, Barry, *The Making of a Modern Saint* (London: Jonathan Cape, 1967).
Vann, Gerald, *Eve and the Gryphon* (London: Blackfriars, 1952).
Ward, Maisie, *The Splendour of the Rosary* (London: Sheed and Ward, 1946).
Werfel, Franz, *The Song of Bernadette* (New York: Viking, 1942).
Williamson, Benedict, *The Sure Way of St Thérèse of Lisieux* (London: Kegan Paul, 1928).
Williamson, Hugh Ross, *The Challenge of Lourdes* (London: Burns and Oates, 1958).
Winckworth, Peter, *The Way of War: a Meditation on the Stations of the Cross in Wartime* (London: Dacre, 1944).
Winstone, Harold E., *Communion under Both Kinds: Its Significance* (London: Catholic Truth Society, 1979).

Selected secondary sources

Alberigo, Giuseppe, *A Brief History of Vatican II* (Maryknoll, NY: Orbis Books, 2006).
Alberigo, Giuseppe, Jossua, Jean-Pierre, and Komonchak, Joseph A. (eds), *The Reception of Vatican II* (Wellwood: Burns and Oates, 1987).
Alberigo, Giuseppe and Komonchak, Joseph A. (eds), *History of Vatican II: Volume I. Announcing and Preparing Vatican II. Towards a New Era in Catholicism* (Leuven: Peeters, 1995).
———, *History of Vatican II: Volume II. The Formation of the Council's Identity. First Period and Intersession October 1962 – September 1963* (Leuven: Peeters, 1997).
———, *History of Vatican II: Volume III: The Mature Council: Second Period and Intersession* (Leuven: Peeters, 2000).
———, *History of Vatican II: Volume IV: Church as Communion: Third Period and Intersession* (Leuven: Peeters, 2003).
———, *History of Vatican II: Volume V: The Council and the Transition: The Fourth Period and the End of the Council: September 1965 – December 1965* (Leuven: Peeters, 2006).

Select bibliography

Ammerman, Nancy T. (ed.), *Everyday Religion: Observing Modern Religious Lives* (Oxford: Oxford University Press, 2007).

Archer, Anthony, *The Two Catholic Churches: A Study in Oppression* (London: SCM Press, 1986).

Aspden, Kester, *Fortress Church: The English Roman Catholic Bishops and Politics 1903–1963* (Leominster: Gracewing, 2002).

———, 'Drinkwater, Francis Harold (1886–1982)' in Brian Harrison and Lawrence Goldman, *Oxford Dictionary of National Biography* (Oxford: Oxford University Press, 2004, online edition) www.oxforddnb.com/view/article/65569?docPos=2.

Atherstone, Andrew, 'The Canonisation of the Forty English Martyrs: An Ecumenical Dilemma', *Recusant History* 30(4) (2011), 573–87.

Beck, George Andrew, (ed.), *The English Catholics 1850–1950: Essays to Commemorate the Centenary of the Restoration of the Hierarchy of England and Wales* (London: Burns and Oates, 1950).

Bellenger, Dominic Aiden, 'Butler, Basil Edward (1902–1986)' in Brian Harrison and Lawrence Goldman, *Oxford Dictionary of National Biography* (Oxford: Oxford University Press, 2004, online edition) www.oxforddnb.com/view/article/39996.

Bellitto, Christopher M., *The General Councils: A History of the Twenty-One Church Councils from Nicaea to Vatican II* (New York: Paulist Press, 2002).

Bingham, Adrian, '"An Era of Domesticity"? Histories of Women and Gender in Interwar Britain', *Cultural and Social History* 1(2)(2004), 225–33.

———, *Gender, Modernity and the Popular Press in Inter-War Britain* (Oxford: Clarendon, 2004).

Bourke, Joanna, *Working Class Cultures in Britain 1890–1960: Gender, Class and Ethnicity* (London: Routledge, 1994).

Boyle, Andrew, 'Bedoyere, Michael Anthony Maurice Huchet de la' in Brian Harrison and Lawrence Goldman, *Oxford Dictionary of National Biography* (Oxford: Oxford University Press, 2004, online edition) www.oxforddnb.com/view/articleHL/31023?docPos=1&anchor=match.

Brierley, Peter, *Prospects for the Nineties: Trends and Tables from the 1989 English Church Census* (London: MARC Europe, 1991).

———, *Pulling Out of the Nosedive: A Contemporary Picture of Churchgoing: What the 2005 English Church Census Reveals* (Eltham: Christian Research, 2006).

Brothers, Joan, *Church and School: A Study of the Impact of Education on Religion* (Liverpool: Liverpool University Press, 1964).

Brown, Callum, 'A Revisionist Approach to Religious Change' in Steve Bruce (ed.), *Religion and Modernization: Sociologists and Historians Debate the Secularization Thesis* (Oxford: Clarendon, 1992), 31–58.

———, *Religion and Society in Twentieth-Century Britain* (Harlow: Longman, 2006).

———, *The Death of Christian Britain: Understanding Secularisation 1800–2000* (2nd ed., London: Routledge, 2009).

———, 'Gendering Secularisation: Locating Women in the Transformation of British Christianity in the 1960s' in Ira Katznelson and Gareth Stedman Jones (eds), *Religion and the Political Imagination* (Cambridge: Cambridge University Press, 2010), 275–94.

———, 'What was the Religious Crisis of the 1960s?', *Journal of Religious History* 34(4) (2010), 468–79.

———, 'Women and Religion in Britain: An Autobiographical View of the Fifties and Sixties' in Callum Brown and Michael Snape (eds), *Secularisation in the Christian World: Essays in Honour of Hugh McLeod* (Farnham: Ashgate, 2010), 159–74.

Brown, Callum and Snape, Michael (eds), *Secularisation in the Christian World: Essays in Honour of Hugh McLeod* (Farnham: Ashgate, 2010).

Brown, Gavin, 'Mass Performances: A Study of Eucharistic Ritual in Australian Catholic Culture 1900–1962' (PhD thesis, Department of History, University of Melbourne, 2003).

Bruce, Steve, *Religion in Modern Britain* (Oxford: Oxford University Press, 1995).

———, *Religion in the Modern World: From Cathedrals to Cults* (Oxford: Oxford University Press, 1996).

———, *God is Dead: Secularization in the West* (Oxford: Blackwell, 2002).

———, *Secularization: In Defence of an Unfashionable Theory* (Oxford: Oxford University Press, 2011).

———, 'Secularization, Church and Popular Religion', *Journal of Ecclesiastical History* 62(3) (2011), 543–61.

Bruce, Steve, (ed.), *Religion and Modernization: Sociologists and Historians Debate the Secularization Thesis* (Oxford: Clarendon, 1992).

Burns, Tom F., 'Hollis, (Maurice) Christopher (1902–1977)' in Brian Harrison and Lawrence Goldman, *Oxford Dictionary of National Biography* (Oxford: Oxford University Press, 2004, online edition) www.oxforddnb.com/view/article/31248.

Caldecott, Stratford (ed.), *Beyond the Prosaic: Renewing the Liturgical Movement* (Edinburgh: T&T Clark, 1998).

Chesser, Eustace, *Marriage and Freedom* (London: Rich and Cowan Medical Publications, 1946).

Christie, Nancy (ed.), *Households of Faith: Family, Gender and Community in Canada, 1760–1969* (Montreal: McGill-Queens University Press, 2002).

Christie, Nancy, Gauvreau, Michael and Heathorn, Stephen (eds), *The Sixties and Beyond: Dechristianization as History in North America and Western Europe, 1945–2000* (Toronto: University of Toronto Press, 2013).

Select bibliography 287

Clark, David (ed.), *Marriage, Domestic Life and Social Change: Writings for Jacqueline Burgoyne (1944–88)* (London: Routledge, 1991).

Coman, Peter, *Catholics and the Welfare State* (London: Longman, 1977).

Conekin, Becky, Mort, Frank and Waters, Chris (eds), *Moments of Modernity: Reconstructing Britain 1945–1964* (London: Rivers Oram, 1998).

Connolly, Gerard, 'The Transubstantiation of Myth: Towards a New Popular History of Nineteenth-Century Catholicism in England', *Journal of Ecclesiastical History* 35(1) (1984), 78–104.

———, 'Irish and Catholic: Myth or Reality? Another Sort of Irish and Renewal of the Clerical Profession among Catholics in England, 1791–1918' in Roger Swift and Sheridan Gilley (eds), *The Irish in the Victorian City* (London, 1985), 225–54.

Cook, Hera, *The Long Sexual Revolution: English Women, Sex and Contraception, 1800–1975* (Oxford: Oxford University Press, 2004).

Corbishley, Thomas, 'Cyril Charlie Martindale (1879–1963)' in Brian Harrison and Lawrence Goldman, *Oxford Dictionary of National Biography* (Oxford: Oxford University Press, 2004, online edition) www.oxforddnb.com/view/article/34911.

Cordeiro, Cardinal Joseph, 'The Liturgical Constitution: *Sacrosanctum Concilium*' in Alberic Stacpoole (ed.), *Vatican II: By Those who were There* (London: G. Chapman, 1986), 187–94.

Cox, Jeffrey, 'Towards Eliminating the Concept of Secularisation: A Progress Report' in Callum Brown and Michael Snape (eds), *Secularisation in the Christian World: Essays in Honour of Hugh McLeod* (Farnham: Ashgate, 2010), 13–26.

Crichton, John Dunlop, 'The Liturgical Movement from 1940 to Vatican II' in John Dunlop Crichton, Harold Winstone and John R. Ainslie (eds), *English Catholic Worship: Liturgical Renewal in England since 1900* (London: G. Chapman, 1979), 60–78.

———, *A Short History of the Mass* (London: Catholic Truth Society, 1983).

Crichton, John Dunlop, Winstone, Harold and Ainslie, John R. (eds), *English Catholic Worship: Liturgical Renewal in England since 1900* (London: G. Chapman, 1979).

Cuncliffe, Charles R. A. (ed.), *English in the Liturgy: A Symposium* (London: Burns and Oates, 1956).

Davidoff, Leonore, Doolittle, Megan, Fink, Janet and Holden, Katherine, *The Family Story: Blood, Contract and Intimacy* (London: Longman, 1999).

Davie, Grace, *Religion in Modern Europe: A Memory Mutates* (Oxford: Oxford University Press, 2000).

Davie, Grace, Heelas, Paul and Woodhead, Linda (eds), *Predicting Religion: Christian, Secular and Alternative Futures* (Aldershot: Ashgate, 2003).

Davies, Andrew, *Leisure, Gender and Poverty: Working-Class Culture in Salford and Manchester, 1900–1939* (Buckingham: Open University Press, 1992).

Davies, John, 'L'Art du Possible': The Board of Education, the Catholic Church and Negotiations over the White Paper and the Education Bill 1943–44', *Recusant History* 22(2) (1994), 231–50.

———, '"Faith of Our Fathers", "Dare to be Daniel": Catholic Processions and Protestant Parades, Liverpool, 1909', *North West Catholic History* 31 (2004), 98–120.

———, 'Catholic-Anglican Relations: Archbishop Downey, Bishop David and the Decree of *Ne Temere*, 1930–1931', *Recusant History* 29(1) (2008), 101–23.

Davies, Michael, *Cranmer's Godly Order: The Destruction of Catholicism through Liturgical Change* (Chumleigh: Augustine Publishing, 1976).

———, *The Tridentine Mass* (Chumleigh: Augustine Publishing, 1977).

———, *The Roman Rite Destroyed* (Chumleigh: Augustine Publishing, 1978).

———, *Communion Under Both Kinds: An Ecumenical Surrender* (Chumleigh: Augustine Publishing 1980).

Deboick, Sophia, 'Image, Authenticity and the Cult of Saint Thérèse of Lisieux, 1897–1959' (Unpublished PhD thesis, University of Liverpool, 2011).

———, 'The Creation of a Modern Saint' in Peter Clarke and Tony Claydon (eds), *Saints and Sanctity* (Woodbridge: Suffolk, 2011), 376–89.

De Fiores, Stefano, 'Mary in Postconciliar Theology' in René Latourelle (ed.), *Vatican II: Assessment and Perspectives. Twenty-Five Years After (1962–1987)* (New York: Paulist Press, 1988), 469–539.

de la Bédoyère, Michael, *The Future of Catholic Christianity* (Harmondsworth: Penguin, 1968).

Delap, Lucy, Griffin, Ben and Wills, Abigail (eds), *The Politics of Domestic Authority since 1800* (Basingstoke: Palgrave Macmillan, 2009).

de Vries, Jacqueline, 'More than Paradoxes to Offer: Feminism, History and Religious Cultures' in Sue Morgan and Jacqueline de Vries (eds), *Women, Gender and Religious Cultures in Britain, 1800–1940* (London: Routledge, 2010), 188–210.

Dixon, Joy, 'Modernity, Heterodoxy and the Transformation of Religious Cultures' in Sue Morgan and Jacqueline de Vries (eds), *Women, Gender and Religious Cultures in Britain, 1800–1940* (London: Routledge, 2010), 211–30.

Dolan, Jay P., *The American Catholic Experience: A History from Colonial Times to the Present* (New York: Doubleday, 1985).

Donnelly, Mark, *Sixties Britain: Culture, Society, Politics* (Harlow: Pearson Longman, 2005).

Doyle, Peter, 'The Catholic Federation 1906–1929' in W. J. Sheils and Diana Wood (eds), *Studies in Church History 23: Voluntary Religion* (Oxford: Basil Blackwell, 1986), 461–76.

———, *Mitres and Missions in Lancashire: the Roman Catholic Diocese of Liverpool, 1850–2000* (Liverpool: Blue Coat Press, 2005).

Select bibliography 289

Duffy, Eamon, *The Stripping of the Altars. Traditional Religion in England, 1400–1580* (London, 1992).

———, *Faith of Our Fathers: Reflections on Catholic Tradition* (London: Continuum, 2004).

Ellis, Alice Thomas, *Serpent on the Rock* (London: Hodder and Stoughton, 1994).

Faggioli, Massimo, *True Reform: Liturgy and Ecclesiology in Sacrosanctum Concilium* (Collegeville, MN: Liturgical Press, 2012).

Fergusson, James, 'Michael Richard Hollings (1921–97)' in Brian Harrison and Lawrence Goldman, *Oxford Dictionary of National Biography* (Oxford: Oxford University Press, 2004, online edition) www.oxforddnb.com/view/article/65225?_fromAuth=1.

Ferraro, Thomas J., 'Not-just-cultural Catholics' in Thomas J. Ferraro (ed.), *Catholic Lives, Contemporary America* (Durham, NC: Duke University Press, 1997).

Field, Clive D., 'Faith in the Metropolis: Opinion Polls and Christianity in Postwar London,' *London Journal* 24(1) (1999), 68–84.

———, '*Puzzled People* Revisited: Religious Believing and Belonging in Wartime Britain 1939–45', *Twentieth Century British History* 19(4) (2008), 446–79.

Fielding, Steven, *Class and Ethnicity: Irish Catholics in England 1880–1939* (Buckingham: Open University Press, 1993).

Finch, Janet and Summerfield, Penny, 'Social Reconstruction and the Emergence of Companionate Marriage, 1945–59' in David Clark (ed.), *Marriage, Domestic Life and Social Change: Writings for Jacqueline Burgoyne (1944–88)* (London: Routledge, 1991), 7–32.

Fisher, Kate, *Birth Control, Sex and Marriage in Britain 1918–1960* (Oxford: Oxford University Press, 2006).

Francis, Martin, 'The Domestication of the Male? Recent Research on Nineteenth and Twentieth-century British Masculinity', *Historical Journal* 45 (2002), 637–52.

Garnett, Jane, Grimley, Matthew, Harris, Alana, Whyte, William and Williams, Sarah (eds), *Redefining Christian Britain: Post-1945 Perspectives* (London: SCM Press, 2007).

Gilley, Sheridan, 'Vulgar Piety and the Brompton Oratory, 1850–60' in Roger Swift and Sheridan Gilley (eds), *The Irish in the Victorian City* (London: Croom Helm, 1985).

———, 'A Tradition and Culture Lost, To be Regained?' in Michael P. Hornsby-Smith (ed.), *Catholics in England 1950–2000: Historical and Sociological Perspectives* (London: Cassell, 1999), 29–45.

———, 'Knox, Ronald Arbuthnott (1888–1957)' in Brian Harrison and Lawrence Goldman, *Oxford Dictionary of National Biography* (Oxford: Oxford University Press, 2004, online edition) www.oxforddnb.com/view/article/34358?docPos=1.

Greeley, Andrew M., *The Catholic Imagination* (Berkeley: University of California Press, 2000).

———, *The Catholic Revolution: New Wine, Old Wineskins and the Second Vatican Council* (Berkeley: University of California Press, 2004).

Green, Simon, *The Passing of Protestant Britain: Secularisation and Social Change c. 1920–1960* (Cambridge: Cambridge University Press, 2011).

Griffith, Edward (ed.), *The Road to Maturity* (London: Victor Gollancz, 1944).

Grimley, Matthew, 'The Religion of Englishness: Puritanism, Providentialism and "National Character"', 1918–45', *Journal of British Studies* 46 (2007), 884–906.

———, 'Law, Morality and Secularisation: The Church of England and the Wolfenden Report 1954–67', *Journal of Ecclesiastical History* 60(4) (2009), 725–41.

———, 'Thatcherism, Morality and Religion' in Ben Jackson and Rob Saunders (eds), *Making Thatcher's Britain* (Cambridge: Cambridge University Press, 2012), 78–94.

Hagerty, James, *Cardinal Hinsley: Priest and Patriot* (Oxford: Family Press, 2008).

———, *The Catenian Association: A Centenary History* (Coventry: Catenian Association, 2008).

———, *Cardinal John Carmel Heenan* (Leominster: Gracewing, 2013).

Hall, David D. (ed.), *Lived Religion in America: Towards a History of Practice* (Princeton: Princeton University Press, 1997).

Hall, Lesley A., *Sex, Gender and Social Change in Britain since 1880* (2nd edition, London: Palgrave, 2012).

———, 'Chesser, Eustace (formerly Isaac Chesarkie) (1902–73)' in Brian Harrison and Lawrence Goldman, *Oxford Dictionary of National Biography* (Oxford: Oxford University Press, 2004, online edition) www.oxforddnb.com/view/article/40923?docPos=2.

———, 'Stopes, Marie Charlotte Carmichael (1880–1958)' in Brian Harrison and Lawrence Goldman, *Oxford Dictionary of National Biography* (Oxford: Oxford University Press, 2004, online edition) www.oxforddnb.com/view/article/36323.

Harris, Alana, 'Bone Idol? British Catholics and Devotion to St Thérèse of Lisieux' in Nancy Christie, Michael Gauvreau and Stephen Heathorn (eds), *The Sixties and Beyond: Dechristianization as History in North America and Western Europe, 1945–2000* (Toronto: University of Toronto Press, 2013), 429–52.

———, 'Gray, Arthur Herbert (1868–1956)' in Brian Harrison and Lawrence Goldman, *Oxford Dictionary of National Biography* (Oxford: Oxford University Press, 2004, online edition) http://www.oxforddnb.com/view/article/102454?docPos=1.

———, 'Houselander, Frances Caryll (1901–1954)' in Brian Harrison and Lawrence Goldman, *Oxford Dictionary of National Biography* (Oxford: Oxford

Select bibliography 291

University Press, 2004, online edition) http://www.oxforddnb.com/view/article/71620.

———, 'Mace, David Robert (1907–1990)' in Brian Harrison and Lawrence Goldman, *Oxford Dictionary of National Biography* (Oxford: Oxford University Press, 2004, online edition) http://www.oxforddnb.com/view/article/101176.

———, '"A place to grow spiritually and socially": The Experiences of Young Pilgrims to Lourdes' in S. Collins-Mayo and B. P. Dandelion (eds), *Religion and Youth* (Aldershot: Ashgate, 2010), 149–58.

———, 'A Fresh Stripping of the Altars? The Reactions of English Catholics to the Second Vatican Council and Liturgical Change' (Unpublished Master's Thesis, University of Oxford, 2004).

Harris, Alana and Spence, Martin, '"Disturbing the Complacency of Religion"? The Evangelical Crusades of Dr Billy Graham and Father Patrick Peyton in England, 1951–4', *Twentieth Century British History* 18(4)(2007), 481–513.

Harris, Ruth, *Lourdes: Body and Spirit in the Secular Age* (London: Penguin, 2000).

Hastings, Adrian, *A History of English Christianity 1920–2000* (4th ed., London: SCM Press, 2001).

Hastings, Adrian (ed.), *Bishops and Writers: Aspects of the Evolution of Modern English Catholicism* (Wheathamstead: Anthony Clarke Books, 1977).

———, *Modern Catholicism: Vatican II and After* (London: Society for Promoting Christian Knowledge, 1991).

Hebblethwaite, Peter, 'St Peter's: A Day to Remember', *The Tablet*, 31 October 1970.

———, *The Runaway Church* (London: Collins, 1975).

Heelas, Paul, Lash, Scott and Morris, Paul (eds), *Detraditionalization. Critical Reflections on Authority and Identity* (Oxford: Blackwell, 1996).

Heelas, Paul and Woodhead, Linda, *The Spiritual Revolution: Why Religion is Giving Way to Spirituality* (Oxford: Blackwell, 2005).

Heimann, Mary, *Catholic Devotion in Victorian England* (Oxford: Oxford University Press, 1995).

Hickey, John, *Urban Catholics: Urban Catholicism in England and Wales from 1829 to the Present Day* (London: Catholic Book Club, 1967).

Hickman, Mary J., *Religion, Class and Identity: The State, the Catholic Church and the Education of the Irish in Britain* (Aldershot: Avebury, 1995).

Hilton, John Anthony, *Catholic Lancashire: From Reformation to Renewal 1559–1991* (Chichester: Philimore, 1994).

Hornsby-Smith, Michael P., *Roman Catholics in England: Studies in Social Structure since the Second World War* (Cambridge: Cambridge University Press, 1987).

———, 'Into the Mainstream: Recent Transformations in British Catholicism' in Thomas M. Gannon (ed.), *World Catholicism in Transition* (New York: Macmillan, 1988), 218–31.

———, *The Changing Parish: A Study of Parishes, Priests and Parishioners after Vatican II* (London: Routledge, 1989).

———, *Roman Catholic Beliefs in England: Customary Catholicism and Transformations of Religious Authority* (Cambridge: Cambridge University Press, 1991).

———, 'Believing without Belonging? The Case of Roman Catholics in England' in Bryan R. Wilson (ed.), *Religion: Contemporary Issues. The All Souls Seminars in the Sociology of Religion* (London: Bellew Publishing, 1992), 125–34.

———, 'Recent Transformations in English Catholicism: Evidence of Secularization?' in Steve Bruce (ed.), *Religion and Modernization: Sociologists and Historians Debate the Secularization Thesis* (Oxford: Clarendon Press, 1992), 118–44.

———, 'The Changing Identity of Catholics in England' in Simon Coleman and Peter Collins (eds), *Religion, Identity and Change: Perspectives of Global Transformations* (Aldershot: Ashgate, 2004), 42–56.

Hornsby-Smith, Michael P., (ed.), *Catholics in England 1950–2000: Historical and Sociological Perspectives* (London: Cassell, 1999).

Jones, Timothy, *Sexual Politics in the Church of England, 1857–1959* (Oxford: Oxford University Press, 2012).

Kane, Paula M., '"She Offered Herself Up": The Victim Soul and Victim Spirituality in Catholicism', *Church History* 71(1) (2002), 80–119.

———, 'Jews and Catholics Converge: *The Song of Bernadette (1943)*' in Colleen McDannell (ed.), *Catholics at the Movies* (Oxford: Oxford University Press, 2008), 83–106.

Kaufman, Suzanne K., *Consuming Visions: Mass Culture and the Lourdes Shrine* (Ithaca, 2005).

Keating, Joan, 'The British Experience: Christian Democracy without a Party 1910–60' in David L. Hanley (ed.), *Christian Democracy in Europe: A Comparative Perspective* (London: Pinter, 1994), 168–81.

———, 'Making a Catholic Labour Activist: The Catholic Social Guild and the Catholic Workers' College 1909–39', *Labour History Review* 59 (1994), 44–56.

———, 'Faith and Community Threatened? Roman Catholic Responses to the Welfare State, Materialism and Social Mobility, 1945–62', *Twentieth Century British History* 9(1) (1998), 86–108.

Kelly, Kevin T., *50 Years Receiving Vatican II: A Personal Odyssey* (Dublin: Columbia Press, 2012).

Kelly, Timothy, 'Suburbanization and the Decline of Catholic Ritual in Pittsburgh', *Journal of Social History* 28(2) (1994), 311–30.

———, *The Transformation of American Catholicism: The Pittsburgh Laity and the Second Vatican Council, 1950–1972* (Notre Dame: University of Notre Dame Press, 2009).

Select bibliography 293

Kelly, Timothy and Kelly, Anthony, 'Our Lady of Perpetual Help, Gender Roles, & the Decline of Devotional Catholicism', *Journal of Social History* 32(1) (1998), 5–26.

Kenny, Mary, *Goodbye to Catholic Ireland* (Rev. ed., Dublin: New Island, 2000).

Knight, Frances, *The Nineteenth-Century Church and English Society* (Cambridge: Cambridge University Press, 1995).

Koopmanschap, Theodore, 'Transformations in Contemporary Roman Catholicism: A Case Study' (Unpublished PhD thesis, University of Liverpool, 1978).

Kselman, Thomas A. (ed.), *Belief in History: Innovative Approaches to European and American Religion* (Notre Dame: University of Notre Dame Press, 1991).

Lamberigts, M. and Kenis, Leo (eds), *Vatican II and its Legacy* (Leuven: Leuven University Press, 2002).

Lane, Peter, *The Catenian Association, 1908–1983: A Microcosm of the Development of the Catholic Middle Class* (London: Catenian Association, 1982).

Langhamer, Claire, 'Love and Courtship in Mid-Twentieth-Century England', *Historical Journal* 50(1) (2007), 173–96.

———, 'Love, Selfhood and Authenticity in Post-War Britain', *Cultural and Social History* 9(2) (2012), 277–97.

———, *The English in Love: The Intimate Story of an Emotional Revolution* (Oxford: Oxford University Press, 2013).

Lannon, David, 'Financing Catholic Schools: Two Aspects of the Situation in 1900' in John A. Hilton (ed.), *Turning the Last Century: Essays on English Catholicism c.1900* (Wigan: North West Catholic History Society, 2003), 27–46.

Laurentin, René, *Bernadette of Lourdes: A Life Based on Authenticated Documents* (London: Darton, Longman and Todd, 1979).

Latourelle, René (ed.), *Vatican II: Assessment and Perspectives. Twenty-Five Years After (1962–1987)* (New York: Paulist Press, 1988).

Lewis, Jane, 'Public Institution and Private Relationship: Marriage and Marriage Guidance, 1920–1968', *Twentieth Century British History* 1(3) (1990), 233–63.

Lewis, Jane, Clark, David and Morgan, David H. J. *'Whom God hath Joined Together': The Work of Marriage Guidance* (London: Routledge, 1992).

Lindsey, Ben B. and Evans, Wainwright, *The Companionate Marriage* (London: Brentano's, 1927).

Lothian, James, *The Making and Unmaking of the English Catholic Intellectual Community, 1910–1950* (Notre Dame: University of Notre Dame Press, 2009).

Marwick, Arthur, *The Sixties: Cultural Revolution in Britain, France, Italy, and the United States, c. 1958–c. 1974* (Oxford: Oxford University Press, 1998).

Massam, Katharine, 'The Blue Army and the Cold War: Anti-Communist Devotion to the Blessed Virgin Mary in Australia', *Australian Historical Studies* 24(96) (1991), 420–8.

———, *Sacred Threads: Catholic Spirituality in Australia 1922–1962* (Sydney: University of New South Wales Press, 1996).
McCaffrey, Peter G. 'Catholic Radicalism and Counter-Radicalism: A Comparative Study of England and the Netherlands' (Unpublished DPhil thesis, University of Oxford, 1979).
McCarthy, Timothy G. *The Catholic Tradition: Before and After Vatican II, 1873–1993* (Chicago: Loyola University Press, 1994).
McClelland, V. Alan and Hodgetts, Michael (eds), *From Without the Flaminian Gate: 150 Years of Roman Catholicism in England and Wales 1850–2000* (London: Longman and Todd, 1999).
McDannell, Colleen, *Material Christianity: Religion and Popular Culture in America* (New Haven: Yale University Press, 1995).
McGuire, Meredith, *Lived Religion: Faith and Practice in Everyday Life* (Oxford: Oxford University Press, 2008).
McKibbin, Ross (ed.), *Marie Stopes, Married Love: A New Contribution to the Solution of Sex Difficulties* (Oxford: Oxford University Press, 2004).
McLeod, Hugh, 'Building the "Catholic Ghetto": Catholic Organisations 1870–1914' in W. J. Sheils and Diana Wood (eds), *Studies in Church History 23: Voluntary Religion* (Oxford: Basil Blackwell, 1986), 411–44.
———, *Religion and Society in England, 1850–1914* (Basingstoke: Macmillan, 1996).
———, *Religion and the People of Western Europe 1789–1989* (Oxford: Oxford University Press, 1997).
———, *The Religious Crisis of the 1960s* (Oxford: Oxford University Press, 2007).
McLeod, Hugh and Ustorf, Werner (eds), *The Decline of Christendom in Western Europe, 1750–2000* (Cambridge: Cambridge University Press, 2003).
McSweeney, Bill, *Roman Catholicism: The Search for Relevance* (Oxford: Basil Blackwell, 1980).
Moloney, Thomas, *Westminster, Whitehall and the Vatican: the Role of Cardinal Hinsley 1935–43* (Tunbridge Wells: Burns and Oates, 1985).
Morgan, David, *Visual Piety: A History and Theory of Popular Religious Images* (Berkeley: University of California Press, 1998).
Morgan, Sue, '"Wild Oats or Acorns?" Social Purity, Sexual Politics and the Response on the Late-Victorian Church', *Journal of Religious History* 31(2) (2007), 151–68.
———, '"The Word Made Flesh": Women, Religion and Sexual Cultures' in Sue Morgan and Jacqueline de Vries (eds), *Women, Gender and Religious Cultures in Britain, 1800–1940* (London: Routledge, 2010), 159–87.
Morgan, Sue and de Vries, Jacqueline (eds), *Women, Gender and Religious Cultures in Britain, 1800–1940* (London: Routledge, 2010).

Morris, Jeremy, 'Secularization and Religious Experience: Arguments in the Historiography of Modern British Religion', *Historical Journal* 55(1) (2012), 195–219.

Morris, Michael and Gooch, Leo, *Down Your Aisles: The Diocese of Hexham and Newcastle 1850–2000* (Hartlepool: Northern Cross, 2000).

National Pastoral Congress (NPC), *Roman Catholic Church, England National Pastoral Congress Discussion Papers* (Liverpool, 1979).

———, *Liverpool 1980: Official Report of the National Pastoral Congress* (Slough: St Pauls Publications, 1981).

Nichols, Aidan, *Looking at the Liturgy: A Critical View of its Contemporary Form* (San Francisco: Ignatius Press, 1996).

Novak, Michael, *The Open Church: Vatican II, Act II* (London: Darton, Longman and Todd, 1964).

O'Malley, John and Komonchak, Joseph A. (et al), *Vatican II: Did Anything Happen?* (London: Continuum, 2008).

Orsi, Robert A., *Thank You, St Jude: Women's Devotion to the Patron Saint of Hopeless Causes* (New Haven: Yale University Press, 1996).

———, 'Everyday Miracles: the Study of Lived Religion' in David D. Hall (ed.), *Lived Religion in America: Towards a History of Practice* (Princeton: Princeton University Press 1997), 3–21.

———, *The Madonna of 115th Street: Faith and Community in Italian Harlem 1880–1950* (Rev. ed., New Haven: Yale University Press, 2002).

———, '"The Infant of Prague's Nightie": The Devotional Origins of Contemporary Catholic Memory', *U.S. Catholic Historian* 21(1) (2003), 1–18.

———, *Between Heaven and Earth: The Religious Worlds People Make and the Scholars who Study Them* (Princeton: Princeton University Press, 2005).

———, 'Everyday Religion and the Contemporary World: The Un-Modern or What was Supposed to Have Disappeared but Did Not' in Samuli Schielke and Liza Debevec (eds), *Ordinary Lives and Grand Schemes: An Anthropology of Everyday Religion* (Oxford: Berghahn, 2012), 145–61.

O'Toole, James M. (ed.), *Habits of Devotion: Catholic Religious Practice in Twentieth-Century America* (Ithaca: Cornell University Press, 2004).

Parsons, Gerald, 'Emotion and Piety: Revivalism and Ritualism in Victorian Christianity' in Gerald Parsons (ed.) *Religion in Victorian Britain: Traditions* (Manchester: Manchester University Press, 1988).

Pasture, Patrick, 'Christendom and the Legacy of the Sixties: Between the Secular City and the Age of Aquarius', *Revue d'histoire ecclésiastique* 99(1) (2004), 82–116.

———, 'Religious Globalisation in Post-war Europe: Spiritual Connections and Interactions', *Archiv für Sozialgeschichte* 51 (2011), 63–108.

Pasture, Patrick and Art, Jan (eds), *Gender and Christianity in Modern Europe: Beyond the Feminization Thesis* (Leuven: Leuven University Press, 2012).

Pasture, Patrick and Van Osselaer, Tine (eds), *Households of Faith: Religion and Domesticity in Twentieth-Century Europe* (Leuven: University of Leuven Press, 2013).

Pearce, Joseph, *Literary Converts: Spiritual Inspiration in an Age of Unbelief* (London: HarperCollins, 1999).

Pereiro, James, 'Who are the Laity?' in V. Alan McClelland and Michael Hodgetts (eds), *From Without the Flaminian Gate: 150 Years of Roman Catholicism in England and Wales 1850–2000* (London: Darton, Longman and Todd, 1999), 167–91.

Perks, Robert and Thomson, Alistair (eds), *The Oral History Reader* (2nd ed., London: Routledge, 2006).

Pope, Barbara Corrado, 'A Heroine without Heroics: The Little Flower of Jesus and Her Times', *Church History* 51(1) (1988), 46–60.

Pratt, Ianthe and Pratt, Oliver, *Becoming the Easter People: Discussion Outlines* (London: Catholic Truth Society, 1981).

Rainer-Horn, Gerd, *The Spirit of Vatican II: Western European Left Catholicism in the Long Sixties, 1959–1980* (Oxford: Oxford University Press, 2013).

Reid, Alcuin, *The Organic Development of the Liturgy* (Farnborough: St Michael's Abbey Press, 2004).

Richards, Graham, 'Psychology and the Churches in Britain 1919–39: Symptoms of Conversion', *History of the Human Sciences* 13(2) (2000), 57–84.

Richards, Michael, *The Liturgy in England* (London: Chapman, 1966).

Rogers, Carole Garibaldi, *Habits of Change: An Oral History of American Nuns* (Oxford: Oxford University Press, 2011).

Rooden, Peter van, 'Oral History and the Strange Demise of Dutch Christianity', *Bijdragen en Mededelingen betreffende de Geschiedenis der Nederlanden* 119 (2004), 524–51.

Roof, Wade Clark, *The Spiritual Marketplace: Baby Boomers and the Remaking of American Religion* (Princeton: Princeton University Press, 1999).

Royal Commission on Population, *Family Limitation and its Influence of Human Fertility during the Past Fifty Years, Volume 1* (London: HMSO 1949–54).

Rubin, Miri, *Mother of God: A History of the Virgin Mary* (London: Allen Lane, 2009).

Ruff, Mark Edward, The Postmodern Challenge to the Secularization Thesis: A Critical Assessment', *Schweizerische Zeitschrift für Religion und Kulterheschichte* 99 (2005), 385–401.

———, *The Wayward Flock: Catholic Youth in Postwar Germany, 1945–1965* (Chapel Hill; University of North Carolina Press, 2005).

Ryan, Desmond, *The Catholic Parish: Institutional Discipline, Tribal Identity and Religious Development in the English Church* (London: Sheed and Ward, 1996).

Rynne, Xavier, *Vatican Council II* (Maryknoll: Orbis Books, 1999).

Schielke, Samuli and Debevec, Liza (eds), *Ordinary Lives and Grand Schemes: An Anthropology of Everyday Religion* (Oxford: Berghahn, 2012).

Schofield, Michael G., *The Sexual Behaviour of Young People* (London: Longmans, 1965).
Scott, George, *The R.C.s: A Report on Roman Catholics in Britain Today* (London: Hutchinson, 1967).
Sewell, Dennis, *Catholics: Britain's Largest Minority* (London: Viking, 2002).
Sheils, W. J. and Wood, Diana (eds), *Studies in Church History 23: Voluntary Religion* (Oxford: Basil Blackwell, 1986).
Spencer, Antony E. C. W. (ed.), *Pastoral and Population Statistics of the Catholic Community in England and Wales, 1958–2002* (Taunton: Pastoral Research Centre, 2004).
Spencer, Dorothy, 'The Second Vatican Council and the English Catholic Novel' (Unpublished PhD thesis, University of Liverpool, 1996).
Stanford, Peter, *Cardinal Hume and the Changing Face of English Catholicism* (London: G. Chapman, 1993).
Stanley, Liz, *Sex Surveyed, 1949–1994: From Mass Observation's 'Little Kinsey' to the National Survey and the Hite Reports* (London: Taylor and Francis, 1995).
Stourton, Edward, *Absolute Truth: The Catholic Church in the World Today* (London: Viking, 1998).
Summerfield, Penny, 'Women in Britain since 1945: Companionate Marriage and the Double Burden' in James Obelkevich and Peter Catterall (eds), *Understanding Post-war British Society* (London: Routledge, 1994).
———, 'Culture and Composure: Creating Narratives of the Gendered Self in Oral History Interviews', *Cultural and Social History* 1(1) (2004), 65–93.
Swift, Roger and Gilley, Sheridan (eds), *The Irish in the Victorian City* (London: Croom Helm, 1985).
Szreter, Simon, *Fertility, Class and Gender in Britain, 1860–1940* (Cambridge: Cambridge University Press, 1996).
Szreter, Simon and Fisher, Kate, *Sex Before the Sexual Revolution: Intimate Life in England, 1918–1963* (Cambridge: Cambridge University Press, 2010).
Tanner, Norman P., *The Councils of the Church: A Short History* (New York: Crossroad, 2001).
Tanner, Norman P., (ed.), *Decrees of the Ecumenical Councils: Volume Two, Trent to Vatican II* (London: Sheed and Ward, 1990).
Taves, Ann, 'Context and Meaning: Roman Catholic Devotion to the Blessed Sacrament in Mid-Nineteenth-Century America', *Church History* 54(4) (1985), 482–95.
———, *The Household of Faith: Roman Catholic Devotions in Mid-Nineteenth-Century America* (Notre Dame: University of Notre Dame Press, 1986).
Taylor, Charles, *A Secular Age* (Cambridge, Mass.: Harvard University Press, 2007).
Tenbus, Eric, *English Catholics and the Education of the Poor, 1847–1902* (London: Pickering Chatto, 2010).

Tentler, Leslie W. (ed.), *The Church Confronts Modernity: Catholicism since 1950 in the United States, Ireland and Quebec* (Washington: Catholic University of America Press, 2007).

Thomson, Matthew, *'Psychological Subjects: Identity, Culture and Health in Twentieth-Century Britain* (Oxford: Oxford University Press, 2006).

Todd, Selina, *Young Women, Work and Family in England, 1918–1950* (Oxford: Oxford University Press, 2005).

Tosh, John and Roper, Michael, *Manful Assertions: Masculinities in Britain since 1800* (London: Routledge, 1991).

Van Osselaer, Tine, '"From that Moment on, I was a Man!": Images of the Catholic Male in the Sacred Heart Devotion' in Patrick Pasture and Jan Art (eds), *Gender and Christianity in Modern Europe: Beyond the Feminization Thesis* (Leuven: Leuven University Press, 2012), 121–36.

Van Osselaer, Tine and Maurits, Alexander, 'Heroic men and Christian ideals' in Yvonne Maria Werner (ed.), *Christian Masculinity – Men and Religion in Northern Europe in the 19th and 20th Centuries* (Leuven: Leuven University Press, 2011), 63–94.

Vasquez, Manuel A., *More than Belief: A Materialist Theory of Religion* (Oxford: Oxford University Press, 2011).

Voas, David, 'The Rise and Fall of Fuzzy Fidelity in Europe', *European Sociological Review* 25(2) (2009), 155–68.

Walsh, Michael, *From Sword to Ploughshare: Sword of the Spirit to Catholic Institute for International Relations 1940–80* (London: Catholic Institute for International Relations, 1980).

———, *The Tablet 1840–1990: A Commemorative History* (London: The Tablet, 1990).

———, 'John Paul II and His Canonizations' in Peter Clarke and Tony Claydon (eds), *Saints and Sanctity* (Woodbridge: Suffolk, 2011), 415–37.

Ward, Conor K., *Priests and People: A Study in the Sociology of Religion* (Liverpool: Liverpool University Press, 1961).

Watson, Natalie K., 'Davis, Charles Alfred (1923–1999)' in Brian Harrison and Lawrence Goldman, *Oxford Dictionary of National Biography* (Oxford: Oxford University Press, 2004, online edition) www.oxforddnb.com/view/article/71960?docPos=3.

Weaver, Mary Jo, 'Sheed and Ward', *U. S. Catholic Historian*, 21(3) (2003), 1–18.

Wildman, Charlotte, 'The "Spectacle" of Interwar Manchester and Liverpool: Urban Fantasies, Consumer Cultures and Gendered Identities' (Unpublished PhD thesis, University of Manchester, 2007).

———, 'Religious Selfhoods and the City in Interwar Manchester', *Urban History* 38(1) (2011), 103–23.

Williams, Sarah C., 'The Language of Belief: An Alternative Agenda for the Study of Victorian Working-Class Religion', *Journal of Victorian Culture* 1(2) (1996), 303–17.

———, *Religious Belief and Popular Culture in Southwark c. 1880–1939* (Oxford: Oxford University Press, 1999).

Williamson, Hugh Ross, *The Modern Mass: A Reversion to the Reforms of Cranmer* (Chumleigh: Britons, 1969).

———, *The Great Betrayal: Some Thoughts on the Invalidity of the New Mass* (Chumleigh: Britons, 1970).

Wolffe, John (ed.), *Religion in History: Conflict, Conversion and Co-existence* (Manchester: Manchester University Press, 2004).

Wolffe, John and Parsons, Gerald (ed.), *The Growth of Religious Diversity: Britain from 1945, Volume III* (London: Routledge, 1994).

Woodhead, Linda, 'Gendering Secularization Theory', *Social Compass* 55(2) (2008), 187–93.

Woodhead, Linda and Catto, Rebecca (eds), *Religion and Change in Modern Britain* (London: Routledge, 2012).

Wuthnow, Robert, *After the Baby Boomers: How Twenty- and Thirty-Somethings are Shaping the Future of American Religion* (Princeton: Princeton University Press, 2007).

Yarnold, Edward (ed.), *The Pope in Britain: Collected Homilies and Speeches* (Slough: St Paul Publications, 1982).

Index

Note: page numbers in *italic* refer to illustrations; 'n.' after a page reference indicates the number of a note on that page.

abortion 45, 170, 182, 245, 265
active participation 7, 58, 78, 100–1
  see also liturgical movement; *Sacrosanctum Concilium* (1963); vernacular
adolescence 103, 110, 152, 159, 162, 164, 213, 259
affluence 2, 44, 157, 177, 183–4, 218
  see also consumption; social mobility
Agatha Christie indult 263–4
  see also Latin; Latin Mass Society; liturgical movement
Alberigo, Giuseppe (1926–2007) 4–5, 24n.10, 24n.18
Anglican 5, 32, 45, 91, 93–4, 101, 148, 221, 234, 259, 264, 265
  see also Archbishop of Canterbury; Church of England; Protestantism
Antony, St 206–7, 231, 249
  see also saints
Archbishop of Canterbury 32, 94, 180, 234
  see also Anglican; Church of England; Protestantism
Archbishop of Westminster 3, 17, 32, 60, 164, 168, 182, 217, 222, 234, 244
  see also Heenan, (Cardinal) John Carmel (1905–75); London
aristocracy 217, 218
  see also class; Establishment; recusant

authenticity 47–8, 70, 106, 173,190n.35; 224–5, 230, 236, 248, 266
authority 2–3, 5, 6, 14, 22, 33, 40, 47, 65, 147, 149–50, 187–8, 225, 266
  papal 32, 109, 166, 183, 268
  see also conscience

BBC *see* British Broadcasting Corporation
Beck, (Bishop) George Andrew (1904–78) 19, 34, 38, 235, 240
  see also Salford, Diocese of
Bédoyère, (Count) Michael de la (1900–73) 18, 25n.20, 29n.107, 87, 124n.127
belief 2–3, 12, 14–15, 17, 21, 40–1, 43–4, 47, 59, 60, 85, 92, 96, 99, 102, 104, 117, 131, 136–7, 152, 174, 182–3, 203, 206, 222–3, 229, 231, 243–5, 249, 259, 266–8
  see also prayer; spirituality
Benedict XVI, Pope (2005–13) 5, 263–4, 269n.12
Benedictines 19, 77, 87
  see also Dominicans; Jesuits; priesthood
benediction 59, 65, 81, 84–5, 104, 173, 182
  see also Eucharist; host; prayer
Bernadette, St 22, 203, 207, 208–33, 247, 248, 249, 262, 265
  see also saints

Index

bible *see Dei Verbum* (1965); scripture
Birmingham 9, 17, 40, 49n.5, 50n.20, 58, 93, 108, 148, 162, 180, 181, 184, 240
  see also Dwyer, (Archbishop) George Patrick (1908–87)
birth control 31n.135, 112, 154, 160, 162–4, 166, 181–3, 265
  see also abortion; contraception; *Humanae Vitae* (1968)
Blessed Virgin Mary *see* Virgin Mary
breadwinner 111, 148, 152, 184, 186
  see also masculinity; work
British Broadcasting Corporation 94, 206, 112, 113, 145
  see also media; television
Butler, (Bishop) Basil Christopher OSB (1902–86) 6, 25n.21, 94, 125n.162

Campaign for Nuclear Disarmament 116, 128n.153
Casti Connubii (1930) 166
catechesis 17, 58, 61, 65, 74, 90, 175, 214, 262, 263
  see also childhood; schools, Catholic
Catholic Action 36, 110
Catholic Marriage Advisory Council 106, 127n.210, 138, 140–1, 160, 161, 162, 164, 166, 169, 190n.52
Catholic Missionary Society 74, 87, 168
Catholic Social Teaching 115, 141
  see also Catholic Action; liberation theology; poverty
Catholic Truth Society 9, 17, 29n.103, 91, 144
celibacy *see* nuns; priesthood; single life
chalice 76, 83, 94, 107, 169, 219
  see also Eucharist, both kinds
chastity 160, 236
  see also purity
childhood 37, 39, 46, 80, 84, 85, 98, 115, 135, 174, 205, 208, 209, 214, 230, 262
  boys and 61, 62, 63, 82, 134, 144, 146, 149, 158–9, 160–2, 168, 237, 258
  girls and 60, 61, 72, 111, 112, 134, 143, 144, 160, 161, 167, 183, 212, 215, 220, 258
  spiritual 66, 208, 211–12, 216, 224, 226, 265
children 22, 35, 58, 60–7, 69, 73, 91, 103, 108, 111, 115, 135, 137, 141, 146–7, 150–2, 155, 158, 162, 177, 178, 183–4, 186, 187, 202, 212, 215, 219, 235, 237, 240, 244, 245, 267
Christology 8, 61, 63, 64, 74, 103, 107, 116, 118, 137, 186, 248, 262, 264
  see also eschatology; incarnational; soteriology; stations of the cross
Christopher, St 10, 206
  see also saints
Church of England 7, 44, 93, 112, 163, 259
  see also Anglican; Establishment; Protestant
class 14, 18, 20, 32, 35–6, 39, 43, 49, 63, 87, 114, 152, 154, 164, 172, 182, 183, 186, 210, 212, 217, 218, 223, 224, 234, 248, 265, 267
  class conflict 72
  see also affluence; aristocracy; middle class; social mobility; working class
clergy *see* priesthood
CMAC *see* Catholic Marriage Advisory Council
CND *see* Campaign for Nuclear Disarmament
Cold War 70, 71, 72, 170, 172, 186, 193n.117, 222, 265
communism 32, 70, 71, 223
confession 3, 81, 96, 126n.174, 163, 177
  see also Humanae Vitae (1968), penance; sin
conscience 89, 93, 95, 155, 164, 167, 181, 212, 242, 248
  primacy of 109, 166, 183, 243, 262, 266, 268
  sensus fidelium 182
  see also authority; *Humanae Vitae* (1968)
consumption 2, 44, 183,

continental Catholicism 20, 27n.67, 29n.97, 87, 98, 128n.249, 213, 242, 252n.73, 254n.131, 265
see also Europe; United States of America
contraception 19, 107, 112, 141, 154, 155, 162, 164, *165*, 168, 171, 180–2, 188
see also birth control; *Humanae Vitae* (1968); pill, the
convent 60, 161, 167, 202, 208, 209, 210, 216, 218, 226, 230, 259
see also nuns
counter culture 29n.115, 101, 116, 128n.249, 143, 167, 227
see also Campaign for Nuclear Disarmament; new age; sixties

Davis, Charles Alfred (1923–99) 89, 124n.134
Dawson, Christopher Henry (1889–1970) 37
Dei Verbum (1965) 127n.194
devotions *see* material religion; prayer; saints; spirituality; tradition
divorce 45, 107–8, 140–1, 170, 171, 180, 222, 261
Dominian, Jack (1929–) 179, 199n.294
Dominicans 81, 116, 133, 138, 155, 166, 216, 217, 226, 227
see also Benedictines; Jesuits; priesthood
Drinkwater, (Canon) Francis Harold (1886–1982) 58, 61, 74, 90, 110, 114, 119n.4, 159, 161
Durham *149*, 156
Dwyer, (Archbishop) George Patrick (1908–87) 93, 98, 162–3, 240

ecumenism 9, 23, 32, 38, 46, 49, 89, 93–4, 104, 109, 132, 145, 164, 173, 177–8, 234, 239, 240–3, 249, 259, 260, 262, 263
see also forty martyrs of England and Wales; recusant
embodiment 6, 15, 47, 59, 60, 61, 68, 73, 80, 82, 86, 97, 99, 103, 105–6, 107, 117–18, 133, 135, 167, 168, 172, 188, 248, 263
encyclical *see individually named*
eschatology 9, 10, 47, 59, 67, 74, 88, 89, 94, 95, 114–16, 169, 171, 172, 175, 206, 248, 263, 265
realised 102, 115, 119
'this-worldly' 23, 48, 59, 82, 89, 101, 107, 132, 204, 206, 227
see also Christology; incarnational; soteriology
Establishment 4, 45, 116, 218
see also aristocracy; Church of England; class
Eucharist 2, 5, 10, 22, 57–60, 65, *66*, 74–104, 106, 107, 108, 110, 112–19, 169, 188, 242, 262, 263, 264
in both kinds 57, 81, 82, 91, 94–7
in the hand 97, 98, 99, 126n.182
see also benediction; host; sacrifice
Eucharistic minister 112, 272, 273, 275, 278
see also Eucharist; priesthood
Europe 3, 11, 14, 20, 31n.137, 34, 35, 37, 44, 75, 78, 86, 98, 213, 230, 264, 265, 270n.33
see also continental Catholicism
experience 4, 14–17, 21, 23, 32, 38, 41, 45, 46–7, 59, 60, 61, 62, 67, 74, 81, 85, 91, 97, 100, 101, 103, 104, 108, 140, 162, 167, 179, 180, 185, 188, 204, 206, 220, 224, 229, 230, 248, 259, 260, 261, 262, 265–8
see also spirituality

family life 11, 21, 23, 88, 130–1, 133, 138, 140–1, 166, 168, 170–1, 176, 179, 186, 188, 244
fashion 106, 142, 157, 173, 186, 234
fasting 80, 86, 117
fatherhood 63, 133, 146, 148–54, 158, 159, 178, 185–7, 230, 244–5, 264
see also masculinity
female ordination 112, *113*, 128n.237, 201n.346, 228

Index 303

see also feminism; nuns; priesthood;
  women's role
feminisation of religion 13, 27n.76
feminism 14, 43, 48, 73, 111, 143, 183–5,
  187, 228
  St Joan's Alliance 114
film 43, 90, 134, 143, 202, 213–15, 219,
  242
  see also music; television; theatre
football 85, 130, 149, 207, 258, 267
forty martyrs of England and Wales
  233–47, *238*, 249–50
  see also Jesuits; Lancashire; saints
France *see* continental Catholicism;
  Europe
Francis of Assisi, St 206, 207, 250n.23
  see also saints
Freudian, 179, 228, 229, 230
  see also psychology

Gaudium et Spes (1965) 9, 165
generation 2, 3, 12, 14, 17, 20, 21, 35, 44,
  59, 61, 62, 76, 78, 82, 85, 91, 96, 100,
  109, 126n.182, 136, 137, 164, 172,
  173–4, 181, 182, 188, 206, 207, 213,
  215, 219, 227, 228, 230, 232, 236,
  262, 265–7
  see also pre-conciliar; sixties
ghetto 20, 21, 34, 36–8, 41, 48, 240
Glasgow 20, 30n.126, 163
  see also Scotland
golden age 21, 37, 48, 131, 151

Haurietis Aquas (1956) 70, 121n.43
  see also Sacred Heart
heaven 4, 9, 10, 12, 22, 39, 58, 67, 69,
  74, 86, 135, 141, 143, 146, 147, 152,
  160, 204, 205, 211, 212, 217, 227,
  233
Hebblethwaite, Peter (1930–94) 38, 233,
  234
Heenan, (Cardinal) John Carmel (1905–75)
  1, 3, 17, 39, 74, 87, 92, 95, 98, 168,
  172, 234, 240

see also Archbishop of Westminster;
  Catholic Missionary Society; London
hell 39, 160, 205, 230, 242
Holland, (Bishop) Thomas (1908–99) 19,
  68, 80, 110, 145, 175, 234
  see also Salford, Diocese of
Hollings, (Rev) Michael Richard (1921–97)
  145, 192n.84, 227
Hollis, (Maurice) Christopher (1902–77)
  34, 95, 100, 126n.170
Holy Communion *see* Eucharist
Holy Family 11, 12, 22, 60, 62, 63, 130–4,
  136, 139, 141, 151, 152, 166, 169,
  170–1, 176–8, 212, 262, 264
Holy Spirit 8, 11, 100, 159, 167, 171, 207
home 11, 35, 59, 63, 65, 69, 72–3, 88, 96,
  106, 107, 108, 111, 115, 131, 133,
  135–7, 139, 141–5, 147–8, 151, 154,
  156, 160, 168, 178, 183, 184, 185,
  188, 205, 208, 212, 218, 223, 244
homosexuality 45, 182
Hornsby-Smith, Michael P. (1932–) 37,
  40–2, 177
  see also sociology
host 22, 57, 59, 64–5, *66*, 67, 75, 76, 80–4,
  86, 87, 94, 95, 97–9, 110
  see also benediction, Eucharist
Houselander, (Frances) Caryll (1901–54)
  64, 67–9, 73, 76, 102, 111, 120n.22,
  135, 152
Howell SJ, (Rev) Clifford (1902–81) 79, 87
  see also Jesuits; priesthood
Humanae Vitae (1968) 19, 112, 160, *165*,
  166, 188
  see also birth control; contraception; Paul
    VI, Pope (1963–78); pill, the
human rights 4, 35, 44, 116, 131, 170,
  263
hymns 4, 84, 123n.111, 176, 258–9, 260
  see also music; Taizé

immigration 2, 14, 19, 20, 35, 48, 79, 175,
  227, 249, 262, 266, 268
  see also pluralism

incarnational 60, 61, 63, 64, 70, 72, 82, 84, 102, 108, 112, 118, 167, 188, 220, 228, 231, 248, 261, 263
  see also Christology; eschatology; material religion
individualism 41–2, 45, 104, 105, 132, 138, 225, 242
intellectuals 33, 35, 37, 89, 167, 202, 227, 234
inter-religious 145, 249, 259, 262, 264
  see also Islam; Judaism; non-Catholic; pluralism
Ireland 2, 20, 34, 35, 36, 73, 130, 134, 137, 144, 146, 147, 187, 236
Islam 28n.81, 145, 264
  see also inter-religious; pluralism

Jarrett OP, (Rev) Bede (1881–1934) 62, 155, 157
  see also Dominicans; priesthood
Jesuits 18, 38, 62, 74, 75, 76, 79, 88, 101, 140, 142, 173, 212, 233, 235
  Farm Street, London 76, 236, 246
  see also forty martyrs of England and Wales; Stonyhurst
John XXIII, Pope (1958–63) 3, 4, 185, 235
John Paul II, Pope (1978–2005) 5, 17, 22, 33, 119, 130–1, 132, 170, 179, 204, 209, 228, 258–9, 260, 263–5
Joseph, St 5, 22, 49, 65, 72, 131, 133, 146, 151–3, 167, 172, 185–8, 264
  see also saints
Judaism 10, 63, 114, 175, 213, 214, 259, 264

Knox, (Mgr) Ronald Arbuthnott (1888–1957) 60, 88, 120n.8, 167, 205, 222

Lancashire 20, 35, 65, 99, 136, 232, 235, *238*, 245, 246, 247
  see also Liverpool; Manchester, recusant; Salford, Diocese of; Yorkshire
Lash, Nicholas Langrishe Alleyne (1934–) 104

Latin 1, 6–7, 57, 58, 75, 77, 78–9, 92, 94, 123n.111, 241, 242, 263
  see also Tridentine mass; vernacular
Latin Mass Society 94, 125n.164, 240
  see also Agatha Christie indult
Lehrer, Thomas Andrew (1928–) 1–2, 3, 32, 57, 130, 202
  see also counter culture; hymns; music; sixties
Leo XIII, Pope (1878–1903) 208
liberation theology 116, 132, 175, 227, 262
  see also Catholic Action, Catholic Social Teaching; poverty
liturgical change 6–8, 19, 38–9, 118, 264
Liturgical Commission of England and Wales 93, 97–8
  see also Dwyer, (Archbishop) George Patrick (1908–87)
liturgical movement 6, 58–9, 75, 78, 118, 263
  dialogue mass 75, 78–9
  see also active participation; continental Catholicism; missal; *Sacrosanctum Concilium* (1963)
Liverpool 2, 9, 11, 17, 20, 30n.125, 30n.126, 30n.128, 34, 40, 74, 91, 101, 172, 175, 181–3, 187, 233, 235, 242
  see also Lancashire; National Pastoral Congress (1980)
Lodge, David John (1935–) 39, 161
London 17, 34, 35, 97, 117, 140, 145, 161, 163, 166, 174, 214, 236, 237, 240
Lourdes 174, 203, 207, 209–10, 213–14, 216, 220, 223, 224, 226, 244, 247, 264
  see also pilgrimage; Virgin Mary; Walsingham
love 10, 11, 12, 48, 62, 65, 69, 70, 72, 74, 87, 89, 105, 106–8, 111, 114, 132–3, 138, 139, 143, 147, 150–1, 154, 155, 157, 160–1, 167–9, 176, 178, 180, 186, 221–2, 241, 258
Lumen Gentium (1964) 8–9, 11, 100, 106, 110, 114, 227

Index

Manchester 19–20, 73, 80, 135, 137, 139, 154, 179, 207, 220, 236, 258–9
  see also Lancashire; Salford, Diocese of
marriage 12, 13, 37, 42, 48, 49, 83, 96, 106–9, 130–88, 212, 244, 261, 264
  'companionate' 137–8, 139, 154
  'mixed' 108, 109, 153, 164, 171, 177, 198n.281, 199n.284, 249
  see also Catholic Marriage Advisory Council; contraception; divorce, *Humanae Vitae* (1968); love
Marshall, (Bishop) Henry Vincent (1884–1955) 19, 72, 78, 80, 133, 139, 144
  see also Salford, Diocese of
Martindale SJ, (Rev) Cyril Charlie (1879–1963) 75, 79, 104, 122n.69, 206, 225, 229
  see also Jesuits; priesthood
martyrdom 9, 23, 34, 69, 93, 204, 206, 207, 219, 223, 233–50
Marxism *see* communism; socialism
Mary *see* Virgin Mary
masculinity 13, 22, 72, 75, 131, 148, 150, 151, 159, 186–7, 223, 264
  see also breadwinner; fatherhood, feminisation of religion, St Joseph
mass attendance 35, 39, 41, 53n.85, 131
masturbation 158–9
  see also sex
materialism 32, 70, 177, 222, 243
  see also affluence; class; communism; socialism
material religion 10, 11, 14, 15, 34, 39, 59, 63, 73, 74, 104, 134, 136, 172, 202, 211, 216, 220, 227, 230–1, 235, 251n.44
maternity 64, 142, 144, 145–7, 150, 163, 178, 183, 188
  see also Union of Catholic Mothers
media 2, 19, 94, 177, 183, 228, 258–9, 262, 268
  see also British Broadcasting Corporation; newspapers; television
Mediator Dei (1947) 81–2, 84, 86, 87, 89, 100

medicine 154, 156, 245–7, 248
  see also psychology; science
metaphysical 103, 132, 134, 249, 261, 265
  see also soteriology
middle class 13, 18, 35, 36, 39, 63, 77, 78, 87, 164, 182, 186, 212, 215
  see also class; social mobility; working class
Middlesbrough 40, 149, 173
  see also Yorkshire
migration *see* immigration
miracle 136–7, 203, 207, 209, 210, 217, 218, 220, 222, 243–8
  see also science
missal 7, 58, 75, 76, 77–9, 97, 125n.151, 240
  see also Latin; liturgical movement
'mixed marriage' *see* marriage
modernity 15, 19, 21, 37, 39, 42–3, 46, 76, 203, 207, 208, 229, 248
morality 13, 19, 22, 33, 40, 42, 44–6, 48, 130, 131, 152, 155–6, 160, 164, 167–9, 171, 179, 182, 184, 221, 224, 260–2
music 1, 3, 4, 7, 85, 174, 221, 230
  see also hymns
Muslims *see* Islam
Mystici Corporis Christi (1943) 81, 86, 87, 97, 100

National Marriage Guidance Council 132, 138, 141
National Pastoral Congress (1980) 2, 11–12, 108, 131, 169, 171, 175–87
  see also Liverpool
Neo-catechumenate 264
new age 47, 173
  see also counter culture; experience; sixties
Newcastle 39, 149
Newman, (Blessed) John Henry (1801–90) 5, 34–5, 101, 109
newspapers 18–9, 29n.113, 29n.116, 43, 134, 141, 164–6, 182
  see also British Broadcasting Corporation; media

NMGC *see* National Marriage Guidance
 Council
non-Catholic 20, 109, 140–1, 148, 162,
 167, 177, 244, 250, 263
 see also Anglican; ecumenism; inter-
 religious; pluralism
novena 39, 70, 136, 207, 232, 265
 see also material religion; rosary
NPC *see* National Pastoral Congress
 (1980)
nuns 70, 96, 102, 108, 112, 128n.232, 157,
 207, 208–9, 211, 215–16, 218, 227,
 259
 see also convent; female ordination;
 feminism; *Perfectae Caritatis* (1965);
 women's role

Oxford 38, 60, 62, 138, 166, 221, 227
 see also university

papal visit (1982) 33, 119, 131, 170, 179,
 187, 258–9, 263, 268
 see also John Paul II, Pope (1978–2005)
paternity *see* fatherhood
Paul VI, Pope (1963–78) 4, 7, 88, 92, 94,
 112, 166, 171, 174, 243
 see also Humanae Vitae (1968)
penance 70, 82, 117, 123n.94, 126n.190,
 209, 223
 see also confession; conscience; sin
Perfectae Caritatis (1965) 112, 128n.128
 see also convent; nuns
peritus 89, 94, 173
 see also Second Vatican Council
 (1962–65)
permissiveness 44–5, 131, 162, 182
 see also homosexuality; morality; pill, the;
 sixties
Peyton, (Rev) Patrick (1909–92) 130–1,
 133–6, 141, 148–9, *149*, 153, 170,
 171, 176, 189n.7
 see also rosary
physiology 67, 132, 154, 156–7, 158, 160
 see also sex

Pickering, (Rev) Aidan (1916–2007) 156,
 158–9
pilgrimage 174, 209, 213, 232, 233, 241,
 248, 262, 264, 265, 268
 see also Lourdes; Walsingham; Willesden,
 Our Lady of
pill, the 45, 164, 185
 see also birth control; contraception;
 Humanae Vitae (1968); Paul VI, Pope
 (1963–78)
Pius XII, Pope (1939–58) 70, 81, 82, 84,
 85, 107, 152, 168, 228
pluralism 41, 44, 45, 46, 48, 261, 262, 268
 see also immigration; inter-religious;
 morality
post-conciliar 3, 16, 38, 40, 88, 103, 105,
 109, 111, 132, 137, 143, 169, 172,
 173–5, 177, 186, 188, 204, 227, 241,
 262
 see also pre-conciliar; Second Vatican
 Council (1962–65)
post-war reconstruction 68, 87, 106, 131,
 133, 138, 140, 141, 142, 147, 148,
 151, 155, 169, 183
 see also Second World War; welfare state
poverty 19, 34, 58, 69, 74, 100, 116–17,
 132, 143, 145, 172, 209, 210, 218,
 220, 223, 227, 247
prayer 9, 14, 32, 40, 59, 62, 68, 70, 72, 76,
 78, 87, 90, 92, 104, 105, 107–8, 110,
 114, 119, 130, 132–6, 137, 141, 146,
 149, 150, 151, 157–8, 167, 173, 174,
 176, 177, 186, 188, 204, 205, 207,
 209, 210, 215, 231, 241, 243, 244,
 245–6, 250, 258, 265
 bidding prayers 112, 117
 Hail Mary 133, 158, 159, 172, 176,
 205
 see also belief; benediction; material
 religion; rosary; spirituality; stations of
 the cross
pre-conciliar 16, 38, 39, 67, 83, 114, 220
 see also post-conciliar; Second Vatican
 Council (1962–65)

Index

priesthood 8, 77, 83, 96, 109, 110, 113, 133, 147, 228, 237, 259
  laity and 8, 78, 110, 113, 228
  married 114
  see also celibacy; female ordination
Protestant 5, 7, 14, 42, 44, 93, 95, 140, 155, 173, 234, 240–3, 259
  see also Anglican; ecumenism; non-Catholic
psychology 7, 9, 23, 46, 49, 62, 67, 107, 145, 146, 152, 154–6, 159, 167, 169, 179, 180, 186, 188, 202–4, 208, 217, 224–5, 228–30, 232, 233, 237, 239, 248, 265, 266
  see also Freudian; science
pub 102, 105, 153
purity 133, 159, 160, 161, 169, 188, 215, 242
  see also chastity

racism 116, 117
'real presence' 65, 82, 88, 91, 94, 95, 98, 99, 100, 107, 109, 110, 117
  see also benediction; Eucharist; host; transubstantiation
recusant 35, 93, 236, 245, 249
  see also forty martyrs of England and Wales; Lancashire; Yorkshire
Reformation 5, 7, 23, 33, 34, 39, 93, 134, 150, 170, 204, 206, 234, 240
  see also forty martyrs of England and Wales; restoration of the Hierarchy of England and Wales; saints
relics 34, 209, 212, 216, 228, 232, 236, 243, 265
  see also material religion
religious orders *see* Benedictines; Dominicans; Jesuits; nuns
restoration of the Hierarchy of England and Wales 32, 34, 38, 260
ritual 2, 15, 43, 60, 134, 136
  see also material religion; pilgrimage; spirituality
rosary 2, 13, 48, 58, 62, 78, 101, 104, 130–7, 146, 148, *149*, 150, 153, 172–5, 182, 188, 244, 262, 264

rosary beads 76, 133, 134, 135, *149*, 209, 39
  see also material religion; Peyton, (Rev) Patrick (1909–92)

Sacred Heart 13, 22, 59, 60, 69–75, 100, 104, 107, 118, 149, 230, 263, 265
  see also Haurietis Aquas (1956); material religion
sacrifice 10, 23, 36, 58, 59, 67–9, 75–7, 80–2, 86–90, 92, 95, 103, 106, 113, 133, 145, 151, 163, 183, 203, 204, 208, 220, 222, 263, 265
Sacrosanctum Concilium (1963) 6–8, 10, 82, 89
  see also active participation; Latin; liturgical movement; vernacular
saints 2, 5, 9–10, 11–13, 23, 39, 48, 49, 64, 68, 81, 87, 144, 147, 148, 174, 185, 186, 188, 203–7, 231, 232, 233, 237, *238*, 244–5, 248–9, 261, 262, 265
  see also Bernadette, St; forty martyrs of England and Wales; Francis of Assisi, St; Joseph, St; Thérèse of Lisieux, St
Salford, Diocese of 17, 19, 20, 34, 68, 72, 78, 80, 90, 108, 110, 116, 133, 136, 139, 142, 145, 166, 177–8, 181, 184, 234, 235, 240, 244, 246
  see also Lancashire; Manchester and *individually named Bishops*
schools, Catholic 13, 35–6, 40, 50n.29, 51n.36, 60, 72, 78, 108, 115, 137, 144, 149, 151, 159, 161, 167, 174, 210, 214, 235, 237, 239, 258, 266, 268
  curricula 90–1, 155–6, 214
  see also sex education; Stonyhurst
science 170, 173, 167, 223–4, 229, 230, 243, 245, 247
Scotland 2, 24n.5, 96
  see also Glasgow
scripture 10, 58, 60, 62, 68, 69, 77, 86, 101, 111, 133, 151, 173, 176, 228, 262

Second Vatican Council (1962–65) 4–10, 15–17, 38–41, 47–8, 89, 93, 94, 95, 96, 100, 110, 112, 114, 118, 132, 168, 173, 185, 188, 227, 240, 260, 263
  see also individually named Decrees and Constitutions; post-conciliar; pre-conciliar
Second World War 2, 16, 21, 23, 32, 33, 37, 47, 67–9, 74, 80, 86, 135, 139, 145, 148, 160, 180, 202, 203, 213, 215, 222, 260, 261
  see also Cold War; post-war reconstruction; welfare state
secularisation 4, 14–5, 22, 33, 41–4, 46–7, 260
secularism 222, 223, 243, 264
sex 12, 21, 48, 131, 132, 138, 179, 180, 261, 264
  marriage and 22, 49, 107, 154–69, 181–3
  pre-marital 160
  see also birth control; homosexuality; *Humanae Vitae* (1968); sin
sex education 141, 154–64, 190n.38; 190n.39; 191n.61
  forum for 155–9, 168–9
  see also Catholic Marriage Advisory Council; National Marriage Guidance Council
Sheed and Ward publishers 37, 38, 52n.55, 57, 69, 269
Sheffield 112
  see also Yorkshire
sin 1, 39, 48, 70, 76, 82, 99, 110, 123n.94, 132, 159, 160–3, 167, 180, 188, 205, 230, 263
  see also confession; conscience, contraception, sex, soteriology
single life 45, 114, 115, 144, 145, 150, 156, 175, 178, 191n.77, 195n.178
  see also celibacy; nuns; priesthood
sixties 2, 3, 4, 14, 22, 33, 37, 38, 43–6, 59, 100, 102, 108, 111, 115, 131, 161, 162, 167, 173, 264

  see also counter culture; morality; permissiveness
social activism 2, 6, 111, 115–16, 227, 249, 262
  see also Catholic Social Teaching; liberation theology; Young Christian Workers
socialisation *see* childhood; schools, Catholic
socialism 19, 70, *71*, 115, 230
  Christian 29n.115, 114–5, *153*
  see also class; communism; materialism; Young Christian Workers
social mobility 22, 30n.129, 33, 35, 41, 109
  see also affluence; class; consumption; middle class; working class
sociology 11, 12, 14, 40, 42, 46–7, 154, 162
  see also secularisation
soteriology 46, 47, 92, 180, 218, 230, 263
  see also Christology; eschatology; metaphysical; suffering
spirituality 2, 13, 15, 23, 40, 41, 47, 59, 85, 101, 102, 105, 109, 115, 117, 118, 131, 137, 146, 149, 155, 162, 173, 177, 204, 218, 223, 227, 230, 246, 248–9, 257n.227; 260; 262; 265; 266; 267
  see also belief; experience; new age; prayer
stations of the cross 67–9, 103
  see also Christology; material religion; prayer
statue *see* material religion
St John-Stevas, (Baron) Norman (1929–2012) 36, 50n.28, 196n.216
Stonyhurst 18, 76, 235, *238*
  see also Jesuits; schools, Catholic
suffering 22, 59, 60, 67–9, 73, 74, 75, 100, 103, 117–18, 119, 120n.30; 179, 203, 204, 207, 211, 218–19, 220–1, 222, 223–4, 228, 230, 237, 244, 252n.73, 265
  see also soteriology

Index

Sword of the Spirit 37, 52n.51, 116
  see also ecumenism; Ward, (Baroness) Barbara (1914–81)

Taizé 85, 124n.114
  see also ecumenism; hymns; prayer
teenager see adolescence
television 1, 116, 134, 177, 239, 262, 268
  see also British Broadcasting Corporation; media; newspapers
theatre 134, 202, 203, 213, 222, 230, 232, 242
  see also film; music
Thérèse of Lisieux, St 22, 23, 202–33, 237, 239, 243, 247–9, 262, 265
  see also saints
tradition 2, 7, 11, 13, 17, 22, 33, 34, 39, 48, 61, 69, 94, 99, 103–4, 111, 116, 130, 134, 135, 139, 140, 144, 160–2, 166–8, 173, 174, 176, 180, 182, 185, 229, 240, 242, 259, 260, 261, 265, 266
  medieval 87, 130, 134
  see also authority; counter culture; pre-conciliar
transubstantiation 57, 61, 82, 87, 91–2, 93–5, 100, 102
  see also benediction; Eucharist; host; 'real presence'
Trent, Council of (1545–63) 34, 81, 92, 96, 125n.148
Tridentine Mass 7, 58, 75, 90, 98, 125n.157, 240, 262, 263
  see also Latin; Latin Mass Society; liturgical movement

Union of Catholic Mothers 142, 155, 184
  see also maternity; women's role
Unitatis Redintegratio (1964) 93
  see also ecumenism
United States of America 1, 2, 6, 11, 12, 13, 16, 44, 75, 79, 101, 116, 130, 213, 221, 267
  see also continental Catholicism; Europe

university 78, 101, 233
  chaplaincy 60, 101, 221
  see also Oxford; social mobility

Vatican II see Second Vatican Council (1962–65)
Vatican II Decrees and Constitutions see individually named
vernacular 1, 7, 78, 79, 92, 261
  see also Latin; liturgical movement; Sacrosanctum Concilium (1963)
Virgin Mary 8–9, 11, 60, 63–4, 111, 112, 119, 130–51, 157–8, 169, 170–5, 183–5, 187, 188, 203, 209, 210, 220, 248, 264–5
  see also Lourdes; Lumen Gentium (1964); maternity; Walsingham; Willesden, Our Lady of
votive candle see material religion

Wales 2, 11, 32, 40, 119, 156, 170, 176, 203, 233, 235, 239, 260, 265
Walsingham 150
  see also Anglican; pilgrimage; Willesden, Our Lady of
Ward, (Baroness) Barbara (1914–81) 116, 128n.250
  see also Sword of the Spirit
welfare state 30n.129, 35, 36, 42, 145, 148, 183
  Beveridge Report 33
  NHS 45, 182
  see also class; post-war reconstruction; Second World War
Willesden, Our Lady of 34, 150
  see also recusant; Reformation
women priests see female ordination
women's role 14, 43–4, 70, 110–13; *113*, 117, 138–9, 142, 144–6, 148, 150, 160, 183–5, 188, 220, 228, 233, 237, 248
  see also female ordination; feminisation of religion; feminism; nuns
Woodruff, (John) Douglas (1897–1978) 18, 29n.112

work 9, 14, 35, 78, 114–15, 116, 147, *153*, 159, 171, 177, 186, 188
   men and 72, 137, 148–54
   women and 44, 78, 139, 143, 144, 145, 147, 150, 157, 183–4, 185, 186, 188, 200n.336, 206, 210
   see also breadwinner; Joseph, St
working class 13, 14, 18, 19–20, 35, 39, 43, 50n.23, 114–15, 143, 147, 152, *153*, 154, 164, 172, 204, 217, 223, 241
   see also class; middle class; social mobility; Young Christian Workers
World War II *see* post-war reconstruction; Second World War

YCW *see* Young Christian Workers
Yorkshire 146, 170, 235, 245
   see also Middlesbrough; recusant; Sheffield
Young Christian Workers 13, 36, 51n.44, 106, 114, 115, 143, 220
   see also Catholic Action; work; working class
youth *see* adolescence

Zen 101
   see also counter culture; new age; sixties; spirituality